The Psychology of Preschool Children

The MIT Press   Cambridge, Massachusetts, and London, England

The Psychology of Preschool Children

A. V. Zaporozhets and D. B. Elkonin, Editors

Translated by
John Shybut and Seymore Simon

Originally published in 1964 by Izdatelstvo "Prosveshcheniye," Moscow,
under the title "Psikhologiya Detey Doshkolnogo Vozrasta," and under the
auspices of the Akademiya Pedagogicheskikh Nauk RSFSR Institut
Psikhologii

Copyright © 1971 by
The Massachusetts Institute of Technology

This book was designed by The MIT Press Design Department.
It was set in IBM Bodoni Book
by Williams Graphic Service, Inc.,
printed on Finch Textbook Offset
by The Colonial Press Inc.,
and bound by The Colonial Press Inc.
in the United States of America.

ISBN 0 262 24013 (hardcover)

Library of Congress catalog card number: 76-166515

Contents

Acknowledgment

We are grateful to Dr. Marilyn C. Barrick, Doris Gold, Barbara A. Rasin, Lowell A. Speckhart, Frances Spires, Elda Peart Wilson, and the Dean's Fund of Northern Illinois University for their assistance and support in the preparation of this manuscript.

Our thanks also go to Susan McCorkendale, John S. Snyder Jr., and Joseph Stein of the M.I.T. Press for their editorial assistance.

J.S.
S.S.

De Kalb, Illinois, October 1970

Preface to the English Translation

Urie Bronfenbrenner[*]

To English-speaking psychologists and specialists in child development, this volume is best described in terms of its closest counterpart in the Western world; namely, the handbook or manual in child psychology associated with such names as Carmichael, Mussen, and most recently, the Hoffmans. This Soviet volume is thinner only because it deals with perceptual processes from birth up to seven years of age. But within that sphere, this book is the standard reference among Soviet psychologists and educators on research in early child development. Edited and partly written by two of the leading Soviet workers in this field, the volume is also widely used as a text in intermediate courses in developmental psychology in universities and pedagogical institutes throughout the Soviet Union, as well as East European countries. Both men are Professors of Psychology at the University of Moscow. Dr. Zaporozhets is also Director of the Institute for the Study of Preschool Children, an independent research center under the aegis of the Academy of Pedagogical Sciences. His colleague, Dr. Elkonin, directs the Laboratory for the Study of School-Age Children at the Institute of Psychology in Moscow.

In making available an English translation of this book, Drs. Shybut and Simon have performed a double service. First, they have given Western specialists access to a systematic survey of the extensive Soviet research in this area. Particularly impressive both in volume and quality are the studies of sensation and perception (reviewed by Yendovitskaya), of language development (Elkonin), and of thinking (Zaporozhets). The remaining four chapters on attention, memory, imagination, and motor development round out the picture of contemporary Soviet work in the developmental psychology of sensory processes.

[*]Professor of Psychology and of Human Development and Family Studies at Cornell University.

In addition to substance, the reader of this book will gain an appreciation of a scientific approach to the process of development rather different from our own. Reflected less in cited references than in the actual formulation of research problems and way of thinking about them, is the pervasive influence of one of the seminal thinkers psychology has produced—Vygotsky. Whether the concern is with the development of movement, attention, language, thought, or social play—and especially the interrelations among these processes—the theoretical ideas which animate and guide the experiments reported in this volume are those of Vygotsky and of his former colleagues and students, now leading psychologists in the U.S.S.R.—Leontiev, Luria, and the two editors of this volume, Zaporozhets and Elkonin.

The hallmarks of this Soviet approach may be characterized briefly as follows:

1. The developing organism is seen not as a passive receptor of stimuli but as an active agent capable of voluntary movement, selective attention, and subsequently, the creative use of language and thought; in short, as Soviet psychologists like to express it, consciousness is conceived as an active rather than a purely receptive process. The infant's psychological capacities develop through his practical activity with the world of material objects, a world that becomes progressively more complex both in content and in structure.

2. The infant's psychological development is shaped primarily through the intervention of other persons as the mediators between the child and his environment; it is their action, or failure to act, that becomes the decisive element in determining the character and course of the child's psychological growth; in short, the child is seen as assimilating the environment presented to him through other people. This orientation has its roots in dialectic materialism. As the editors state in their foreword:

In contradiction to those Western European and American psychologists who assert either that psychological development of a child takes place seemingly as a result of the spontaneous realizing or maturing of inborn abilities (Bühler, Stern, and others), or moves along the path of adaptation and individual adjustment to the surrounding environment (a line of reasoning generally espoused by Spencerite psychologists and "strict behaviorists," and in a more refined form represented in the latest works of Piaget), Soviet psychologists (Vygotsky, Leontiev, and Rubinshtein), having translated into concrete terms certain well-known philosophical propositions of Marxism-Leninism, have shown convincingly that the psychological development of individuals follows a path of "social inheritance" (Engels) or a path of "appropriation" (Marx) of social experience.

The application of these principles in the context of child development is nicely illustrated in the following passage from Chapter II:

The main factor in the establishment and development of the reciprocal relation between the young child and his surrounding environment is the social interaction of the child with the socializing adult. The emergence of the two-sided interaction of the adult with the child is marked by the appearance in the child of two and three months of age of a characteristic arousal reaction evoked by the sight of the adult. During such interaction it is possible to capture the child's attention and to organize his familiarization with the surrounding environment by evoking sensory reactions to a given object. In the course of interaction the adult first begins to utilize indicatory gestures and then words to attract the child's attention. By doing so the adult seems to strengthen the object's direct influence and to divert the child from other things. Subsequently, the child begins to utilize first the indicatory gestures and later words. The timing in the use of words depends on the rate of mastering speech. As a result of utilizing gestures and words, the child learns to isolate objects from the surrounding environment and to attract the attention of another human being.

3. As illustrated in the foregoing passage, language soon becomes the principal avenue of interaction between child and adult. Thus, it is language which shapes and controls the behavior of the child, first from without and then internally, as he begins to use the concepts and instructions of others as tools for structuring and controlling his own behavior.

4. Given the preceding propositions, the development of thought is closely related to language development and to the context

from which the latter derives, namely social relationships and social structure.

5. Finally, given the power of the man-mediated environment in shaping the development of the child, *training*, especially in early life, becomes of critical significance. Hence, the concern in Soviet experimentation with the acceleration of psychological development through the process outlined in the quotation cited above; that is, by focusing the attention of the child on differentiated aspects of the environment chiefly through the medium of language, and by inducing activity which makes use of the new discrimination, the experimenter, or trainer, seeks and—as the experimental evidence shows—often succeeds in enhancing the child's competence in such diverse areas as auditory discrimination, visual perception, language usage, thought processes, and imaginative play.

The distinctive character of the Soviet approach to psychological development is perhaps reflected most sharply in the occasional glimpses that the volume affords of Soviet views of Western theory and research in this area. Especially in the chapters by Zaporozhets and Elkonin, the work of non-Soviet investigators, notably Piaget but also Isaacs, Russell, Bühler, Lashley, the "Gestalt" psychologists, and others, are examined from the Soviet theoretical perspective. Especially illuminating along these lines is the critique of Piaget for his failure to recognize the social basis of what he calls "egocentric speech."

Along with its merits, the volume has some shortcomings from the point of view of the English reader. The first of these is inherent in a work of this kind; the descriptions of any single study are necessarily brief, especially on matters of method and experimental detail, a circumstance that is especially frustrating when the original sources cited are in a foreign language.

A second deficiency is specific to this first American edition of Zaporozhets and Elkonin's work, since it covers only the first of two volumes they have published on the psychology of preschool children—that devoted to the development of sensory processes, which appeared in 1964. A second volume, entitled "The Psychology of Personality and of Activity in the Preschool Child," issued a year later, reviews Soviet research in such areas as the development of volition, emotions, motivation, and personality. In addition, it discusses Soviet investigations on different aspects of children's activity, including games, work, and learning. It is to be hoped that this second volume also will soon be published in English and, in the meantime, that the studies cited in the present edition will become familiar references in Western publications.

Ithaca, New York, June 1970

Foreword

This book concerns the development of cognitive processes in early and preschool childhood. It represents the first part of a collective monograph *Psychology of Preschool Children*, prepared by the co-workers of the Laboratory of the Psychology of Preschool Children at the Institute of Psychology, APN RSFSR.* The volume summarizes and evaluates theoretically the results of years of investigations in our laboratory, the work of other Soviet authors, and the work of many foreign psychologists. While extensively utilizing a variety of factual material available in child psychology in the preparation of this monograph, we do not plan to limit the writing to a mere compendium of the available investigations in the area of the psychological development of the child. In addition to reconstructing a general picture of the formation of various cognitive processes in preschool childhood, we attempted, as much as possible, to expose conditions and principles of their formation, relying on established theoretical positions and taking into account those practical problems which are confronting Soviet planners of preschool upbringing today.

The enormous growth of nurseries and kindergartens requires a quality of medical services and pedagogical training that insures optimal physical and mental development of all children and that increases their level of preparation for schooling. The role of preschool training is extremely important in the general process of personality formation. In the course of the first seven years of life the child undergoes extensive physical and mental development. The classical writers of Soviet pedagogy, Krupskaya and Makarenko, indicate correctly that not only does an intensive accumulation of various knowledge and skills occur in preschool age, but also that different abilities are constructed, bases of character are established, and certain moral qualities of personality are formed. In order to make this process manageable and to

*APN-RSFSR-Academy of Pedagogical Sciences, Russian Soviet Federated Socialist Republic.

provide optimal conditions for the multilateral development of the child's personality, preschool pedagogy must rely on a knowledge of psychological principles in this development and the characteristics of their manifestations at various developmental stages. While highly praising Soviet psychological attainments in the solution of actual pedagogical problems, Krupskaya wrote as early as 1932: "For many years methods of influencing children rested on empiricism on the one hand and on idealistic psychology on the other. The scientific approach was either lacking in the old methods or was inaccurate. Now scientific materialistic psychology, relying on the accomplishments of contemporary neurology, presents a more valid scientific base on which scientific methods may be constructed."*

Since 1932, Soviet investigations in the area of general and child psychology have advanced markedly, and the utilization of psychological data in theory and practice of pedagogical training of children has become indispensable. Furthermore, the number of studies in child and pedagogical psychology during the past years has increased considerably. Many of these studies are printed in various journals of limited edition and are presently considered bibliographical rarities. In spite of this, a large number of these articles addressed themselves to specific questions of child psychology, and the reader interested in constructing a total picture concerning the development of certain psychological aspects of child behavior must perform the enormous task of comparing and evaluating data obtained from various sources. Under these conditions, utilization of psychological data presents difficulty not only for educators but also for scientists in the areas of pedagogy and psychology. In addition, a need exists for the preparation of synopses and abstracts of works in child psychology that would systematize for the reader the essentials of investigations conducted in a given area.

Similar works published abroad (e.g., in the U.S.A., *Child*

*N. K. Krupskaya. Selected pedagogical works. M. Pub. by APN RSFSR, 1948, p. 177.

Psychology and Methods of Psychological Investigations of Children, edited by Murchison, Carmichael, Mussen, and others) undoubtedly are of definite interest to the specialist-psychologist. However, due to unfamiliar methodological approaches and one-sided selection of factual material, these investigations are less suitable for a wider circle of readers, especially for those with a pedagogical orientation. The existing gap in summarized studies on child psychology has to be narrowed to some extent by relying on such Soviet books as Zaporozhets's *Psychology*; Elkonin's *Child Psychology*; and Lyublinskaya's *Outline of the Psychological Development of a Child*; or those published in other democratic countries, Piryov's *Child Psychology with Defectology* (Bulgaria); Klauss and Gibsh's *Child Psychology* (East Germany), and others. However, being written as texts or study guides, they can only in part fulfill the indicated function, since the volume of the attractive material and the thoroughness of its examination are limited by the scope of the given course and the didactic problems confronting the authors. Consequently, the preparation of a summary of studies concerning problems of child psychology pertaining to psychological development in early and preschool childhood remains indispensable for theory and practice of Soviet preschool training.

In preparing this book we relied upon theories proposed in Soviet psychology concerning motivational causes and upon basic principles of the ontogeny of human psychology. Propositions applying to psychological development in early childhood have been under study for many years in our laboratory. In contradiction to those Western European and American psychologists who assert either that psychological development of a child takes place seemingly as a result of the spontaneous realizing or maturing of inborn abilities (Bühler, Stern, and others), or moves along the path of adaptation and individual adjustment to the surrounding environment (a line of reasoning generally espoused by Spencerite psychologists and "strict behaviorists," and in a more refined form represented in the latest works of Piaget), Soviet psychologists (Vygotsky, Leontiev, and Rubinshtein), having translated into concrete terms certain well-known philosophical propositions of Marxism-Leninism, have shown convincingly that the psychological development of individuals follows a path of "social inheritance" (Engels) or a path of "appropriation" (Marx) of social experience. Recent theoretical and experimental genetic investigations by Leontiev and his co-workers revealed a deeply embedded uniqueness in the ontogeny of the psyche of man in contrast with that of animals. If in animals two forms of experience play a decisive role, generic, fixed in the inherited nervous organization of separate individuals, and individual, acquired via the path of adaptation of inborn abilities to the present environmental conditions, then in human development the dominant role is assumed by a third form of experience, completely lacking in animals. This experience, called socialization, is fixed in the products of material and nonmaterial culture created by humanity and acquired individually during childhood.

Vygotsky was the first Soviet psychologist to introduce propositions concerning the leading role of training in the psychic development of the child. His theoretical and experimental investigations reveal that the socialization process not only enriches the knowledge and skills of the child; it precipitates essential changes in various psychic processes and engenders a genuine development of the child's psyche as well.

Furthermore, numerous investigations in psychology (Zaporozhets, Kostyuk, Leontiev, Elkonin, etc.) and in pedagogy (Usova, Leushina, Sakulina, Flyorina, and others) of preschool children confirmed this proposition and thus extended its application to areas of psychic development previously considered "naturalistic," i.e., moving along the path of the adaptation of an individual's biological abilities to existing environmental conditions. Studies of this kind led, for example, to a clarification of the decisive role of the mastery of social experience in the development of sensory processes and in the formation of a child's motor activity.

Clarification of specific aspects of the special type of the child's psychic development permits one to approach an old problem of psychology and pedagogy in a new way: the problem of the role of inheritance and environment in the formation of human identity. It is useless to argue, as has been done in the past, which of these is more important. The presence of specific natural predispositions in the form of hereditarily fixed features of the human nervous system, as well as their normal process of maturation in ontogeny, is an indispensable condition for the full psychic development of the child. One must be born with a human brain in order to become a man. Investigations which attempted to train in a humanlike fashion offspring of the highest organized animals—anthropoid monkeys (Ladygina-Kots, D. and K. Kellog, and others)—produced negative results and convincingly demonstrated that without the presence of corresponding natural predispositions the formation of human personality is impossible. In addition, data of neurological and defectological clinics indicate that substantial defects of a child's nervous system or disturbances in its maturation due to illness lead to more or less essential inadequacies of the psyche.

Finally, recent investigations of general and partial typological attributes of the human nervous system (Teplov, Leytes, and Merlin) permit one to assume that individual differences in innate dispositions create different opportunities for development and determine various paths for the attainment of similar results.

Thus, the presence of certain natural predispositions is not just merely important, but an absolutely indispensable condition in the ontogeny of the human psyche. However, these predispositions are not at all the motivational cause of the psychic development of the child.

In contrast to animal offspring, maturation of the child's nervous system is not in a position in and of itself to contribute to the development of any kind of species-specific form of activity, either practical or theoretical. This maturation merely provides certain opportunities for that development which might be realized only in the presence of a definite social environment and training. Only through the acquisition of social musical culture can man's musical abilities develop, just as mastery of the knowledge and the ways of thinking accumulated by society may insure the development of man's intellect. Along with changes in our ideas concerning the role of predispositions in the psychic development of the child, the role of the environment in this process comes to be examined in a different light.

If for animal offspring environment is only the sum of conditions to which it has to adjust, then for the child his specific social environment is not merely an external condition, but a source of development. This environment contains the centuries-old experiences of mankind, defined in terms of tools of labor, means of communication, etc., which the child must master in order to become a man, i.e., a full-fledged participant in social achievements and social development. Mastery of this social experience is an unusually complex process and cannot be obtained through a passive approach, an approach of mere contemplation of the surrounding reality.

Theoretical and experimental investigations of Soviet psychologists (Vygotsky, Leontiev, and Rubinshtein) have shown that psychic development takes place in the process of activity and is dependent on the conditions and character of such activity.

At each qualitatively distinct level of development a dominant role is assumed by a specific type of leading activity, which determines the forms of mastery and to a large extent the character and extent of the acquired content. Such leading types of activity at an early age are object manipulations; for preschool-age children, games; and for school-age children, learning combined with various types of participation in mutually useful tasks.

The ongoing activities are not exclusive to a particular level of development, but rather comprise a dominant nucleus of the entire system of activities, on which depend the formation and mode of executing these activities at a given age. Thus, a preschooler not only plays, but learns and also takes part in simpler forms of tasks. The character of these activities must therefore be taken into account when studying psychic development in the child. The study of orienting activity was of great importance in gaining an understanding of the dependence of psychic processes, and in part cognitive processes, upon the character of a child's activity, (Galperin, Zaporozhets, and others). The fact is that cognitive processes do not form and develop by themselves, but as individual exploratory acts comprising an indispensable organic part of an integral activity of the child (practical, playful, etc.), and fulfilling in it orienting and regulating functions.

In connection with the realization of activities differing in content and structure, the child is confronted with various cognitive tasks which require different methods for their solution, methods differing in the nature of their orienting and cognitive actions. Thus, a shift from object manipulation, characteristic of an earlier age, to games with a plot and productive activities of preschool childhood demands a basic restructuring of the orienting aspect of activity, since here it is necessary to take into account not only the directly perceived but also the imaginary surroundings and to control one's actions not only by the prevailing conditions but by some known manner or principle. In other words, those changes in perception, memory, thinking, etc., which are observed, for example, during the shift from infancy to preschool age, cannot be understood without taking into account more general changes in the character of the mutual relationship of the child to the surrounding reality as well as the content and structure of ongoing activity occurring at a given developmental level.

Although the second half of this monograph contains a special examination of the psychological problems of a child's play, his learning, and his performing, a constant attempt has been made throughout this work to single out the dependence of these and other cognitive processes upon the general character of the child's activity and upon that orienting function which these processes fulfill.

The scope of this presentation has been to encompass the entire period of childhood from birth to seven years. However, because the psychological investigation of early age until recently has been less scrutinized than that of preschool age, this task has been only partially realized and not to the degree desired. In some chapters (e.g., those concerning motor activity and the development of sensation and perception) material concerning early age is more substantial; in other chapters (e.g., those on thinking and memory) material is brief and sometimes sketchy.

While attributing considerable importance to age-specific morphological changes and the process of maturation of nervous mechanisms needed for the ontogenetic development of the psyche, the authors have been unable to elucidate this question thoroughly due to lack of available information. As a result of investigations by Soviet authors, the matter concerning the study of the ontogeny of higher nervous activity comprising the physiological bases of the psychic development of a child has been more adequately treated. The examination of data obtained from these investigations, rather than being confined to a single chapter, has been included whenever it seemed appropriate in conjunction with analyzing mechanisms of concrete psychic processes in children of different preschool ages.

In conclusion, the authors well recognize shortcomings of their work. While the book was in preparation, the demands of psychological science grew constantly, and as a result studies in psychology and related fields expanded greatly. Whereas this book largely reflects that which has already been attained in child psychology, new research is needed in order to fulfill these increasing demands completely and to become fully acquainted with complementary achievements of scientific thought. Nevertheless, publication of this monograph is indispensable, because in order to advance in the area of pedagogical and psychological investigations of preschool childhood a sufficiently systematic and general account of previously conducted work is needed.

A number of co-workers of the Laboratory of Psychology of Preschool Children, Institute of Psychology, APN RSFSR, took part in the preparation of this book. Separate chapters have been written by the following authors: Chapter 1—"Development of Sensation and Perception"—T. V. Yendovitskaya, V. P. Zinchenko, and A. G. Ruzskaya; Chapter 2—"Development of Attention"—and Chapter 3—"Development of Memory"—T. V. Yendovitskaya; Chapter 4—"Development of Speech"—D. B. Elkonin; Chapter 5—"Development of Thinking"—A. V. Zaporozhets, V. P. Zinchenko, and D. B. Elkonin; Chapter 6—"Development of Imagination"—T. A. Repina; Chapter 7—"Development of Movements and Formation of Motor Habits"—M. I. Lisina and Ya. Z. Neverovich. The last chapter serves as the connecting link between the first and second parts of our monograph, since in the second half problems of the development of volitional and emotional processes of preschool-age children are examined.

A. V. Zaporozhets and D. B. Elkonin

The Psychology of Preschool Children

1. Development of Sensation and Perception

During the early years of a child's life perception processes pass through a complex developmental path that encompasses various aspects of the processes. The emerging operational side of the perceptive processes undergoes a refinement, and the means of getting acquainted with the surrounding environment become more adequate with respect to the tasks confronting the child. A corresponding development occurs in the active side as the child's perceptive images become more orthoscopic and more ably reflect the surrounding reality. A motivational sphere also develops, in which perceptive processes acquire purposeful characteristics. The rapidly growing number of studies on sensory learning and development support this view of perceptual development. This position differs from that expressed by adherents of the Gestalt theory and some other theories which assume that the main structural aspects of perception are present in the child at birth. Currently, the debate between these contradictory positions on the understanding of perception is not as intense as it had been during earlier arguments between nativists and empiricists. The question of what kinds of perceptual operations are inborn, not needing learning, and which ones are a result of sensory learning is very important, especially when one considers that the child's sensory development is accomplished under conditions of the organism's ongoing physiological maturation.

In embryology and embryomorphology divergent views exist about the ontogenetic process in the prefunctional or prenatal period. This difference of opinion is analogous for psychology to the traditional opposing views between nativism and empiricism. The essence of this disagreement has recently been summarized by Arshavsky (4).

According to the views of one group of embryo-physiologists, preliminary construction of a "machine" occurs in the early stages of ontogenesis. From the moment of inception the emerging functions have no adaptive significance for the developing organism during the entire embryonic and fetal periods, but represent either the expression of genes or preadaptive foresight, i.e., some exercise of those functions that will become useful to the organism only after birth (Barcroft, 6, and others). These ideas are being expanded by Anokhin and his co-workers. According to Anokhin (2), the essential biological significance of the embryonic period is that it provides for that critical moment in the newborn's life when for the first time he encounters the enormous conglomeration of outside factors which comprise the specific conditions of his existence.

A second point of view, developed by Arshavsky, is based not on preadaptation but on adaptation of structural functions organized in the prenatal period. This viewpoint may be used to explain the anatomical, physiological, and embryological facts about the irregular development of various analyzers in the ontogeny of man. Skin receptors in man, e.g., Meissner's and pacinian corpuscles, proprioceptors of skeletal muscles and the vestibular apparatus, take shape during the intrauterine period (Obelin, Puzik, and others). According to Arshavsky, this is necessary in order to insure a permanent postural tonus which is species-specific. With skin receptor stimulation the reflexory tonic contraction of skeletal muscles in turn becomes a stimulus for muscular proprioceptors, whose excitation reinforces the species-specific posture. Arshavsky also considers the early morphological formation of the sucking apparatus as a form of adaptation to prenatal environmental conditions and not as a form of preparation for that function, which will become useful to the organism only after birth. He discovered that after the formation of the musculature of the mouth and the respiratory system the fetus begins to process pericarpial waters with the help of sucking and breathing movements, thus fulfilling an omnitrophic form of nutrition. This discovery enables one to understand the investigations of Ignatyeva, who discovered a more intense growth of nerve tracts innervating muscles of the mouth and the tongue.

In connection with the formation of optical and acoustical receptors during the prenatal period, Arshavsky, referring to the work of Benua and Markelov, states that during this period these receptors fulfill a trophic function in relation to the nerve centers until they begin to fulfill their specific visual and auditory functions. These specific functions are still absent in newborn children; they are capable of responding to auditory and visual stimulation by a change in the rate of breathing and heart beat and by a generalized motor reaction, and to visual stimulation by a defensive visual reaction. Furthermore, desynchronization of electrical activity of the cerebral cortex which occurs in response to auditory and visual stimulation, typical for adults, is absent in the newborn. Desynchronization of electrical activity of the cortex occurs in response to the stimulation of the hunger center and to the execution of sucking movements.

Arshavsky's findings concur with results showing a much earlier formation during the prenatal period of cortical cells in the corresponding nuclei of the motor analyzer, as compared with the development of cortical cells in the optical and acoustical analyzers (Kukuyev, Minayeva, Preobrazhenskaya).

From Arshavsky's line of reasoning, a valuable general proposition applicable not only to embryogenesis but also to psychological development emerges. One cannot utilize the criteria characteristic of an adult organism to determine the morphological maturity of a structure. Aside from essential differences, the various functions as well as the corresponding structures are mature at each stage only to the extent to which they provide a corresponding form of adaptation to those specific environmental conditions with which the organism interacts in each developmental period.

Polyakov's (60) findings concerning the development of separate areas of the cerebral cortex connected with the activity of individual analyzers are of interest from this point of view. The areas of the cortex that are connected with the nuclear zones of the analyzers mature earlier than the other areas. For instance the frontal, the lower parietal, and the temporal-parietal-occipital subareas, which are involved in a complex interaction of the analyzers, develop in the adult brain much later.

Polyakov presents evidence proving that "the organism comes into the world with a structural analyzer that has attained a certain degree of maturity for the interaction between cortical and subcortical formations, by means of which cortical regulation of the positioning of analyzers with respect to the activity of stimuli is attained . . ." (60; p. 8).

Only toward the beginning of the second year of life does the system of projective-associative connections attain a relative degree of maturation. The latest to develop and mature is the system of associative cortical connections. Polyakov assumes that the latter are involved in the highest and most complex forms of cortical analysis and synthesis and in functional connections among the analyzers, which are formed during the initial years of life (60; pp. 12, 13). Without citing additional data concerning embryogenesis of analyzers, let us merely note the complexity of the problem of maturation and development.

At the present time, no systematic data exist concerning the interrelation, in the formation of cortical endings of analyzers, of tracts and the level of the receptors' specialization at any given developmental period with the means of perceiving a given set of characteristics of the environment. Ascertainment of these interrelations represents a very important problem for the psychology and the physiology of childhood.

Sensory Development in Early Childhood

Activity of Receptive Systems in the Newborn
Visual reception. The visual apparatus of the newborn, as can be determined by a chain of reactions produced in the newborn by light stimuli, begins to function at birth. Some investigators point out that at birth the characteristic response to a light stimulus is a

change in the general motor activity of a child (Irwin and Weiss, 35; Weiss, 85; Irwin, 34, and others). They indicate that the character of changes in the motor activity—its increase or decrease—depends, on the one hand, on the intensity and the duration of the light stimulus and, on the other hand, on the composition of visual receptors (light-adapted or dark-adapted eye). There is evidence concerning the appearance in the newborn of the visual-pupillary reflex upon sudden exposure to light of sufficient brightness or following drastic change in general illumination. Observations of the newborn show a movement of the eyes and head toward the source of light as well as a continuous movement of the eyes in response to a moving light stimulus. These movements appear after one to two weeks of life. Pursuing movements of the eyes in relation to an object moving in a vertical sphere appear later than the visual pursuit of a light stimulus moving across a horizontal plane.

As the stimulus in his experiment Chase (15) used the movement of a colored spot of light on a colored background of a different shade but of the same brightness as the moving spot. He considered pursuing movements of the eyes as an indicator of the presence of color vision in the newborn. He observed pursuing movements of the eyes in response to colored dots in fifteen-day-old infants. At the same time, an absence of pursuing movements is reported where colorless dots are presented moving on a colorless background of a different brightness.

Aside from the presence of a whole series of visual reactions to outside stimulation, the visual apparatus of the newborn does not yet possess the mechanism that would provide for the ability to distinguish between spatial relations of objects. In the newborn the coordinating mechanism is not yet formed; consequently, sustained visual fixation is absent. According to Ling (46), neither convergent nor binocular fixation takes place in the neonatal period. Attendant divergence and compensatory coordinated eye movements were registered by Ling (on film) on the thirty-second day after birth.

Auditory reception. Numerous investigators point out that the following reactions of a newborn infant give evidence of a sensitivity to sound: changes in general motor activity, wrinkling of the forehead, movement of the eyelids, tremors, changes of rhythm and rate of breathing, turning of the eyes and head to the source of sound, and inhibition of sucking responses (Denisova and Figurin, 20; Bronshtein and Petrova, 12; Pratt, 61). The appearance of a reaction and the degree of its expression depend primarily upon the intensity of the auditory stimulus. For example, Figurin and Denisova point out that only intense auditory stimuli evoke in the newborn child corresponding reactions in the form of blinking and tremors of the entire body. Stubbs (76) regulated the intensity of sound and registered the number of corresponding reactions. He discovered that the number of reactions in the newborn grows with increasing loudness of the sound. The loudest sounds (85, 70, 50, and 30 sensory units of intensity) produced the greatest motor activity, i.e., the greatest number of eyelid closures and breathing movements. Stubbs presented the newborn with sounds of four frequencies: 128, 256, 1024, and 4096, holding intensity constant with a duration of ten seconds. The recorded movements of his subjects showed no difference in the nature of responses to sounds of different frequencies. However, the lowest frequency sound evoked responses in a smaller number of cases than did the highest frequency sound.

A study of activity of the newborn's auditory analyzer has recently been conducted by Soviet scientists (Bronshtein and Petrova, 12; Bronshtein, 13; Bronshtein, Petrova, Bruskina, and Kamenetskaya[*]). In their investigation they used the delay (inhibition) of the sucking responses following the unconditioned orienting reaction to the auditory stimulus as an indicator of auditory sensitivity. They recorded the exact nature of the sound stimuli and the corresponding reactions. They discovered that an infant in the first days of life not only reacts to sounds of a tonal

[*]The complete reference was not provided in the original.

and nontonal nature, but also is able to differentiate them according to pitch and timbre. The investigators relied on the following fact to account for the presence of this differential sensitivity. After the infant's orienting reaction to the sound stimulus had extinguished, the application of a sound stimulus differing from the initial one in pitch or timbre again aroused the orienting reaction—the inhibition of sucking movements.

The limits of differential auditory sensitivity were not established in this study; however, data indicating that the newborn could distinguish sounds separated by one octave (660 and 330 Hz) were presented. Findings pertaining to the development of conditioned reflexes to sound stimuli in very early stages of the newborn's life are contradictory. According to Kasatkin and Levikova (39, 45), attempts to produce conditioned reflexes to sound stimuli in the newborn do not lead to successful results. On the other hand, some authors point out that conditioned reflexes to sound stimuli can be obtained during the first ten days of life, e.g., appearance of sucking movements and inhibition of general motor activity (Marquis, 48); inhibition of sucking responses (Bronshtein and Petrova, 12).

Tactual sensitivity. Tactual sensitivity is highly developed in the newborn. According to Carmichael (14), tactual sensitivity is the earliest form of sensitivity phylogenetically as well as ontogenetically. It emerges during the prenatal period in the area of the mouth-nose cavity and spreads throughout the entire surface of the body in the early postnatal period.

In the first few days of life, a touch on the infant's cheek evokes exploratory responses—opening of the mouth, wrinkling of the lips, and sucking movements (Denisova and Figurin, 20, and others). Denisova and Figurin refer to this type of reaction as orienting-nutritive. It is possible to elicit a palmar reflex in the first period of postnatal life, through stimulation of the skin of the palm. Figurin and Denisova also observed in the newborn a reflex opposite to the palmar—a straightening of the fingers in response to stimulation on the back of the hand and fingers.

Olfactory sensitivity. The majority of investigators concerned with early childhood hold that olfactory sensitivity in the newborn is either absent or minimal.

Taste sensitivity. Using mimic and sucking reactions to taste stimuli as an indicator of taste sensitivity, some authors (Pratt, Nelson, and Sun, 62; Stirnimann, 73; and others) indicate that the newborn distinguishes the taste qualities of sweet, sour, and salty.

Temperature sensitivity. A number of investigators cite indisputable studies showing the infant's sensitivity to changes in temperature (Pratt, Nelson, and Sun, 62; Stirnimann, 74, and others). These investigators, using cold and warm stimuli applied to various parts of the body, obtained clearly expressed responses: withdrawal of the body from the stimuli, tremors of the entire body, and vegetative reactions, i.e., respiratory and vasomotor reactions.

Development of the Sensory Sphere during the First Year of Life

More or less systematic data concerning the development of analyzer activity during the entire first year of life are presented in a study by Denisova and Figurin (21), dealing with characteristics of the developmental stages of children from birth to one year. The remaining investigations present ideas pertaining only to isolated aspects of the development of the sensory apparatus and relating usually to only one of the stages of a given period in the child's development. Therefore, discussion here of the general sensory development during the first year of life shall be based principally upon the data of Figurin and Denisova. The developmental periods formulated by these authors are as follows: first period—from birth to the end of the first month; second period—from the beginning of the second month to the third month; third period—from three to six months; fourth period—from six to twelve months.

First period (from birth to the end of the first month). From the first days of life the child exhibits a number of defensive and orienting visual reactions: the pupillary reflex, partial closing of the eyes upon exposure to bright light, turning of the eyes and head toward the light and to an object vibrating at the periphery of the visual field, steplike visual pursuit, and the turning of the head in the direction of a slowly moving object.

During the first month of life new visual reactions appear. Usually in the second-third *week uncoordinated movements of the eyeballs in response to optical stimulation disappear and convergence appears. Initially convergence is produced only with difficulty, i.e., only with the use of shining objects; convergence ceases at a distance of approximately 10 cm from the infant's eyes. The reaction improves rapidly.

Immediately following the start of convergence in the third-fourth week of the first month, visual fixation or sustained attention to an object appears. In addition to the previously mentioned visual pursuit and convergence, which coincide with simultaneous inhibition of general motor activity, fixation upon an immovable object can now be observed.

Initially, in order to evoke visual fixation it is necessary to catch the infant's eye; the length of such fixation is only about five seconds. Subsequently, the length of visual fixation increases rapidly; during the second month of life, the infant can fixate on an object for several minutes.

During the first month of life, the distance from which an infant can observe moving objects increases. Whereas pursuing eye movements occur in relation to a moving object located 20-30 cm from the infant's eyes at birth, by the end of the first month of life the infant can keep an eye on a moving object at a distance of 1-1.5 m.

Little data concerning the development of the auditory analyzer during the first month are available. Figurin and Denisova note that approximately in the second-third week of the first month a new reaction to a relatively strong auditory stimulus appears. This reaction—in contrast to reactions already present at birth such as

*The use of hyphens in age designation has been retained from the original. Its meaning should be interpreted in terms of the context.

trembling, closing of the eyelids, etc.—is expressed in terms of inhibition of general motor activity. Drawing an analogy to visual fixation, they call this reaction "auditory fixation." Shortly after this occurs, during the third-fourth week, auditory fixation can be obtained, not only in response to a relatively loud noise, but also to verbal expression by an adult. In contrast to these findings, Bronshtein and Petrova (12) present data indicating that inhibition of motor activity in the form of sucking movements in response to auditory stimulation occurs during the first nine days of life. This reaction occurs in the absence of general motor activity.

According to Figurin and Denisova, the appearance of visual and auditory fixation during the first month of life is of critical importance for the further development of the analyzing activity and of the behavior of the child as well. They point out its biological significance in relation to the child's adaptation to new visual and auditory stimuli encountered during the shift from intrauterine to extrauterine existence. Biologically the essence of fixation, evoked by distance receptors, is that it provides the best conditions for the activity of these receptors by inhibiting all other activities.

Second period (from one to three months). In the second-third month visual reception begins to play the leading role in the child's development. According to Bekhterev and Shchelovanov (7), beginning in the second month the speed of visual reaction to a given stimulus increases; inhibition of other reactions is also accelerated and the length of visual fixation is gradually extended up to ten minutes. Approximately in the same period visual fixation appears, not only in situations involving direct visual stimulation, but also spontaneously. The beginning of the spontaneous visual fixation is observed in terms of independent eye movements in the direction of some object.

Furthermore, beginning with the second half of the third month, visual fixation time constantly increases and becomes the predominant component of the child's behavior. At the same time, one observes visual searching evoked by another receptive system—turning of the head and eyes toward the sound of objects not in the field of vision.

Rosenhart-Pupko asserts simply that the third month of life is the main period of development of visual perception during the first year of life, for during this time active perception appears: "The infant begins to look in order to see an adult, thereafter a moving toy in the hands of an adult and, finally, a fixed toy, to which an adult tries to attract the child's attention" (66; p. 22).

Stimuli pertaining to other receptive systems—auditory and tactile—arouse visual reactions in the three-month-old infant. In response to the sound of the human voice, children of this age immediately turn their heads and visually search for the person speaking; if they accidentally touch a suspended toy with their hands, they immediately look at it. During this period visual perception is the main medium for getting acquainted with the surrounding world and is tightly linked to the emotional sphere of the child.

During the third month of life, as noted by Rosenhart-Pupko, a child interacts with an adult primarily through visual perception. Figurin and Denisova also note the prevalence of visual perception, pointing out that during this period the child is always visually exploring something and that the length of fixation is 7-10 minutes. According to their data, the visual pursuit reaction is formed in the first to third month. During the second month the child observes a moving object at a distance of 2-3 m, during the third month at a distance of 4-7 m. There also appears the visual pursuit of objects being variously displaced in the visual field, e.g., in line with a semicircle, in contrast to the previous period during which the child could follow an object moving only in one plane—from right to left or from top to bottom.

During the same period, conditioned-reflexive blinking begins and is readily observable whenever an object on which the child has fixated is quickly moved toward the child. Subsequent to this reaction, even a small movement (2-3 cm) of an object in the direction of the child's eyes is sufficient to evoke blinking. In some cases the blinking reaction is evoked by sudden withdrawal or, in general, sudden movement of the object.

As evidence of substantial progress in the area of auditory perception during this period, Figurin and Denisova point to the appearance of the localization of sound in space. This is expressed initially by moving the head from one side to the other toward a sound presented laterally, then by raising the head toward a sound above the head. The authors emphasize that the shifting of the head toward the source of sound—its localization in space—results from training.

With regard to skin sensitivity, this period is characterized by the appearance of localized skin reactions. Judgments of stimulus localization can be made on the basis of hand movement toward the stimulated part and rubbing of that part.

Initial indicators of localized reaction—movement of the hand toward the part being stimulated—can be observed as early as the end of the first month. But localized reactions in their perfected form, which includes rubbing, do not appear until the second-third month of life. These reactions begin first at the eyelids and later at the nose.

During the third month of life intersensory connections, i.e., connections between orienting reactions emerging in the various receptive systems, begin to form. This is indicated by the appearance of an orienting sensory reaction in connection with a stimulus directed toward another receptor, as for example in the turning of the eyes and head upon activation of an auditory or a tactual receptor. The appearance of intermodal reactions along with facts concerning the production of conditioned reflexes, to be cited below, indicates the relative functional maturity of cortical divisions of analyzing systems.

The feeding behavior of the child assembles an interesting array of facts. Observations show that the nutritive orienting-exploratory reactions (turning of the head from side to side, distortions of the lips, and opening of the mouth) in an infant of two-three months of age begin to be evoked not only by internal organic stimuli, as they are during the first month of life, but also by external stimuli, in part by stimuli directed to the visual receptors. Apparently this indicates on the one hand development of receptive reactions and, on the other, the appearance of intersensory connections.

The fact that it is possible to produce conditioned reflexes in all receptors from the second month on is evidence of the presence of orienting reactions in all sensory organs and the functional readiness of the cortical component of analytic systems at this period.

That conditioned reflexes can be produced during the second month with auditory and visual stimuli on the basis of nutritive and defensive unconditioned reflexes has been shown by Denisova and Figurin (21), Levikova (45), Kasatkin (39), and Shriftzettser (70).

Investigations by Nemanova (55, 56, 57) indicate that during the second month it is possible to produce relatively stable conditioned reflexes with olfactory and taste stimuli. Such reflexes can also be produced by stimulation of the vestibular apparatus.

Available data show that in the second-third month it is possible to produce, through the method of conditioned reflexes involving nutritive and defensive unconditioned reflexes, gross and relatively unstable differentiations between external stimuli.

Kasatkin (39) obtained relatively unstable differentiation between a green light and a contrasting yellow (or red) one with a few children in their third month of life. He obtained gross differentiation between two qualitatively different auditory stimuli (sound of a bell and sound of an organ pipe) in three youngsters in their second to third month.

Kasatkin obtained a relatively stable differentiation between two tones, differing by almost an octave (eleven and one-half tones), in three children in their third month. With continued application of the differentiated tone, however, there followed a rapid drop in the constancy of the positive conditioned reflex.

Denisova and Figurin (22), on the basis of the defensive blinking response, were able to produce in one child toward the end of its third month a more refined (four tones), even though unstable, differentiation.

Differentiations of smell, olfactory as well as trigeminal, are especially unstable in children during their second-third months, as indicated by the experiments of Nemanova (56) and Kasatkin (39).

Denisova and Figurin (22) demonstrated a relatively stable distinction of localization of skin-tactual stimulation during this second period. One youngster of two months and four days gave evidence of differentiation involving the tactual analyzer by distinguishing between a pin prick on the chest and one on the foot.

According to experiments by Nemanova (57), it is possible to assume that during the second half of the second month some taste differentiation may emerge, and that during the third month the child is capable of distinguishing the basic taste qualities of sweet, salty, and sour. During the third month, gross differentiations in vestibular stimulation, such as rocking from one plane to another (55), can be obtained. Even though the differentiations obtained during the first months of life are gross and relatively unstable, they indicate that even in the first stages of postnatal life an initial analysis of activity in the external environment is possible. In other words, it indicates that discriminations between external influences are now capable of regulating the behavior of the child—of activating or inhibiting unconditional reflexes.

Third period (from three to six months). This period is characterized by active development of the hand as an organ of action and cognition. During this period feeling movements of the hand emerge. They are evident first in the feeling of one's own hands —i.e., holding one hand next to the other and moving one hand over the other—and subsequently in the feeling of an object by moving the hand over it. Thereafter it is possible to evoke prolonged holding of the hand near the object and movement of the hand in pursuit of a withdrawing object. Later the directional positioning of the hand toward a visible object appears. These developments are followed by visual exploration of hands and objects and by the retention of hands and objects in the field of vision with a relatively prolonged fixation of the hands in one position.

During the fifth-sixth month, according to Rosenhart-Pupko (66), the child exhibits independent exploration for and manipulation of objects. That is, this activity occurs independent of adult participation. Children of this age hold a toy in their hands for a relatively long period of time, simultaneously turning and examining it. Sometimes they may shake it and listen to the sounds it makes.

In children of this age there is an ongoing enlargement and development of intermodal connections in the visual-kinesthetic and visual-tactual spheres. Reactions such as moving the hand toward a visible object, simultaneously feeling and examining an object, maintaining the hands in a given position and examining them, holding a visible object, and maintaining the hand in a certain position while holding an object are also observed. Other reactions, turning of the head toward the point of contact and visually fixating upon that point, are expressive of visual-tactual connections.

Toward the end of this period, the relationship between visual perception and movements of the hand undergoes a change. Whereas before touch evoked visual perception and seemingly guided it, i.e., direct contact with an object evoked visual fixation and the eyes continually followed the touching movements of the hand now, to the contrary, visual perception evokes movements of the hand toward an adult or toward an object and regulates the duration of such movements with respect to direction and form.

Denisova and Figurin's data indicate fundamental progress in the development of the kinesthetic sphere of the child during this period. This progress manifests itself in two ways. It is expressed by the occurrence of a prolonged tonic tension due to stimulation of the child's eyes and skin, e.g., holding an object, examining it, and feeling it, as noted above. It is expressed also by the fact that during the period from three to six months differentiated movements of the skeletal musculature emerge, indicating differentiated innervation of the muscles. The first distinct movement reactions are movements of the hand—feeling and grasping.

During this period the skin analyzer undergoes further development. Localized reactions on the forehead, ear, stomach, and chest occur. In addition to the expansion of localized reactions of the skin, some new types of reactions evoked from the skin begin to appear in the form of grasping of the hands, diapers, and toys, and of the turning of the head upon contact with visual fixation upon the point of contact. Furthermore, a distinctly original form of the orienting-adjusting reaction emerges. Drawing an analogy from visual and auditory fixation, Denisova and Figurin call this form of reaction "tactual fixation." Its distinctiveness arises from a child's tendency, as the authors put it, to "freeze totally" in response to stimulation on some portion of his skin instead of reaching the hand toward the portion being stimulated. During the time of stimulation all movements stop; total inhibition of motor activity ensues, and the child seems to be listening to, or to be tuned in to, the ongoing stimulation. These authors report that toward the sixth month of life the development of tactual reactions essentially comes to an end. Thereafter, the development of each analyzer is directed toward perfecting the reactions with respect to speed, accuracy, and differentiation.

During this period, for the first time, recognition of compound and complex stimuli appears. During the fifth-sixth month of life, the child begins to recognize his mother and can distinguish her from other people by her external appearance. Whenever the child is hungry or disturbed, sight of the mother leads him to turn, cry, etc. During the quiescent period, sight of the mother makes him more active—he begins to breathe deeply, smile, mumble, and move around. The appearance of a strange face often evokes negative emotional reactions. Rosenhart-Pupko notes that in addition to being able to distinguish people close to him and especially in being able to distinguish his mother from strangers, children of five-six months recognize such situations as feeding, preparation for sleeping, etc.

The common improvement in perceptual processes during this stage of development depends upon the fact that external actions begin to acquire predominant significance in regulating the child's behavior: they give rise to and exert a critical influence on its course. Movements and actions of the child become more differentiated and more adapted to the conditions of the surrounding environment due to the fact that they begin to be regulated and controlled not only proprioceptively, but also by means of other sensory systems. Their formation and development occur primarily under the control of visual reception.

In comparison with the previous period, the possibility of the production of relatively stable and refined differentiations involving various receptors at this time indicates a higher level of maturity of the analytic systems.

As the data of all investigators working on the development of differentiation in children during the first half of their first year indicate, relatively stable differentiation can be obtained beginning with the fourth month of life. Kasatkin asserts that a more stable differentiation of two quantitatively different light stimuli is possible only during the fourth month of life (39; p. 179).

Differentiations between auditory stimuli also become more stable. Using children in their fourth month, Nechayeva (53) developed a relatively stable differentiation of a sound, differing from the basic positive sound by seventeen tones. Levikova and Nevmyvako (45) obtained, during the fifth month of life, stable differentiation between sounds differing by one octave.

In children of this age differentiations of external stimuli, developed through the unconditioned reflex, also become more precise. Kasatkin (39) obtained differentiation of sounds differing by five and one-half tones in children in the fourth month and at the beginning of the fifth month, and differentiation of several smells at the beginning of the fourth month; whereas during the previous period, it was possible to obtain differentiation between only two kinds of smells.

Fourth period (from six to twelve months). The major innovation of this period consists of connection of movements in a sequential order under the control of one or another perceptual organ, in the formation of motor systems. Apparently this is directly related to those fundamental gains that occur in proprioception in the area of the motor analyzer, during the second half of the first year of life. During this period, complex locomotor movements are formed indicating a high degree of coordination of separate muscle groups under the control of proprioception.

This stage of development also witnesses the beginnings of what appear to be new forms of sensory responsiveness: reproduction of a presented pattern, and modeling of external influences. This type of responsiveness is first expressed in the early form by the child's imitation of an adult's motor behavior. Clapping hands in patty-cake fashion and placing rings on a stem under the direction of an adult are typical of this type of responsiveness, as is the imitation of an adult's vocal reaction.

From our point of view, the new aspect here consists of external influences evoking a specific reaction in such situations, that is, eliciting an attempt to reproduce the objective properties or qualities of the external influence, e.g., a form of movement or the qualitative character of sound.

Imitation of hand movements, that is, reproduction of the pattern of movement, can be observed at seven to nine months; vocal imitation of individual syllables at the seventh month; and repetition of separate syllables ("da-da-da," "ba-ba-ba," etc.) at ninth-tenth month. In general, according to Figurin and Denisova, any imitation up to the end of the first year is performed with difficulty and is quite imperfect. At the end of the first year an abrupt change occurs after which copying behavior is easily evoked. The child then begins to imitate, more or less precisely, diversely, and frequently without any special arousal.

Aside from reproducing the elements of the auditory composition of words, children in the second half of the first year, according to these authors, make an attempt to imitate the tonal or rhythmic character of an auditory pattern.

Rosenhart-Pupko also indicates that during the period from six to twelve months imitation occurs in the form of reproducing patterns. In the child of this age visual perception is constructed by imitating the process of an adult's visual perception during joint visual exploration. Then the child's eyes follow the movements of the adult's eyes, which thus become a pattern for imitation. The introduction of speech into this process during the ninth-tenth month serves first to direct the process and second to enlist the process as an aid in developing an understanding of speech and verbal instructions.

The experimental findings of Barbashova (5) substantiate the key role played by visual perception in the development of the understanding of words in children toward the end of the first year of life. She experimentally explored the role of different analyzers in the forming of connections between an object and its verbal meaning. By combining the verbal definition with the visual, the auditory, and the tactile-kinesthetic methods of presenting an object, she attempted to determine the number of trials needed to develop a conditioned-reflexive, orientational reaction to an object, as indicated by turning of the head, the eyes, or the entire body. Results of the experiment showed that the orienting reaction to an object in children of ten to twelve months of age appears most readily under conditions when the verbal definition is combined with visual presentation of the object (after five to ten trials); that it is somewhat more difficult in combination with the auditory image of an object (eleven to nineteen trials); and that it is most difficult with the tactile-kinesthetic image (seventeen to twenty-eight trials).

Data concerning the development of conditioned reflexes and differentiations in children in the second half of their first year are sparse. Nechayeva's data (53) indicate that in six-seven-month-old children it is possible to obtain fine differentiations in pitch with an accuracy of about half a tone.

Using the forms of the cone, prism, sphere, and cylinder, Denisova and Figurin (20) have shown that during the eighth month it is possible to develop differentiation of form. Similarly, working with the colors green, red, yellow, and blue and employing the method of conditioned reflexes with food as the reinforcement, they observed at the same age an ability to differentiate color. The authors noted certain peculiarities in the development of this type of visual differentiation at that age. First, one of the essential conditions for the development of differentiation is the simultaneous presentation of the stimuli to be differentiated. Second, visual differentiation obtained as a result of simultaneous impact of both alimentary and nonalimentary stimuli is immediately disrupted upon presentation of only one object. In this case, the alimentary reaction is observed in relation to the alimentary stimulus as well as the nonalimentary one and is accompanied by a markedly shorter latency period than the one observed with the presentation of both objects.

Denisova and Figurin recorded interesting observations with respect to the process of visual distinction between two simultaneously presented objects. They noted that the decisive factor in this development was the transfer of sight from one object to another and an alternating fixation upon each object.

Volkelt's experiments (81) also indicate that differentiation of form is possible for the five- to twelve-month-old child. Using food as reinforcement, Volkelt trained the child to distinguish the various forms of feeding bottles. As choices, the child was presented with four different forms of bottles—square, triangular, oval, and violinlike. The bottles were quite similar in all other respects. Each bottle was topped with a nipple; however, only one of these nipples had a hole in it. Consequently, the child was able to obtain milk only by selecting the bottle of a given form. As a result of this training, the child learned the various forms presented to him.

Recently, Walk and Gibson (83), relying on extremely ingenious methodology, obtained data concerning visual depth differentiation in children during the second half of their first year (from six and a half to fourteen months). With thirty-six children they employed the following design. Each child was placed on a platform in the center of a table covered with thick glass. Under the glass there was colored linoleum. On one side of the child the linoleum was placed immediately under the glass; on the other side it was placed four feet below the surface of the glass, directly on the floor. The mother of the child approached the table, either from one side or the other, and stood there for a period of two minutes. She offered toys to the child and verbally encouraged him to come to her. Whenever the mother stood on the side of the platform with the linoleum placed directly under the glass, 75 percent of the infants crawled to her; the others remained in the center of the table. In those cases where the mother stood on the side of the table with the colored surface directly on the floor, only 8 percent of the children approached her, 62 percent remained in place, and 30 percent crawled in the opposite direction. Walk and Gibson conclude that as soon as children are capable of moving around, they begin to show visual perception of depth.

As far as it is possible to determine on the basis of available data and assuming sufficient contact with a nurturing adult, adjustment mechanisms and adaptational perceptual reactions of all sensory systems develop during the first half of the first year of life. Under the category of adjusting reactions are included visual fixation on an object, visual pursuit of a moving object, auditory fixation, localization of sound in space, etc., as well as vegetative components of orienting sensory reactions—vasomotor and respiratory reactions. Development of the elementary reactions of the sensory apparati is a necessary preliminary stage in the development of the essentially psychological process of sensory reflection of the objective world, i.e., those sensory activities on the basis of which it is possible to construct a sensory image reproducing the objective characteristics of the external object with all the accompanying connections and relationships.

During the second half of the first year, on the basis of already formed elementary sensory reactions, essentially sensory actions consisting of attempts to reproduce motor activity of the external influence by imitation of an adult's actions begin to be formed.

Theories concerning the mechanisms of sensory reflection formed principally by Sechenov and developed recently by Soviet psychologists (Leontiev, 44, and others), as well as certain experimental investigations, present a basis for assuming that the formation of essentially sensory actions appears possible only under the conditions of objective activity. These actions emerge, in other words, only with direct, uninterrupted—for rather prolonged periods of time—mutual interaction of the sensory organ with the external object.

Analysis of the child's psychological development shows that the object relationship becomes not only a necessary condition for the formation of the mechanism for sensory action, but also one of the decisive factors in the genesis of sensory activity. Thus, it is only due to interaction with objects that the child develops the need to take into account objective signs and qualities and to adjust his instrumental responses in terms of their characteristics. As a result of this internalized activity, cognitive sensory activity appears and is directed at familiarization with objects. This process is expressed by a visual examination of the object prior to the instrumental act or by tactual exploration interspersed with instrumental activity. This sensory activity in the presence of an existing cognitive task may be transformed into essentially perceptual rather than instrumental activity.

Data introduced in this chapter concerning development of the child's sensory sphere during the first stages of life refer to that aspect of sensory feedback that is defined by Sechenov as a relationship on "sensation"—"sensation" to movement and actions, and the ability of that "sensation" to evoke biologically expedient reactions directly from the area of the sensory apparati as well as from the other types of organismic activity.

The process of formation and development of essentially perceptual activity channeled into construction of the sensory image of the external objects, and the question of maintenance of the sensory image in children during the early stages of ontogeny have not been investigated. Therefore, the data illuminating this important psychological aspect of the young child's sensory development are not discussed in this chapter. These questions must still be exposed to thorough experimental analysis.

Development of Sensation and Perception During Pre-preschool and Preschool Age

Perceptual activity and its development in children of pre-preschool and preschool age have been explored generally from two points of view. First, psycho-physiological methods helped to establish the sensitivity levels of various sensory systems and to study the dynamics of the development of accuracy and precision in differentiating between individual properties and signs of external objects during the preschool age. Second, experiments were conducted investigating separate aspects of perceptual activity in general. An attempt was made to study the process of sensory feedback of the surrounding reality with respect to organization, duration, and in part, conditions of formation of the sensory image and its maintenance.

Visual Sensitivity

Visual acuity. Foucault's (25) data presented in Table 1 indicate that beginning with later preschool age through fourteen-fifteen years, visual acuity increases steadily. To measure it Foucault utilized methodology ordinarily employed in medical practice. This methodology relies on verbal report as the single criterion for determining whether or not the subject can distinguish external stimuli. Yendovitskaya's (86) study concerning the development of visual acuity in preschool children showed that its increase with age is also noted within the limits of preschool childhood. Measuring the maximal distance from which children at various preschool ages were able to detect the break in Landolt's ring—the diameter of the ring was 7 mm and the break was 1 mm—Yendovitskaya showed that for children from four to five years, the average distance was 2 m and 10 cm; for children from five to six years of age, 2 m and 70 cm; and for children from six to seven years, 3 m. He also found that the visual distance for children of various age groups increased whenever verbal description of the location of the break in Landolt's ring was not required. In other words, the visual distance for children of various age groups was greater when the child was required merely to orient himself toward this break by some type of action. Such action might involve, for example, pointing out in which of a number of similar boxes, distinguished only by the location of the break on a picture of Landolt's ring pasted on the boxes, a picture was hidden.

This study also examined the relationship between visual acuity and the conditions of activity. The data obtained indicate that visual acuity among children of preschool age increases under

Table 1
Visual Acuity of Children

Age (years)	Mean Distance (cm)
6	299
7	326
8	350
9	355
10	360
11	375
12	404
13	440
14-15	475

those conditions where success of determining the position of the break in Landolt's ring becomes the decisive factor in the fulfillment of the required activity. A comparison of the visual distance determined by the regular method, i.e., by simply presenting the child with the task of identifying the break in the Landolt ring, with the visual distance measured under the condition of active play, showed that in the latter case the distance increases for children of four to five years on an average of 17.2 percent; for children of five to six years, 29.8 percent; and for children of six to seven years, 30.2 percent.

Differentiation of Color. A series of experimental investigations by Brazhas (11), Arkin (3), Istomina (36, 37), and Danyushevskaya (17, 19) explored fineness and exactness of color differentiation in children. These experiments made use essentially of two basic methods to determine sensitivity of color distinction. In the first case, children were asked to interact with objects, taking their color into account without naming the colors; in the second case, verbal definition of the color was used, provided either by the experimenter or by the child himself.

Brazhas used only children in the first half of preschool childhood (three to five years). In one case he asked the children to match objects according to color by placing differently colored balls of wool into correspondingly colored boxes. In another case he asked the children to select an object among other objects, merely by having someone name the color of the object. And in a third case he asked them to name the color of the presented object. The data obtained indicate that the first method—matching objects according to color—enables children to obtain relatively better results in color differentiation than is possible in the other two methods. That is, children make substantially fewer mistakes in the first method than in the second or third. The third method, requiring the children to identify the color of a presented object, yielded the greatest number of mistakes. The technique of matching colors by "direct comparison" yielded not only the fewest errors, but the errors it did precipitate were not as gross as those in the remaining two methods. In this series of trials children tended to mix only those colors in close proximity to one another on the spectrum—yellow and orange, violet and blue—in contrast with the other two series in which children tended to mix colors quite distant from one another on the spectrum.

Arkin and Istomina explored the dynamics of color distinction during the period of preschool age. Both of these investigations show that accuracy of color distinction increases with age.

The experiments conducted by Arkin asked in one case that children fill in the centers of large circles of different colors with small circles corresponding in color to that of the large circles. The second case utilized the method of naming; the children were asked to state verbally the color of a given circle. The results of the first series of experiments showed that the children in the first half of preschool childhood made mistakes in 24 percent of the cases; under conditions of the second series, 52 percent. Children in the second half of preschool childhood recorded an error rate of 5.5 percent for condition one and 30.5 percent for condition two.

A comparison of these results indicates that the percentage of error for both age groups is much lower in situations where color enters only as a cue directing the actions of the child than in those where the child is required to define the color verbally. For children in the younger age group, the number of errors in the second series of experiments rises to 28 percent and for children in the older age group it increases to 25 percent.

Istomina conducted experiments not only with children of preschool age, but also with older children of pre-preschool age. These experiments implemented intermediate hues as well as basic colors. The results showed that up to the age of two years children can directly perceive four basic colors: red, yellow, green, and blue. However, children experienced difficulties in distinguishing the intermediate colors of orange, light blue, and violet. Thus, in grouping tones of color according to a given picture, the children of pre-preschool age (two to three years) solved the problem most easily when the pictures corresponded to basic colors, making in this case 40 to 50 percent mistakes. Whenever they were asked to match the intermediate colors the percentage of errors rose to 70-80 percent. Furthermore, children of this age do not yet form a stable connection between the color and its name, even in the case of the basic colors.

Istomina therefore concluded that the ability to differentiate color, either through direct perception or by naming, improves throughout the preschool period. Furthermore, beginning at the age of five years, all children perform errorless sorting and grouping of both basic and intermediate hues. With respect to the basic colors, a rather stable connection between the color and its name appears at the beginning of the fourth year. A fairly stable connection between the intermediate hues and their names appears beginning at age five. Beginning with this age, in grouping colored pictures children take into account not only hue, but also brightness.

Danyushevskaya showed that recognition of relative color brightness also may occur with children of younger preschool age whenever it is required by the conditions of the task confronting the child, especially when the relative brightness acquires stimulus properties. Perception of brightness relationships improves with age. Training sessions witness a decrease in the number of presentations of pairs of objects similar in hue but differing in brightness, necessary to evoke a response not to the absolute brightness, but to the relationship of brightness. Quick and accurate discrimination of relative brightness and transfer of this relativity to other situations, such as the presentation of a pair of objects of a different hue, occur whenever such relationships are defined by a generalization—e.g., "dark, light."

A series of experiments by Cook (16) shows that two-year-old children are capable of matching shades of the basic colors (red, green, blue, and yellow) that vary in saturation. Accuracy in distinguishing shades of color approximately doubles by six years of age. Cook also remarks that distinguishing colors by naming presents a more difficult problem to all preschool children.

The nature of the connection between color and the object plays an important role in isolation of color as a specific quality by preschool children. An experiment by Gordon (28) included color discrimination by children during play. Under the first set of conditions, the object's relationship to color was completely absent; the child was presented with colored surfaces. In the second set of conditions, color occurred as an incidental indicator of the object; children were asked to differentiate between two colored boxes. The third set of conditions presented color as the characteristic sign of the object, its natural color. The results showed that the most favorable conditions for discrimination are the ones in which color occurs as an inseparable characteristic sign of an object. Under these conditions, a preschool child begins to orient his actions in terms of the absolute sign of color, whereas with the other two sets of conditions, the child perceived the color in its relative sense and was guided in his actions by the differences between colors.

Auditory Sensitivity

Auditory Acuity. Tonal acuity in children up to the age of thirteen is lower than that of adults with respect to all frequencies, and is especially so in the area of lower frequencies. Results of experiments by Suzuki and Hakaoka (78) confirm other findings that the acuity of tonal hearing improves with age, i.e., preschool children show lower acuity than adults. Comparing the auditory threshold of children three-four and five-six with auditory threshold for adults (up to twenty-five years), measured in relation to seven frequencies with a range of 125-6,000 Hz, Suzuki and Hakaoka discovered that thresholds of the younger group exceed the adults' threshold by 7-11 db, and those of the older group exceed the adults' by 5-8 db. A comparison of the auditory threshold within the preschool group by the same investigators showed that an increase in the acuity for tonal hearing during this period develops unevenly. According to the data obtained on 418 children, the thresholds of children three and four, just as well as five and six, show little difference, whereas between the ages four and five a noticeable gain in the acuity for tonal hearing is observed.

Kogan (41) determined that children's auditory acuity for speech is also less refined than that of adults. The threshold of preschool children (four-seven) for this type of hearing exceeds that of adults by 14-16 db. A comparison of developmental indicators for the relationship between hearing and verbal stimuli lead Kogan to conclude that the auditory acuity for speech increases with age. Furthermore, he remarks that in the preschool period the lowering of the speech threshold is accomplished more gradually than in the subsequent developmental periods. The data obtained in the measurement of tonal and speech thresholds with children of preschool age show an appreciable difference between the thresholds in these children. The level of the speech threshold exceeds the level of the tonal threshold by 18-22db. This means that children of preschool age perceive a word only when its sound exceeds the loudness at which they perceive the sound of simple tones.

Differential sensitivity of pitch. Relying on theoretical developments concerning formation of human hearing, Leontiev formulated a hypothesis stating that in correspondence to the two basic aspects of auditory reality—sounds of speech and of music—man develops two qualitatively different receptive systems: reception for speech, or the phonemic system, and reception for music, or the tonic system. Leontiev (44) points out that perception of the sounds of speech and of music requires separation of qualitatively different components of auditory reality. He notes too that the surroundings, in terms of which the auditory state is reflected, are determined by the attributes of "a set" reflected in the sensations of qualities. That is, "a set" of these qualities comprises the essence of the different systems of hearing—systems on the one hand specifically related to speech, and on the other, related to pitch.

Until now, there has been neither systematic investigation of the mechanisms involved in the formation of the phonemic and the tonic audition, nor study of the correlation in the development of the two systems in childhood. However, as indicated by some observations of speech development, as well as by certain recent experiments in the development of the tonic hearing, the development of these two auditory systems does not proceed in a parallel fashion.

Speech hearing begins to develop relatively early: from the end of the first or the beginning of the second year of life. As a rule, at the beginning of the preschool age the child differentiates practically all sounds of his native language in accordance with their phonemic signs; he understands speech and actively utilizes it.*

A somewhat different pattern appears in the development of tonic hearing. Yendovitskaya and Repina have shown that the differentiation of pitch relationships presents considerable difficulty for children in the first half of the preschool period (from three to four and one-half or five years).

Yendovitskaya (88) arranged the experimental setting in such a way that the children were required to be directed in their play activities by two sequential sounds differing in pitch. Only children in the second half of the preschool age—older than five —were able to complete the task successfully. After presentation of eighty to ninety-six complex sound stimuli of both equal and differing pitch and with a gradual reduction in the difference of pitch between each subsequent pair of stimuli, the children were able to develop a relatively refined pitch discrimination. Differential thresholds in the five to six- to seven-year-old group they the limits of 9 to 25 Hz; in the six- seven-year-old group they ranged between 8 to 20 Hz.

Children of middle preschool age showed some difficulty in differentiation whenever it was necessary not only to state the presence or absence of the difference in pitch of a pair of sounds,

*See "Development of Speech," Chapter 4.

but also to indicate the direction of the difference—higher or lower—between the two members of the pair.

Repina's data indicate that children older than five, unlike younger children, are capable of giving a verbal appraisal of pitch relationships. They can say whether two sounds presented to them differ or are the same in pitch and, after special training, they can state verbally which one of the two sounds is higher.

These experiments facilitate formulation of certain principles concerning development of tonic hearing in childhood. Specifically, the training of younger preschool children is successful whenever the child masters the method of active reproduction of pitch relationships.

Mediational ways of modeling pitch relationships by relying on already mastered relationships from another sphere of reality and by including other sensory systems into the modeling process were used in several of these training experiments.

In Yendovitskaya's experiments modeling of pitch relationships was accomplished by arm movements within a well-defined space, equivalent in terms of its parts to the pitch of sounds presented in a sequence. The modeling process consisted of having the child execute arm movements corresponding in amplitude to the relationship between the pitch of sounds. A play situation was used for training the children to perform a movement of predetermined amplitude corresponding to the pitch interval of the presented sounds. During training, the correspondence of pitch to the amplitude of movement was rigidly enforced. For any increase in the difference of the pitch of sounds by a predetermined number of cycles per second, the amplitude of arm movement was also relatively increased by a corresponding number of spatial units (squares). As a result of this type of training, younger preschool children began to distinguish pitch relationships—reporting presence or absence of a difference in the pitch of sounds—merely by listening, i.e., without employing the motor reproduction of the impinging auditory relationships.

Repina trained younger preschool children to discriminate pitch relationships by relying on visually perceived object size relationships. The high tones were conditionally associated with sounds of small animals, whereas low tones were paired with sounds of large animals. This visual reproduction of pitch relationships was conducted in the context of play activity and resulted in the children's learning to perceive pitch relationships directly, i.e., without relying on the visual, external support.

Ilina's data (32) also indicate that pitch hearing in younger preschool children is not yet formed. Children three to five years of age do not reproduce a pitch pattern of a melody, but exhibit a monotonous singing in a "comfortable" tone. Ilina characterizes this type of singing in younger preschool children as "rhythmic singing" because it reproduces only the rhythmic curve.

Older preschool children also will experience difficulty in pitch discrimination. Belyayeva-Ekzemplyarskaya (8) indicates that when children in this age group perceive a musical composition they detect primarily its dynamic aspect—the rhythm and the tempo. They do not as readily perceive aspects of pitch—melody and harmony. Of the latter two, they perceive melody more easily than harmony because they are capable of reproducing it vocally. This vocal reproduction serves as the basis for recognition of musical compositions. The harmonic aspect remains unidentified because the child cannot vocally reproduce it.

Kinesthetic and Tactile Sensitivity

The preschool age is also characterized by development of the joint-muscular and tactile sensations, which play a major role in the analysis of various properties and qualities of the surrounding world—such as surfaces, weights, dimensions, forms, etc. Sukhanova (77) studied the development of accuracy and fineness of differentiations in association with passive angular displacements of parts of the body (upper extremities), the development of fineness in analysis of the degree of muscular tension, and the development of the ability to localize motor response with respect to an outside stimulus. Sukhanova conducted the experiment within the framework of a conditioned reflex methodology. With the help of the Zukovski kinematometer, she used displacement of the arm to a predetermined angular distance as a signal for the reciprocal movement. The results showed that fineness of differentiation under the condition of passive angular displacements improves during the preschool age. The majority of four-year-old children tested were capable of firmly distinguishing only an angle of seven degrees, whereas the majority of seven-year-old children differentiated a difference of one degree or less.

Ability to analyze the degree of muscular tension also improves with age. According to Sukhanova's data, responses to auditory stimuli develop significantly faster in children of six-seven years of age than they do in four-year-old children. Sukhanova's experiment involved submitting the child to the auditory stimuli of a whistle and a horn and verbally reinforcing his activity in one set of conditions with "press hard" and in a second set of conditions with "press easily." Sukhanova found too that the four-five-year-old children exhibit characteristic significant fluctuations in their strength of pressing, both during development of the conditioned reflex as well as during differentiation, whereas in the older children (six-seven years) reactions are more stable.

Consequently, during the initial stages of preschool childhood the analysis of proprioceptive impulses emerging from the muscular-joint apparatus of the arm is obviously inadequate. However, it improves appreciably within the limits of preschool age.

Sukhanova, relying on the development of conditioned motor reflexes to visual and auditory stimuli, also studied the ability of children to produce a localized motor reaction. Sukhanova's experiment to determine this ability recorded not only the reactions of the right arm, on which the reflexes were being developed, but also the movements of the left arm, as well as the movements of both feet. The investigations showed a decrease with age in diffuse motor responses. The number of diffuse reactions in the seven-year-old was four times less than that in the four-year-old children. In other words, the motor reaction becomes specialized and localized with age.

Sukhanova's study also yielded data pointing to an increase during preschool age in the precision of estimating the weight of objects. In selecting a cube equivalent in weight to the presented standard, four-year-old children allowed on the average an error rate of 90 percent; whereas seven-year-old children allowed a rate of only 26 percent. (In estimating the weight of the cube, the child took the cubes sequentially with the same hand.)

According to Jakobson's data, during the preschool age perceived weight differences are reduced by more than half, from one-fifteenth to one thirty-fifth of the weight being estimated.

Olfactory Sensitivity

Zimmerman (90) presents some relevant findings illuminating the question of the level of olfactory sensitivity development in preschool children. Her experiments utilized water emulsions of four olfactory substances: mint, pine, rose, and anise butter. She placed each emulsion into identical dark glass containers. With ten subjects from each year of age, children from ages four to seven were asked to smell the emulsions and to identify the smell. Each child had been previously informed of the names of the smells involved. In those cases where the child had difficulty in identifying the smell, the experimenter reinforced the pairing of a given smell with its name by giving the child a candy, the color of which was conditionally associated with the given smell. Furthermore, during the course of the experiment, whenever the child could not name the presented smell, he was given the choice of candy. The selection of the appropriately colored candy was accepted as a correct response.

The results obtained, presented in Table 2, indicate that all the experimental subjects demonstrated differentiation of smell and that, with the increase in age, a fewer number of trials was necessary for correct discrimination.

Zimmerman indicates that the majority of children of all ages utilized the verbal definition as well as the color of the candy in

Table 2
Olfactory Sensitivity of Preschool Children

| Age (years) | Number of Children Reaching Errorless Identification of Smell | |
	Less Than 10 Trials	More Than 10 Trials
7	8	2
6	7	3
5	6	4
4	2	8

differentiating the smell. Five children, of the six to seven age group, use the verbal definition only. Three children in the four to five-year-old group did not initially employ the verbal definition of a smell, but instead chose the appropriately colored candy. After a number of trials, even these children began to employ the names of smells.

Perception of Space

Perception of spatial relationships serves as a basis for the distinction of objects in terms of the most salient cues—form, size, position in space, etc. This form of perception gradually emerges during the period of pre-preschool and preschool age. The preschool child gradually begins to distinguish spatial relationships with some degree of accuracy. He begins not only to direct his behavior to the form, size, and relationship of objects in space but also to isolate these relationships as particular cues and to comprehend them.

While still in early childhood the child learns to isolate objects in space and to distinguish their form, size, and position in space, as well as their displacement in a given direction. He acquires the ability to distinguish spatial relationships visually, in connection with the development of muscular sensations brought about by accommodation, convergence, movement of the eyes during visual exploration of objects, etc.

Sechenov (67) ascribes a very important role to "the muscular sensation" in the development of perception of spatial relationships. He showed that movement of the eyes and the head while looking at something played a main role in spatial discrimination, in distinguishing mutual positioning, size, distance, and physical characteristics of the surrounding objects. "If, during the development of the child," wrote Sechenov, "his visual actions were not accompanied by movements of the eyes and the head—exploratory movements—he would never learn to distinguish the interrelationships of parts of the visual field; because the seeing of the right and the left and the upper and the lower part of the visual field would not have been accompanied by the differential reaction of the visual apparatus. With the assistance of exploratory movements he receives for each one of the movements of the eyes—up, down, left, right, and all the intermediate ones—separate, i.e., distinguishing (and for each particular movement, always the same) sensory cues which guide him in distinguishing up from down, left from right, etc." (67; pp. 255-256).

The distinguishing of "sensory cues"—those proprioceptive, kinesthetic sensations arising during the movement of the eyes and head—serves as the basis for the development of perception of spatial relationships—form, size, distance, etc. The closest assistant to the eye in the process of distinguishing spatial relationships is the hand.

Orientation in space. As Kolodnaya's investigation (42) indicates, differentiation of spatial relationships, their isolation and comprehension in the process of orientation to the surrounding environment, begins to develop in the preschool child on the basis of differentiation of spatial relationships of his own body. Initially, the child isolates and begins to identify his right hand correctly. On the basis of discriminating between his left and his right hand, the child begins to differentiate the paired parts of his body and the arrangement of objects in space. The isolation of the right hand occurs in the context of activity, with the direct participation of the motor and the visual analyzers.

Kolodnaya observes that the preschool child, while distinguishing the paired organs of his body in response to a request to show the right eye or the right ear, at the beginning always identified his right hand through some kind of movement—making a fist or moving it slightly to the right. And only after that is the child able to show his right eye or his right ear. In determining the spatial relationships of the surrounding objects, not only the hand movements take part, but also the eye and the head movements. Determining the position of surrounding objects follows, analogously, identifying the spatial relationships of one's own body, so that the child first not only makes movements with his right hand, but also looks at it—identifies it visually. Furthermore, by shifting his visual focus from one object to another and frequently by extending his hand in the object's direction he determines the object's position in relation to his own body.

The inclusion of words in the perception process plays a very important role in the development of perceiving spatial relationships. According to Kolodnaya, in speech the child verbally differentiates his right hand earlier than the left hand. This occurs because, while establishing connections between the word "right" and the corresponding hand, the child relies on numerous visual-motor connections which have been developed during activity of the given hand. During a certain stage of development, in response to a request to show his right hand the child says with the right hand I eat, draw, and greet people; therefore, that is the right hand.

Speech plays an especially important role in the development of perceiving spatial relationships among objects. While still in the pre-preschool age, the child takes into account spatial positioning of objects in his actions. However, it is only in the preschool age that the child begins to actively distinguish their spatial relationships and to abstract them in his understanding. The latter is accomplished in connection with the acquisition of verbal labeling of such relationships. A precise perception of spatial relationships is attained only under conditions in which the child utilizes their differentiated verbal descriptions. Following this line of reasoning, Lyublinskaya (47), analyzing Kozyreva's experiments in

which children from a younger kindergarten group were asked to
arrange model furniture precisely in the same way as it was found
in their living room, has shown that the correct reproduction of
spatial relationships occurs only under conditions in which the
child employs in his speech, accompanying his activity, such
words as *ahead of, next to, in the middle of, between,* etc. On the
other hand, whenever the child limits himself to common, undifferentiated, verbal descriptions of space that do not reflect relationships (such as *here, there, right here*), he is not able to complete the task successfully.

Inclusion in the child's verbal repertoire of such words as *on,
under, above, in front of, behind, to the right, to the left,* etc.,
indicating spatial relationships of objects, facilitates the isolating
and the abstracting of spatial relationships and the forming of
spatial representations.

Perception of size. Usually children of pre-school and preschool age separate form first as the main distinguishing cue in
the perception of an object. Size plays a considerably smaller role
in recognition and identification of objects in preschool age. For
example, a large difference between the image and actual size of
an object does not create much of a problem in recognizing the
conceptualized object. Portrayal of relative size requires a great
effort on the part of children this age. A distortion of actual size
relationships in a representation of several objects may impair the
adequate perception of the objective content of the situation.

In a series of studies Rosenfeld (65) presented children with
plastic figures (ovals) of different sizes and somewhat different
forms and asked them to select, in one case tactually and in
another visually, the one that most resembled the presented
standard (ellipse). As the author indicates, under both sets of
conditions the younger preschool children chose the figure most
like the presented standard in form, yet considerably different in
size. The older preschool children, under both sets of conditions,
attempted to find a figure that would be in close agreement with
the standard in form and not too different in size. None of the

children chose a figure approximating the standard in size but differing in form.

However, a fine differentiation of object size can be developed with pre-preschool and preschool children whenever size is used as a stimulus. Volkelt (81) used the method of choosing between two objects, one of which emitted a ringing sound when touched, to show that even the children of pre-preschool age (two to three) attain considerable fineness in size discrimination. By gradually decreasing the size difference of two circles Volkelt showed that children of this age are capable of distinguishing the circles, even when one circle was greater than the other only by one-fiftieth of its size.

Danyushevskaya (18) studied the perception of size relationships in preschool children. She employed a choice behavior as the methodology in which a picture sought by the child was always found in an envelope carrying a picture of an object— triangle, square, or circle—larger in size than the one on another envelope. It was found that preschool children of all ages (from three to seven) can determine the size relationships. Furthermore, the speed of acquiring correct responses (choosing larger objects) and transfer of this relationship to new objects increases with age (see Table 3).

The author of this investigation points out that the age differences in correct perception of size may be leveled off to some

Table 3
Perception of Size Relationships in Preschool Children

Age(years)	Average Number of Trials Necessary to Establish a Reaction	Average Number of Cases of Transfer (%)
3-4	11	85
4-5	8	70
5-6	1	99
6-7	2	94
7-8	3	99

degree by organizing the child's activity involved in comparing the objects of choice.

Perception of form. Numerous investigators have studied form perception by children of different preschool ages. It was found that the perception of form represents a heterogeneous process, which may be better interpreted as a system of operations which differ in their tasks, methods, and results. Differences in operations which accompany perception of form are found among children of the same age, as well as among children of different preschool ages.

Recently, a systematic investigation of the process of form perception by preschool children has been conducted by Venger (79). He assumes correctly that the data from the study by Volkelt, Ling, Figurin, and Denisova on differentiation of form by five-month-old children using the conditioned reflex methodology with food as reinforcement, cannot be accepted as characterizing the lowest age limit for form differentiation in children. The above-mentioned authors made attempts to obtain discrimination between a square, a circle, a triangle, an oval, and a cross, using movements of the hands and the body in the direction of the experimental object and grabbing the object as an indicator of differentiation. In his study, Venger made an attempt to answer the question: Is it possible for children who have not yet developed the act of grabbing to distinguish form?

As an indicator of form differentiation, he used the orienting response. The experiments were carried out with three-four month old infants. In the training stages the infants were presented two three-dimensional geometric figures (rectangular prism and sphere). It was found that the length of the visual fixation upon each of these objects was approximately the same for each child. Following this, in order to extinguish the orienting reaction to one of the objects, the object was suspended over the crib containing the child. Finally, the children were again presented with a pair of figures in controlled experiments. The orientation to one of these figures was extinguished; the second figure was a new one. In these experiments, the children directed their sight to the new figure and fixated upon it for a longer period than the fixation period for the old familiar one; this was accepted as an indicator of differentiation. On the basis of his experiments, Venger concludes that the discrimination of three-dimensional, as well as flat, geometric figures may be observed during the third-fourth month, i.e., prior to the appearance of clearly differentiated, grasping movements and tactile explorations. Furthermore, he points out that the change in spatial orientation of the figure evokes the same visual fixation as the presentation of a new figure. This, on the other hand, indicates the restricted possibilities for discrimination and also raises a question concerning the utilization of cues in the discrimination of figures. Venger is correct in assuming that the solution to this question lies in a detailed investigation of the connection between the eye movements involved in the fixation upon a stationary object and the appearance and development of visual form discrimination. As for the eye movements, they still retain adjusting and executive characteristics. The children as yet do not visually explore the contours of the figures; they do not model the properties of these stimuli. Even more critical is the issue concerning the nature of the elementary forms of distinguishing and differentiation, which are observed prior to the isolation of such quantities as contour, size, or some other properties of an object. It is possible that the orientation involved in differentiation of form depends on a complexity of cues. However, it is necessary to note that in Venger's experiments with older children as well as in other experiments the construction of such a complex of cues requires a relatively long time and does not occur spontaneously, as postulated by the Gestalt psychologists.

Thus, a comparison of Venger's data with the findings of Volkelt, Ling, Figurin, and Denisova suggests a variety of indicators of the discriminating process. In employing an indicator, such as selective fixation in place of grabbing or movement in the direction of an object, one is more likely to discover discrimination of form in younger children. However, the issue of whether distinction of form obtained by different methods also differs as a sensory product still remains an open issue.

In another series of experiments the child's objective actions were used as an indicator of visual discrimination of form. These actions were simultaneously interpreted as a means for the organization of form perception. According to Abramovich-Lekhtman, Venger (79), and others, these objective actions give rise to the practical acquisition of form through the developmental process of elementary hand movements. In the course of practical activity the children not only isolate various qualities of objects, but also clarify certain relationships existing between them.

In an experiment by Venger, two-three-year-old children were given a task which required dragging a geometric figure with the square, right angle or triangular plane facing the subject through one of the openings in an experimental grill. To do this it was necessary to select the opening corresponding to the form of the figure. Initially, all children solved the problem through manual manipulation, i.e., by trial and error. The two-year-old children, even after many trials, did not advance beyond this level; as for the three-year-olds, the actual relationship between the form of the figure and the opening served as a base for establishing a frequent visual comparison. The child frequently shifted his sight from the figure to the opening, as if visually putting one next to the other, and therefore attained an errorless practice solution, even under an entirely new set of conditions.

Pressman's (63) investigation also attributes a very important role to objective activity in the development of form perception. Form board performance of pre-preschool children indicates that the process of perception is not yet separated from objective activity; as a matter of fact, it still is a part of it. Only during the preschool age do specific visual reactions appear—inspection of contours and comparison of the form of the figure and of the opening occur prior to the execution of practical activity. Analogous results were obtained by Boguslavskaya, who studied children's perception of new objects. While only occasional glancing at an object, attempting to grab it and to manipulate it are characteristic of younger preschool children, a relatively detailed visual familiarization with an object prior to the phase of practical activity is performed by older children. As a result of this visual exploration the effectiveness of the solution to a given problem is appreciably enhanced. It is necessary to note that the perceptual actions being formed "borrow" from the practical problem-solving method and, subsequently, separate as an independent stage in the fulfillment of practical activity. Irrespective of the fact that perceptual actions already begin to separate from the practial actions at the age of three-four, the results of familiarization via practical activity exceed, for a relatively long period, the results obtained by visual or tactual familiarization.

In experiments by Zinchenko and Ruzskaya (92), children of different preschool ages were asked to become familiarized with flat figures of irregular form through the following distinctive methods: (a) visual exploration, (b) tactual exploration, (c) visual exploration and tactual exploration, and (d) practical activity, i.e., activity involving placement of the figures into appropriate apertures. Sensory effects of these exploratory methods were checked in controlled experiments where the children were required, also by different methods, to recognize a previously perceived figure located among unfamiliar ones. Two methods of identification were used, visual and tactual. The results of the experiment are summarized in Table 4. For purposes of comparison, the table also includes the data of two special series of experiments (lines six and eight) in which the children were not required to remember the figure. In one of the series of experiments, the figure was placed directly in front of the subject while he was tactually trying to find a similar figure; in the second series the procedure was reversed.

The data obtained indicate that in younger children (three and four years) purely sensory familiarization with a new object produces poorer results than practical manipulation. And only later, toward the fifth year, does formation of perceptual activity (in this case, actions of the eye) attain a level comparable in its identifying effectiveness to that produced by the process of practical manipulation. High indices, obtained with practical activity used as the means of familiarization with an object, may also be explained on the basis of a greater acceptance by preschool children of object recognition tasks than of object familiarization tasks. In the case of the form board method, the object familiarization task is not involved, but is replaced by practical activity. It

Table 4
Average Percentage of Errors for Each Age Group Under Different Conditions of Presentation and Selection of Objects

Conditions for Solution of the Problem		Age (years)				Average Percent of Errors
Method of Familiarization	Method of Selection	3-4	4-5	5-6	6-7	
Form board	Visual	15.4	10.5	0	0	6.5
Visual-tactual	Visual	30.8	21.0	11.5	1.9	16.3
Visual	Visual	50.0	28.5	0	2.5	20.2
Form board	Haptic	37.0	24.7	24.7	5.3	24.3
Tactual	Visual	47.7	42.3	25.0	23.1	34.5
Tactual-visual comparison		71.0	50.0	24.5	27.0	43.1
Visual-tactual	Haptic	70.8	45.5	19.2	19.2	43.7
Visual-tactual comparison		61.0	62.0	54.5	8.2	46.4
Tactual	Haptic	70.5	42.3	38.5	40.4	47.9
Visual	Haptic	100.0	73.0	34.0	23.2	57.5
Mean percentage of errors for each age group	Haptic	55.4	40.5	23.1	15.1	—
Variance		24.1	17.7	15.5	12.3	—

is possible to assume that having completed other tasks requiring practical manipulation of an object, one would obtain even higher indices, not only with visual, but also with haptic selection of the test object.

Analysis of the data presented in the table shows the following. In all the series of trials one observes a regular decrease in the number of errors with an increase in age. However, according to the absolute indices as well as to the rate of decrease in the number of errors, significant differences are noted that may be attributed to the different conditions of perceiving and choosing. The average percent of error across all ages varies in the different series from 6.5 to 57.5. Almost the same kind of fluctuation is obtained in differential age analysis of the subjects. Here the average percent of error taken across all series for each age varies from 55.4 among the younger preschool children to 15.3 among the older. However, with respect to the older age groups, a decrease in the general number of errors is accomplished by a marked leveling off of indices in the various experimental series. The conditions of presentation and selection of the test object among the older preschool children exert a lesser influence on the success of the solution to the problem.

For each age there are specific, optimal conditions for familiarization and selection. Thus, for the visual selection, with three-five and six-seven-year-old children visual-tactual familiarization creates such conditions. For the five-six-year-old children, higher indices are obtained with visual familiarization. Apparently, information added through the children's tactual sensitivity of this as well as of younger ages may lead to confusion of figures similar in form.

With respect to haptic selection, for three-four-year-old children the most appropriate conditions are obtained through visual-tactual comparison; in the four-five-year-old group, tactual and visual-tactual familiarization yielded similar results; for the five-six-year-old children, the obvious preference is for visual-tactual familiarization with the test object; and finally, among the older

preschool children the best results are associated with visual-
tactual comparison of figures. It is necessary to note that as far as
the method of haptic selection is concerned, visual familiarization
alone results in extremely poor performance in three-five-year-
olds.

The above-stated findings are in agreement with the data previously presented by Jakobson (38), who studied object form
recognition in children of various preschool ages. She found that
two-four-year-old children were able to recognize an object
according to form more easily when first allowed to examine it
tactually before being asked to find it in a group of three objects
presented visually, rather than initially having perceived the
object visually and then being required to find it among other
objects manually. From the obtained results the author concludes
that tactual perception of form in preschool age occurs considerably ahead of visual perception. And while perception of
form in the younger preschool age is accomplished via tactual perception without visual assistance, the tactual component of perception is indispensible for visual perception of form.

Jakobson also showed the importance of tactility for abstraction, i.e., the distinguishing of form from the conditions of its
surroundings in the visual perception of form. Movements of the
grasping hand play a very important role in the organization of
continuous visual exploration of an object's contours during
formation of its visual image. Construction of an exact visual
picture of the form by means of the organization of sight movement was possible with children older than four years of age.
With younger children, an attempt to form an orderly visual pursuit failed even with the inclusion of hand movement around the
contours; consequently, the children were not able to attain exact
reproduction of form.

Volokitina's (82) data, obtained while training children to
analyze the form of flat figures visually, also point out that the
inclusion of tactility into the process of visual perception brings
about a noticeable increase in the accuracy of form reproduction

in children over four years of age. Furthermore, Volokitina indicates that the tactual-motor component becomes superfluous
for visual analysis of form in children six-seven years old.

In one respect, the conclusions of Jakobson and Volokitina regarding the role of tactility in visual perception of form are not
exactly correct. The hand does indeed play an essential role in the
development of visual perception; although not as an organ of
tactility, but as an organ of activity with objects.

The previously mentioned results of Zinchenko's and Ruzskaya's experiments indicate that the effectiveness of familiarization and selection basically depends on whether the problem is being solved visually or tactually or whether both of
these modalities operate in the process. This means that between
vision and tactility relatively complex relationships exist which
cannot be expressed by a formula—"the hand teaches the eye."
As indicated in Table 4, in a number of cases the eye succeeds
much more rapidly in problem solving than its "teacher"—the
hand. Furthermore, the hand itself to a great degree requires
some form of teaching by the eye. This is indicated by results obtained in solving the same kinds of problems by the hand and by
the eye. The data in Table 4 indicate that, in a series of cases, the
hand needs help from the eye. However, the reverse relationships
are also correct: certain problems are solved much more easily
with the participation not only of vision, but also of touch.
Finally, in the process of familiarization with the figure, there are
also cases where the mutual activity of both sensory modalities
produces poorer results than either vision or touch alone. Thus,
there is a series of problems still inaccessible to the hand, and
there are problems which cannot be solved by the eye without
the help of the hand.

Investigations by Ginevskaya (27), in which blindfolded children
were asked to familiarize themselves with objects through tactual
exploration, indicate that in younger and middle preschool age
children the special tactual movements of the hand are not yet
formed. The character of the movements of the exploring hand

changes with age. In younger preschool children these movements are still primitive and are inadequately differentiated from instrumental movements. Children, upon the first contact with objects, try to manipulate them one way or another, for example, by rolling, knocking, or pulling them, and in the process of this type of practical activity familiarize themselves with these objects. Later, feeling actions of the hand become separated from practical, instrumental actions. But even among four-five-year-old children, the movements are not exploratory, but are by habit still basically adjusting, fixating in character. In attempting to discover the nature of an object, the child merely presses the object with the motionless hand without making some kind of exploratory, feeling movements. Finally, with older preschool children, in addition to the above-mentioned methods of tactual exploration, more advanced procedures also show a marked development. Thus, feeling movements of the hand appear which aid in examining an object's contours, strength, texture, etc. Consequently, the child's tactual images become richer in content and closer in correspondence to the qualities of the perceived objects.

Sokhina (72) studied the role of objective activity in the visual analysis of form. Continuing Luria's well-known experiment, she showed that without appropriate training three-seven-year-old children cannot visually isolate elements of a complex form—for example, they cannot indicate the elements that compose a complex figure. However, after a series of practical exercises in construction by actually building a figure from elements of different forms and sizes, children begin to conduct figure analysis by purely visual means, anticipating in the process the paths and results of their practical activity. The effect of such training can be widely transferred to new conditions and may be identified by the child's ability to select the required element out of a complex whole.

The fact that perception of form in younger and middle-aged preschool children is included in their objective activity does not mean that children of this age poorly perceive or distinguish the shape of objects. On the contrary, the child very early distinguishes objects on the basis of their form; however, at the beginning of preschool age form is not yet isolated as a cue to an object, i.e., it is not yet abstracted, but remains inseparably tied to the object. This is indicated by the fact that the younger preschool children easily recognize a given object among contour and silhouette drawings of various shapes and also by numerous studies related to identifying geometric forms (Shebalin, 68, and Rosenfeld, 65). At the beginning of preschool age children usually call a square—"block," "window"; a circle—"balloon," "wheel," "ball"; a triangle—"house," "roof," etc.

Toward the end of the middle and during the older preschool age, children begin to isolate form as one of an object's cues; they begin to abstract it and realize its general meaning. The middle and older preschool children do not identify the shape with an object, but only relate or compare their own concepts of different forms with that of the presented object. When presented with sketches of geometric forms whose names they do not yet know, children of this age only point to the object's similarity with some other objects: "this is like a wheel," "this is like a ball" (circle), "this is like a barrel," "resembles a cup" (cylinder).

Whenever children of this age were asked to recognize an object depicted by a silhouette or contour drawing, they did not identify it by immediately referring to another object (after a quick glance at the drawing) as was done by the younger children, but carefully inspected the drawing, especially while perceiving the form, which reflected a number of alternative relationships, and frequently named several objects having a similar form (Shebalin).

The abstraction of form and familiarization with it require a shift from the objective-practical stage in perception development to an essentially perceptive activity. The practical action is directed toward attainment of a given result. Familiarization with certain aspects of the object occurs as a by-product of interaction with it. The formation of recognition activity, which in many different investigations is used as an indicator of perception, is based on practical activity with objects. The recognition process relies on orientators or points of reference that are isolated in practical activity. However, the isolated orientators do not always suffice for adequate identification and even more so for reproduction of an object. In line with the limited recognition effects of practical activity, a system of perceptual actions begins to be formed, especially intended for a more complete object familiarization. During its formation certain orientators, i.e., object-specific cues, are identified. In form perception this is accomplished through special movements of the receptive apparati, which are distinguishable from instrumental movements (such as manipulation or observation of a moving object).

A characteristic aspect of perceptual activity is its expansiveness and successiveness, which create an opportunity for observing the development of the process of form perception in children through the use of recordings of eye and hand movements. By utilizing movements of the perceptual apparati as indicators of the perceptual process, it is possible to examine the relationship between trajectory movements of the hands and of the eyes and the properties of the observed or felt object. A movie recording of manual and optic movements in children during familiarization with new objects and recognition of more-or-less known objects was used in a series of studies by Zinchenko, Ruzskaya, Lavrentyeva, and Tarakanov (91, 92, 93). The investigators found that these processes are different and that it is necessary to speak about distinct types of perceptual activity: familiarization activity and recognition activity.

First of all, let us examine the genesis of tactual and visual actions. The experimental investigation of tactility used the following method. The child was placed behind a curtain, in front of which on a platform was fixed a flat figure or irregular form. The child was asked to familiarize himself with it tactually in such a way as to be able to find the form later visually among other figures. His trials were registered on film. The picture of tactual exploration of each figure continued for sixty seconds.

Comparison of the data obtained with children of different ages permits one to characterize development levels of the hand movements used during tactual exploration. Thus, the hand movements of three-year-olds resemble grabbing more than exploring. Quite frequently the youngsters, instead of examining a figure, play with it. One child, for example, having placed the palm of his hand on the edge of the figure, patted it with his fingers. During this activity his palm remained immobile through almost the entire period of object exposure.

Hand movements of four-five-year-olds closely resemble those of three-year-olds; however, some new elements are present in these movements. One observes the same attempt to grab an object with the phalanges of four fingers and the palm positioned on the edge of the figure. However, the hands of a four-year-old do not remain very long in this immobile position and relatively quickly shift to a more active familiarization with the object, which is conducted by the palm and also by the frontal surface of the phalanges. The tips of the fingers in this process of groping are relatively uninvolved. The groping is conducted usually with only one hand.

Five-six-year-old children exhibit simultaneous tactual exploration of figures with both hands, which are either moving in the direction of or away from one another. However, systematic exploration of the entire contour of the object is still lacking. Children usually limit themselves to a thorough exploration of some characteristic of the figure, elevations and depressions for example, neither relating them to each other nor clarifying their localization on the figure. And only among six-year-olds is it possible to observe sequential exploration of the entire outline of the figure with the finger tips, as if the children are reproducing, i.e., modeling its form, by their tactual movements. The shift to these new, more advanced methods of object familiarization brings about a higher effectiveness of perception, as was discovered in controlled experiments with visual recognition of figures presented earlier for tactual familiarization. Whereas children up to five years made a large number of errors during recognition, the six-year-olds, having thoroughly examined the contours of the figure by hand, later recognized it without error.

Marked age-specific changes in the nature of perceptual activity are also reported in experiments in which eye movements during the perception of an object were recorded on film. In three-four-year-old children the eye movements in connection with a given sensory problem are few. The alternating periods of fixation are appreciably longer than among older children. These movements are contained within the limits of the figure, sometimes (momentarily) following its axis. Children's attention is frequently diverted by the camera. There is a complete absence of pattern movement representing the contour of the figure. Such a primitive method of familiarization produced relatively poor results in figure recognition. Half of the answers incorrectly included figures which were markedly different in form.

With four-five-year-old children, the eye movements during visual exploration, for the most part, also are contained within the limits of the figure. The number of movements is twice that observed with younger children, and correspondingly there is a decrease in the duration of fixations. Based on the trajectory of the eye movement, it is possible to assume that they are oriented toward the dimension and the area of the figure. One observes many large-scale sweeping movements which, as it appears, are directed toward measurement of the perceived object. Even though at this age the contour examining movements are absent, there are noticeable groups of fixations closely positioned to one another and directed at the figure's most pertinent characteristics.

In controlled experiments this method of familiarization yields better results in figure recognition than that observed with the three-year-olds.

Among five-six-year-old children eye movements appear to

pursue the contour of the perceived figure. However, they usually seize upon one particular, most characteristic part of this contour while other parts of the figure remain unexplored. The eye movements of five-year-olds during the exposition are approximately equal in number to those of the four-year-olds. Many of these movements are still not too informative with respect to solving the problem and are contained, for example, within the limits of the figure. In spite of this, however, such a method of exploration appears to be sufficient for subsequent recognition of the perceived object, and in controlled experiments five-year-olds give errorless responses.

With six-seven-year-old children, the eye movements primarily follow the outline of the figure as if reproducing or modeling its form. One simultaneously observes movements across the field of the figure which, while measuring the area of the perceived object, apparently also fulfill an important orienting function. There is an increase in the number of movements during exposition compared to that recorded with younger children. At this time further decrease occurs in the duration of fixation. With such an active and accomplished method of familiarization one not only reaches 100 percent accuracy in recognition under controlled conditions, but also creates the opportunity for solving more complex sensory problems associated with an adequate reproduction of the perceived figure through a process of drawing, modeling, construction, etc., as indicated by Boguslavskaya and others.

Although the most detailed examination of the development of perceptual activity is presently possible in the visual and tactual areas, there are bases for assuming that similar changes occur in other sensory modalities.

Perceptual activities that are being formed in childhood do not remain unchanged; they continue to become more differentiated and more specialized. In this process of differentiation and specialization, sensory training methods exert a great influence upon the developmental level of these activities. The perceptual actions formed serve as a base for the formation of recognition activity. Ruzskaya, working with children of different preschool ages, studied the shift from perceptual to recognition activity by the process of differentiating geometric figures. Placed on the table before the child were two activating keys. Nearby was a garage containing a model automobile. A small screen was fastened above the garage. With the help of a special setup, geometric figures were projected on this screen. Upon the appearance of one set of figures (triangles), the child had to press the left key; when other signs were shown (rectangles), the right one. The correct selection was reinforced by a playmobile moving out of the garage.

During training trials, the children were taught to distinguish form on the basis of one pair of frequently appearing figures. Having developed differentiation, the children were put through controlled experiments. In these experiments numerous variations of the presented figures placed in various positions were projected to the children. All preschool children made a large number of errors in selecting the required figure. The number of errors was especially high for three-four-year-olds.

This indicates that the perceptual images formed under these conditions of training are neigher adequately stable nor adequately generalized; consequently, they do not contribute to the child's capability for solving complex sensory problems.

Relying on the above-stated deduction concerning the genesis of perceptual activities, Ruzskaya attempted in subsequent experiments to train children to form the means for familiarization with the perceived objects. Children were given cardboard figures that they could feel and manipulate. Under these conditions, all the younger children and some of the older ones utilized rather primitive ways of familiarizing the figures. They shifted the figures from one hand to the other, touched their corners, and stacked them into piles without careful examination. Subsequently, the children were given special training designed to expose them to a more rational way of familiarizing themselves with objects. They were taught to follow the contour of the figure sequentially with their fingers, while changes in the direction of movement at the corners were emphasized through accompanying counting.

Examination of rectangles alternated with the examination of triangles, together with an explanation of differences in their dimensional structure, i.e., differences in the number of angles and sides. Thus, the child acquired a system of exploratory actions which allowed him to recognize any variant in a figure formed by a broken line in a variety of positions. However, in the initial formative stages of the exploratory and modeling functions the tactile movements of the hand performed a key role, while the eye served in an auxiliary role by merely registering and pursuing the movements of the hand. Subsequently, the eye acquired an opportunity for independent solving of perceptual tasks by systematically inspecting the figure's contour, as was done previously by the hand.

Some interesting transitory forms were noted at the time when the child visually distinguishes the figures, but accompanies eye movement with abortive movements of the hand which, at a distance, models the object's form and thereby organizes and adjusts the process of visual exploration of this object.

Later the children switch to a purely visual orientation, when during the initial stages, according to Zinchenko, the eye movements are quite unrestricted, continuously observing the entire contour of the perceived figure and modeling its properties in detail.

During the last stages in the formation of the perceptual process, for example, after the child has had a long training in recognition and differentiation of a given type of figure, the exploratory eye movements are successively shortened and decreased, fixating on the distinct, most informative characteristics of the object. At this stage a higher internalization of the perceptive process is accomplished, when on the basis of the formerly obtained, external models (for example, formed with the help of the hand or eye movements), which have been frequently contrasted with the object and corrected in relation to its properties, an internal model—a constant and orthoscopic perceptual image—is finally formed.

Now, without extensive exploratory actions, a quick glance at an object directed to a particular characteristic aspect of the object can actualize the entire "internal" model in a child and, in such a way, lead to an instantaneous judgment of the qualities of the perceived object.

In this fashion, Gestalt psychologists were describing the perceptual process incorrectly, asserting that it originates in ontogeny and is apparently determined by the physical laws of structural organization. In reality, a given form of perception is the product of an extended development which is largely accomplished in a child through practical experience and training. Only genetic investigation can uncover the origin of this perceptual process and its dependence on the child's practical and exploratory activity.

In conclusion, it is necessary to emphasize that the development of the child's perception does not occur spontaneously, but is guided by practice and training. In this process the child acquires mastery of socio-sensory experience and becomes adapted to the sensory culture created by mankind. Adults form in the child the means of familiarization with the surrounding environment; they acquaint him with the systems of musical tones, speech phonemes, geometric forms, etc., developed by humanity and also teach him how to identify them with the help of language. As a result, the child masters a known system of general sensory standards, which he later applies to his perceptual activity, especially in analyzing reality and reflecting it in synthetic, sensory images.

This process of sensory training may proceed in an unorganized, spontaneous fashion, and in such a case it appears to be relatively unproductive. However, if one succeeds in organizing it according to the psychological principles of the formation of perceptual activity, then the effectiveness of such training may be substantially increased.

References

1. Agenosova, N. L. Razvitiye proizvolnogo vospriyatiya u detey doshkolnogo vozrasta. (Development of voluntary perception in preschool children.) Kand. diss. Moscow, 1948.

2. Anokhin, P. K. O morfogeneticheskikh zakonomernostyakh razvitiya funktsy v embryogenese zhivotnykh i cheloveka. (Concerning morphogenetic principles in the development of functions in the embryogenesis of animals and man.) Tezisy dokladov VI vsesoyuznogo syezda anatomov, fiziologov i embriologov. (Theses of presentations of the VI national convention of anatomists, physiologists, and embryologists.) Kharkov, 1958.

3. Arkin, Ye. A. Doshkolny vozrast. (Preschool age.) Moscow. Uchpedgiz, 1948.

4. Arshavsky, A. I. K kharakteristike razvitiya nekotorykh form retseptsii v svyazi s analizom stanovleniya i preobrazovaniya skeletno-myshechnykh i reflektornykh reaktsy v ontogeneze cheloveka. (Toward characterization of the development of certain forms of reception in connection with the analysis of establishment and reorganization of skeleto-muscular and reflectory reactions in the ontogeny of man.) V Kn: Struktura i funktsii analizatorov cheloveka v ontogeneze. (In: Structure and functions of analyzers in the ontogeny of man.) Moscow. Medgiz, 1961.

5. Barbashova, Z. I. Rol razlichnykh analizatorov v obrazovanii uslovnykh svyazey na slovesny razdrazhitel u detey rannego vozrasta. (Role of various analyzers in the formation of conditioned responses to a verbal stimulus in children of early age.) Izvestia APN RSFSR. No. 75, 1955.

6. Barcroft, J. Research on prenatal life. New York. Oxford, 1941.

7. Bekhterev, V. M., and Shchelovanov, N. M. K obosnovaniyu geneticheskoy refleksologii. (Toward establishing genetic reflexology.) Sb. Novoye v refleksologii i fiziologii nervnoy sistemy. (New developments in reflexology and physiology of the nervous system.) Moscow, 1925.

8. Belyayeva - Ekzemplyarskaya, S. N. Muzykalnye perezhivaniya v doshkolnom vozraste. (Musical experience in preschool age.) Moscow, 1925.

9. Boguslavskaya, Z. M. Vydeleniye tsveta i formy detmi doshkolnogo vozrosta v zavisimosti ot kharaktera ikh deyatelnosti. (Identification of color and form by preschool children in relation to the nature of their activity.) Doklady (presentations of) APN RSFSR. 1958, No. 1.

10. Boguslavskaya, Z. M. Osobennosti oriyentirovochno-issledovatelskoy dyeyatelnosti v protsesse zritelnogo vospriyatiya formy u detey doshkolnogo vozrasta. (Characteristics of orienting-exploratory activity in the process of visual perception of form in preschool children.) Doklady (presentations of) APN RSFSR. 1961, No. 3.

11. Brazhas, V. P. Eksperimentalno-psikhologicheskoye issledovaniye tsvetovykh vpechatleny u detey. (Experimental-psychological investigation of the color impressions of children.) Trudy pervogo vserossyskogo syezda po Eksperimentalnoy pedagogike. (Works of the first all-Russian conference on experimental pedagogy.) Moscow, 1911.

12. Bronshtein, A. I., and Petrova, Ye. P. Issledovaniye zvukovogo analizatora novorozhdyonnykh i detey rannego vozrasta. (Investigation of the auditory analyzers of neonates and children of early age.) Zhurnal vysshey nervnoy deyatelnosti. (Journal of higher nervous activity.) Vol. 2, No. 3, 1952.

13. Bronshtein, A. I. Sravhitelnaya otsenka razvitiya slukhovogo analizatora detey i nekotorykh zhivotnykh v pervyye mesyatsy zhizni. (Comparative evaluation of the development of the auditory analyzer in children and certain animals during the initial months of life.) Izvestia APN RSFSR. No. 75, 1955.

14. Carmichael, L. The onset and early development of behavior. In "Manual of Child Psychology," ed. L. Carmichael, 2nd. ed. New York. Wiley, 1954, 60-185.

15. Chase, W. P. Color vision in infants. J. exp. psychol, 1937, 20, 203-222.

16. Cook, W. M. Ability of children in color discrimination. Child development, 1931, 2, 303-320.

17. Danyushevskaya, T. I. Rol rechi v vospriyatii i obobshchenii svetlot obyektov u detey doshkolnogo vozrasta. (Role of speech in perception and generalization of brightness in preschool children.) Doklady (presentations of) APN RSFSR. 1958, No. 1.

18. Danyushevskaya, T. I. K voprosu o roli oriyentirovochno-issledovatelskoy deyatelnostsi v vospriyatii otnosheny mezhdu obyektami u detey doshkolnogo vozrasta. (Concerning the role of orienting-exploratory activity in the perception of relationships between objects in preschool children.) Doklady (presentations of) APN RSFSR. 1958, No. 3.

19. Danyushevskaya, T. I. Razvitiye vospriyatiya otnosheny svetlot i velichin u detey doshkolnogo vozrasta. (Development of the perception of brightness and of size relationships in preschool children.) Voprosy Psikhologii, (Questions of Psychology). 1958, No. 4.

20. Denisova, M. P., and Figurin, N. L. Opyt refleksologicheskogo izucheniya novorozhdyonnogo. (An experiment in reflexological study of the neonate.) Sb. Novoye v refleksologii i fiziologii nervnoy sistemy. (New developments in reflexology and physiology of the nervous system.) Moscow, 1925.

21. Denisova, M. P., and Figurin, N. L. K voprosu o pervykh sochetatelnykh refleksakh u grudnykh detey. (Concerning the first combinative reflexes in infants.) Voprosy geneticheskoy refleksologii (Questions of genetic reflexology), Vol. 1. Moscow. Gosmedizdat, 1929.

22. Denisova, M. P., and Figurin, N. L. Ranniye uslovnyye refleksy u grudnykh detey. (Early conditioned reflexes in infants.) Sovetskaya pediatriya (Soviet pediatrics). 1936, No. 6.

23. Figurin, N. L., and Denisova, M. P. Opyt eksperimentalno-refleksologicheskogo izucheniya rannikh differentsirovok sochetatelnykh refleksov u detey v mladencheskom vozraste. (An experimental-reflexological study

of early differentiation of the combinative reflexes in young children.) Sb. Novoye v refleksologii i fiziologii nervnoy sistemy. (New developments in reflexology and physiology of the nervous system.) Moscow, 1925.

24. Figurin, N. L., and Denisova, M. P. Etapy razvitiya rebyonka ot rozhdeniya do odnogo goda. (Stages in the development of the child from birth to one year.) Sb. Voprosy geneticheskoy refleksologii (Questions of genetic reflexology). Moscow, 1929.

25. Foucault, M. L'acuité visuelle et l'acuité auditive chez les écoliers. L'année psychologique, 1925.

26. Ginevskaya, T. O. Znacheniye kompozitsii v vospriyatii detmi risunka illyustratsii. (Significance of composition in the perception of illustrative drawings by children.) Uchyonyye zapiski Kharkovskogo ped. in-ta. (Scientific notes of the Kharkov Pedagogical Institute.) Vol. VI, 1941.

27. Ginevskaya, T. O. Razvitiye dvizheny ruki pri osyazanii. (Development of hand movements in touch.) Izvestia APN RSFSR. No. 14, 1948.

28. Gordon, Ye. V. Rol predmetnosti v vospriyatii rebyonkom akhromaticheskikh tsvetov. (Role of objectiveness in the child's perception of achromatic colors.) Kand. diss. Moscow, 1947.

29. Guernsey, M. A quantitative study of eye reflexes in infants. Psychol. Bull., 1929, 26, 160-161.

30. Hooker, D. The origin of the grasping movement in man. Proc. Amer. Phil. Soc., 1938, 79, 596-606.

31. Hooker, D. The origin of overt behavior. Ann Arbor. University of Michigan Press, 1944.

32. Ilina, G. A. K voprosu o formirovanii muzykalnykh predstavleny u dosh-kolnikov. (Concerning the formation of musical representations in preschoolers.) Voprosy Psikhologii. (Questions of Psychology.) 1959, No. 5.

33. Irwin, O. C. The latent time of the body startle in infants. Child Development, 1932, 3, 104-107.

34. Irwin, O. C. Effect of strong light on the body activity of newborns. J. comp. psychol., 1941, 32, 233-236.

35. Irwin, O. C., and Weiss, L. A. The effect of darkness on the activity of newborn infants. University of Iowa Stud. Child Welfare., 1934. 9, 163-175.

36. Istomina, Z. M. Vospriyatiye i nazyvaniye tsveta u detey doshkolnogo vozrasta. (Perception and naming of color in preschool children.) Doklady (presentations of) APN RSFSR. 1957, No. 2

37. Istomina, Z. M. O vzaimo-otnoshenii vospriyatiya i nazyvaniya tsveta v rannem vozraste. (Concerning the interrelation of perception and naming of colors in early age.) Doklady (presentations of) APN RSFSR. 1959, No. 3.

38. Jakobson, S. G. K voprosu o razvitii vospriyatiya formy. (Concerning the development of form perception.) Rukopis. (Manuscript.) Moscow, 1947.

39. Kasatkin, N. I. Ranniye uslovnyye refleksy v ontogeneze cheloveka. (Early conditioned reflexes in the ontogeny of man.) Moscow. Lzd-vo AMN SSSR, 1948.

40. Khomenko, K. Ye. Vospriyatiye izobrazheniya prostranstvennykh i perspectivnykh otnosheny u detey mladshego vozrasta. (Perception of spatial and perspective relationships in young children.) Uchyonyye zapiski Kharkovskogo ped. in-ta. (Scientific notes of the Kharkov Pedagogical Institute.) Vol. VI, 1941.

41. Kogan, A.D. K voprosu o stanovlenii tonalnogo i rechevogo slukha. (Concerning the formation of tonal and verbal hearing.) Doklady na nauchnom soveshchanii po voprosam fiziologicheskoy akustiki. (Presentations delivered at the scientific conference on physiological acoustics.) Moscow, 1954.

42. Kolodnaya, A. Ya. Razvitiye differentsirovki napravleniya "pravogo" i "levogo" u detey doshkolnogo vozrasta. (Development of differentiation in the directionality of "right" and "left" in preschool children.) Izvestia APN RSFSR. Vyp. 53, 1954.

43. Kozyreva, A. Ye. K voprosu o pervonachalnom razvitii vospriyatiya prostranstva u detey. (Concerning the initial development of space perception in children.) Leningrad. Izd-vo LGU, 1949.

44. Leontiev, A. N. O mekhanizme chuvstvennogo otrazheniya. (Concerning the mechanism of sensory feedback.) Problemy razvitiya psikhiki. (Problems of psychic development.) Moscow. Izd-vo APN RSFSR, 1959.

45. Levikova, A. M., and Nevmyvako, G. A. K voprosu vospitaniya sochetatelnykh reaktsy i ikh differentsirovok u mladentsev. (Concerning the growth of combinative reactions and their differentiation in young children.) Sb. voprosy geneticheskoy refleksologii. (Questions of genetic reflexology.) Vyp. I. Moscow, 1929.

46. Ling, B. C. I. A genetic study of sustained visual fixation and associated behavior in the human infant from birth to six months. J. genet. psychol., 1942, 61, 227-277.

47. Lyublinskaya, A. A. Rol rechi v razvitii zritelnogo vospriyatiya u detey. (Role of speech in the development of visual perception in children.) Sb. Voprosy detskoy i obschchey psikhologii. (Questions of child and general psychology.) Moscow. Izd-vo APN RSFSR, 1954.

48. Marquis, D. V. Can conditioned responses be established in the newborn infant? J. genet. psychol., 1931, 39, 479-492.

49. McGinnis, J. M. Eye movements and optic nystagmus in early infancy. Genet. psychol. monogr., 1930, 8, 321-430.

50. Mistyuk, V. V. Vospriyatiye rebyonkom izobrazheny dvizheny. (The child's perception of the representation of motion.) Uchyonyye zapiski Kharkovskogo ped. in-ta. (Scientific notes of the Kharkov Pedagogical Institute.) Vol. VI, 1941.

51. Mukhin, S. V. Vospriyatiye tsveta i formy v doshkolnom vozraste. (Perception of color and form in preschool age.) Uchyonyye zapiski Moskovskogo gos. ped. in-ta. (Scientific notes of the Moscow State Pedagogical Institute.) Vol. XXVII, Vyp. 2, 1941.

52. Munn, N. L. Psychological development: An introduction to genetic psychology. Boston. Houghton Mifflin, 1938.

53. Nechayeva, N. P. K funktsionalnoy kharakteristike slukhovogo analizatora rebyonka rannego vozrasta. (Concerning functional characteristics of the auditory analyzer in the child of an early age.) Zhurnal vysshey nervnoy deyatelnosti. (Journal of higher nervous activity.) Vol. IV, Vyp. 5, 1954.

54. Neklyudova, A. I. K voprosu o razvitii protsessov vospriyatiya u detey doshkolnogo vozrasta. (Concerning the development of perception processes in preschool children.) Sb. Opyt obyektivnogo izucheniya detstva. (Objective study of childhood.) Moscow, 1924.

55. Nemanova, Ts. P. Nayboleye ranniye polozhitelnyye i otritsatelnyye zashchitnyye i pishchevyye refleksy na vestibularnyye razdrazheniya u grudnogo rebyonka. (The earliest positive and negative defensive and nutritive conditioned reflexes in connection with vestibular stimulation in an infant.) Voprosy pediatrii. (Questions of pediatrics.) Vol. III, 1935.

56. Nemanova, Ts. P. Uslovnyye refleksy na oboronitelnyye razdrazheniya u grudnykh detey. (Conditioned reflexes in connection with defensive stimulation in breast-fed infants.) Fiziologichesky Zhurnal. (Physiological Journal.) SSSR, 27, 6, 1939.

57. Nemanova, Ts. P. Uslovnyye refleksy na vkusovyye razdrazheniya u detey pervykh mesyatsev zhizni. (Conditioned reflexes in connection with taste stimulation in children during the initial months of life.) Fiziologichesky Zhurnal. (Physiological Journal.) SSSR, 30, 4, 1941.

58. Ovsepyan, G. T. Razvitiye nablyudeny u rebyonka. (Development of observation in a child.) Uchyonyye zapiski ped. in-ta im. Gertsena. (Scientific notes of the Herzen Pedagogical Institute.) Vol. XVIII, 1940.

59. Peyper, A. Osobennosti deyatelnosti mozga rebyonka. (Characteristics of the activity of the child's brain.) Moscow. Medgiz, 1962.

60. Polyakov, G. I. Nekotoryye itogi issledovany po razvitiyu neyronnogo stroyeniya korkovykh kontsov analizatorov u cheloveka. (Certain results of investigations concerning the development of neural constructions of the cortical endings of analyzers in man.) V kn.: Struktura i funktsii analizatorov. (In: Structure and function of analyzers.) Moscow. Medgiz, 1961.

61. Pratt, K. C. The effects of repeated visual stimulation upon the activity of newborn infants. J. genet. psychol., 1934, 44, 117-126.

62. Pratt, K. C., Nelson, Amalie K., and Sun, K. H. The behavior of the newborn. Ohio State Univ. Stud. Contr. Psychol., 1930, 10, ix-237.

63. Pressman, A. A. O roli predmetnogo deystviya v formirovanii zritelnogo obraza u rebyonka. (Concerning the role of objective activity in the

formation of the visual image in a child.) Sb. Problemy Psikhologii. (Problems of Psychology.) Leningrad. Izd-vo LGU, 1948.

64. Raney, E., and Carmichael, L. Localizing responses to tactual stimuli in the fetal rat in relation to the psychological problem of space perception. J. genet. psychol., 1934, 45, 3-21.

65. Rosenfeld, F. S. Osobennosti osyazatelnykh vospriyaty rebyonka-doshkolnika. (Characteristics of the tactual perception of a preschooler.) Izvestia APN RSFSR. Vyp. 17, 1948.

66. Rosenhart-Pupko, G. L. Rech i razvitiye vospriyatiya v rannem detstve. (Speech and the development of perception in early childhood.) Moscow. Izd-vo AMN SSSR, 1948.

67. Sechenov, I. M. Izbrannyye filosofskiye i psikhologicheskiye proizve-deniya. (Selected philosophical and psychological investigations.) Moscow. Gospolitizdat, 1947.

68. Shebalin, S. N. Vospriyatiye formy doshkolnikami. (Perception of form by preschoolers.) Uchenyye zapiski Ped. in-ta im. Gertsena. (Scientific notes of the Herzen Pedagogical Institute.) Vol. XVIII, 1939.

69. Shif, Zh. I. Podbor skhodnykh tsvetovykh ottenkov i nazvany tsvetov. (Selection of similar shades and names of colors.) Sb. Voprosy psikhologii glukhonemykh i umstvenno otstalykh detey. (Questions of the psychology of deaf-mute and mentally retarded children.) Moscow, 1941.

70. Shriftzettser, M. O. Opyt ispolzovaniya zashchitnogo refleksa na silny svet dla vyrabotki nayboleye rannikh uslovnykh refleksov u grudnogo rebyonka. (An experiment in the utilization of the defensive reflex to a strong light for the production of the earliest conditioned reflexes in a breast-fed infant.) Zhurn. Voprosy pediatrii. (Questions of Pediatrics.) Vol. VII, Vyp. 6, 1935.

71. Shvachkin, N. Kh. Eksperimentalnoye izucheniye rannikh obobshcheny. (Experimental investigation of early generalizations.) Izvestia APN RSFSR. Vyp. 54, 1954.

72. Sokhina, V. P. O vydelenii figury iz fona doshkolnikami. (Concerning separation of the figure from the ground by preschoolers.) Doklady (presentations of) APN RSFSR. 1962, No. 1, 2.

73. Stirnimann, F. Der Saugwulst der Neugeborenen. Kinderärztl. Prax., 7, 1936.

74. Stirnimann, F. Versuche über die Reaktionen Neugeborener auf Wärme-und Kältereize. Z. Kinderpsychiat., 5,1939.

75. Stirnimann, F. Über das Farbenempfinden Neugeborener. Ann. Paediat., 1944, 163.

76. Stubbs, E. M. The effect of the factors of duration, intensity, and pitch of sound stimuli on the responses of newborn infants. Univ. Iowa Stud. Child Welfare, 1934, 9, 75-135.

77. Sukhanova, P. V. K voprosu o razvitii taktilno-kinesteticheskogo analizatora u detey doshkolnogo vozrasta. (Concerning the development of the

tactual-kinesthetic analyzer in preschool children.) Izvestia APN RSFSR. Vyp. 75, 1955.

78. Suzuki, S., and Hakaoka, Y. Normal acuity of hearing in young children measured by the peep-show test. J. pract. oto-rhino-laryngol., Basel, 1958, 20, N 4-5.

79. Venger, L. A. Razlicheniye formy predmetov detmi rannego vozrasta. (Distinguishing the form of objects by young children.) Doklady (presentations of) APN RSFSR, 1962, No. 2.

80. Volkelt, H. Neue Untersuchungen über die kindliche Auffassung und Wiedergabe von Formen. Vorträge a. d. IV Kongress für Heilpädagogik. Leipzig, 1928.

81. Volkelt, H. Eksperimentalnaya psikhologiya doshkolnika. (Experimental psychology of the preschooler.) Moscow & Leningrad, 1930.

82. Volokitina, M. N. Osobennosti vospriyatiya i izobrazheniya ploskostnykh figur v doshkolnom vozraste. (Aspects of the perception and conceptualization of plane figures in preschool age.) Uchyonyye zapiski in-ta psikhologii. (Scientific notes of the Institute of Psychology.) Vol. 1, 1940.

83. Walk, R. D., and Gibson, Eleanor J. A study of visual depth perception in the human infant with a visual cliff. Paper read at EPA in April, 1959.

84. Watson, J. B. Psychology from the standpoint of behaviorist. Philadelphia. Lippincott, 1919.

85. Weiss, L.A. Differential variations in the amount of activity of newborn infants under continuous light and sound stimulation. Univ. Iowa Stud. Child Welfare, 1934. 9, 1-74.

86. Yendovitskaya, T. V. Dinamika elementarnykh sensornykh funktsy v doshkolnom vozraste. (Dynamics of the elementary sensory functions in preschool age.) Kand. diss. Moscow, 1947.

87. Yendovitskaya, T. V. K voprosu o razvitii ostroty zreniya v doshkolnom vozraste. (Concerning the development of visual acuity in preschool age.) Izvestia APN RSFSR. No. 64, 1955.

88. Yendovitskaya, T. V. O zvukovysotnoy razlichitelnoy chuvstvitelnosti u detey doshkolnogo vozrasta. (Concerning differentiation of pitch in preschool children.) Doklady (presentations of) APN RSFSR. 1958, No. 5.

89. Zakharov, A. N. Usloviya formirovaniya obobshcheny u detey doshkolnogo vozrasta. (Conditions for the formation of generalizations in preschool children.) Kand. diss. Moscow, 1954.

90. Zimmerman, A. N. Uchastiye obonyatelnogo analizatora v analitiko-sinteticheskoy deyatelnosti u detey 4-7 let. (Participation of the olfactory analyzer in the analytic-synthetic activity of children from four to seven years of age.) Izvestia APN RSFSR. Vyp. 75, 1955.

91. Zinchenko, V. P. Vospriyatiye i deystviye. (Perception and action.) Soobshcheniya 1-XII. Doklady (presentations of) APN RSFSR. 1961, No. No. 2, 5.

92. Zinchenko, V. P. Ruzskaya, A. G., Lavrentyeva, T. V., Lomov, B. F., and Tarakanov, V. V. Sravnitelny analiz osyazaniya i zreniya. (Comparative analysis of tactility and vision.) Soobshcheniya I-XI. Doklady (presentations of) APN RSFSR. 1959, No. 5; 1961, No. 4, 6; 1962, No. 1, 3.

93. Zinchenko, V. P., Van Chzhi-tsin, and Tarakanov, V. V. Stanovleniye i razvitiye pertseptivnykh deystvy. (Establishment and development of perceptual activity.) Voprosy Psikhologii. (Questions of Psychology.) 1962, No. 3.

2. Development of Attention

During preschool age considerable gains are noted in the development of attention. Involuntary attention continues to grow with noticeable increase in its stability and span. One also observes the beginnings of premeditated, voluntary attention. At this age the child learns to be attentive, i.e., he learns to isolate those elements in the surrounding environment that are important in regulating behavior and activity correspondent to the tasks set by adults.

In the earliest stages the child's attention is attracted, first of all, by the novelty of a stimulus as well as by the changes in the surrounding environment. The strength of the stimulus is a very important factor in attracting the child's attention. Loud sounds, a bright light, or a sudden touch evoke in a child orienting reactions directed toward familiarization with these stimuli. Somewhat later, the child's attention is attracted by stimuli having characteristics of stable, meaningful cues, and also by objects associated with acute emotional experiences. The significance of cues is directly related to the satisfaction of the child's needs.

At a very early age, unconditioned-orienting reactions to the impinging stimuli are first signs of attention. Shchelovanov, Figurin, and Denisova label these initial unconditioned-orienting reactions, which appear during the first month of life, fixation reactions. They are characterized by an optimal orientation of the sensory organ towards the object and an elevated sensitivity of this organ, which in combination provide the best conditions for perception. Thus, in response to a loud sound the child turns his head toward the source of the sound and orients the auditory receptor to the most favorable position. Upon introduction of bright, shiny objects into his field of vision, the child directs his vision towards them, and his vision remains stationary for a relatively long period of time. Upon accidentally touching some object with his hand, the child squeezes it, which enables him to obtain the most contact between the surface of his hand and the object.

To the extent to which the development of interaction between the child and the surrounding media has progressed, more complex forms of attention may appear. These are exemplified by reactions directed toward a more extensive familiarization with the surrounding environment—*orienting-exploratory reactions.* The child, following the positioning of the receptor, begins to examine the object by feeling it.

The main factor in the establishment and development of the reciprocal relation between the young child and his surrounding environment is the social interaction of the child with the socializing adult. The emergence of the two-sided social interaction of the adult with the child is marked by the appearance in the child of two-three months of age of a characteristic arousal reaction evoked by the sight of the adult. During such interaction it is possible to capture the child's attention and to organize his familiarization with the surrounding environment by evoking sensory reactions to a given object. In the course of interaction the adult first begins to utilize indicatory gestures and then words to attract the child's attention. By doing so the adult seems to strengthen the object's direct influence and to divert the child from other things. Subsequently, the child begins to utilize first the indicatory gestures and later words. The timing in the use of words depends on the rate of mastering speech. As a result of utilizing gestures and words, the child learns to isolate objects from the surrounding environment and to attract the attention of another human being.

With expanded experience, a greater number of objects and events begin to attract the child's attention, evoking positioning and orienting exploratory reactions. Dunayevsky (2) reports that, with age, the number of objects attracting the child's attention increases, and his actions begin to be subservient to those objective relationships which the child establishes among the objects.

For instance, a two—two and one-half-year-old child in contrast to a one—one and one-half-year-old one does not just plainly rotate, knock, or place the figures given to him into his mouth, but orienting himself to the form of one figure and the opening of the other, makes an attempt to unite them.

Dunayevsky notes that Pavlov's characterization of animals, orienting reflex as a "what is it?" reflex remains the same for children, but this reflex may be characterized now also as a "what can be done with this?" reflex. While recognizing the common characteristics of the orienting reflex in animals and children, for example, its extinction with repeated presentation of stimuli, the author refers to the specificity of the orienting reflex in children. Thus, if the object of the child's activity is somewhat complex, the child may again and again *return* to that object, finding in it new relationships and new possibilities for action. All new and recently acquired forms of action are included in the common base of the orienting reflex, meaning that the question "what is it?" brings about a fundamental change in the child's functional equipment. The indicator of the effectiveness of the orienting reflex also is altered. If the decisive factor for an animal, aside from precision in distinguishing changes in the surrounding environment, is the speed of the orienting reaction, then for a child its stability, capacity for continuing exploratory activity along available channels, is of special significance.

As early as pre-preschool age, the child can examine with concentration some kind of an object for a relatively long period—feel it and interact with it. Toward the end of pre-preschool age, the child can already remain somewhat attentive, not only to objects perceived through sensory modalities, but also to their verbal description which provides clear and distinctive images. A two and one-half—three-year-old child can already listen attentively to short poems, fairy tales, and stories and imagine that which is conveyed in them.

A characteristic aspect of the child's attention during the pre-

preschool and the beginning of preschool age is its nonpre-
meditated, involuntary nature. Attention is entirely determined
by the conditions of primary qualities of objects, such as their
newness, attractiveness, etc. The pre-preschoolers and the
younger preschoolers cannot yet isolate various elements of a
given situation on the basis of a designated goal corresponding to
a given task. Purposeful, deliberate attention begins to form in the
child only during the preschool age, becoming during this period
more stable, wider in scope, and more productive. Familiarization
with a situation becomes effective, in the sense that it is performed in shorter time and leads to a more adequate—from the
point of view of the object of activity—image of the surrounding
environment.

Development of Separate Properties
of Attention in Preschool Age

Numerous investigations indicate an increase in the stability of
attention during preschool age. Thus, Beyrl's results on the study
of maximal duration of play among children of different ages indicate that attention stability in preschool age increases more intensively than in pre-preschool age (Graph 1).

Agenosova's (1) data also confirm the marked growth in attention stability during the preschool age. While controlling the
length of time for visual exploration, she asked preschool children
to examine a picture of simple content. Especially noted was the
interval of time between the moment when the child first looked
at the picture and the moment when he turned away from it,
shifting his sight to the experimenter or to the surrounding environment (three—four-year-old children as a rule did not resume
exploring the picture). The average time used by children of different ages in examining the picture shows that the attention stability—concentrated exploration—increases from the younger to
the older preschool age almost twofold (from 6.8 to 12.3 seconds).

In an experiment by Petukhova (9), children were given a rather

Graph 1.
Maximal Duration of Play in Terms of Averages for Each Age Group

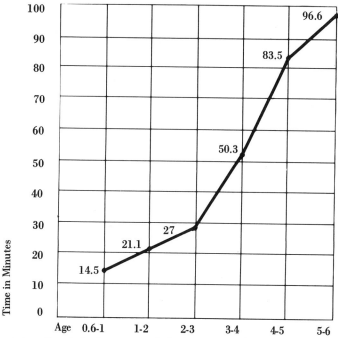

uninteresting task that required placing pieces of colored paper into boxes according to color. The data, in terms of the average time devoted to this type of activity and the average time of being distracted from it, for children of various age groups show considerable differences in the attention stability (see Table 5). The older preschool children not only continue with an uninteresting task (one assigned by an adult) for a longer period of time, but they also turn away from the task less often than the younger preschool children.

During preschool age, an increase in attention stability is accompanied by an increase in the attention span. Furthermore, as far as it is possible to determine on the basis of experimental findings, this applies to voluntary as well as involuntary attention.

Table 5.
Stability of Attention to Activity in Children

Age (years)	Duration of Activity (minutes)	Duration of Distraction (minutes)
2.5-3.5	17.5	7.8
3.5-4.5	37.4	7.5
4.5-5.5	51.4	6.4
5.5-6.5	62.8	1.6

Godovikova (5) reports a growth in the span of involuntary attention, i.e., in the number of elements in a situation and the relationships among them that directly evoke orienting responses. In her experiments, the child was not given any task, but was exposed to several visual and auditory stimuli. The child was seated in front of a screen on which a series of colored bulbs were turned on in a predetermined order. Now and then a red light appeared to the left of the screen, following which a bell rang. The bell was located to the right of the screen. The time interval between the light and the sound of the bell varied. All of the child's reactions were recorded.

The tendency for familiarization with the surrounding environment was least pronounced in the youngest of the preschool children (three—four-year-olds). With these children, occasional orienting reactions were observed in response to the stimuli. Some children, three out of ten taking part in the experiment, did not turn to the bell even while it was ringing. In the others, the first presentation of the bell evoked turning the head to the source of the sound, but in two of these children this reaction was immediately extinguished, and upon a second presentation of the bell it did not reappear. For the rest of the children, the reaction was extinguished during the sixth-eighth presentations. Under such conditions, only a few of the three—four-year-old children showed conditioned orienting reactions to the bell—anticipated ringing of the bell, expressed by turning the head to the location of the bell or by pressing the ears and closing the eyes in anticipation of its ringing. But even these reactions were not stable. For this age group, the first ten presentations of the bell resulted, on the average, in 4.5 unconditioned and 1.2 conditioned orienting reactions (Graph 2).

In a postexperimental interview, designed to determine the level of familiarization with the situation after twenty presentations of the light and the bell, many children could state that the bell would always ring after the appearance of the light.

In contrast, four—five-year-old children engaged in a great deal of activity during familiarization: they showed many orienting reactions that were extinguished relatively slowly. In all children of this age, the orienting reaction occurred with the first presentation of the bell and remained stable over a relatively long period of time: for half of the children, over the fourteen-fifteen presenta-

Graph 2.
Orienting Reactions of Children in Familiarization with Environment

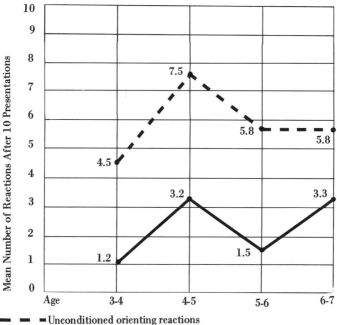

tions; for the other half, till the end of the experiment. Conditioned orienting reactions were observed in many of the children quite early, beginning with the second-fourth presentations of the bell. In the rest of the children, this reaction appeared with the sixth-fifteenth presentations. On the average, after ten presentations of the bell 7.5 unconditioned and 3.2 conditioned orienting reactions were recorded for this group of children (Graph 2).

The question period revealed that after twenty presentations of light and sound, 80 percent of these children were able to verbalize the temporal relationship between them by stating that initially the red light would go on, and thereafter the bell would ring.

In the five-six and six–seven-year-old children, orienting reactions occurred during the first presentation of the bell, but they were just as quickly extinguished (during the second-fourth presentations). Conditioned orienting reactions appeared also during the second-fourth presentations, but they were quite unstable. Relating the light and the bell during pauses occurred only infrequently.

A postexperimental interview revealed, however, that a decrease in the number of externally expressed reactions does not yet indicate weakening of attention. Thus, 90 percent of the five-six year-old group and 100 percent of the six–seven-year-old group responded correctly when asked to state both the stimuli used in the experiment and their relationship. These data indicate that toward the end of preschool age the process of attention seems to be expressed less externally and more through a complex path. It seems that at this stage direct orientation toward elements of the external reality begins to be replaced by orientation toward the child's imagined reality. A very important role in this process is attributed to words—the linguistic mediation of reality.

Yendovitskaya's (14) investigations also confirm the increase in preschool children's span of voluntary attention. Viewing a card with drawings of six geometric figures presented tachistoscopically for a duration of three seconds, the child was confronted with the task of determining the most attentive way of examining the drawings so that a report consisting of two parts, verbal (naming the figures) and actual (selecting the previously presented figures now mixed with others), could subsequently be given. Thereafter, the child was asked to lay out the figures on a table, observing the same spatial relationships which had been depicted on the card. Three cards, differing from one another in the composition of figures (five of them were the same on all cards and one was different) and their spatial positioning, were used in this study.

The conditions of presentation varied. The first card was shown without any kind of preparatory work with the child. Before seeing the second card, the child received a set of figures from which, after the presentation, he would have to select the necessary ones, and the experimenter encouraged the child to verbally identify each one of the figures (if the child had difficulty in naming a figure, the experimenter helped him). After this, the figures were removed and the card was flashed on the screen. Prior to showing the third card, the experimenter through special instructions organized a map of visual inspection of the figures for the child. He was told that during the card's presentation it would be necessary to try to examine all the figures and was shown how this could best be done through special instruction and the visual scheme. The results obtained in these investigations indicate that the length of voluntary attention increased during preschool age (Table 6).

The data characterizing the attention span of children three-four years of age are not included in Table 6. With these children, a relatively clear picture was difficult to obtain. They either did not give a verbal report at all or gave a common name to all figures, e.g., "these red blocks." Whenever asked to select out of a number of figures only those which had been seen on the screen, they proceeded to take every figure, accompanying this by such expressions as: "I saw this one" and "That one was there."

These experiments show that under conditions stimulating the

Table 6.
Average Number of Correctly Named and Chosen Figures (out of Six)
After Each Presentation

Age (years)	First Card		Second Card		Third Card	
	Naming	Choosing	Naming	Choosing	Naming	Choosing
4-5	0.6	1.6	1.7	2.6	1.3	3.5
5-6	1.3	2.2	2.7	3.6	2.5	3.6
5-7	1.4	2.2	2.6	3.6	3.4	4.5

child's attention (presentation of the second and third cards), the span of attention increases for all age groups. This is evident with naming as well as with choosing figures. The most effective was the condition that included the organizational map of the visual movements (this was especially clearly demonstrated in the actual selection of figures). The greatest result with this method occurred in the six–seven-year-old group: after presentation of the third card, half of the children in this group correctly distinguished five out of the six figures.

Furthermore, it is apparent that in most cases of distributed attention, i.e., attention distributed between the form of the figures and their spatial positioning, belong to the older age groups. Thus, in laying out figures six–seven-year-old children correctly fixed the position of individual figures in twenty-two cases and the spatial relationship of two or three figures in twelve cases. For the five–six-year-old children, correct positioning of figures occurred in twelve cases and interrelationships in four. The four–five-year-old children correctly positioned the figures in three cases and identified their relationship in one case.

During preschool age, the child's attention becomes not only more stable and wider in scope, but also more effective. This is especially noticeable during the formation of some type of complex, voluntary action. As a rule, the success of such action primarily depends upon isolating with adequate precision those elements of the situation and their relationships that are responsible for its afferentiation. Clarification of the conditions of action becomes the first stage in its formation. This stage in some cases is anticipated by the instrumental link of the action and in other cases is realized in the course of its execution.

Poddyakov (10), studying aspects of automatization of action in preschool children, obtained data indicating an increase in the effectiveness of attention during the formation of activity throughout the preschool years. In this experiment, the child was asked to extinguish differently colored bulbs that were turned on at a panel in a predetermined sequence. In order to do this, the child had to push a button on the panel corresponding to a given bulb.

Results show that three and one-half—four-year-old children, in the process of determining the location of the bulbs and the buttons and their relationship, turned their heads sharply, frequently shifting their sight from the bulb to the button and vice versa. For four—five-year-old children, the number of orienting reactions to the signals (bulbs) and the objects of action (buttons) was appreciably smaller, and the form of the visual orienting reaction itself changed. Preschool children of five—six and one-half years of age were able to find the signal with only one or two head movements.

The extensiveness of orienting reactions and their external expression observed among these young children was not attended by some kind of effective action. For a relatively long period of time, three and one-half—four-year-old children could establish neither the distribution of signals in space nor the sequence of their activation, which exerted an inhibitory effect on the action formation. Visual orienting reactions to the signal resisted extinction even after a large number of trials. Registering the sequence of signals when pressing the button had to be done without the appearance of signals and was observed only after numerous repetitions.

The difficulty in reproducing the necessary system of movement in the absence of signals depends on imperfection in the orienting activity rather than on the complexity of the system of movements. This is indicated by the following conditions. With simplification in the subsequent trials of spatial and temporal relationships between signals, the number of repetitions required to achieve the correct reproduction of the order of pressing buttons without signals dropped appreciably. Under these conditions, the number of orienting reactions also dropped and their extinction occurred more rapidly.

Surkhaykhanova (11) studied attention during the action formation under conditions lacking such external stimuli as would directly arouse orientation. Children were forming the habit of moving across a maze without relying on vision. The child was asked to transport a fir tree on a model automobile from the store (beginning point of the maze) to the kindergarten (end point of the maze). He also was told to carry the tree as quickly as possible, that is, via the shortest possible path. After preliminary periods, during which the child was allowed to feel the maze and to find the shortest path, he was asked to deliver the tree.

These experiments revealed marked differences in the behavior of younger and older preschool children. For three—four-year-old children, a characteristic was the absence of attention to the conditions of action. The problem did not evoke in them attempts to explore the maze. Orienting movements, performed only after complementary stimulation by the experimenter, were elementary and rarely improved in a process of repetition. The child could not isolate even the initial and the end points of the maze on his own; he could not find and show the correct path.

The behavior of four—five-year-old children differed only slightly from the behavior described above. Like the younger children, they did not make independent attempts to explore the maze. The experimenter found himself constantly stimulating the child to explore and helping him to move his hand from the starting to the finishing point of the maze. The children did not make tactual movements that would explain the position of various paths within the maze. The process of familiarization with the maze was accomplished very slowly. As a result, the children could neither show the correct path nor tell how they were going to move through it. The child's movements while guiding the automobile were similar to his initial orienting movements during familiarization with the maze, i.e., the child was acting as if he were in a new, unfamiliar situation.

An increase in the level of attention during the performance of orienting activity was noted in five—six-year-old children, who carefully explored the maze. After the first tactual inspection, they were able to isolate the beginning and the end points of the maze. As a result, these children were able to point out not only the shortest path, but also the longest one. Consequently, on the basis of their familiarization with the maze, they had formed some mental image of it. The transfer of experience from the exploratory, orienting movements to instrumental movements was reflected in the quick and confident manner in which the children moved the automobile through the maze, independently noting their own mistakes. However, the presence of errors shows that the children were not able to utilize fully their initial familiarizing experience with the maze, i.e., they encountered difficulties in relating instrumental movements to the concept of conditions for action, which bespeaks the weakness of their attention.

Older preschool children (six-seven), on the other hand, engaged in a thorough and detailed tactual exploration of the maze, as a rule, accompanied by a verbal orientation ("this is a fence; this is an orchard; this is a dead end; the car cannot get through"), showing relatively quick comprehension of the relationships among the various aspects of the maze. After initial tactual exploration, they were able to isolate the beginning and the end points and to point them out. The image of the situation, formed on the basis of extensive orienting activity and a careful familiarization with the object of action, guaranteed them a flawless maneuvering of the automobile through the maze.

The experiments thus show that toward the end of the pre-school age, the child's attention increases appreciably in scope, becomes relatively stable, and most important, permits the child to reveal the main aspects of the conditions in which actions are formed.

The Development of Voluntary
Attention During the Preschool Age

Voluntary attention, in contrast to involuntary, which depends on the intensity of external influences or on the direct attractiveness of the objects, is evoked and maintained by motives not directly related to its object.

A question concerning the genesis and development of voluntary attention during childhood was raised in Soviet psychology by Vygotsky (12, 13), and Leontiev (6, 7). In analyzing the nature of voluntary attention, they emphasized the role of sociohistorical conditions of life in the appearance of voluntary attention in man. The voluntary regulation of attention is evoked by the requirements of socio-industrial activity and is actualized with the help of language. Each man in the process of his development through socialization acquires historically formed methods of organizing attention. The formation of voluntary attention in ontogeny begins in this way: the adult, with the help of words, expressive gestures, and other actions, attracts the child's attention to various aspects of reality. Gradually, the child learns to utilize these means for organizing his attention, which as a result acquires mediating, voluntary character.

As a number of studies indicate (Leontiev (6, 7), Elkonin (3), and others), the child's living conditions and activity are of decisive significance in the formation of attention. Thus, the shift during preschool age to a more complex form of play action, to learning type activities, and to fulfillment of simple labor tasks, in which the child has to take into account known rules and requirements of the adults, and of the child's community, exerts an essential influence on the development of voluntary attention.

Vygotsky's (12, 13) experiments describe the formation of the initial stages of voluntary attention. Children during play were asked to guess which of the covered cups placed before them contained peanuts. The cups were covered with pieces of cardboard in dark and light gray colors. Whenever the child guessed correctly, he took the peanuts; if he made a mistake he paid a penalty. The children, solving the problem by trial-and-error, were unable to note or fix their attention on the fact that the peanuts were found only in cups with darker covers. Multiple repetition of their attempts (forty-five—forty-nine trials) did not result in improvement. Only after the experimenter's introduction of a special method for attracting them to the distinguishing cue, the darker cover, did the five-year-old children solve the problem. The following method was used: while the subject was looking, the experimenter placed a peanut in one of the cups and covered it with a dark cover, silently pointing to it with his finger. With his next movement, he pointed to the light gray cardboard covering on an empty cup. This indicatory gesture sufficed for attracting the child's attention to the necessary cue so that he could isolate it and utilize it for guiding his actions. In the controlled experiments, whenever the covers were changed (in one case to black and gray, and in another to gray and white) the child unerringly opened up cups with the darker cover.

In another set of experiments in which an indicatory gesture for attracting the child's attention was used with the situation slightly changed, Vygotsky obtained analogous results. In these experiments the covers were of chromatic colors; for example, the cups were covered with orange and blue tops. The color of the "positive" cover was changed on each trial. Narrow gray stripes were used as an identifying cue. These stripes were pasted on the covers—darker on the "positive," lighter on the "negative." In this situation, the child had to act not on a trial-and-error basis as he did before, but by relying on the experience of preceding experiments had to figure out beforehand which color would lead to success, and at once pick up the right top. The five-year-old child could not solve this problem solely by himself; however, it was sufficient for the experimenter to point to one of the narrow gray stripes, and by doing so, attract the child's attention to the identifying cue when the child would give the correct response. From there on the child, relying on this cue, immediately identified the stripes and correctly made the choice between the colors of the covers.

The indicatory gesture, however, plays only a helping role in the genesis of voluntary attention. Speech is of decisive significance in this process. Martsinovskaya (8) presents interesting data, indicating that by using verbal instruction it is possible to direct the attention of preschool children to the components of the situation, which by themselves would not attract attention; by so doing they can be distracted from very potent stimuli. Preschool children were trained to develop motor reaction to a complex stimulus formed by a strong and a weak component. In the first series of experiments, employing conditioned reflex methodology and verbal reinforcement, a simple reaction to a lighted red circle and a weak-sounding bell was developed. After mastering the reaction (ten-fifteen correct consecutive reactions) the subjects were interviewed. The interview showed that, as a rule, preschool children of all ages associated their motor reaction with the appearance of the lighted circle, i.e., they paid attention only to the strong component of the complex.

In the second series of experiments, special verbal instructions directed the children's attention to the weak component of the complex so that they would isolate it as a signal for their actions. Initially, the children were trained in a choice reaction involving a complex stimulus consisting of a weak and a strong component (bright red circle on a pale yellow background and green circle on a white background). The children were required to press one button or another, depending on the quality of the stimulus, with one group of children guided by the strong component (the color of the circle), and the other by the weak component (color of the background). In order to make the choice easier, sheets of paper corresponding to those colors were placed under the buttons.

Verbal inquiry conducted after formation of the choice reaction showed that in the first group all children (from three to seven years), in 100 percent of the cases, pointed to the color of the circle as the determinant of their button choice. In the second group, the majority of the three- to four-year-old children, in spite of verbal instructions that were supposed to direct their attention to the weak component, oriented themselves in accordance with the strong one, the color of the circle, for the button selection. The number of cases in which children pointed to the weak component (color of the background) as the signal determining the button choice increases with age. Among the four- to six-year-old children there were 70 percent such cases; among the six- to seven-year-old children, 90 percent.

In order to verify the verbal report and the explanation of what it really was that the child relied upon in guiding his selection of the button, Martsinovskaya used an ingenious method. After the choice reaction had been well established, the strong components of both complex stimuli—red and green circles—were interchanged. If in the process of formation of the conditioned reaction the red circle was presented on a light yellow background, now it was presented on a white background, and vice versa. The results of this experiment showed that for the first group, in which verbal instructions oriented one to the strong component of the stimulus, children of all ages in 100 percent of the cases acted in accordance with the instruction, paying attention to the color of the circle and verbally indicating it during the inquiry.

A somewhat different result was obtained with the second group, in which verbal instructions directed the children's attention to the weak component. In this group, more than half of the three- to four-year-old children and one-fifth of the four- to five-year-old children acted in terms of the circle's color, and not in terms of the color of the background as the instructions directed.

Five-to seven-year-old children, as a rule, followed the verbal instructions in their actions. They paid attention to the color of the background while choosing the button. Only a part of this age group—30 percent of children from five to six and 10 percent from six to seven—reported errors that resulted from occasional utilization of the strong component as a qualitative basis for their selective procedures.

The postexperimental interview indicated that in this situation, for a given group, all children from three to four associated their motor reaction with the color of the circle, and all children from six to seven, with the background color.

Thus, Martsinovskaya's investigation showed that as early as preschool age it is possible, by ascribing cue significance through verbal instructions to the weaker component of the complex to direct the child's attention to the weaker element and by doing so, to level off the stronger component's activity.

Attention regulation through speech, as early as preschool age, permits one to direct the child's attention somewhat independently of the direct stimulation of external influences, and thereby to make his behavior freer and more adequate to the situation. Verbal presentation of certain goals and tasks, which the child in turn learns to present to himself, assures the isolation of any elements of the situation and the reliance upon them during execution of the action.

Data on preschool children obtained in an investigation by Godovikova (4) indicate that it is possible to switch the child's attention by means of verbal influences. With the assistance of preparatory verbal instruction, the children, ages three to seven, in a situation in which a little window with a burning bulb was open, were required to act in this manner: to depress the right key upon illumination of a red bulb and left key for a yellow bulb. In another situation, in which the lateral window was closed, it was necessary to act in a contrary manner. The child had to notice the change in the situation on his own, and at the same time shift to an activity pattern stipulated in the preliminary instructions. The child could judge the correctness of his actions on the basis of a practical result: when he acted according to the verbal instructions, the bulb extinguished; in a case of incorrect action, it remained burning.

The experiment showed that it is possible by means of preliminary verbal instruction to prepare children of all preschool ages for a predetermined voluntary shift from one type of action to another, in correspondence with changes of elements of the situation in which the action occurs. The experiment also demonstrates, however, that formation of the adjusting reaction that ensures the shift and the nature of the already formed reaction exhibit different characteristics at different age levels. Only for children in the second half of preschool age was verbal instruction sufficient to create a set for the shift with a change in the situation. For all the six- to seven-year-old children, the correct (verbally stipulated) shift from one type of action to another occurred with the first change of the adjusting signals. Among members of the younger group (five to six years), half of the children were able—only on the basis of verbal instruction—to change actions immediately in correspondence with the changes of the adjusting signals.

Formation of the adjusting reaction was accomplished through active mastering of the instruction, characteristic of the older children. As a rule, all children in the six- to seven-year-old group and a part of the five- to six-year-old group carried out some preparatory work while listening to the instructions. They paid attention to all elements and relationships of the situation pointed out in the instructions, as observed by their visual-motor orienting reactions to the elements of the situation. In spite of preparatory orientation, these children, while executing the action accompanying the change of adjusting signals in the situation, exhibited a verbal orienting reaction which was sometimes joined by an orienting hand movement. For example, with the appearance of the adjusting signal the child said: "Now, the red one is here," and touched the right button with his hand. A

majority of the children during the change of adjusting signals
used their hands for performing orienting movements, accompanying them with such words as: "Now, this one to this one,
and this one to this one"—apparently understanding by the
words, "this one," the color of the activating signal. In the postexperimental inquiry these children were able to give a verbal
account of their actions. They also could explain what caused
them to change their patterns of action.

In the three- to five-year-old children, verbal instruction—even
after its numerous repetitions—did not produce the adjusting
reaction. To obtain this, it was necessary to repeat several times
the shift from one to the other type of action as dictated by the
change of the adjusting signal. In addition, the experimenter had
to repeat the verbal instructions with each repetition. The children of this age listened to the preliminary instruction passively,
without showing any attention to the concrete conditions of action. They did not exhibit orienting reactions.

Even greater differences in voluntary attention are observed
when the child has to act with concrete objects according to verbal instructions (Petukhova, 9). The children were presented with
the following task: they were asked to select out of ten cards
(each card containing six pictures of animals) those containing at
least one of the pictures mentioned in the instructions (for example, a chicken or a horse); under no circumstances, however,
were they to take cards which contained a picture prohibited by
the instructions (for example, a bear). The child was given an
opportunity to select cards five times in a row. The first, second,
and fifth time the same pictures (a chicken and a horse) were
cited in the instruction as positive and a bear as negative. The
third and fourth time both the negative and the positive pictures
were different. Prior to the first selection, the child received no
instruction about the course of action. Starting with the second
trial, the experimenter invited the child, each time just prior to
the choice, to look carefully at all the pictures on the cards, to
think about what was said in the instructions (which cards are

allowed to be taken and which are not), and to repeat them aloud.

Three and one-half- to four and one-half-year-old children had great difficulty in fulfilling the task wherein they had to rely on the relationship between three elements. The number of correct solutions for children of this age, even at the end of the experiment, i.e., after some training, was small. However, all children of the older preschool age solved the task correctly beginning with the third presentation, in spite of the fact that new elements were introduced, starting at that time. Children of this age actively utilized speech for organizing their attention in the process of card selection.

It is apparent that during the fulfillment of the task the repetition of instructions aloud increases with age. Thus, verbal repetition of the elements of the instructions (two positive and one negative representation) was observed in the younger children only ten times during the course of the experiment, as compared with 107 such observations in the older children. An even greater difference exists in the number of repetitions of the prohibited representation. Twelve such repetitions were recorded for the younger children, as compared with 147 for the older children.

Leontiev's (6) investigation indicates even greater difficulty children have in completing an action according to verbal instructions within a verbal scheme. Under these conditions, children's attention has to be regulated completely with speech determined by purely verbal connections. The children were required to answer questions while adhering to specific verbally defined conditions. In reply to questions concerning the color of a given object (there were only seven such questions), presented to them among some other questions, the children were not to name two colors stated in the instructions, and not to repeat the same color twice.

Carrying out this task was difficult not only for the children of preschool age (in these experiments school-age children also took part), but also for children of younger school age. All children made mistakes in their replies; preschool children made a greater number of errors than younger school-age children. In contrast with preschool children, however, school-age children, under conditions when supportive means in the form of nine colored cards were provided, were able to utilize these supports and with their help to organize their attention, resulting in a drastic reduction of the number of wrong answers. The school-age children, as a rule, selected cards with the forbidden colors and set them aside, placing the rest of the cards in front of them. Prior to naming the color, they visually fixated the forbidden colors, thus protecting themselves from the possibility of naming them. While naming a certain color, they turned the card over so as not to repeat the color. The preschool children, on the other hand, were unable to utilize the colored cards in organizing their attention. They could not do it even after being prompted about the method for their utilization. As a result, the average number of wrong answers in the series with colored cards was approximately equal to that in the series without cards.

Among the younger school-age children, the number of wrong answers in the series of experiments with cards was reduced twofold, and among the medium school-age children, tenfold.

In conclusion, psychological investigations indicate that voluntary attention already begins to form during preschool age, and that the development of voluntary attention is tightly connected to an increase in the role of linguistic components in regulating the child's activity. These components may occur in the form of verbal instructions from an adult, as well as in the form of linguistic autosignalling, i.e., verbal designation by the child himself of those elements in the situation which require attention during the fulfillment of activities.

The correct organization of the child's activity plays an important role in the development of voluntary attention. How clearly the task of action, its goals, and conditions are specified and whether or not the situational elements, which are significant for the fulfillment of activity, are adequately identified determines the level of the child's attention. The cultivation of voluntary, premeditated attention is one of the important problems of preschool pedagogy and one of the important conditions in the child's preparation for training in school.

References

1. Agenosova, N. L. Razvitiye proizvolnogo vospriyatiya u detey doshkolnogo vozrasta. (Development of voluntary attention in preschool children.) Kand. diss. Moscow, 1948.

2. Dunayevsky, F. R. Popytka izucheniya razvitiya vysshey nervnoy deyatelnosti pri eksperimentalnom rasshirenii vozmozhnostey yeyo proyavleniya u detey pervykh et zhizni. (An attempt to study the development of higher nervous activity under experimental facilitation for its expression in children during the first few years of life.) Izvestia APN RSFSR. Vyp. 75, 1955.

3. Elkonin, D. B. Detskaya psikhologiya. (Child psychology.) Moscow. Uchpedgiz, 1960.

4. Godovikova, D. B. Obrazovaniye uslovnykh ustanovochnykh reaktsy u detey doshkolnogo vozrosta. (Formation of conditioned adjusting reactions in preschool children.) Doklady (Presentations of) APN RSFSR. 1957, No. 3.

5. Godovikova, D. B. Rol predvaritelnogo zritelnogo oznakomleniya s usloviyami zadachi v formirovanii dvigatelnogo navyka u detey doshkolnogo vozrasta. (The role of a preliminary visual familiarization with the conditions of a task in the formation of a motor habit in preschool children.) Voprosy psikhologii. 1959, No. 2.

6. Leontiev, A. N. Razvitiye vysshikh form vnimaniya. (Development of higher forms of attention.) Razvitiye pamyati. (Development of memory.) Ch. IV. Moscow-Leningrad. Uchpedgiz, 1931.

7. Leontiev, A. N. Problemy razvitiya psikhiki. (Problems in the development of the psyche.) Moscow. Izd-vo APN RSFSR, 1959.

8. Martsinovskaya, Ye. N. Razvitiye osoznaniya elementarnykh deystvy u detey doshkolnogo vozrasta. (Development of performance of elementary actions in preschool children.) Rukopis. (Manuscript.) Moscow, 1952.

9. Petukhova, T. V. Razvitiye proizvolnogo vnimaniya u detey doshkolnogo vozrasta. (Development of voluntary attention in preschool children.) Uchenyye Zapiski Pyatigorskogo ped. in-ta. (Scientific notes of the Piatigorsky Pedagogical Institute.) Vol. 9, 1955.

10. Poddyakov, N. N. Osobennosti avtomatizatsii deystvy u detey doshkolnogo vozrasta. (Aspects of automatization of actions in preschool children.) Rukopis. (Manuscript.) Moscow, 1957.

11. Surkhaykhanova, U. M. Sootnosheniye oriyentirovochnykh i rabochikh dvizheny v processe vyrabotki navyka u detey doshkolnikov. (The relation-

ship between orienting and manual movements in the process of the development of a habit in preschool children.) Rukopis. (Manuscript.) Moscow, 1952.

12. Vygotsky, L. S. Razvitiye activnogo vnimaniya v detskom vozraste. (Development of active attention in childhood.) Trudy AKV im. Krupskoy. (Works of Krupskaya AKV.) Sb., Voprosy marksistkoy pedagogiki. (Questions of Marxist pedagogy.) Vol. I, 1929.

13. Vygotsky, L. S. Razvitiye vysshikh form vnimaniya v detskom vozraste. (Development of the higher forms of attention in childhood.) Izbrannyye psikhologicheskiye issledovaniya. (Selected psychological investigations.) Moscow. Izd-vo APN RSFSR, 1956.

14. Yendovitskaya, T. V. Vliyaniye organizatsii oriyentirovochnoy deyatelnosti na obyom vnimaniya u detey. (The influence of the organization of orienting activity on the attention span in children.) Doklady (presentations of) APN RSFSR. 1957, No. 3

3. Development of Memory

Observations of the psychic development of children, as well as specially conducted studies, indicate that a child's memory develops with age. Its scope, as well as its qualitative aspects, undergoes a change.

In the history of psychology there have been several theories explaining principles of memory development in ontogeny. In Western European and American psychology, for instance, a false concept receiving wide circulation was that memory represents an innate, organic faculty, consisting of a passive storage for the imprints of former activities, in much the way that sand preserves the imprints of footsteps or wax, the imprints of a touching finger (Gering, Simon*).

This concept, in essence, rejects the development of memory, recognizing only the quantitative changes of its plasticity—its initial expansion due to maturation of the nervous system and the subsequent decrease due to aging of the organism. Adherents of this point of view regard progress in the area of voluntary and logical memory not as a result of mnemonic activity per se, but as a product of the intervention "of higher psychic factors," i.e., the will, thinking, etc. In contrast to these unscientific propositions concerning memory development, Soviet psychologists examine its genesis and development in terms of a process determined by the interaction of the subject with the surrounding environment, in which of essential significance is the subject's activity as defined by its goals and its content. The child does not merely passively record a variety of external activities, but he actively retains what he contributes to the interaction and upon which depends the attainment of a positive result of his activity.

Development of memory depends on the fact that during different periods of his life a child's goals change, and the character of his interaction with the surrounding environment is also altered.

*The complete reference was not provided in the original.

Memory as a separate psychic process, a mnemonic activity, is not passed on to the child in its final form at birth. It is constructed and modified during the developmental process under the influence of environmental conditions.

The most elementary form of memory—the imprinting and recognition of those external actions which are of significance to the vital processes of the organism—appears in the first stage of a child's life. As the studies of higher nervous activity indicate (Krasnogorsky, 12, Kasatkin, 6, and others), the simplest form of imprinting in children is observed as early as the first month of life. It is expressed in the form of a stereotyped reaction to a stimulus, based on actualized conditioned connections due to repeated influence of the stimulus.

Around the third-fourth month of life, appearance of a more complex form of imprinting based on an elementary analysis of complex stimuli is noted. This in turn leads to formation and imprinting of an image of the impinging object. It is essentially these formations that become the foundation of the child's memory, identifiable in terms of recognition of previously perceived objects.

Special investigations, as well as diary material, indicate that three—three and one-half-month-old children exhibit recognition in the visual and auditory spheres. Most frequently, the first objects of recognition are the mother's face and voice. In such cases, recognition is expressed by the child through special movements: raising the head, turning the body in the direction of the mother, the appearance or disappearance of crying, etc.

Observable during the third-fourth month is a recognition of objects connected with the feeding situation: pulling up the head with the mouth open, towards the bottle from which the infant is always fed (Shchelovanov, 18), sucking responses at the sight of a spoon nearing the mouth, etc.

The sphere of recognizable objects expands subsequently beyond the limits of the feeding situation. During the fifth-sixth months, the child begins to recognize familiar people and to distinguish them from strangers.

During the seventh-eighth month of life, in the process of socialization of the child with an adult a distinctive form of memory is observed—recognition mediated by language. It is expressed initially by visual fixation on an object named by the adult and its shifting from object to object, depending on verbal designation.

Subsequently, children begin to associate words not only with objects, but also with their own movements. Among eight—nine-month-old children it is possible to observe reproduction of movements to a verbal signal: clapping hands to the word "patty-cake," waving a hand to the word "good-bye," etc. Many parental diaries note that at the end of the first and at the beginning of the second year there appears a new form of reaction to naming objects—the pointing gesture of the hand.

Depending on the child's progress of socializing with an adult, at the end of the first year and the beginning of the second year the objects of memory become words themselves. At this time, naming an object evokes not only movement response, such as shifting the eyes to the named object or the pointing gesture by the hand, but also a reproduction of the word. At the beginning as a rule, the child's utterance of the word immediately follows the adult's naming an object, but thereafter the child begins independently to name the object upon seeing it.

According to diary materials, the period between perception of an object in a situation and subsequent recognition becomes longer with age. During his second year, the child recognizes familiar people and common objects even after several weeks; during the third year, after several months; and during the fourth year, even after a year.

A very important aspect in the development of the child's memory is the separation of memory from the perception process, i.e., the ability to create an image of an object in the absence of the latter. Initially, the causative factor in the recollection of an object seen previously is perception of another object connected with the former by situational, spatial, or temporal relationships. For example, a child passing a place where he once saw chickens demands that they be shown to him again (one year, eight months, thirteen days). Thereafter, in order to recall a picture of something previously perceived, it is enough to have the presence of another percept related in some way with the object of recollection. Subsequently, with the development of speech, the mental image of an object is produced on the basis of its verbal designation.

In the pre-preschool age, a child's memory may be characterized as unintentional and involuntary, i.e., the child remembers anything without setting remembering as a specific goal himself. Remembering and recalling are achieved during the process of socializing with an adult and are primarily detected in the form of recognition.

In the preschool age, the child's activity becomes more and more goal-oriented. Simultaneously, there is an increase in demands imposed on the child by adults with respect to the fulfillment of his activity. In part, adults begin presenting the child with such tasks as remembering and recalling something specific in order to perform some action successfully (practical, playful, learning). On this basis, in addition to further development of involuntary memory, new forms of memory emerge.

According to psychological investigations (Leontiev, Zinchenko, and others), mnemonic activity per se, with its specific goals, applications, and methods, begins forming in preschool age. This leads to emergence of voluntary, premeditated memory. During preschool age, the child learns to govern this process, to present himself with a goal for remembering or recalling something. Special mnemonic actions are formed during this period.

The shift to conscious governing of mnemonic activities is a complex process that includes a series of stages. Initially, the child distinguishes and realizes the mnemonic goal. Thereafter, he begins to utilize actions and operations corresponding to this goal.

Initially, the mnemonic goal, such as to remember or to recall, is presented to the child by an adult and is formed verbally. With the help of an adult presenting the corresponding tasks, however, the child gradually develops an intention to remember something to be recalled in the future: he learns to present himself independently with a mnemonic goal.

This process of isolation and realization of mnemonic goals was studied by Istomina (2, 3). She reports that isolation of this goal by the preschool child occurs when he is confronted with conditions requiring active memorization and recall. This condition alone is not sufficient, however. Isolation and realization of the mnemonic goal by the child depends, in addition, on its relationship to the motive of the activity within which the mnemonic action has to be realized. Only the presence of definite motives makes the mnemonic goal itself meaningful for the child. Memorizing is necessary to be able to carry out successfully some form of objective or mental activity in the future (transmitting a message, mastering knowledge, etc.). Remembering therefore must always be motivated, and the activity of memorizing or recalling should lead to attainment of a significant—for the child— goal.

Istomina's investigation studied experimentally the dependence of isolating mnemonic goals upon the character of the activity pursued by the child (laboratory-type tasks, play, and practical activity). In one case, the child was presented with a goal to memorize and thereafter to recall a series of words (laboratory-type tasks). In other cases, the child was required to isolate this goal for himself in the course of play and practical activity. Analysis of the results indicates that in the laboratory type of experiments, the motive arousing the child to participate in them was based on the child's desire to socialize with the experimenter; the mnemonic goal, which was presented to the child by the experimenter, did not arise primarily from this motive. In play and practical activity, on the other hand, the mnemonic goal was directly connected with a common motive arousing the child to act, since the fulfillment of play or the practical task was possible only with performance of the mnemonic activity. Thus, under conditions of play and practical activity, the special goal to memorize and to remember acquired for the child a concrete meaning.

Istomina's data, characterizing the efficiency of memorization under a variety of conditions (Table 7), show that the optimal condition for appearance in the child of the intention to remember and to recall something is fulfilling an assignment given by an adult, in the process of accompanying activity.

The fact that the fulfillment of practical assignments creates optimal conditions for remembering is also supported by results of observations of various aspects of children's actions. During performance of a practical assignment, the children not only isolated the mnemonic goal more easily, but also began to apply special methods in order to remember better. The application of mnemonic methods was observed among children beginning at five years of age.

The data obtained allow us to assume that the optimal conditions for formulation of the mnemonic goal and of remembering

Table 7.
Average Number of Reproduced Words (out of 5)

Conditions	Age (years)			
	3-4	4-5	5-6	6-7
Laboratory types of tasks	0.6	1.5	2.0	2.3
Fulfillment of a play assignment within playful activity	1.0	3.0	3.2	3.8
Fulfillment of an assignment within practical activity	2.3	3.5	4.0	4.4

and recalling as special acts occur under living conditions that require the child to fulfill some type of "important" task assigned by an adult.

Similar circumstances may also be reproduced in the play situation. Under the preschool child's limited opportunities to participate in practical activity with an adult, a play activity presents complementary conditions for the successful development of voluntary memory.

Istomina's data also indicate that recall acquires a voluntary character earlier than memorizing. This apparently occurs because the child actually confronts himself in the reproducing situation with the necessity of acting in order to solve the mnemonic task—to recall what is required. This condition evokes a search for methods of recall. In the process of recall, one also discovers that something has been forgotten, and this leads one to assume that in the past there was not enough activity expressed while memorizing the material which presently has to be remembered.

The memorizing situation itself does not contain a special necessity for heightened activity so that one can memorize. This necessity first emerges in a child under the influence of requirements for active recall. The latter exerts an influence on the formation of the memorizing activity.

Experimental materials obtained by Istomina indicate that the child, having discovered his own failure during fulfillment of a given assignment, recognizes the fact that he had not been sufficiently active during listening to the presentation of the assignment and had done nothing in order to remember it.

Even though it is already possible to observe elements of voluntary memory among children of middle preschool age, the predominant form of memory during the entire preschool age continues to be involuntary and unintentional. This is expressed in that preschool children mainly remember a situation, words, objects, and their interrelationships in the course of fulfilling some type of activity (practical, play, learning), and to the extent to which that activity is expressed in the process of performance.

This is supported by the fact that during preschool age the efficiency of unintentional remembering remains higher than that of intentional remembering.

Zinchenko (25, 26) studied the relative effectiveness of voluntary and involuntary remembering in preschool children. In the course of the experiments, children were asked in one series to distribute (classify) pictures according to their content into five groups defined by the experimenter as associated with a kitchen, an orchard, a yard, etc. In the second series, another group of children of various ages were given the task of simply remembering the pictures while utilizing grouping as the means for memorizing.

After fulfillment of the task, the experimenter determined the extent of the memorized material. The results showed that the efficiency of both forms of remembering (involuntary in the first series, as well as voluntary in the second) increases with age; at the same time the efficiency of involuntary remembering, however, surpasses the efficiency of voluntary remembering at all levels of preschool age (Graph 3).

It is characteristic that the younger preschoolers who generally performed poorly on the classification task in both series did not show any special activity, and their efficiency in remembering is in both cases very low.

A general increase in remembering efficiency during preschool childhood has been noted by many Soviet authors. Thus, Leontiev (13) demonstrated an increase in the effectiveness of memorizing words. In an investigation by Korniyenko (11) an increased effectiveness of memorizing both visual and auditory material has been reported (Table 8).

Similar results have been obtained by the foreign psychologists. Thus, McElwee (15) ascertained the development of memory for objects in preschool children; Lumley and Calhoun (14) noted the emergence of memory for words for this age group. Winch (20), using Stern's method requiring the child to describe the content of a picture previously presented to him, obtained results

Graph 3.
Efficiency of Voluntary and Involuntary Memorizing

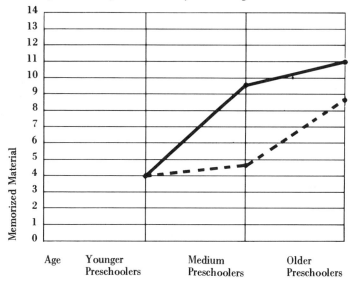

━━━━ Involuntary memorizing
■ ■ ■ Voluntary memorizing

Table 8.
Effectiveness of Memorizing Words and Objects (Mean Numbers)

Age (years)	Reproduced Objects	Reproduced Names of Familiar Objects (out of Ten)	Reproduced Names of Unfamiliar Objects (out of Ten)
3-4	3.9	1.8	0
4-5	4.4	3.6	0.3
5-6	5.1	4.6	0.6
6-7	5.6	4.8	1.8

also indicative of an increased scope in the memory of preschool children (Table 9).

What then determines the increased effectiveness of memory in preschool children? As far as is possible to determine on the basis of experimental findings, this increase is dependent on development of the content of activity carried out by the child in relation to the objects being memorized, and also by formation and development of the means for memorizing. Data from numerous experiments indicate, for example, that preschool children while memorizing begin more often to arrive at simpler forms of generalization, to relate remembered objects to a definite category, and to group them by meaning.

The systematization of representations emerging in the process of children's activity serves as a base for this type of generalization and unification. According to Zankov (22), unification of objects related to some category is accomplished initially on the basis of the child's using them jointly; subsequently, they are perceived during fulfillment of various types of activity: eating, washing, drawing, etc. On the basis of this, for example, such objects as a plate, a spoon, a fork, a cup, paper, a pencil, paints, a brush, etc., become associated and unified.

Later on, systematization of representations is accomplished, not only during the process of the child's direct practical activity with objects, but also on the basis of verbally conveyed descriptions of objects, their definition, and methods of utilization.

The systematization of representations, their unification into semantic groups, serves as an essential support for memorizing to

Table 9.
Effectiveness of Memorizing Pictures (Mean Numbers)

Age (years)	Reproduced Elements of a Picture
3-4	8.3
4-5	16.1
5-6	26.5
6-7	30.0

a preschool child. The investigation of Zankov and Mayants (23) showed that five- to seven-year-old children remember objects much better when they are presented to them not one by one, but in pairs; and especially when they are presented in such a combination that it is possible to create a semantic connection between the objects of each pair or to relate them to some kind of a common category.

Generalization of remembered material and its unification into semantic groups is also reported by Korniyenko (11), who studied children of all preschool ages. Having analyzed reproduction of ten names of objects with which the children were quite familiar, he identified three methods of recall. The first method consists of an unsystematic recall of the words (the words were reproduced in random fashion). In the second method, the order of recall reflects the order of the words' presentation. The third method includes a semantic grouping of the words. The number of cases where semantic grouping was utilized increased with age.

A rise in the cases applying semantic grouping in memorizing throughout preschool age and the expanding role of analysis of the remembered material reflected in generalization, were found in an investigation by Yendovitskaya (21) that specifically studied intellectual operations used by a child as means for memorizing words—especially in a case when outside supports (pictures) were provided. The research showed that preschool children, while memorizing, establish the most distinctive connections between words, but with age the relative weight of these connections changes. Moreover, the most progressive type of connection is a semantic grouping performed on the basis of a generalization by relating words to a homogeneous group of objects (Graph 4).

The utilization of semantic grouping by preschool children in the memorization process by itself attests to the intelligent nature of their memory and may serve as one of the bases for disproving propositions about the so-called mechanical character of preschool children's memory.

Graph 4.
Application of Semantic Grouping in Memorizing

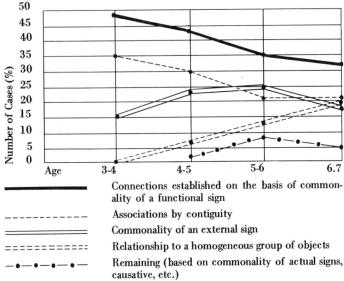

Connections established on the basis of commonality of a functional sign

Associations by contiguity

Commonality of an external sign

Relationship to a homogeneous group of objects

Remaining (based on commonality of actual signs,
causative, etc.)

Numerous psychologists have thought that one of the fundamental characteristics of childhood memory is its mechanical
nature. Stern, Kolenare, and Treter spoke about the advantage of
mechanical memorizing among small children. Mayman asserted
that the acquisition of logical memory may be ascribed only to
thirteen—fourteen-year-old children.

Investigations of Soviet psychologists indicate that the effectiveness of remembering in preschool children increases in direct
relationship to meaningfulness of the presented material. Table
10 presents data of Leontiev (13), supporting the greater effectiveness in remembering meaningful words as compared to non-
sense syllables.

Korniyenko (11) reports an increase in the effectiveness of
memory, depending on the level of meaningfulness, i.e., the
child's understanding of the memorized material (Table 11).

In the preschool age, verbal mediation plays an ever greater role
in the comprehension of material.

Table 10.
Relationship of Meaningfulness of Material to Memorizing

| Age (years) | Mean Number of Reproductions | |
	Nonsense Syllables	Words
4-5	0.25	1.45
6-7	2.2	4.7

Table 11.
Effect of Understanding Material on Memorizing

| Age (years) | Mean Number of the Reproduced Words | |
	Quite Familiar	Not Familiar
3-4	1.8	0
4-5	3.6	0.3
5-6	4.6	0.4
6-7	4.8	1.2

In an experiment conducted by Kazheradze (7), children were asked to group a variety of objects. One series of trials required grouping objects, the collective names of which were well known to the children; the second series included objects whose naming presented difficulty to the child; the third series contained objects to be identified by a collective name, producing even greater difficulty for the child. Each series had a fixed number of objects to be remembered in the grouping process. The data indicate a direct relationship between the child's utilization of a word common to the objects during grouping and the the effectiveness of memorizing (Table 12).

Yendovitskaya (21) investigated the influence of verbal mediation in the course of building semantic connections on the effectiveness of remembering. In order to better memorize the words presented to them, preschool children were asked to select pictures corresponding in their meaning to the words and to clarify verbally their reasons for selection. Thereafter, the selected pictures were presented sequentially, and the children were asked to reproduce the words that were used at the time of the original

Table 12.
Relationship Between Collective Naming and Memorizing

	Mean Number of Reproduced Objects			
Nature of Material	Age (years) 4	5	6	7
Easily named by a collective word	3.2	3.4	6.0	8.2
More difficult to name	0.4	1.4	3.4	3.8
Extremely difficult to name	0	0	0.6	1.4

selections. This study showed that presentation of a formerly chosen picture assures recall of the associated word only when the basis for selection (the established semantic connection) was formed verbally. Reproduction of a word occurred, for example, when the child in responding to the word "kitten" selected a dog's picture. He expressed the following reasoning: "This is because it is also a domestic animal and also a small one." In response to the word "house," a picture of a red apple was selected. This response was justified by saying, "The apple is red and the house can be red, made of bricks." Such a verbal description of the semantic connection was observed with middle and older preschool children.

Furthermore, the children (most frequently, younger preschool children from three to five) who selected pictures close in meaning to the words, i.e., "lunch"–picture of a plate or "kitten"– picture of a dog, but were unable to verbally formulate their basis for selection, were subsequently unable to reproduce these words.

The participation of speech in the establishment of semantic connections within the material being remembered is one of the central factors in memory development during preschool age. The replacement of graphic-visual connections, present during the first stages of preschool age, by semantic connections indicates a shift to an internally-mediated memory, which provides for the formation of verbal-logical memory. As Korniyenko's (11) data indicate, during preschool childhood the tempo of memory development for verbal material surpasses the tempo of the formation of memory for visual material. Furthermore, the greatest shift in memory development for verbal material is observed from four to five years of age (Table 13; the data for the three- to four-year-old group are taken as 100 percent).

Korman (8, 9, 10), analyzing various aspects of reproduction of connected verbal material, such as reading of a fairy tale, showed that even four—five-year-old children can remember and reproduce with sufficient logical sequence relatively complex prosaic material (in this investigation, a fairy tale that could be comprehended by the children was used). Children's narration of the formerly presented material indicates that they did not reproduce the text of the fairy tale in a mechanical manner, but were restating its meaningful content. Korman notes that the children frequently departed from the original sequence of events, but accompanied such a departure by logically explainable "jumps." Logically conceived reproductions of the fairy tale are evident in that while repeating the story the preschool children omitted certain episodes, especially those of lesser importance to the main idea. They could remember only events that were essential to the logical relationship of elements of the main activity, leaving out what was related to circumstances.

According to Korman, the nature of the reproduction of a connected text changes with age. During the process of recalling a fairy tale, the four—five-year-old children taken in by the

Table 13.
Effectiveness of Memorizing Visual and Verbal Material in Comparison to the Three—Four-Year-Old Group

Age (years)	Reproducing Visual Material	Reproducing Verbal Material
3-4	100%	100%
4-5	112	200
5-6	130	255
6-7	143	266

dynamics of the unfolding main events, as a rule reproduced only the episodes necessary for the unfolding of the fairy tale. The links related to the precision and the details of the setting in which the main action occurred were omitted. Six-year-old children gave a more detailed and precise, in a textual sense, reproduction of the fairy tale.

The formation and cultivation of memory in preschool children, just as the formation of other psychological processes, occurs in the process of activity. The nature of memory to a large extent depends on the features of the activity structure during preschool age. This activity is characteristically directed toward immediate and concrete goals. Therefore, the content of remembered and recalled material is determined by what the child considers directly necessary and interesting. Memorizing in order to accumulate material to use later, i.e., "learning by heart," is performed with great difficulty and only toward the end of the preschool age.

The memory of the preschool child is mainly unintentional in character. Its effectiveness depends basically upon the child's activity evoked and sustained by the direct goals and motives of the action, and by that direct relationship which the child forms toward what he perceives. In addition, children's numerous special pursuits—didactic games, drawing, constructions, exercises for developing speech, etc.,—create favorable conditions for the development of intentional and meaningful remembering and recalling.

In specially organized children's activity, whenever the child is presented with a task requiring attainment of a specific result, he experiences a necessity of isolating various objects and their interrelationships from the surrounding environment and remembering them. This serves as a base for isolating and formulating the special mnemonic goal. Initially, this goal is usually presented to the child by an adult, who points out what should be isolated and remembered and the reason, prompting the child in methods for remembering and reinforcing (by approval or reproach) the obtained result. Thereafter, the child—again with the help of an adult—learns to isolate and verbally formulate the mnemonic goal himself. During the various periods of preschool age, both the adult's and the child's speech is an important condition for developing meaningful and intentional memory.

Correct organization of the nurturing process in general and the organization of the child's activity in particular play an important role in the formation of memory in the preschool child. The way in which the child's activity is organized—e.g., presenting him with a special goal to remember and to recall the necessary material; connecting a memorizing task with general motives of his activity; forming methods for memorizing, etc.—to a large extent determines the effectiveness of his memory development.

Creating favorable conditions in the preschool age for the development of intentional and meaningful processes of memory—more specifically the formation of the elements of intentional memory—is of great significance in the child's further psychological development. Cultivating at this age elements of purposeful memory, forming the ability to present oneself consciously with a goal to remember, and forming the ability to recall and to utilize the methods and means necessary to accomplish this goal are the essential preconditions for the successful training of the child in school.

Features of Memory at the Various Levels of Preschool Age

Younger Preschool Age (Three-Four Years)

Memory processes as special actions directed toward memorizing and recall are still absent in children of younger preschool age. The child of this age cannot yet set himself a goal to memorize or to recall. Memorizing, like recalling, is accomplished unintentionally at this age. Imprinting and reproducing something occur without the child's intentional attempts in the process of some practical or play acitivity.

The three—four-year-old children mainly memorize and recall connections formed by constantly repeating spatial or temporal contiguity of impinging objects and phenomena. Recall appears in the form of recognition of either formerly perceived objects or something closely resembling them. Essential reproduction, recall of specified, assigned material in the absence of the objective situation facilitating it, is accomplished by the younger preschool child within very narrow limits.

Experimental data show that children of this age are able to reproduce, on the average, not more than four objects or their representations out of ten to fifteen objects presented to them (Zinchenko, 26 and Korniyenko, 11). The limited scope of the material being memorized is even better illustrated in experiments requiring memorization of individual words as they are presented to the child. According to a number of authors (Leontiev 13; Istomina, 2, 3; Korniyenko, 11, and others), three—four-year-old children memorize on the average not more than two words.

A young child does much better in memorizing a connected text—poems, stories, and fairy tales. In this case, along with a large number of repetitions, a number of conditions are present that favor memorizing. Zhukovskaya (24) studied the kinds of sayings and poems that are best memorized and reproduced by children of the younger preschool age. Certain conditions favoring their memorization and reproduction of a poetic text were uncovered. An especially important condition appears to be the emotional content of the text. Those poems which evoke clear images, stimulate imagination, give rise to the idea of being helpful (mental and direct activity), and evoke empathy are easily remembered by the children and are eagerly reproduced. Sonority and clear rhythm of the poetic text play an important role. The latter facilitates construction of a verbal-motor image, which serves as a support for memorizing and reproducing. Correspondence of the rhythm of speech with the rhythm of body movement is another relevant factor in memorizing poems by three—four-year-old children. These facts further support a well-known proposition in child psychology concerning predominance in young children of motor and visual-graphic types of memory.

Middle Preschool Age (Five Years)

This age is characterized by the appearance and gradual development of intentional memorizing and recalling. A four—five-year-old child is able to accept a mnemonic goal set by an adult and is also capable of constructing such a goal for himself, especially when conditions of activity favor it.

The first sign of the presence of such goal orientation is the simple repetition of material that must be retained in memory. Such a goal-setting at first, however, is not recognized by the child as the means for memorizing and is not consciously utilized as such. Isolation of the mnemonic goal does not entail immediate application of special actions directed toward memorizing. Indeed, the five-year-old's ability to present himself with such a goal defines the appearance of the first attempts to utilize special methods and means for memorizing and recalling. In five—six-year-old children, with appropriate organization of their activity, there begin to form special mnemonic actions directed toward memorizing and recall.

Near the end of middle preschool age there appear, along with an elementary mnemonic method—simple repetition of what is necessary to remember—such methods as subsequent repetition and elementary systematization of the material with the goal of remembering it, as well as methods of memorizing based on a logical analysis of the material. In connection with the development of speech and the child's thinking activity, develops his verbal-logical memory.

The development of the memory process during middle preschool age leads to an increase in the range of the material memorized. Children of this age already are able to reproduce, on the average, five out of ten to fifteen objects momentarily presented to them (Zankov and Mayants, 23 and Korniyenko, 11) and about four unconnected words out of a series of ten to fifteen words (Leontiev, 13; Istomina, 2, 3; Korniyenko, 11, and others). There is also an increase in the amount of memorizing connected text. Moreover, Korman (8) points out that there is not only an improvement in the quality of material remembered, but also a change in the content of what the child can remember. Retelling a fairy tale, a four—five-year-old child restates not only its main events, but also makes an attempt to pass on details and to reproduce the fairy tale more in the context of the text, that is, to pass it on in terms of the same verbal expressions used by the author.

Older Preschool Age (Six-Seven Years)

During this age, the processes of intentional memory and recall acquire the form of specially developed action that is directly subservient to the mnemonic task—a task to recall or to memorize. In terms of its efficiency, voluntary intentional memorizing begins to approach involuntary memorizing (Zinchenko, 26). The child learns to govern his memory, utilizing various mnemonic methods and means, among which a leading place is occupied by verbal mediation.

In older preschool age, appreciable development is noticed in the verbal-logical memory. The six—seven-year-old child utilizes words easily in forming semantic connections while memorizing. Relying on the word, he analyzes the material being remembered, groups it according to a predetermined category of objects or phenomena, and establishes logical connections. This procedure also facilitates an increased amount of remembered material. A six—seven-year-old child memorizes on the average seven objects or their representations out of ten to fifteen after their momentary presentation (Zankov and Mayants, 23; Korniyenko, 11; Leontiev, 13; and Istomina, 2, 3). Characteristically, in contrast with younger preschool children who show a distinctive difference in the efficiency of memorizing objects and words, children of older preschool age memorize verbal material (separate words) almost as successfully as object material.

An important role in the improved efficiency in memorizing during older preschool age may be attributed to the fact that toward six-seven years, representations of the surrounding environment begin to be systematized. Various objects are placed by the child into various categories of objects or phenomena. The latter facilitates forming logical connections between objects and semantic connections, in general, which facilitate memorization.

References

1. Gordon, Ye. V. Osobennosti razvitiya protsessov pamyati u detey. (Aspects of the development of memory processes in children.) Doshkolnoye vospitaniye. (Preschool upbringing.) 1953, No. 9.

2. Istomina, Z. M. Razvitiye proizvolnoy pamyati v doshkolnom vozraste. (The development of voluntary memory in preschool age.) Izvestia APN RSFSR. Vyp. 14, 1948.

3. Istomina, Z. M. K voprosu o razvitii proizvolnoy pamyati u detey doshkolnogo vozrasta. (Concerning the question of the development of voluntary memory in preschool children.) Doshkolnoye vospitaniye. (Preschool upbringing.) 1953, No. 4.

4. Ivanov-Smolensky, A. G. (ed.) Sb. Opyt sistematicheskogo issledovaniya uslovnoreflektornoy deyatelnosti rebyonka. (Systematic investigation of the child's conditioned reflex activity.) Moscow, 1934.

5. Ivanov-Smolensky, A. G. (ed.) Sb. Na puti k izucheniyu vysshikh form neyrodinamiki rebyonka. (Toward an understanding of higher forms of neurodynamics in the child.) Moscow, 1934.

6. Kasatkin, N. I. Ranniye uslovnyye refleksy v ontogeneze cheloveka. (Early conditioned reflexes in the ontogeny of man.) Moscow. Medgiz, 1948.

7. Kazheradze, Ye. D. Razvitiye pamyati v doshkolnom i pervom shkolnom vozraste. (The development of memory in preschool and early school age.) Kand. diss. Tbilisi, 1949.

8. Korman, T. A. O dinamike myshleniya i vosproizvedeniya. (Concerning the dynamics of thinking and recall.) Doshkolnoye vospitaniye. (Preschool upbringing.) 1944, No. 3-4.

9. Korman, T. A. Razlichiya slovesno-smyslovoy pamyati mladshikh i starshikh doshkolinkov. (Differences in verbal-semantic memory of younger and older preschoolers.) Doshkolnoye vospitaniye. (Preschool upbringing.) 1945, No. 7.

10. Korman, T. A. K kharakteristike aktivnogo vosproizvedeniya u doshkolnikov. (Toward the characteristics of active recall in preschoolers.) Sovetskaya pedagogika. (Soviet pedagogy.) 1945, No. 9.

11. Korniyenko, N. A. Uznavaniye i vosproizvedeniye naglyadnogo i slovesnogo materiala detmi doshkolnogo vozrasta. (Recognition and recall of visual and verbal material by preschool children.) Kand. diss. Moscow, 1955.

12. Krasnogorsky, N. I. Razvitiye ucheniya o fiziologicheskoy deyatelnosti mozga u detey. (Development of studies concerning the brain activity of children.) Sb. Ob osnovnykh mekhanismakh raboty bolshikh polushary u detey. (Concerning the basic mechanisms of activity of the hemispheres in children.) Moscow-Leningrad. Medgiz, 1939.

13. Leontiev, A. N. Razvitiye pamyati. (Development of memory.) Moscow-Leningrad. Uchpedgiz, 1931.

14. Lumley, T. H., and Calhoun, S. W. Memory span for words presented auditorially. J. Appl. Psychol., 1934, 18, 773-784.

15. McElwee, E. W. Further standardization of the Ellis memory for objects test. J. Appl. Psychol., 1933, 17, 69-70.

16. Rubinshtein, S. L. Osnovy obshchey psikhologii. (Basis of general psychology.) Moscow. Uchpedgiz, 1946.

17. Sechenov, I. M. Izbrannyye proizvedeniya. (Selected studies.) Vol. 1. Moscow. Izd-vo AP SSSR, 1952.

18. Shchelovanov, N. M., and Aksarina, N. M. (ed.) Vospitaniye detey rannego vozrasta v detskikh uchrezhdeniyakh. (Training of young children in children's institutions.) Moscow. Medgiz, 1955.

19. Smirnov, A. A. Psikhologiya zapominaniya. (Psychology of memorizing.) Moscow. Izd-vo APN RSFSR, 1948.

20. Winch, W. H. Children's perceptions. Baltimore: Warwick and York, 1914.

21. Yendovitskaya, T. V. O razvitii oposredstvovanogo zapominaniya v doshkolnom vozraste. (Concerning the development of mediational thinking in preschool age.) Rukopis. (Manuscript.) Moscow, 1954.

22. Zankov, L. V. Pamyat. (Memory). Moscow. Uchpedgiz, 1949.

23. Zankov, L. V., and Mayants, D. M. Zapominaniye i vosproizvedeniye predmetov u slushashchikh i glukhonemykh doshkolnikov. (Memorizing and recalling objects in hearing and deaf-mute children.) Sb. Voprosy psikhologii glukhonemykh i umstvenno otstalykh detey. (Questions of the psychology of deaf-mute and mentally retarded children.) Moscow, 1940.

24. Zhukovskaya, R. I. Zapominaniye i vosproizvedeniye stikhotvoreny malenkimi detmi. (Memorizing and recalling of poems by small children.) Doshkolnoye vospitaniye. (Preschool upbringing.) 1947, No. 12.

25. Zinchenko, P. I. Problema neproizvolnogo zapominaniya. (Problem of involuntary memorization.) Uchyonyye zapiski Kharkovskogo ped. in-ta inostran. Yazykov. (Scientific notes of the Kharkov Pedagogical Institute of foreign languages.) Vol. I, 1939.

26. Zinchenko, P. I. O formirovanni neproizvolnogo i proizvolnogo zapominaniya. (Concerning formation of involuntary and voluntary memory.) Sovetskaya pedagogika. (Soviet Pedagogy.) 1954, No. 4.

4. Development of Speech

General Characteristics of Speech in Preschool Age (Development of the Forms and Functions of Speech)

In early childhood the child's speech, appearing as a means for socializing with adults and other children, is directly related to his practical activity or to the vivid situation in which or because of which socialization is taking place. The activity of a child this age usually is accomplished either together with adults or with their help; therefore, his socializing may be characterized as situational. This imparts on speech a special form—that of situational speech having dialogic character in most cases. This speech represents either answers to an adult's questions or questions to an adult in connection with tasks arising during activity, demands about satisfaction of various needs, or finally, questions arising during familiarization with objects and phenomena in the surrounding environment.

The dialogic form of speech in early childhood may be viewed as evidence and also expression of a child's insufficient independence or lack of separation of his activities from those of adults.

The shift to preschool age consists of actual changes in the child's developmental conditions and most of all, in his relationships with adults. His expanded abilities and adults' demands for his greater independence, coupled with his own tendency toward this activity lead to the emergence of real independent activity. This serves as a basis for rapid development of various types of action in children: creative role-playing, imaginary activity (drawing and pasting), construction, and elementary forms of physical activity. A more important aspect is the creative character of these activities, consisting of the child's independent realization of his own intentions. The formation of the creative and the productive forms of activity provides the base for an intensive development of the children's collective life; this in turn is utilized for the formation of children's collectives, united by common activity and intentions.

A significant increase in the child's scope of vital relationships occurs now, reaching far beyond the limits of direct, joint activity with adults. The child becomes acquainted with life and people's activities; access to objects other than ones he can reach, not only those that he is able to recognize directly, becomes available; objects, people, and relationships, with which he is acquainted through adults' narrations, books read to him, and exploration of pictures occupy a greater place in his life.

Change in the child's way of life, the appearance of new relationships with adults, and new forms of activity lead to differentiation of functions and forms of speech. New socialization tasks arise, consisting of the child's conveying his impressions to an adult, obtained outside of direct contact with adults. Informative speech appears as a type of monologue-story about what was experienced and seen, intentions for play and completed work, an observed children's film, stories heard, interrelationships with friends, and all that occurred in the life and the activity of the child outside of his direct association with adults. On the basis of the developing life in the collective arises a necessity for reaching agreement about common intentions in activity, distribution of functions, and control in the fulfillment of rules, etc. Depending on the nature of the collective activity emerge the problems of instruction, evaluation, etc. On this basis the development of dialogic speech continues with the appearance of its new forms: commands, evaluations, agreements for activity, etc.

In connection with the development of independent practical activity, the child encounters the need for forming his own intentions, for defining activity, and for reasoning concerning the means for fulfilling activity.

Functions and forms of speech during the preschool age become extremely diversified. The child masters all the basic forms of the spoken language characteristic of an adult. New needs for socializing and activity, bringing about new forms of speech, inevitably lead to an intensive mastery of the language, its verbal content, and grammatical structure as a result of which the child's speech becomes more connected. The degree of connectedness depends first of all on the task, the situation in which the interaction takes place, and on the content of interaction.

Leushina conducted a special investigation concerning the development of connected speech in preschool children. Following Rubinshtein, she identifies a special form of speech, "situational speech," and contrasts it with "contextual speech." According to Leushina, *"situational speech does not fully reflect the content of a thought as expressed in verbal forms.* Its content becomes *clear* to the interlocutor only *when he takes into consideration that situation* about which the child is narrating, and also *when he takes into account gestures, movements, mimicry, intonations, etc. Contextual speech* differs in that *its content is revealed in the context itself,* and thus becomes understandable to the listener, independent of whether or not he takes a given situation into account" (19; p. 22).

Having confronted the problem of learning the developmental features of connected speech forms, Leushina has collected a considerable amount of material concerning children's narrations under various task requirements and conditions of social interaction.

The investigation shows that children's narrations based on their everyday experiences are characterized by situationality in speech during the entire preschool age. A large drop in this characteristic is observed even with the youngest children when they are narrating previously heard stories, but speech again becomes situational when pictures are introduced into the activity and the children begin to rely on them. Among children of older preschool age, a drop in situationality is noted in independent narrations of themes taken out of their own lives, even in instances utilizing pictures; in retelling stories (with or without the pictures), a marked contextual character of speech is retained.

Thus, Leushina demonstrated that for the same children speech might be more situational or more contextual, depending on the nature of the tasks and the conditions of social interaction. The above-stated conclusions indicate that situationality of speech is not entirely an aspect of age, characteristic of preschool children, but that even among the youngest preschool children, given certain conditions of social interaction, one observes the emergence and expression of contextual speech. Furthermore, during preschool age there is an appreciable drop in signs of situationality and an increase in contextual features of speech, even under conditions pressing for situational forms. On the basis of her data, Leushina concludes that it is not a monologue but dialogue that is the primary form of a child's speech.

The basic specific feature of situational speech is its conversational character. As the means for the child's direct social interaction with familiar people who can understand his subtle hints, it is less grammatically formulated. What Piaget conceptualizes as not taking into account the listener's point of view, which for him is proof of children's egocentricism, Leushina considers as separate aspects of the situationality of children's speech. The latter is no doubt a clearly expressed form of social speech serving the tasks of social interaction. According to Leushina (19; p. 57), "from exclusive domination by situational speech, the child moves toward mastery of contextual speech, the relative weight of which increases, depending on the extent to which the child in his relationship with the surrounding environment moves beyond the framework of direct sensory experience."

Toward the end of preschool age, both forms of speech coexist, and the child utilizes either form depending on a given task and the conditions of interaction. On the basis of her study, Leushina comes to the correct conclusion that it is not the word but the sentence (connected speech) that is the unit of speech and consequently, the development of connected speech plays the leading role in the process of the preschool child's linguistic development. During his development, the forms of connected speech undergo restructuring. The shift to contextual—connected—speech remains tightly associated with the acquisition of vocabulary and the grammatical structure of the language; the mastery of the native language is prerequisite to the voluntary utilization of all of its means.

The decrease in situationality of children's expressions was also observed by Istomina in an investigation designed to study the influence of a verbal model and visual material on speech development in the preschooler (13). Istomina asked preschool children to retell a story without a picture, with a picture, and also to narrate independently while relying on a picture. The decreased situationality was expressed on the one hand by the reduced number of indicative particles and locational adverbs replacing other parts of speech, and on the other hand, in the lesser role of expressive gestures accompanying narration.

On the basis of her data, Istomina concludes that the verbal model plays a decisive role in the formation of the connected speech form and in the elimination of situational aspects; furthermore, she indicates that reliance on the visual model strengthens the situational aspects of the child's speech, reduces the elements of connectivity, and increases the aspects of expressiveness.

A noted decrease in situational aspects of speech during the sixth year and an equal degree of speech connectivity in narrations utilizing a verbal model, as well as in the ones not using it, underscores the significance which the mastery of linguistic forms has for the development of connected—contextual—speech.

Mastering the forms of language apparently makes possible a transition to more connected kinds of expression. The work of Penevska, Leushina, and others shows that narration training has a leading role in developing a connected form of expression in preschool children. Thus, a shift from dialogic forms of speech to open expressions is determined not only by essential changes in the tasks, content, and conditions of the child's social interaction with adults, but also mainly by the mastery of grammatical forms of open expressions.

Relying on studies of Leushina, Zvonitska, and others, Rubinshtein formed the basis of his concept of speech development, which he contrasted with the one suggested by Piaget (26; p. 29).

Piaget argues that the main line of speech development moves from egocentric speech, during which the child constructs his expressions without taking the listener into account, to socialized speech, in which the listener's point of view is taken into account. Piaget's investigations regarding egocentric speech are in essence illustration and evidence of his general conception of the development of the child's cognitive awareness.

Rubinshtein quite correctly points out that situational speech is also directed to another human being—the listener and the interlocutor; it has the same social directionality as any speech, "which is even more direct and clearly expressed than in contextual speech" (28; p. 11). However, Rubinshtein is inclined to recognize the presence in the child of involuntary tendencies of the egocentric type. Thus, he indicates that

"The child tends involuntarily to construct his speech on the basis of what he directly knows and understands. However, the action of this involuntary tendency seems to be broken up by the emerging cognizance of the necessity to take the listener into account, and to build the concept in such a way that the content of speech would be understandable to the other person. This latest aim has not as yet been adequately reinforced. Therefore, it does not determine speech construction from the very beginning, but only enters into it complementarily, disrupting its predominantly situational method of presentation (28; p. 9).

According to Piaget, the acting force in speech development is the displacement of the egocentric point of view by the social. Rubinshtein, while not rejecting the change in points of view, explains it as a change in the objective, semantic content of speech rather than displacement. He points out that a shift in points of view and in forms of verbal interaction has to have its own material base within the new objective content. In view of the fact that this content goes beyond the limits of the immediately experienced situation, a child's speech has to be realistically restructured. In the composition of this content, a necessity arises for new forms of speech and for a different verbal construction. Thus, Piaget's concept that egocentric speech is displaced by social receives new basis. Rubinshtein points out that "the mastering of the new form of speech that might be understood on the basis of its context, depends on the new requirements confronting speech whenever it is directed to an object beyond the limits of the immediate situation of the speaker, and is intended for any listener" (28; p. 12). Inclusion of the listener within the new content must be accomplished through other methods, as compared with situational speech. The essence of these methods consists of imparting on speech a connective form. Connectedness, according to Rubinshtein, means *"adequacy of the verbal appearance of the speaker's or the writer's thought, from the point of view of its understandability* for the listener or the reader" (28; pp. 6-7). The main line of speech development with respect to its connectedness consists of a shift from exclusive dominance by only situational speech to contextual speech, i.e., connected speech. "A preschool child takes only the first steps in this direction. Further development of connected speech relates primarily to school age. It is associated with the mastery of the written language" (Rubinshtein, 28; p. 13). According to his view, new aims arising out of the new content of expressions produce connected speech.

The above-stated proposition takes into account certain conditions that are necessary but not sufficient for the formation of connected speech. Rubinshtein accounts for one aspect of the matter but fails to consider a more important condition for the development of connected speech—mastering the language as a means of social interaction.

Language represents a vast—in terms of its complexity—system of means allocated for social interaction and developed by mankind in the course of historical growth. It represents for the child a concrete reality such as all other objects, a reality which the child masters according to the same principles used in the mastery of other objects, i.e., practically utilizing linguistic means in his verbal activity.

One cannot agree with Rubinshtein's proposition that the development of connected speech refers primarily to school age.

This is not in agreement with the data relating to the child's mastery of the grammatical structure of language. Thus, Gvozdev, in his penetrating work concerning this question, presents material indicating that by the third year of life the child already reflects in his speech all basic forms of connected speech.*

Gvozdev notes that the child prior to school learning masters the daily conversational style of speech; the grammatical elements of the literary style, however, remain unmastered. The mastery of grammatical elements characteristic of literary language occurs during school age.

Thus, the conclusions of Rubinshtein are in contradiction to the factual course of events in preschool children's mastery of the language. Rubinshtein undervalues the command of the daily conversational style of language in the development of the connected form of speech and on the other hand, overvalues the significance of the literary style. This occurs as a result of identifying dialogic speech with situational, and contextual with connected speech. Such an identification is incorrect; it leads to the assertion that contextual, i.e., connected speech, develops only in connection with command of the written language (with the mediational forms of interaction) and is associated with an orientation toward the reader and the listener in general.

Social interaction during the preschool age has a directional character; the preschool child in his narrations always keeps in mind a definite, usually familiar person (parents, nurturing figures, familiar children). However, the daily conversational style of speech includes in itself ample possibilities for the formation of connected speech, consisting not of separate sentences unconnected with one another, but representing a connected narration—a story, a report, etc. Within the limits of the daily conversational style, a decrease in the situational aspects of speech is observed, and there is a shift to understanding essentially based on linguistic means.

*See pp. 130f.

Thus, the mastering of the basic linguistic means (grammatical structure) during preschool age provides the child with an opportunity for the realization of social interaction through linguistic means.

In 1923, Piaget published his first work concerning the problems of the development of children's speech functions. In accordance with his own general concept of cognition development in children, Piaget distinguishes between socialized speech, which fulfills the function of interaction, and egocentric speech, which does not fulfill that function, simply being speech for oneself (26).

Piaget found that in the preschool age egocentric speech comprises a significant part of all the expressions of children, reaching 56 percent in the third and dropping to 27 percent toward the seventh year. The increasing socialization of speech, according to Piaget, is associated with the development of joint activity in seven—eight-year-old children.

From Piaget's point of view, egocentric speech plays a dominant role during the earlier ages and is gradually replaced by the socialized forms. This replacement occurs because of the child's adjustment to the socialized thinking of adults. Piaget's discovery of a speech form not having the function of social interaction is of unquestionable interest. Even though Piaget's general conception based on the primary autism of the child's awareness is quite unacceptable, the facts of his investigations are quite accurate.

The data concerning egocentric speech published by Piaget were subjected to validation in a series of investigations. Stern points out that Piaget undervalues the significance of the social surroundings in which children are raised, and most of all the family situation and social play with other children (34). Muchow, in an investigation conducted in Hamburg's kindergarten where children are found in a closer interaction with one another than the Geneva children studied by Piaget, reports significantly lower coefficients of egocentrism (33 percent against 45 percent reported by Piaget). The coefficient of egocentrism was found to be even lower in a study by Katz and Katz (15). They studied the conversations of children with their parents and with each other. These investigations showed that whenever children expressed themselves in the presence of their parents, their speech did not have the egocentric character. According to the data of this investigation, the conversations between two brothers also were not egocentric, and only in conversations with strangers or relatively unfamiliar children did the experimenters observe certain elements of egocentrism in this sample of boys. With minor exceptions, almost all conversations reported in the book are examples of highly developed social speech and of complete mutual understanding between the children and their parents and between the two brothers—participants in the conversations.

McCarthy and Day (24) obtained significantly lower indications of egocentrism. Having expanded the category of social expressions somewhat in conversational situations between children and adults, during an examination of toys and picture books McCarthy received from 1.3 to 6.5 percent of egocentric expressions, and Day even lower indicators, 1 to 2 percent.

These data permit one to assume that the appearance of egocentrism does not represent a simple function of age development, and that the influence of social conditions is of decisive significance for its emergence. But, however important the data relating to the extent of children's egocentrism obtained by these authors may be, they do not undermine the significance of facts obtained by Piaget.

In the third edition of his book (1948) Piaget examines the findings obtained by other authors and enters into polemics with them. First of all, Piaget discards without criticism all those findings obtained by authors who ascribed to the concept of egocentrism a meaning different from his own; secondly, he agrees that the results do change in connection with the situation to the extent to which there is some freedom for speech, the nature of activity, and the degree to which nurturing figures exert influence on the child's speech; finally, Piaget points out that the child's social interaction with adults is of great significance. In view of the stated differences, Piaget publishes new data obtained by Leizinger-Shuler during observations of her son and three other children three to four years old. Reviewing the data from the available investigations, Piaget continues to insist that the coefficient of egocentrism is a function of age and that it drops with age fairly regularly. He views as significant a decrease in the egocentrism coefficient under various environmental conditions, for it is not surprising that in an environment different from that of the "home of a child" in Geneva, children's speech may become just as socialized as that of adults. The reason for changes of egocentrism under various environmental conditions may be associated with the child's activity as well as his relationships with people in the environment. In connection with the surrounding environment, according to Piaget, there are two factors in the reduction of egocentrism: commonality of interest between the child and his friends, and an increase in the influence of the adults.

The facts of the above-mentioned investigations regarding the change of the egocentrism coefficient within different environmental conditions do not touch upon the basic question—the nature of egocentric speech. Consequently, the essence of the matter depends not on the demonstration of facts attesting to the presence of egocentric speech, but in the discovery of its nature. For Piaget, egocentric speech is only a symptom of egocentricity of consciousness, growing out of the child's autism, its directionality to essentially inner experiences and states; this transitional step from autism to socialization indicates that the child does not distinguish himself adequately and clearly from the surrounding world, but projects into this world the content of his own subjective world. Piaget's conception in general, and the concept of egocentric speech in particular, have been subjected to a sharp and fundamental critique, both theoretical and experimental, in Soviet psychological literature first of all by Vygotsky (37).

According to Piaget, egocentric speech emerges from inadequate socialization of the initially individualistic speech. In contrast, Vygotsky formulated a hypothesis concerning initially socialized speech and the emergence of egocentric speech as the result of inadequate isolation, differentiation, and separation of individual speech. In order to determine which of the two points of view is the correct one, Vygotsky adopted an experimental investigation, having as its goal clarification of the effects of the weakening or strengthening of social elements in a situation on the child's egocentric speech.

If the egocentric speech of a child stems from the egocentrism of his thinking and from inadequate socialization, then any weakening of the social elements in the situation, any circumstances favoring the child's isolation and freeing him from connections with the collective, any assistance in his psychological isolation and the loss of psychological contact with other people, any liberation from the necessity to adjust to the thoughts of others, and consequently, to utilize socialized speech—must unavoidably lead to a sharp increase in the coefficient of egocentric speech at the expense of socialized speech, because all this has to create most favorable conditions for an unrestricted and complete exposure to the inadequate socialization of the child's thought and speech. (37; p. 349).

And conversely, if egocentric speech is derived from an inadequate individuation of the initially socialized speech, lack of isolation, and lack of separating speech to oneself from speech to others, then any weakening of the social aspects in the situation should be reflected by a sharp decline in egocentrism.

In the first series of experiments, weakening the social aspects of the situation was attained by removing the illusion of being understood by other children, which is present in egocentric speech. A child whose coefficient of egocentrism was predetermined in a preliminary situation corresponding to Piaget's experiments, was placed into a group of either totally non-communicative (deaf and dumb) children, or into a collective of children speaking a different language. In this situation, the child performed the same kind of activity as in the preliminary trials. The illusion of understanding which was present in the first situation was removed in the second. The experiments showed that in the situation where the illusion of understanding was absent, the co-efficient of egocentrism in a majority of cases approached zero, and in the remaining ones was reduced eightfold on the average.

In the second series of experiments, weakening the social aspects was attained by exclusion of opportunity for a collective mono-logue. Here, the child whose coefficient of egocentrism had been previously determined under conditions where opportunity for a collective monologue existed was placed either among entirely unfamiliar children, isolated from the children (behind another table in the corner of the room), or finally, worked entirely alone without any group or opportunity for interaction with the experi-menter. The elimination of opportunity for collective monologue leads to a sharp drop in the egocentrism coefficient, approaching zero. The average relationship of the coefficient in the first and the second situation of this experiment was 6 to 1. Even though different methods for the exclusion of the collective monologue gave different degrees of reduction of egocentric speech, a general tendency for the decrease was clearly demonstrated.

In the third series of experiments, the opportunity for vocaliza-tion of egocentric speech was excluded. Here also, following the measurement of the coefficient of egocentrism in the basic situa-tion, the child was transferred to another situation in which the possibility for vocalizing was either impeded or absent. The child was seated a long distance away from other children, or else a noise was created behind the walls of the laboratory overshadow-ing the children's speech. In these experiments a drop in egocen-tric speech was also discovered. The relationship between coef-ficients was 5.4 to 1.

Thus, all three series of experiments show a consistent drop in the egocentrism of speech whenever the possibilities for socializa-tion of children were either impeded or absent. These facts led Vygotsky to a well-founded assertion that egocentric speech is social by its nature and stems from the womb of social speech, being isolated but not yet completely separated from social speech in its own distinct form (37; pp. 351-353).

Piaget's point of view concerning emergence of egocentric speech from initially individual speech thus appears to be disproven experimentally.

In line with his own concept of egocentrism, Piaget also investigated the functions of egocentric speech. According to him, egocentric speech has no realistic function in the child's activity but merely accompanies it, without contributing to the child's activity. Naturally, such a useless function atrophies. This then is supported by the drop in the egocentrism coefficient toward the end of preschool age.

Vygotsky, in cooperation with Luria, Leontiev, Levina, and others, conducted special experimental investigations clarifying the question of the causes of egocentric speech. To accomplish this, experimental disruptions and impediments were introduced into the child's spontaneous activity. The investigations showed that the coefficient of egocentrism during an impeded process of activity increases twofold, in comparison with the coefficient obtained in the activity situation without an impediment.

On the basis of these investigations, Vygotsky concludes "that apparently egocentric speech, besides having a purely expressive function and a function of discharge, besides merely accompanying the child's activity, very readily becomes a means of thinking in its own sense, i.e., it begins to fulfill the function of formulating a plan for the solution of a problem emerging in the course of behavior" (37; p. 80). From this, Vygotsky decides that egocentric speech does not merely disappear but is transformed into internal speech.

In the above-mentioned experiments, the question of egocentric speech was studied primarily from the point of view of its dependence on the social interaction situation. Its origin was examined separately from the character and content of activity. The question of the connection of egocentric speech with various forms of activity was raised by Syrkina (35), who investigated egocentrism on the one hand in relation to various conditions of interaction, and on the other hand in relation to the nature of activity. She measured the coefficients of egocentrism first in a situation with an unfamiliar experimenter (first series); secondly, in a situation with unfamiliar children (second series); and finally, in a situation of interaction with familiar children (third series). In all of these situations, the coefficients of egocentrism were measured under the conditions of free drawing activity and in the solution of practical problems. The results obtained are presented in Table 14.

The results obtained by Syrkina permit us to make the following conclusion: in the case of free drawing activity as well as during solution of practical problems, the highest coefficient of egocentrism was obtained in the situation of interaction with an unfamiliar person (experimenter), a lower one in the situation with unfamiliar children, and finally, the lowest coefficient—approaching zero—in the situation with familiar children, under practical problem solving conditions.

Thus, the higher the opportunity for interaction, the lower the coefficient of egocentrism. This conclusion is contradictory to the data obtained by Vygotsky, according to whom any weakening of opportunity for interaction (exclusion of the illusion of understanding, of an opportunity for collective monologue, and of an opportunity for vocalization) leads to a decrease in the co-

Table 14.

Changes in the Coefficient of Egocentrism in Relation to the Type of Activity and the Situation of Interaction (According to Syrkina)

Groups	Drawing			Solving Practical Problems		
	Series			Series		
	I	II	III	I	II	III
Youngest	0.98	0.67	0.32	0.47	0.21	0.06
Middle	0.83	0.44	0.20	0.62	0.15	0.08
Oldest	0.69	0.06	0.21	0.75	0.07	0.04

efficient of egocentrism. However, this contradiction is only an apparent one.

In Vygotsky's experiments the interaction of the child was restricted by various types of external barriers, i.e., the opportunity for interaction was either made difficult or was absent altogether. In the experiments of Syrkina, the external opportunities for interaction were preserved in all situations: the illusion of understanding, opportunity for collective monologue, and opportunity for vocalization. The change of the situation consisted of a change in the real opportunities for interaction, collaboration, participation, and help. The greatest opportunities for realistic collaboration are found in the situations of interaction with familiar children, the least in the situation of activity in the presence of the unfamiliar experimenter. Thus, with the presence of identical external conditions for interaction, the coefficient of egocentrism essentially depends on the real (intimate) conditions of collaboration. The child of preschool age apparently has a strong tendency toward collaboration with adults; however, the situation of a strange adult does not provide conditions for its realization. The tendency toward collaboration and social interaction, in the absence of internal conditions for its realization, leads to high indicators of egocentrism: the same tendency, in the presence of internal conditions for its realization, leads to a decrease in egocentrism. Syrkina's data convincingly indicate the social nature of egocentric speech and its directionality toward another person.

In view of the above-mentioned facts, egocentric speech occurs in the form of collaboration whenever *internal conditions* for the realization of collaboration are absent. This is a call for participation, for help, and for mutual activity. In terms of such a proposition, the drop in egocentrism is associated with the child's growing independence; one can also understand the increased egocentrism in respect to the difficulties encountered in an activity associated with the natural growth of the tendency for collaboration with others. Naturally, the forms of collaboration differ first of all in terms of the content of the activity. It would be possible to postulate that the function of egocentric speech will also differ under various types of activity. An answer to this question is given in Table 15.

As indicated in the table, the most typical function of speech for drawing is a *statement* (naming of objects or narration accompanying the course of drawing), which reflects the child's attempt to draw the people around him into the realm of the content of his activity. In the case of solving practical problems, the emphasis is clearly on *plan* and *analysis* (planning of anticipated activity and analysis of failure), which are associated with the difficulties of the task and express a tendency to resort to the help of those present. This tendency is clearly expressed, especially in relation to familiar children. During the problem solving, *exclamations* are clearly dominant whereas during the drawing *distractions* are more frequent.

Functional analysis reveals a high dependence of the function of egocentric speech on the character of activity and, associated with it, opportunity for collaboration. This dependence is also noted in the grammatical analysis of egocentric expressions (Table 16).

Table 15.
Functional Analysis of Egocentric Speech (%) (According to Syrkina)

Function of Speech	Drawing			Solving Practical Problems		
	Series			Series		
	I	II	III	I	II	III
Plan and analysis	33.1	21.3	35.2	24.4	35.7	46.9
Statement	51.1	61.1	52.8	34.5	43.7	38.2
Reference to an object	0.0	0.0	0.5	13.4	0.0	0.0
Exclamation	3.6	1.2	3.5	26.2	6.3	14.9
Distraction	11.5	15.0	8.0	0.9	12.5	0.0
Other	0.7	1.3	0.0	0.6	0.0	0.0

The table indicates that during the drawing activity, egocentric speech in general has a more connected character than during problem solving. Furthermore, during the drawing activity there is an appreciable number of connected sentences and a relatively small number of fragmentary words; during the problem solving fragmentary words are predominant, with connected sentences occupying a secondary position. The expressions by which the object of activity or the activity itself is defined are also interchanged. During the drawing, the number of definitions of objects is greater than definitions of activity; during the problem solving, vice versa. Such relationships are to be expected if one takes into account that during drawing the main task of social interaction consists of an attempt to attract those present to the objective content, and not to the modes of activity, whereas during the solving of practical problems the main task is to get those present to collaborate in resolving difficulties encountered in the task and in the fulfillment of various actions.

Table 16.
Grammatical Analysis of Egocentric Speech (%) (According to Syrkina)

Function of Speech	Drawing			Solving Practical Problems		
	Series			Series		
	I	II	III	I	II	III
Extended sentence	17.3	35.0	21.8	0.3	12.5	4.3
Designation of object of action	8.3	2.5	6.2	2.7	0.0	4.3
Designation of object	28.4	32.5	3.2	7.7	0.0	0.0
Designation of action	16.2	10.0	13.3	27.6	18.7	38.3
Incomplete infinitive sentence	0.3	3.7	3.1	3.6	6.3	14.8
Disconnected words and expressions	29.5	16.3	23.6	58.1	62.5	38.8

On the basis of the conducted investigations, it is thus possible to formulate the following proposition concerning the nature and functions of egocentric speech. Egocentric speech grows out of social speech and real collaboration of children and adults in practical activity. Its appearance and development are associated with the tendency of younger preschool children toward collaboration and cooperative interaction with adults. This tendency is greater the less independent the child and the more difficulties are evoked by his activity. Emerging under a set of conditions which impede real collaboration, egocentric speech has a social directionality and is a distinctive speech equivalent of practical collaboration in some type of activity. The content of egocentric expressions changes depending on the concrete activity and the opportunity for real collaboration.

When difficulties are encountered in intellectual activity, egocentric speech reflects the child's desire for maintaining collaboration and assistance. By the same means, egocentric speech objectively fulfills a regulatory function in relation to activity.

Thus, the regulatory function emerges from social orientation and contains the same aspects as speech accompanying realistic practical collaboration. The curtailment of egocentric speech is dependent on the degree of the child's independence.

Interesting material concerning the functions of speech accompanying practical activity is presented by Lyublinskaya in her work pertaining to analysis of the child's visual-effective thinking (22).

Lyublinskaya showed that such speech may fulfill, first of all, the function of formulating the problem at a time of difficulty, and secondly, the function of planning a course of action. At first, speech is included in activity for the length of its duration, but with age, is gradually concentrated primarily at the beginning of activity, thus representing a prototype of internal planning.

In this connection there occur changes in activity. Toward the end of preschool age, there appear to be two stages in the child's activity: first, adoption of a solution and planning expressed verbally; and second, the practical execution of the adopted solution and plan.

One can assume that during preschool age a new speech function is formed which ought to be called the intellectual function, i.e., one accounting for the planning and regulating of practical activity.

Related to the question concerning emergence of this type of speech function, of some interest are the data concerning preschool-age children's understanding of verbal instructions in relation to a given task. This question was explored by Morozova (25). Her data indicate substantial gains during the preschool age in children's response to verbal instructions. First of all, opportunities for delayed fulfillment of instructions increase; secondly, one observes the following of instructions related not only to the theme of the task, but also to the methods of action. The delayed performance of instructions related to the theme (the object) of the task and above all, to the means of executing the task, indicates that the methods of action have become isolated already from the process of fulfillment and that consequently, opportunities have arisen for the preliminary planning of one's own actions.

The Development of Vocabulary and Grammatical Structure of Speech

Broadening of experiential relations and increasing complexity of the child's activity and interaction with adults during the preschool age lead to a gradual growth of vocabulary. In view of the pronounced influence of environmental conditions on the development of vocabulary, it is difficult to obtain mean quantitative indicators of the absolute composition of vocabulary as well as of its increase with age. Growth of vocabulary, as well as the mastery of grammatical structure, depends directly on the conditions of life and upbringing, and individual differences here are much greater than in some other psychological spheres of development.

The most detailed data on the development of vocabulary are presented by Smith (Table 17).*

Bühler, presenting data on vocabulary learning by thirty children, ages one to four years, indicates minimal and maximal vocabulary for each age and shows individual differences that are present (Table 18).

Arkin presents the following data on growth of vocabulary: 1; 0–9 words, 1; 6–39 words, 2; 0–300 words, 3;6–1,110 words, 4; 0–1,926 words (2).

According to Arkin, the vocabulary of a four-year-old is distributed among various grammatical categories as follows:

Nouns (including nine pronominal nouns)	968	(50.2%)
Verbs	528	(27.4%)
Adjectives (including twenty pronominal adjectives)	227	(11.8%)
Adverbs	112	(5.8%)
Numbers (cardinal and ordinal)	37	(1.9%)

Table 17.
Development of Vocabulary in Preschool Children

Age	Number of Words	Increase in the Number of Words	Age	Number of Words	Increase in the Number of Words
0; 10	1	1	3; 0	896	450
1; 0	3	2	3; 6	1,222	326
1; 3	19	16	4; 0	1,540	318
1; 6	22	3	4; 6	1,870	330
1; 9	118	96	5; 0	2,072	202
2; 0	272	154	5; 6	2,289	217
2; 6	446	174	6; 0	2,589	273

*These data concerning the growth of vocabulary on non-Russian children are extracted from the book by Rubinshtein (29; pp. 425-426). Let us also note that in designating age we adhere to the adopted system in which the first number indicates years and the second, months; e.g., 1; 6—one year six months.

Table 18.
Differences in Maximal and Minimal Vocabulary in Children Aged
One to Four

Age	Maximal Vocabulary	Minimal Vocabulary
1; 0-1; 2	58	3
1; 3-1; 5	232	4
1; 6-1; 8	383	44
1; 9-1; 11	707	27
2; 0-2; 3	1,227	45
2; 3-2; 6	1,509	171
3; 0-4; 0	2,346	598

Conjunctions	22 (1.2%)
Prepositions	15 (0.8%)
Interjections and particles	17 (0.9%)

The following distribution of contents was obtained for the
nouns in the vocabulary (percentages):

Dwellings (furniture, utensils, lodging)	15.2%
Food	9.6%
Clothing	8.8%
Animals	8.8%
Plants	6.6%
Town surroundings (including means of transportation)	5.1%
Parts of body	4.7%
Professions, technology, instruments	4.6%
Inanimate objects	3.3%
Time	3.4%
Social phenomena	3.3%
Patrimonial concepts	1.6%
Geometric forms	0.9%
Swearwords	0.9%
Abstract concepts	0.7%

It is necessary to note that determining the number of words irrespective of their relationship to the content in the speech of
adults cannot characterize the development of vocabulary. A

child's mastery of the verbal composition of his native language is not exhausted by its quantitative growth. In this process, of great significance is the development of word meanings.

Vocabulary per se presents merely the building material, which only through combination of words into sentences according to grammatical rules of the language, can serve the goals of social interaction and familiarization with reality. In the development of the child's speech, the most essential question concerns itself with acquisition of the grammatical structure of the native language.

In the area of speech development, an exceptional investigation of the highly qualified linguist Gvozdev, entitled "Formation of the grammatical structure of Russian language in a child," presents a systematic analysis of the language mastery process and various aspects of speech development: syntax, morphology, processes of word building, and word changing (12). In comparison with the previously published diary materials by Russian as well as foreign authors, this word presents the most complete, systematic, and qualified investigation. Therefore, in describing the process of mastering the language, we shall primarily rely on this work. Being a linguistic study, Gvozdev's work obviously cannot give an answer to questions pertaining to the psychological and physiological mechanisms in the process of language mastery. However, by providing the external logic of mastering a language, such an investigation is a fundamental one for any psychological analysis. He covers the process of formulation of grammatical structure from the appearance of the first word to the beginning of school age, and describes this process from many different perspectives.

On the basis of a carefully conducted study of grammatical structure development of the Russian language, Gvozdev identified the following formative periods:

First Period—from one year three months to one year ten months. It is a period of sentences consisting of amorphous word-roots, which are used in one and the same form in all situations wherever they are spoken. This period is clearly subdivided into two stages: a) stage of a single-word sentence (1;3 to 1;8)*; and b) stage of sentences including several words, mostly two-word sentences (1; 8 to 1; 10).

Second Period—from one year ten months till three years. This is the period of mastering the grammatical structure of the sentence, connected with the formation of grammatical categories and their external expression. It is characterized by a rapid growth of simple and complex sentences, in which parts of the sentence are expressed through the syntactic means of the language. This period has three stages: a) formation of the initial forms (1; 10 to 2; 1); b) utilization of inflected system of the Russian language for the expression of syntactic connections (2; 1 to 2; 3); and c) mastery of linking words for the expression of syntactic relationships (2; 3 to 3; 0).

Gvozdev notes that this period is "radically separated from the first period, but is not clearly delineated from the subsequent period" (12; p. 190).

Third Period—from three to seven years. This is the period of mastering the morphological system of the Russian language, characterized by command of various types of conjugations and declensions. During this period there is a separation of previously mixed synonymous, morphological elements according to individual types of conjugations and declensions. Simultaneously, to a large extent, all singular, individually isolated forms are mastered.

In describing the results obtained by a child toward the eighth year in mastering the grammatical structure of the Russian language, Gvozdev writes: "The mastery level of the native language by a child approaching school age is very high. At this time the child exhibits such a command of the entire complex system of grammar, including the sharpest distinctions found in the Russian language concerning principles of syntactic and morphologic order, and also consistent and unmistakable usage of multiple individual aspects of structure, that the Russian language being

*Indicating one year and three months to one year and eight months.

mastered becomes indeed a native language. And the child receives in it an accomplished tool for interaction and thinking" (12; p. 189).

Thus, during the ages two to seven, the child fulfills a tremendous task in connection with mastering all the basic forms of the native language.

Bühler in his time suggested that at the base of the entire process of acquisition lies the child's *discovery* of the inflectional nature of the language. After this discovery, the child begins to understand the basic principle of the inflected languages: that relationships may be expressed via the sound changes in the morphological parts of the words. Such a suggestion cannot be accepted. Bühler overintellectualized the language recognition process of the child. Furthermore, even if the child were to come up with the indicated discovery, it should only serve as a crowning touch to the process of mastering—be its result, but not serve as a base of the development.

A number of psychologists, linguists, and pedagogues argued for a special sensitivity for language supposedly present in a child of two to five-six years that allows him to make the distinctions between some of the more complex linguistic formulations. In Russian prerevolutionary literature an exceptional expert on child's language, the writer Chukovsky, repeats emphatically that during the period from two to five years the child possesses an unusual sensitivity for language, and that this sensitivity and the mental work involved in mastering the language associated with it form a base for the ongoing process. Furthermore, Chukovsky correctly emphasizes the active nature of the language mastering process and opposes the theory of a mechanical and passive mastering of the native language.

Without such an elevated sensitivity to phonetics and morphology of expression, one bare imitative instinct would be entirely helpless and would not be able to lead wordless youngsters to a full mastery of the native language. Certainly, one should not forget that this mastery in all cases—without a single exception— is the result of mutual collaboration of the child with those who sur-round him. However, all the efforts of adults would be entirely useless if the children of younger age were not to show this high sensitivity to composition and pronunciation of words (5; p. 68).

Chukovsky's contribution is not only his opposition to mechanistic theory and his support of the active nature of language mastery, but also his accumulation of diverse, abundant material on children's verbal composition.

Gvozdev also underscores a special linguistic ability in preschool-age children. He writes: "The child constructs forms, freely manipulating meaningful elements, relying on their meaning. An even greater degree of independence is required in formulating new words, since in such cases a new meaning is created; to do this requires a versatile observation, an ability to isolate known objects and phenomena and to find their characteristic aspects. The accuracy of children's observations and an artistic clarity of many children's words are well known; they are very close indeed to that verbal creativity which is practiced by artists of expression. Therefore, one notices a real creativity here, attesting to the exceptional linguistic ability of children" (12; p. 187).

One cannot equate children's verbal creativity with that of writers as has been attempted frequently by Chukovsky and Gvozdev. However, that the preschool age is the period in which there is the highest sensitivity toward linguistic phenomena is, without a doubt, a well-established fact.

Independent word formation is a process expressing mastery of the system of suffixes. Here too, the process of mastery has its logic. An investigation by Gvozdev thoroughly explored the issue of word formation. Command of the diminutive, pejorative, augmentative, and hypocoristic suffixes is observed up to the age of three years. Suffixes for description of objects according to action or quality were noted only in isolated cases. Mastery of all the other suffixes occurs after the age of three and is continued throughout the entire preschool age.

In this connection it is necessary to note that mastery of word formation occurs during a later age than does mastery of those morphological elements that designate various syntactic relationships. This attests to the greater difficulty in mastering word formation.

At the same time, Gvozdev notes unusual ease in the construction of new diminutive words utilizing corresponding suffixes by his son Gregory at the age of three years five months.

Gvozdev describes an original game with his son. Gregory tells his father; "I am a mishulchyk (a made-up word), and you are a bear." Father: "And if I am a lion, who are you?" Gregory: "livunchik" (lionling) (12; p. 199).

The game continued as follows: the father asked the question and the child answered. The following words were formed in reply to the father's questions: tigr—*tigrichek malenky* (tiger—small tiger + d.s.*); slon— *ya byl sloniska* (elephant—I was an elephant + d.s.); krokodil— *ya krokodilchik* (crocodile—I'm crockodile + d.s.); olen— *a ya olenchik* (deer—and I'm deer + d.s.); loshead—*zherebenochek malenky* (horse—colt + d.s. (little one); korova—*ya bylaby telka, ya byl by malenkaya korovka* (cow—I would be a heifer, I would be a small cow + d.s.); volk—*mishulchik* (wolf—a made up word with a d.s.); svinya—*porosenochek* (pig—suckling pig + d.s.); sobaka— *ya byl by malenkaya sobachka* (dog—I would be a small dog + d.s.); zebra—*ya byle be malenky izeberchyk* (zebra—I would be a little "izeberchyk," a made-up word with a d.s.); los—*losik malenky* (elk—a small elk + d.s.); lisa—*lisinchik malenky* (fox—a small "lisinchik," a made-up word with a d.s.); kenguru—*kengurinchik malenky* (kangaroo—a small "kengurichik," a made-up word with a d.s.); zhirafa—*zhivarchik* (giraffe—"zivarchik," a made-up word with a d.s.); krolik—*krolichik* (rabbit—rabbit + d.s.); zmeya— *smiyka* (snake—"zmiyka," a made-up word with a d.s.); tarakan— *tarakanchik* (cockroach—cockroach + d.s.); mukha—*tozhe mukha* (fly—also a fly); zhuk—*ya byl by komar* (beetle—I would be a mosquito).

*d.s. = dimunitive suffix.

The presented facts indicate the relative ease with which the child utilizes appropriate word-forming suffixes.

Bogoyavlensky experimentally explored the question concerning the understanding of certain suffixes and their usage in word construction (4; p. 261). In the first series of experiments, Bogoyavlensky investigated children's understanding of word-forming suffixes. With this in mind, he presented children with words containing suffixes but formed with roots which were unknown to children: lar—defined for the child as an animal; lafeet—sweet as juice; kashemir—beautiful material. After the children became acquainted with the meaning of these new words, they were told a "fable." The "fable" included words formed out of these new words and the following suffixes—yenok, -ishche, -nits, and -shchik, e.g., lar*yenok*, lar*ishche*, lafit*nitsa*, kashimer-*shchik*. Five—six-year-old children took part in the experiments. The results show that suffixes -yenok and -ishche are well understood by the children, in spite of the fact that the children had to deal with new, unknown words. Suffixes -shchik and -nits appeared to be more difficult. Somewhat easier was the suffix -nits, but even this one was found to be harder than the suffixes -yenok and -ishche.

Bogoyavlensky explains the relative difficulty of understanding suffixes -nits and -shchik as follows: in the construction of words using these suffixes there is a change in the lexical meanings of the words, while in the formation of words using diminutive and hypocoristic suffixes the basic lexical meanings of the words remain unchanged. It is possible to assume that this may serve to explain the later appearance of word construction in which there is a change in lexical meaning of words and a rather early mastery of word changing in comparison with word forming.

With the second series of experiments, Bogoyavlensky studied children's independent (active) word forming. He asked five—six-year-old children to form diminutive words from these basic ones: giraffe, oats, chestnut, oak, lion, balloon, nose, wolf, nail, ostrich. The majority of the children easily fulfilled the task.

Thus, Bogoyavlensky's work further supports the fact of the preschool child's mastery of word forming.

Children's independent word forming, or so-called word creativity, has been cited by some authors (Chukovsky and Gvozdev) as primary evidence of the presence of special linguistic sensitivity in a preschool child. It appears to us that word creativity is not something exclusive, but must be viewed as a manifestation, a symptom of the child's *mastery* of linguistic reality.At the base of children's word creativity lie principally the same rules that are found at the base of mastery of the inflected system of language. Realistically, the child performs not a lesser nor a less active task during mastering, for example, of such an abstract and entirely formal category as gender, having a very important significance in Russian language, and agreements in gender of verbs in the past tense and adjectives associated with it.

The phenomena of word forming, like that of word changing, are uniordinal. They are indications of the child's work conducted in mastering language as the objective reality and, at the same time, of that concrete experience in the course of which this mastering takes place.

Two circumstances interfered with a correct understanding of the processes of the child's mastery of native language as the objective reality. Assumptions of special linguistic sensitivity, linguistic instinct, and special linguistic giftedness, as nonanalyzable internal forces, leading to an intensive formation of the grammatical structure of language, were great obstacles. Obviously, such assumptions blocked the paths for clarification of objective rules for the language mastery process.

Not a lesser hinderance was the so-called glass theory. Luria formulated the content of this theory as follows:

As numerous experimental investigations conducted in Soviet psychology during the last ten to fifteen years (investigations of Rubinshtein, our investigations, works of Bozhovich, Morozova, and Slavina) have shown, the first significant period in the child's development is characterized by this: while actively utilizing grammatical language and while defining with words the corresponding objects and actions, the child still *cannot make a word and verbal relationships the object of his awareness.* During this period, the word may be used but not noticed by a child, and *frequently it presents things seemingly like a glass,* through which the child looks at the surrounding world, not making the word itself the object of awareness, and not suspecting that it has its own existence, its own aspects of construction (italics ours D.E.), (21; pp. 61).

The child's cognizance of the acoustic, material system of linguistic means, without which there is not and cannot be any language at all, Luria attributes to the period of school learning. "The initial training in reading and writing," Luria points out, "makes an object of awareness not the concrete thing or action, but separate, related entirely to the system of language sounds and letters, by means of which—much later—the student begins to see, defined by the combinations of these sounds and letters, objects. In the training of writing and reading, a word, as a unit of the system of language, for the first time acquires its own concreteness and sensitivity, it becomes an object of child's awareness" (21; pp. 61-62).

If one were to accept this theoretical conception, then in order to explain the formation of the grammatical structure of a child's language, facts of word changing and word forming, it is indeed necessary to adopt the notion of verbal instinct or some special linguistic sensitivity, with whose help the child becomes acquainted with the linguistic reality.

In reality, the matter is quite different. Pavlov repeatedly noted that a word is just as real a stimulus as any other. From the first moment of language mastery, a word is perceived by the child first of all in terms of its material, acoustic aspect. As a matter of fact, the child responds to this aspect initially when learning to understand the first words, and even more so when learning how to pronounce them. All this colossal work, performed by the child in learning to tell one word from the other, is primarily work performed on the material, acoustic aspect of language. This is noticed to an even greater degree during the child's acquisition of articulation of separate sounds, etc. Furthermore, observant pedagogues, e.g., Fausek, have noticed that little children aged one and one-half to four or four and one-half years and sometimes older, like to pronounce some kind of a word, frequently distorted or meaningless, just because they like the sounds of it (8). Chukovsky in his book has gathered much material concerning the large task performed by a child with respect to the material, acoustic aspect of the language. "Rhyme-making during the second year of life is an unescapable stage of our linguistic development. Children who do not perform such linguistic exercise are abnormal or ill. These activities are indeed exercises, and it is difficult to think of a more rational system of practice in phonetics than such frequent repetition of all possible sound variations," points out Chukovsky quite correctly (5; p. 178).

Just as the mastering of objective reality is not possible without formation of activity with objects, exactly in the same manner is language mastery not possible without formation of activity with language as the material object with its concrete form.

Thus, there are ample grounds to assume that the material, acoustic casing, as the carrier of all the richness of the language, very early becomes an object of the child's activity and of his awareness. It cannot be otherwise, for in the world surrounding the child there are few objects as important as language, which he confronts so early, and which surrounds him constantly.

Sokhin studied experimentally the child's formation of an understanding of the preposition as a grammatical form expressing relationships between objects (32, 33).

The investigation's methodology consisted of clarifying the understanding of an instruction containing a preposition that fulfills its basic grammatical function in relation to concrete, sensory aspects of objective relationships. Grammatically, the instruction was always the same: "Put (name of object) on (name of another object)." In its object-content, the instruction was changed every time. In the first series, the objects were a circle and a cube, approximately equal in size, and the child, according to the instruction, had to put one object on the other in an alternating sequence. Variations of this experiment were introduced by changing the relationship of the objects' size (a little circle and a large cube; a little cube and a large circle). In a second series, the objects were identical and of equal size (two circles and two cubes), and variations of this experiment also consisted of changes in the relationship of the size of objects. Subjects were children from one year to three years five months.

As the result of the investigation concerning the nature of understanding and fulfillment of the instruction, all children were classified into three groups representing various degrees of mastery of the preposition.

The results of the first and second series of the experiment are presented in Table 19. The numbers indicate the percent of those attempting the task; the sign "+" means the fulfillment of the instruction; the sign "−" means negative solutions.

As the table indicates, the children of the first group did not fulfill the instruction. Such failure may be considered as a lack of isolating the preposition as an independent element of the phrase. Incorrectly fulfilling the instruction in the experimental condition, the children of the first group correctly responded to an analogous phrase in nonexperimental situations (such phrases as

Table 19.
Understanding the Preposition as a Grammatical Form
Expressing Relationships in an Instruction

	Nature of Problems							
	Series I (Different Objects)				Series II (Identical Objects)			
Groups of Children	Circle on Cube		Cube on Circle		Circle on Circle		Cube on Cube	
	+	−*	+	−*	+	−*	+	−*
1st	−	100	−	100	−	100	−	100
2nd	45	54	58	41	9	91	14	86
3rd	95	5	97	3	88	12	94	6

*Negative solutions included: for the first group—failure to fulfill the instructions; for the second and the third groups—reversal of relationships with respect to the ones stated in the instructions.

"Put the ball on the carpet"). The understanding of the phrase, as the experiment indicates, depended on the simple logic of relationships between objects, whereas in the experimental conditions the object relationship was not presented as simply and conveyed two alternative orientations.

The children of the second group (from 2; 3 to 3 years) did not ignore the preposition in the phrase, and always correctly responded to the general content of the instruction. However, the concrete form of object relationships in many cases was incorrectly established; a reversal of the relationships stated in the instructions was observed. Here the preposition was found to be a distinct element of the phrase; however, understanding of the phrase was still largely dependent on the concrete form of object relationships within the context of which fulfillment of the instruction took place. This may be deduced on the basis that in the second series of experiments, where the logic of object relationships is not expressed and the child must orient himself entirely by the meaning of the preposition, the instruction was not carried out. This is also supported by a complementary series of experiments in which the logic of object relationships was strengthened. Thus, with a presentation of a large cube and a small circle, the instruction "Put the circle on the cube" was correctly fulfilled in 92 percent of the cases, and incorrectly in only 8 percent; with the opposite instructions—"Put the cube (large) on the circle (small)"—the correct solution dropped to 30 percent, and the incorrect solution increased to 70 percent. In the variation of the second series of the experiments, where identical objects of equal size were replaced by identical objects of different sizes, the correct solutions of the instruction increased considerably, and almost all children under these conditions fulfilled its demands.

Thus, this group of children, even though isolating the preposition as a separate grammatical element of the phrase, failed to separate its meaning from the concrete, directly perceived object relationships. The children of this group did not yet abstract the meaning of the preposition.

Only the children of the third group (from 2; 5 to 3; 5 years) executed the instructions well, independently of object relationships. This indicates that here the preposition fulfills its indicatory function under a higher degree of abstraction from the concrete aspects of object relationships. The meaning of the preposition is of a more generalized nature for these children than for the children of the first group.

Sokhin on the basis of his investigation makes a series of deductions. He points out that during the early stages of speech development an understanding of grammatically formed expressions is to a great extent determined by nongrammatical features and is dependent on the logic of object relationships. Thereafter, the grammatical element is isolated and it becomes a signal of objective relationships. Initially, however, the grammatical element is connected with the concretely objective form of these relationships and only gradually becomes separated from it, becoming a grammatical form expressing object relationships apart fron concreteness.

Sokhin's study discloses the basic developmental stages of the meaning of grammatical forms. It is possible to assume that this path is followed not only in the formation of the meaning of prepositions, but also in the meaning of case endings, suffixes, prefixes, etc. Initially, a given objective relationship is expressed by vocabulary with reliance on the concretely perceived objective situation; thereafter, a grammatical form is isolated that begins to express this relationship within the objective situation; finally, there appears separation and generalization of relationships defined by a given form.

Fradkina has demonstrated that the child's understanding of the adult's words depends initially on the objective situation and that only gradually does social interaction become, in the true sense, a verbal one, where understanding depends on linguistic means (9).

However, the key question of how a given grammatical form (morpheme) becomes isolated in speech remains unanswered. The importance of this question is further enhanced by the fact that certain subtle grammatical relationships are purely formal, in which the correct use of the word depends not so much on the connection of a given morpheme with some objective relationship as on the connection with a form of another word.

Clarification of this question was attempted by Popova, who studied formation of gender agreement between past tense verbs and nouns (27).

Obviously, the category of gender is the most characteristic of nouns. Furthermore this category does not have a distinct meaning other than a formal one. Agreement in gender of a past tense verb with a noun depends on morphological cues of the noun (its ending in the nominative case of a singular form). Without identification of the morphological form the agreement in gender is impossible. Thus, investigating the process of agreement formation in gender must clarify the occurrence of isolation of morphological elements in the absence of clearly expressed meanings of such elements.

Gvozdev points out that the formation of gender agreement undergoes a long path of development and is mastered relatively late. His material also contains evidence indicating that during the early developmental stages of speech, agreement in feminine gender predominates; thereafter, agreement in masculine gender and confusion is observed; and finally the correct agreement is attained. According to Gvozdev, toward the third year gender agreement in the past tense is mastered.

In the first series of her investigations, Popova studied the general course of mastering agreement of past tense verbs with nouns according to gender. With this in mind, fifty-five children ages one year ten months to three years six months were given four forms of nouns to be put in agreement with the verbs. These forms were: animate nouns of masculine and feminine gender with a different degree of gender appearance; animate nouns of masculine and feminine gender having morphological appearance appropriate for the gender, identifiable in terms of sex[yezh (M)—(male hedgehog; yezhikha (F)—(female hedgehog)]; animate nouns of masculine gender, whose gender can be determined only by a cue of sex; inanimate nouns with appropriate morphological appearance of gender. The experiment showed a presence of four distinct levels of mastery of agreement. First level: feminine gender clearly predominates; second level: masculine gender is the predominant one; third level: predominance of confusion between masculine and feminine genders; fourth level: the correct agreement. A detailed analysis of correct as well as incorrect agreement patterns led Popova to conclude that at the base of agreement formation is the child's orientation to the noun's form. How this orientation comes about, however, was not discovered by the attempts of the first series. An assumption was made that the basis of the appearance of such orientation is the child's varied practice of interaction with adults. This proposition was tested in a second series of experiments, which consisted of training the children to form the right agreements. Training was conducted through specially organized play in the course of which the experimenter repeated sentences consisting of two parts (noun and verb in the past tense); the child, having repeated these sentences, was asked to construct them on his own. All errors were corrected. These exercises were continued until the child mastered the right agreement between the words used in the experiment and transferred the principle of agreement to other words. Twelve children participated. The results are presented in Table 20.

The table indicates that only one child out of five at the first level of mastery was able to form the correct agreement (after 180 repetitions); the remaining four children, in spite of the large number of repetitions (from 312 to 534), were not successful in forming an agreement. Among children who were at a higher level prior to the training trials—second and third level—an agreement was obtained, but for some of them only after a large number of repetitions. For four of the children (three of them at the beginning of learning trials were at the third level, and one at the

Table 20.
Formation of Gender Agreements Between Nouns and Past-Tense Verbs

Subjects	Age at the End of Training	Level of Agreement at the Beginning of Training	Number of Repetitions of Phrases by Experimenter*	Level of Agreement at the End of Training
N.M.	2; 8	I	534	III
S.B.	3; 2	I	528	II
I.K.	2; 11	I	312	II
N.M.	3; 5	I	204	III
O.I.	2; 9	I	180	IV
T.O.	3; 4	II	438	IV
U.G.	3; 6	II	84	IV
T.F.	3; 0	II	216	IV
T.L.	3; 1	III	258	IV
G.R.	3; 0	III	84	IV
V.S.	3; 3	III	60	IV
U.K.	2; 10	III	12	IV

*The number of times that the phrases were repeated by the children. This number does not include the results of the first three days of training, during which the experimenter verbalized phrases and the child repeated them.

second) only a small number of repetitions were necessary (84, 60, 12).

Thus, even though simple repetition of the correct word agreements and listening to them in adults' speech finally lead to the formation of agreement, the task is very difficult and requires a great effort. Popova points out that during such training children did not notice their mistakes and did not correct them, and that the process of forming agreement passed sequentially through all the intermediate steps. Nonproductivity of such an approach to agreement formation is attributed to the fact that the children did not show an orientation toward the form of the word; their activity with the word was not at all organized.

The obtained results necessitated constructing the study in such a way that during its course the child would form an orientation toward the formal elements of the word (in this case toward the gender-specific endings of nouns).

The last series of experiments included a new method of learning, which was conducted in a form of playing "the tower" game. Children were asked to lead animals (three males and three females) into the tower. The door of the tower would open and the animal was allowed to enter only if the child correctly stated the agreement in response to the experimenter's questions: "Who went to the tower?" and "Who has arrived in the tower?" If the child answered incorrectly, the door would not open and the experimenter pointed out the mistake. If the child immediately and without the help of the experimenter corrected his mistake, the door would open; if, however, there was no self-correction, the experimenter told the child how to say it correctly, and the game was repeated with another animal. Thus, the child's answer entered into the chain of open practical actions, occupying among them an essential link in the correctness of execution on which depended the success of the entire activity in general. Of special importance was the opportunity given to the children for independently correcting the mistakes they made in the construction of grammatical agreement. All these conditions favored the organization of orientation toward the word's form. Children quickly learned to verbally isolate the endings of nouns and verbs.

Twenty children, ages one year eleven months to three years four months, took part in this experiment. In Table 21 the data of the experiment are summarized.

The table shows that training according to the method used in this series of experiments was significantly more effective. Effectiveness is indicated first of all by the fact that all children without exception were able to form the agreement; secondly, by a significant decrease in the number of required repetitions; thirdly, that 25 percent of the children formed agreements "instantly," i.e., after only three training days.

Table 22 presents the number of children (percentage) who required various amount of repetitions.

These data clearly indicate significantly higher effectiveness of the second training method, by which 75 percent of the children

Table 21.
Effect of Orientation Toward Formal Elements in Word on Gender Agreement

Subjects	Age at End of Training	Level of Agreement at Beginning of Training	Number of Repetitions of Phrases by Experimenter	Level of Agreement at the End of Training
L.Z.	1; 11	I	0	IV
I.B.	2; 3	I	0	IV
I.F.	3; 3	I	0	IV
S.D.	2; 1	I	12	IV
M.P.	2; 3	I	24	IV
A.E.	2; 9	I	36	IV
U.Zh.	3; 0	I	36	IV
N.K.	2; 7	I	48	IV
T.K.	3; 1	I	60	IV
Zh.S.	2; 3	I	84	IV
L.M.	2; 1	I	132	IV
V.D.	2; 3	I	156	IV
L.P.	2; 6	I	192	IV
S.G.	3; 4	II	24	IV
I.P.	2; 8	II	156	IV
L.Sh.	3; 1	II	156	IV
V.M.	2; 3	III	0	IV
G.E.	2; 6	III	0	IV
N.M.	3; 2	III	36	IV
V.S.	2; 4	III	84	IV

Table 22.
Number of Children Requiring Repetitions in Formation of Gender Agreement

Method of Training	Number of Repetitions			
	0	0-100	100-200	200
I	––	33	8	59
II	25	50	25	––

formed agreement with a number of repetitions not exceeding 100, in spite of the fact that in the second group the number of children at the lowest (first) level of mastery of agreement was relatively greater than in the first group.

Analysis of agreement formation during the training process in the second method showed that children quickly develop an orientation toward the sound form of the word. The emergence of such an orientation leads the children to arrive at the correct agreement by bypassing the first of the established stages of its formation. In light of the facts obtained by Popova, formation and generalization of stereotypes, with a predominance of agreement in masculine or feminine gender, indicate a lack of the differentiated orientation to the sound form of the word. Establishment of such stereotypes in the course of a spontaneously ongoing process of interaction acts as an inhibitor in the formation of orientation to the word's sound form.

The essence of Popova's investigation is the discovery that the most important condition in mastering the grammatical structure of language is the formation of orientation toward the sound form of the word. In turn, an important factor for forming orientation toward the sound form of the word is an organization of the child's activity with the words, during which orientation enters as one of the decisive links, determining the success of the entire activity. No less important is the fact that simple exercise and accumulation of experience may not lead to a positive result.

The principle meaning of this investigation seems to us to lie in the fact that it discloses the essence of so-called sense of language. In the light of obtained data, a sense of language is nothing more than an orientation toward the sound form of the word, occurring during definite organization of the child's activity with words.* This also indicates a possibility for the active formation of a sense of language in preschool children.

The child's orientation toward the sound form of the word is the basis of a whole series of phenomena occurring during the preschool age, noted by a number of observers.

Thus, Gvozdev observes the appearance of first attempts to establish the word meanings and to ascribe to them etymological explanations during the fifth year. Gvozdev points out that these

*This does not mean that a sense of language is always taken in this way (another meaning is quite possible). For mastering the grammatical structure of language in preschool age, a sense of language related to the sound form of the word is of significance.

attempts are made by a child on the basis of comparing some words with other consonant words. This leads to misleading similarities of words. For example, the word *gorod* (town) is equated with the word *gory* (mountains); *trava* (grass) with *otravit* (to poison); *derevnya* (village) with *derevya* (trees), etc. In all of these cases, the affinity in meaning follows the acoustic comparison of words.

Chukovsky presents a large amount of children's poetic creativity at whose base undoubtedly lies an orientation, first of all, towards the sound form of the word. Poetic rhyme, as well as rhythm, is not possible without this orientation.

It is possible to assume that a noted acuity in semantic perception of words and semantic constructions arises in children on the basis of an intensive formation of orientation toward the sound form of words.

Using preschool children, Zakharova investigated the mastery of case categories of nouns (40). The basic task of the experiment consisted of explaining the factors to which the child orients himself during the construction of case forms and the conditions which favor a more successful flow of this process. Zakharova found that during the preschool age there is an appreciable increase in the number of relationships expressed by each case. The progress in mastering case constructions depends on this: in speech, with the help of case forms, one expresses all the new types of objective relationships; also, the objective relationships are expressed through an ever increasing variety of methods. Thus, for example, the speech of younger preschool children expresses temporal relationships through the accusative and instrumental cases, and the speech of older children also begins to express the same relationships through the genitive and the dative cases.

Zakharova showed that mastery of the declension forms occurs in preschool children under the prime influence of the child's orientation to the word's form (its ending) in the nominative case. Formation of a system of connections, occurring with orientation towards form, takes place in a definite sequence throughout the entire preschool age.

First of all, orientation appears toward nouns of feminine gender ending with an "a" and of masculine gender with a hard base. The number of mistakes during the construction of case forms from words of this type, even among younger children, is small. Somewhat later, declension of masculine and feminine nouns with a soft base is mastered.

Mastery of declension of neuter nouns occurs somewhat later and with great difficulty. Zakharova determined that with respect to acquisition, these nouns can be divided clearly into two groups: more rapidly mastered are the declensions of neuter nouns with accented endings and less rapidly, those unaccented. Such a definite separation of the process affirms the leading importance of the orientation toward the acoustic form of the word. Zakharova has shown that the younger preschool children, while declining neuter nouns, are not yet always oriented toward their endings in the nominative case and thus mix the endings of the first and second declension. The older preschool children construct case forms according to the type of declension. They already orient themselves to the endings in the nominative case and, depending on the pronunciation, construct the forms— according to the first or second type of declension. If the unaccented ending was perceived and pronounced by them as "a," they used endings of the first declension in all the cases; if they perceived the ending as a reduced "o," they employed endings of the second declension in all the cases.

Consequently, the older preschool children express orientation toward the sound form of the word quite distinctly. For the younger ones the orientation appears not as clear—it is only in the process of being formed; but even these children already begin to orient themselves toward the sound form. Zakharova points out that even among the younger preschool children one can find cases of "double" declension of the same word, depending on how it is pronounced in the nominative case. Thus, for example, pronouncing the word *ograda* (fence) correctly, the child declines it according to the first declension, but pronouncing this word as "ograd," the child ascribes to it the endings of the second declension in all cases.

Thus, Zakharova's investigation points out that mastery of the morphological system of the Russian language, so intensively reflected during the preschool age, is carried out on the basis of the child's development of orientation toward the sound (material) form of words.

As to the question of the content of this orientation, regrettably there are not any reliable data. It is possible only to assume that at the very beginning orientation occurs toward the common sound characteristics of a morpheme, without taking into account its precise phonemic composition, and only thereafter occurs further differentiation. During mastering the grammatical structure of the native language, the preschool child follows the path from orientation toward the sound form of a morpheme to orientation toward separate phonemic cues. Cultivation of phonetic hearing occupies one of the leading roles in this process.

Almost all authors involved in the study of the process of speech development during preschool age have emphasized the importance of practice of the child's verbal interaction with surrounding adults in mastering the native language. This obviously is correct and important. Only in the practice of interaction linked with practical and cognitive activity by the child, and only during the process of familiarization with an increasingly greater sphere of the surrounding reality is the development of speech possible.

Of great significance is not only listening to the grammatically correct and phonetically precise speech, but also the child's independent practice in utilizing all forms of connected speech. The development of connected speech in all its forms undoubtedly assists the child in the task of mastering the grammatical structure of the native language.

However, as it appears to us, that activity of the child in which the word is an object from the point of view of its acoustic, material makeup is undervalued. A series of observers (first of all, Chukovsky) point out that among children self-created games with words are widespread. Repetition of the same word, continuous manipulation of a word by changing it, and composition of purely nonsensical rhymes and rhythms are observed. In our pedagogical literature it is customary to hold that manipulation of material objects is quite acceptable and even desirable. An absence of such manipulative activity during early childhood immediately evokes concern. And, indeed, the meaning of such an activity is tremendous. Maintained by means of orienting-exploratory reflexes, this activity has great significance in the formation of correct images of objects' separate qualities. As soon as a preschool child begins to manipulate a word as a sound complex, however, the pedagogues exhibit concern: "Isn't this type of activity nonsensical and should it be allowed under these circumstances?" At the same time, it is possible to assume that such activity with words is a powerful means for mastering the sound, material form of words, primarily because during this activity the sound complex is liberated from the lexical meaning and appears before the child in terms of its material aspect; and, consequently, it refines the child's orientation toward this aspect of the language. It may be argued that the development of orientation toward the acoustic form of language should be introduced into the organized channel of pedagogical work in the preschool institutions.

A child's mastery of the grammatical structure of the language includes not only acquisition of the grammatical forms, but also of the verbal composition of speech. The question of the realization by a preschool child of the verbal composition of speech was studied by Karpova (14). She explored two issues: first of all, what kinds of difficulties arise for the preschool child whenever he is required to isolate separate words in a sentence, and what are the elements of isolation at different developmental stages at this age; and secondly, how are these isolating actions formed, and what are the conditions that can make this process easier.

In the first series of her investigation, Karpova determined that for the children of preschool age recounting of a series of unconnected nouns does not represent any special difficulties. If, however, in the series categories of words other than nouns are also included, e.g., adjectives or verbs, the situation changes considerably: for younger and medium-age preschool children, this creates difficulties, and consequently they prefer nouns and leave out words in other categories; older preschool children in the majority of cases succeed in this task. The relative ease in recounting the nouns, according to Karpova, hinges on the fact that the intonational units (words) correspond with the objective units (objects defined by these words).

In a second series of experiments, the children were asked to recount a conceptual whole—a sentence consisting of different categories of words. The investigation showed that children encounter great difficulty in this task. In terms of the level of success in this task, the children were found to be at various stages in relation to the conceptual whole.

The first stage included children who characteristically displayed a direct relation to the content of the sentence. These children (mainly younger preschoolers) generally did not subdivide the sentence into parts.

The second stage was comprised of children who at the beginning of the experiment treated the sentence as an indivisible whole, but who in response to the experimenter's repeated questioning shifted to a semantic analysis of the sentence and isolated its objective components; thereafter, in response to complementary or leading questions they shifted to a formal analysis of the sentence structure. However, the semantic aspect always governed, and the child again reverted to isolating the material components of the sentence.

In the third stage were children who were able to isolate in the sentence almost all the words, with the exception of prepositions and conjunctions.

In a third series of studies, Karpova formed in the children a mental action for separating a meaningful whole into individual words. This formation was accomplished by introducing external action with external supports into the process of separation. Each word was marked with a right-angled plate and the child, while recounting the words, was required each time to remove one plate, thus helping him note a given word. Studies of this series show considerable improvement in the task fulfillment. These studies were conducted with children who, on the basis of previous series, were classified as being in either the first or second stage. Table 23 presents data indicating the number (percent) of children at the first stage (direct relation to the sentence), showing progress in the solution of the task under conditions of external supports.

As the table indicates, all children showed some improvement. The most considerable improvement was noted in middle and older preschool-age children who, in the majority of cases, shifted to a higher stage. As Karpova points out, however, for younger children activity accomplished with external supports does not lead to a shift to mental activity without supports. Whenever these children were asked to carry out the task without external supports, they shifted to the stage at which they were operating initially (i.e., the first stage). In the older children, one noticed the possibility of transfer of methods mastered with the help of external supports, to isolation of words without such supports.

For the second group of subjects, placed at the second stage on the basis of the previous series, progress was notable. As a result of activity with the external supports, all the children of this group shifted to the highest stage, i.e., isolated all the words presented to them (besides prepositions and conjunctions), and most important, transferred the adaption of this analysis, developed with the help of the external supports, to action without this external assistance.

Table 23.
Progress in Solution of Task Under Conditions of External Supports

Levels of Improvement	Age		
	3.5-5	5-6	6-7
Remained at the first stage	53%	22%	––
Shifted to the second stage	37%	14%	––
Shifted to the third stage	10%	64%	100%

Thus, Karpova's studies showed that ability to isolate words is formed in a child slowly—throughout the entire preschool age. However, special forms of training help considerably in the advancement of this capability.

Development of the Phonological Aspect of Speech During the Preschool Age

" 'The soul' from the very beginning carries a damnation—to be 'burdened' by material things, which appear here in the form of moving layers of air, sounds—in other words, in the form of language" (23; p. 29). These words clearly delineate the meaning of the external, material aspect of language for social interaction. Language is the means of interaction for people, namely the impact of its material phonological nature. Specifically, it permits, on the one hand, to perceive and on the other to transmit words of language.

It is quite clear that the formation of connected speech in the child and the closely associated mastery of grammar are impossible without command of the sound system of speech. This mastery represents a base on which the acquisition of language as a chief means of interaction is built.

It is regrettable that scientific studies pertaining to the child's mastering phonological aspects of the native language are very few.

Two interrelated processes enter into mastery of the phonological aspect of the Russian language: developing perception of sounds of the language or, as it is called, the development of the phonemic audition, and sound pronunciation.

The child's first verbal utterances appear very early and are associated with crying and babbling. A variety of sounds go into their composition. One encounters sounds that are present in the language as well as some that are absent. Gvozdev has indicated the child loses the ability to produce these sounds and their combinations during the period of mastering his own language.

The significance of this period ("crying and babbling") is that, in the process of sound pronunciation, the auditory perception and articulatory apparatus are perfected. This in turn leads to an opportunity for imitating the language sounds which the child hears in the speech of surrounding adults.

Mastery of the phonological aspect of language begins at the moment when language begins to serve as a means for interaction. This consists of both understanding words directed to the child by adults, and the first independently articulated words by the child.

The child's early understanding of words and even instructions pronounced by adults is built not on the perception of the phonemic content, but on the capture of the common rhythmic-melodic structure of a word or phrase. During this stage of development, a word is perceived by the child as a singular undivided sound possessing a definite rhythmic-melodic structure. Therefore, with a change in the sound composition, but with preservation of the rhythmic-melodic structure, understanding is retained anyway. Movement of the child in response to verbal signals is formed in the type of temporal connection in which the adult's word appears as a conditioned stimulus, and the unconditional orienting reflex serves as a reinforcement.

As shown by Fradkina (9), in all these cases of primary significance is the intonation of the pronounced words or question, rather than their objective meaning (this has been shown also by other authors, for example, Preyera and others). Fradkina substituted the word *gudit* (buzzes) for the word *vozmi* (take), and the words *kapitan-kapitan* (captain-captain) for the words *ladushki-ladushki* (patty-cake-patty-cake), and obtained the corresponding motor reactions.

Only at the next level does there emerge an understanding of words based specifically on linguistic characteristics, i.e., on the basis of meaning connected with a specified sound composition. Special experimental investigations were conducted in order to substantiate the position that among seven—eight-month-old children the word is not distinguished from any other primary auditory stimulus, and that toward the end of the first year reactions to the word acquire specific character. In the first series of these experiments, Fradkina developed conditioned reflexes to verbal signals and also simply to auditory signals. For seven—eight-month-old children, during the formation of temporal connections no differences were observed; for ten—eleven-month-old children, a comparison of the development of conditioned reflexes to auditory signals and to a word indicates that, in forming the conditioned reflex to a word, four times less reinforcement is needed.

In the second series, Fradkina, having developed a conditioned reflex to one word, exchanged it for another with the same exact intonation; under this condition, it was found that for the older children (ten and eleven months) reaction to the new word does not appear. This shows that, toward the end of the first year, the word begins to serve as an instrument of social interaction and acquires the nature of linguistic means.

The period during which understanding of speech is not based on the perception of specific linguistic means (phonemes), Shvachkin calls the period of prephonemic development of speech.

The next period, in which the understanding of speech is more dependent on perceiving specific linguistic means (phonemes), he calls the period of *phonemic speech*. From the external point of view, this period is characterized by a rapid increase in the passive vocabulary, i.e., by an increase in the understanding of adult's speech and by the appearance of the first childish words. Shvachkin examined in detail the development of the phonemic perception of speech during this period (31). He studied the child's understanding of words differentiated only by one kind of phoneme. With this in mind, he developed a special collection of words including all the phonemes of the Russian language. Shvachkin taught children to understand these words (each word represented an object of some kind) and thereby explained to what extent understanding is based on perception of the word's phonemic composition, and in which sequence words are differentiated or distinguished from each other by some kind of phoneme.

On the basis of carefully conducted experimental investigations, Shvachkin determined a sequence of phonemic development in eleven-month to one year ten-month-old children.

According to Shvachkin's data, toward the end of the second year the child utilizes in his understanding of speech phonemic perception of all the sounds of the Russian language.

Rzhevkin states: "Characteristic properties of different consonants are for the most part so indistinguishable that they are on the border of sensitivity of objective physiological analysis. One must be surprised only by the sensitivity of hearing which easily distinguishes a difference there, where physiological analysis is for the most part ineffective" (30).

In reference to the last stages of phonemic perception development, Shvachkin especially underscores the significance of hearing for differentiating the most refined acoustic nuances. Thus, he writes: "This differentiation (voiced and unvoiced consonants) is complicated not only because between these sounds there is only a very fine acoustic nuance, but because a close resemblance in articulation of voiced and unvoiced consonants also leads the child into error. He is required to be guided not by similarity of articulation, but to sharpen his auditory perception of sounds to distinguish between the most refined nuances; he is required to be guided by hearing and only by hearing.

"The child thus begins basically with acoustic differentiation of sounds; thereafter, articulation is introduced and finally the process of differentiation of consonants is again accomplished, mainly through acoustic differentiation. And yet, how great the difference between the first and the final acoustic differentiation!

During the initial distinction between sonorant and articulated voices, there is a rather gross, primitive auditory differentiation of consonants; in this period the child articulates very few of the consonants; primarily he is guided by his hearing. During the final stages of differentiation between the voiced and unvoiced consonants, the child's hearing attains high perfection. At this time the child follows a complex path of development under the conditions of interaction of hearing and articulation. He must now master not only articulation of sounds, which orients him differentiating these sounds, but also the opportunity for *not always considering articulation, and in spite of articulatory similarity to distinguish the given sounds only by hearing* (31). In Shvachkin's proposition, it is very important to single out the meaning that he attributes to hearing (acoustical differentiation) in differentiating consonant sounds in the Russian language, and a contradiction which may arise between articulating similarities and phonemic differences.*

The development of phonemic perception is simultaneously accompanied by the intensive development of active vocabulary and mastery of pronunciation. The question of mastering the acoustic composition of the language and the means of its utilization in the child's active speech is subjected to a detailed scrutiny in the previously-mentioned work by Gvozdev, which presents not only the results of his own observations, but also accounts of all diary material of Russian authors related to this question.

The first childish words tend to have separate syllables. In the compositional structure of Russian words, it is characteristic that the center of the word is the accented syllable and unaccented syllables connected it it have a comparatively different strength. The child learns to perceive all the syllables of a word gradually. The relative strength of individual syllables is the main reason for the retention of some syllables and omission of others.

Krasnogorsky points out that "new observations indicate that in

*This proposition appears to be important to us primarily because in the sequential development, in the training of literacy, analogous relationships appear between articulation and phonemic perception.

the formation of a word the strength of the stimulus is of great significance, i.e., the tonal strength of the phoneme or the syllables from which the word is formed. The child first of all acquires and reinforces through repetition the first, the last, or the strongest accented syllable in the perceived word" (18).

Mastery of the sound composition of language occurs together with the expansion in the word supply. The quantity of the child's correctly pronounced sounds is in a close relationship with the repertoire of actively utilized words.

Gvozdev notes that his son's vocabulary toward one year and nine months of age consisted of eighty-seven words with the following consonant sounds missing: labiodental fricatives—v and ph; hard varieties of plosive dental sounds—n, d, and t; affricates—ts; hard varieties of dental fricatives—s, z, l, and n; a soft sounding variety of z toward the silent s; all palatals (sibilants)—sh, zh, sh', shi, sh', and ch'; and dental trills—r and r'.*

Analyzing mastered as well as nonmastered groups of sounds, Gvozdev indicates that the absence of entire sound groups may be explained on the basis of the child's not having learned certain aspects of articulation. The absent sounds are replaced, as a rule, by other sounds in the process of speech.

Gvozdev determined that most frequently in place of the absent sound in the child's speech a sound appears that is closely related to the missing sound in its articulation. "The system of substitution (replacement) is based mainly on the articulated nature of sounds, first of all by their grouping according to the place of formation, and then according to the manner of formation," indicates Gvozdev (11).

One feature of sound transmission during the initial learning period is the instability of articulation in pronouncing these sounds. The latter indicates that during this period the child does not have finely differentiated phonemes and he is still operating with his selfmade diffuse sounds, characterized by the instability of their separate components.

*$'$ indicates softness of the corresponding sound.

Mastery of a new sound in most cases does not come about immediately but gradually, through intermediary sounds. Gvozdev indicates that especially noticeable among these intermediary sounds is a group of variations which represent a transitory sound between the substitute and the new sound.

Gvozdev emphasizes exceptionally early dates for appearance of auditory control over the pronunciation of newly acquired sounds, pointing out that "Sometimes the new sound appears during inattention to pronunciation, whereas during purposive pronunciation the old substitute appears" (11; p. 29). To illustrate this, Gvozdev presents an excerpt from a diary of observations on his one year ten-month-old son, Jerry. "He pronounced 'volk' (wolf) with a hard *l* (which he still did not have in his repertoire; if anything he only had semisoft *l*) but, however, when he began to repeat the word with apparent effort, then he departed considerably from his pronunciation—there occurred: 'voyk, yoyk'. The first variation occurred as if by itself without any particular effort on his part" (11; p. 29).

The mastery of individual sounds requires a different length of time. So for example, according to Gvozdev, for his son the mastery of individual sounds was of the following duration: *t*—twenty days; *l*—one month and one day; *n*—one month and eight days; *v*—two months, twenty-four days; *l*—two months and one day; *s*—one month and twenty-two days; *z*—one month and twenty-four days; *r*—two months and eleven days; *sh*—one month and eighteen days; *zh*—two months and seven days; *sh′ sh′*—fifteen days; *zh′ zh′*—nineteen days; *ch′*—two months and four days.

In examining the question of factors determining the mastery of phonetic aspects of speech, Gvozdev especially underscores the role of the motor sphere. He writes, "The first place in this regard is attributed to the role of the motor sphere, to which pertain the motor centers of speech in the main brain as well as speech motor apparatus" (11; p. 44).

Listing proofs in favor of such a deduction (distribution of mastered and nonmastered elements according to the articulative

cues, replacement occurring on the basis of articulative relationships and the appearance of groups of new sound closely resembling each other in their vocalizing aspects), Gvozdev notes:

All this indicates that out of an intricate complex of psycho-
physiological conditions necessary for the mastery of a known
phonetic element, the last to appear are the speech motor components. Upon formation of these components, no further
obstacles are encountered for the appearance of a phonetic element in the child's speech. In other words, if there were any
other obstacles in the form of insufficiently distinguished auditory perceptions, for example, such a sequence would not be
possible. Therefore, the mastery of phonetics is determined
basically by development of the speech motor sphere (11; p. 44).

In order to prove this proposition, Gvozdev presents materials
indicating that the auditory sphere is formed earlier. He writes:

The auditory sphere is the leading one in the sense that, due to
the early development of hearing, the child first of all learns to
distinguish various phonetic elements by hearing; their exact
auditory presentations become regulators for their development
in his own pronunciation. However, for their occurrence in the
child's speech articulative habits are necessary in addition to these
auditory presentations. As the above-indicated analyses show,
these habits develop later and with their development, auditory
elements enter directly into the child's speech.

From this point of view, formation of the motor sphere appears
to be the determining factor in the entire process of mastering the
phonetic aspect of the native language" (11; p. 47).

Without diminishing the importance of the speech motor sphere
in mastering the phonetic aspect of the language, it is necessary to
note that Gvozdev attributes to it an exaggerated significance and
undervalues development of phonemic hearing, the development
of the perception of speech sounds. First of all, it is necessary to
point out that mastering sounds of the native language, i.e., the
ability to pronounce them, is the content of this process, and on
these grounds alone cannot be the motivating reason, the determining factor in acquisition. Furthermore, as it appears to us,
Gvozdev does not take into account the following circumstances:
the motor image of the sound pronounced by a child does not
directly correspond to the sound heard by the child in adults'

speech. This correspondence is reached *through the phonetic image* of the sound being pronounced by the child himself. Thus, articulating movement and its image in the cerebral cortex of the two hemispheres seems to be situated between two auditory images: between the sound appearing in the speech of adults and the sound pronounced by the child. Obviously, their differentiation lies at the base of correspondence in the articulation of sound. The mastery of sound and the associated correct pronunciation appear then when these two sound images coincide with one another, i.e., whenever they are identical. At the foundation of the concept suggested by Gvozdev lies a proposition that the child not only correctly perceives sounds of adult speech (that is, at a very early stage his perception exhibits tone differentiation), but also that he correctly hears his own mistaken pronunciation. Even if one were to assume that the child perceives the sounds of adult speech quite correctly, this is far from assuming that by the same token he quite adequately hears his own sounds.

Let us present as an example a dialogue between a little girl and an adult reported by Bernshtein (instead of "r" the girl was pronouncing a bilabial sound "v"):

Girl: "Day mne kvandash." (Give me a pencil.)

Father: "Zachem tebe kvandash?" (Why do you need a pencil?)

Girl: "Ne kvandash, a kvandash."(Not a pencil but a pencil.)

Father: "Nu ya i govoru 'kvandash. " (Well, I'm saying 'pencil'.)

Girl: "Net, ty govorish 'kvandash.' Ne umeyesh, tak e ne govory." (No, you're saying 'pencil'. If you don't know how, don't talk.)

From this example it is obvious that the girl already hears an incorrect pronunciation by the adult and is even making an attempt to correct the adult. Apparently, she already has the image of the sound "r"; however, she still hears herself incorrectly and mixes up the sound image of her pronunciation of the sound "v" with the sound image of "r." She does not say that she does not know how to pronounce this sound, but seems to be proving that the adult is pronouncing it incorrectly.

Thus, phonemic hearing is noted twice during the mastery of the phonological aspect of the language. First, it serves as a base for an image; later as a result of action. The main condition for mastering the language's phonological aspect is a precise differentiation of the presented sound from the sound actually pronounced by the child. Bernshtein, in his book dealing with the learning of pronunciation of a foreign language, indicates: "The main difficult during mastery of the pronunciation of a foreign language is that the learners perceive the acoustic aspect of the foreign language according to their familiarity with the phonetic system of their native language. Having developed stable habits of hearing and pronunciation of the sounds of the Russian language, they tend to fit their perception and pronunciation of the unaccustomed, foreign language sounds into the same framework" (3; p. 13). And furthermore: "The phonetic system of the native language influences the perception of sounds in the foreign language to such an extent that, in the majority of cases, those sound images which the learners are attempting to personify in their pronunciation turn out incorrectly. It is possible to assert that we hear absolutely correctly only those sounds of speech which we are able to pronounce" (3; p. 15).

It is possible to assume that something analogous occurs during children's mastery of the phonetic system of their native language, with only this difference: during the learning of a new sound, formerly pronounced—correctly and incorrectly—sounds comprise the phonetic system in terms of which new sounds are perceived. One may assume that every nonmastered sound is perceived originally in terms of its substitute, i.e., it is heard as the pronounced sound which serves in its place.

In psychological literature, the question concerning the development of phonemic hearing and its significance in the mastery of sounds is carefully elaborated by Levina.

Levina, on the basis of extensive experience and psychological studies of children with various speech defects, attributes a more important meaning to the development of phonemic hearing in mastering the phonetic aspects of speech.

Thus, she writes:

It is correct to assume that the mastery of pronunciation is entirely subservient to the child's facilities of speech motor activity, and that it comes into existence as a mechanical compiling of sounds based on the degree of their accessibility to the pronouncing apparatus. The act of pronunciation of a sound, to a degree, should be viewed more likely as *the termination* of the acoustical process directed toward isolation of the corresponding sound, i.e., its distinctiveness among other sounds. The sound image of a phoneme emerges as a generalized one out of different 'versions', which are realized through the motor formula of pronouncing the sounds of speech. Thus, pronunciation depends largely on the acoustic generalization of a sound (20; p. 10).

Under appropriate child-rearing conditions, by the age of three years the child masters all the basic sounds of the language. However, there are frequent cases where even among older children there appear to be defects in pronunciation, indicating that mastery of the language's acoustic aspect is still not completed. Certain defects in pronunciation are also found in the younger school-age children.

In connection with the particular importance assigned to the development of phonemic perception, of great interest are the developmental stages of linguistic awareness in the child. Levina identifies five stages.

During the first stage, there is a complete absence of sound differentiation; neither the understanding of speech nor the active speech of the child is present. This is the prephonemic stage in speech development.

During the second stage, the distinguishing of the most remote phonemes is evident; there is, however, an absence of differentiation of similar phonemes. During this period, the child hears the sound differently than we do. His pronunciation is incorrect, distorted. The child does not distinguish correct and incorrect pronunciation of other people, and he does not notice his own pronunciation. He reacts alike to the correctly pronounced word as well as to the words pronounced in such a manner as he himself pronounces them.

During the third stage, decisive gains are evident. The child at this time begins to hear the sounds of the language in correspondence with their phonemic cues. He recognizes the incorrectly pronounced words and is able to make a distinction between the correct and the incorrect pronunciation. During this stage, there is a coexistence of the formerly inarticulate and newly developing linguistic background. The speech still remains inaccurate, but in it are the beginnings of adaptation to the new perception being expressed by the appearance of intermediate sounds, i.e., sounds located between the one pronounced by the child and by adults.

During the fourth stage, there is a prevalence of new images in the perception of sound. However, the linguistic awareness has not yet displaced the preceding form. The child at this stage still recognizes the incorrectly spoken words. The active speech of the child attains almost complete accuracy.

During the fifth stage, the process of phonemic development is concluded. The child hears and speaks correctly. During this stage, the child stops recognizing the incorrectly pronounced words. He forms distinct and differentiated auditory images of words and separate sounds.

The first three stages occur during early childhood (up to three years of age); during the preschool age, the child goes through the remaining two stages.

Gvozdev points out especially that, beginning from two to three years of age, children begin to realize peculiarities of their own pronunciation and even engage as "competitors" for correct pronunciation. He introduces numerous examples depicting the child's realization of the norms for pronunciation and an active struggle for their command. However, Gvozdev does not attribute to the development of linguistic awareness that role in mastering the language's phonological aspect which in reality belongs to it.

The development of awareness of the language's phonological aspect is the central point in its complete mastery during the preschool age, for it increases the child's opportunities for orienting himself in the complex relationships of grammatical forms, beyond which always lie the relationships of one sound form to another. However, it is also important because it represents one of the most essential preconditions for the new stage in the mastery of the phonological aspect of speech, the one associated with learning literacy—reading and writing.

Toward the end of the preschool age, the child correctly hears every phoneme of the language; he does not mix it up with other phonemes, and he masters their pronunciation. However, this is still insufficient for a transition to the training in literacy.

Almost all psychologists and methodologists concerned with the issues pertaining to literacy training unanimously emphasize that for the acquisition of literacy, it is necessary that the child should not only correctly hear and pronounce separate words and the sounds contained in them, but also—and this is important—he should have a clear conception about the phonetic composition of the language (words) and should be able to analyze sound composition of words. An ability to hear each separate sound in a word, to separate it clearly from the one next to it, and to know out of which sound the word is composed, i.e., the ability to analyze word sound composition, is a very important precondition for the correct training in literacy. At the same time, literacy training is advanced as one of the most important stages in developing awareness of the language's phonological aspects. Taking into account the entire preceding path of the phonemic development, training in literacy emerges as a higher stage in this development.

In connection with this, of interest is an investigation of the child's abilities to analyze sound composition of words. Gvozdev correctly asserts (as have previously a number of other authors) that "even though the child notices the difference in the separate sounds, the separation of words into sounds is not carried out by him independently, and the implementation of such an analysis during the period of training in literacy represents a new stage in the realization of sounds; herein lies the difficulty of such an analysis" (11: p. 59).

Yegorov presents data obtained in Carlson's investigation concerning the ability of children to isolate separate sounds out of words at the time when the children have just entered school (from the fourth to the thirteenth of September), i.e., prior to the beginning of learning how to read (38; pp. 53-54). The study investigated the ability to isolate hard and soft consonants in the frontal and terminal positions (soft "l," hard "l"; soft "r," hard "r"; soft "n," hard "n"; soft "s," hard "s"; soft "m," hard "m") by some children who were, and others who were not, able to read. Children who are just beginning to acquire literacy are unable to analyze the sound composition of words; they do not single out the consonant sounds located either at the beginning or at the end of words. Children who know how to read have less difficulty in solving this problem; even with these children, however, only half of them perform satisfactorily.

Normally, on the basis of such data, deductions are made concerning relative difficulty in isolating the given sounds in a word. However, it appears that these deductions are not adequately substantiated since they do not take into account the experience of *forming* the ability for isolating sounds.

Fausek, in work previously cited by us, presents a large number of facts indicating that at the age of four, under appropriate conditions, children can rather easily solve the problem of analysis and rapidly acquire this ability.

"While observing children in the Montessori kindergarten for a prolonged period (in my experience over nine years), we became convinced that the majority of children between the ages of four to six, at whose disposal are the necessary materials for learning to write, *become lovers of sound*," writes Fausek (8; p. 56) (italics ours). Our own observations on the development of a son, show that at the age of five he was freely able to analyze sound composition of words. If one is aware that as a matter of fact, during the preschool age, the child forms a relation with the sound composition of the language, then there is nothing surprising in this information. More surprising is that there are children who have neither the interest in the language's sound composition, nor the ability to analyze sounds in words. This is undoubtedly a consequence of the conditions of their development, under which special sensitivity to the sound composition of the language, appearing as a rule during the preschool age, was neither picked up nor developed.

Dettsova, relying on the factual material in literature related to a sporadic analysis of the phonological aspect of speech in preschool-age children, assumed that the problem of isolating sounds in a word, regardless of its difficulty, is feasible for a child (6). She assumed that the inability to isolate sounds in words is not a developmental aspect, but is associated only with the absence of presenting such a problem to the child, in other words, his own lack of necessity for it in his practice of verbal interaction with others.

She invited kindergarten children of all different age groups to participate in the task of recognizing and isolating sounds in words. She used twelve sounds (three vowels: *a*, *u*, and *e*, and nine consonants: *m*, *n*, *z*, *s*, *t*, *n*, *b*, *sh*, and *ch*). The children of the younger group were not able to recognize the sound at the beginning of a word; in the middle age group, 50 percent of the children solved this problem; in the older group, 95 percent. The children of the younger group were not able to cope with the problem of recognizing sounds in the middle of the word; in the middle group, 5 percent of the children solved this problem; in the older group, 75 percent.

Independent isolating of a sound at the beginning of a word was observed in 25 percent of children in the middle group and 95 percent of children in the older group; when the task was to independently isolate sounds in the middle of the word, no one among the children in the middle group succeeded; 60 percent of the older children succeeded at this task.

The data obtained by Dettsova are contradictory to those of Carlson, and indicate that already in the middle age group of kindergarten the children are able not only to recognize distinct sounds in a word, but are able also to isolate sounds independently (25 percent of the subjects in this group were able to do this). In the older group, this problem was solved by more than half of the children. However, Dettsova's investigation is only descriptive in character and does not say anything about the children's possibilities concerning the formation of the ability to analyze the sound composition of words.

Khokhlova studied the process of forming mental activity pertaining to the sound analysis of words with children of older preschool age (16). Operating on the assumption that an adequate operation for sound analysis of words is their distinctive pronunciation, Khokhlova, in the first series of her experiments, taught the children to analyze the sound composition of words through such a method. The methodology of training consisted of having the experimenter pronounce a word and ask the child to separate it into individual sounds via loud pronunciation. If this was not immediately attained by a child, the experimenter helped him by raising questions: "Which is the first sound in the word? Which is the second?", etc., and conducted the partitioning of the word along with the child. After this, the child repeated the sound composition of the word, pronouncing individually one sound after another. For the purpose of exercise, monosyllabic, bisyllabic, and finally multisyllabic words were presented. In total, there were forty to forty-five words. Each child received from five to seven twenty-minute exercises.

Training children according to this method was found to be rather ineffective. Having analyzed forty to forty-five words with the help of an adult, the children showed almost no improvement in their ability to separate the word into the sounds composing it; toward the end of the trials, difficulty did not decrease and the number of mistakes was not reduced. This series of investigations helped to clarify the essence of the children's difficulty in isolating the first and the second sounds in a word. The basic difficulty that children encounter in partitioning a word into sounds consists of their inability to hear the vowels and to separate consonant from vowel sounds in a word.

Surmounting the complex system of articulation, an essential aspect of verbal speech, presents the main difficulty for children. This is due to the fact that children, in partitioning the word into sounds, orient themselves not to the auditory perception but to articulation; they strive to pronounce the word, if possible, more accurately and articulate it more clearly; however, this does not lead—and cannot lead—to the necessary result.

The results of the first series of studies showed that the simple exercises of children in partitioning words into the sounds that compose them via the paths of loud, separate pronunciation of each sound, do not lead to the expected result.

Previously, Fausek had shown that "the analysis of something continuous is impossible and therefore speech must be *materialized*, i.e., the word has to be depicted in terms of graphic signs, which for a six-year-old and even sometimes five-year-old kindergarteners of Montessori, appears to be quite a simple matter" (8; p. 65). We have assumed that the main difficulty for the child during analysis lies in the continuity of sounds during the pronunciation of a word.

In his investigations concerning formation of mental activity, Galperin has determined that full-fledged mental activity may be formed only in that case when its mastery goes sequentially through a series of stages. The main stages in the formation of mental activity, according to Galperin, are: 1) mastering the task; 2) mastering operations with objects; 3) learning operations in the scheme of loud speech; 4) transferring operations into a mental plan; 5) the final formation of mental activity; and 6) the most important stage after getting acquainted with the task, the mastery of activity with an object under the conditions of maximal full-scale activity.

The object of a child's activity in the word sound analysis is the sounds of speech; the only action which may be performed along with it is pronunciation. Only in writing, when each sound is depicted by a letter (material object), a number of practical activities with the sounds becomes possible. Writing is an activity with sounds, in which they appear in their most materialized form. However, it entails a number of difficulties. Essentially, these difficulties arise due to the fact that the children of preschool age may not even know the letters yet, and consequently, the materialization of the analysis process by designating individual sounds with letters is precluded.

We suggested to Khokhlova in the second series of experiments to use chips of different colors, which would replace the letters. Thus, the child was given a task to conduct the word sound analysis, conditionally "recording" it, i.e., marking each isolated sound by a chip; at the end of the analysis as many chips as sounds in a word were lined up in front of the child.

From then on, training continued in the same fashion as in the first series. After the child had analyzed forty to forty-five words according to this method, he was asked to analyze a series of words without the aids (i.e., without chips), but only on the basis of pronunciation.

The results of this type of training in general appear analogous to the ones obtained by the first method but however, somewhat surpass them. For 75 percent of the children an attempt to formulate an activity for the sound analysis did not succeed; for 25 percent only partial activity was formed, i.e., these children correctly analyzed more than 50 percent, but less than 75 percent of all the presented words. Even the children who had mastered this activity with the aid of chips made many errors when required to perform the analysis without the aid of chips. A proposition was set forth that under these conditions the child's attempt to formulate the necessary activity failed, because the word that the child was partitioning into sounds was presented to him in a continuous form. Subsequently, a procedure was introduced whereby the materialization of the word's sound analysis would be accomplished according to a graphic scheme in which each little square would represent an individual sound, and during analysis a chip could be placed into each little square.

In this series of investigations, a picture was placed before the child, under which there was a graphic representation of the sound composition scheme of the word to be analyzed. The child received a small card with a representation of an object below which was a graphic scheme of a word's sound composition (little squares corresponding to the number of sounds in a word), and he was required, after having named the object depicted on the card, to perform a word sound analysis, placing into the scheme a chip in place of each sound. After the children had mastered this activity under conditions of maximal materialization, they were asked to conduct the sound analysis without the graphic scheme of the word's sound composition, but only with the utilization of supporting means (chips), and finally to conduct the sound analysis without any aids, simply by pronunciation out loud.

The results of this method of analysis formation differ sharply with the former. Only 6 percent of the children failed to formulate the activity; 12 percent showed formation of partial activity (i.e., in the analysis without any aids they committed more errors than in the 50 percent of the words); 82 percent formed the activity successfully (children either did not make any mistakes or made only a few).

The number of words correctly analyzed without any aids under the different methods of training is as follows:

After training in the first series (without the help of either the supporting means or the materialized scheme of the word's sound composition) 0%

After training in the second series (with the help of aids, but without the scheme) 31%

After training in the third series (with the shift to the second series) 81%

In the final series, activity for sound analysis was completely formed in 82 percent of the children. In the first and the second series, the completely formed activity did not appear at all.

Investigations by Khokhlova convincingly indicate that the children of older preschool age formulate fairly easily (after five to seven exercises of twenty minutes each, during which the child analyzed forty to forty-five words) a full-fledged activity for the analysis of a word's sound composition, i.e., the child learns to isolate the separate sounds in words and to determine the quantity and the character of the sounds composing the word. However, in order to form this type of activity, it is necessary initially to materialize and to expand the activity with sounds to the maximum, by bringing it closer to the realm of material activity with objects.

Under these conditions according to Khokhlova's data, children easily acquire a set for articulatory analysis, and shift to essentially sound analysis.

The fact that a child of older preschool age is able to master rather easily the activity of the word sound analysis prior to or without familiarity with the letters of the alphabet is extremely important. Khokhlova's investigation indicates that a child of this age can easily be accelerated in his phonemic development to the level necessary for the mastery of literacy, and raises a question about the possibility of mastering literacy during the older preschool age, obviously under the conditions of special methodology, which would take into account the aspects of phonemic hearing development as well as phases of forming mental activity pertaining to reading.

In light of the obtained data, it is possible to assume that the potentialities of the preschool child regarding awareness of the phonological aspect of speech are far from being totally utilized, and that this certainly results in some damage to the child's entire further development.

All the materials reviewed by us indicate that during the preschool period, i.e., at the age of three to seven years, the child appears to be extremely sensitive to learning language. The basis for this heightened sensitivity is the occurrence of increased demands for socialization in early childhood and the preschool age.

Based on this orientation to the sound form of a word and its intensive development during the preschool age, the child follows the path beginning with isolating a morpheme to isolating a phoneme.

The facts newly obtained by Soviet investigators about the development of speech during the preschool age present an opportunity for making certain general assumptions for charting a direction for further investigations, and for illuminating certain issues pertaining to practical problems encountered in the study of speech development.

First of all, these investigations confirmed that the preschool age is a period of an extremely intensive development of speech form and function and of mastery of grammatical structure and the native language's phonological composition. Furthermore, the obtained data indicate that the potentialities for development of speech during such a period are not being fully utilized.

Keeping in mind the great significance that mastery of language has for the entire psychological development of the child, it is necessary to explore fully the potentialities and conditions favoring their full utilization.

The lack of theoretical and practical soundness of the conceptions that attempt to explain the process of language mastery by the child through "intuitive discoveries" of a word's nominal function and the inflected nature of the language has been demonstrated by these investigations. Even though based only on examples of acquisition of separate grammatical categories, it has been convincingly demonstrated that such "discoveries" arise not prior to mastery of language, but are generalizations occurring according to known principles during the process of learning, under the conditions of proper organization of such a process. Investigations also showed the total untenability of the theory regarding the existence of a special unconscious sensitivity or "an instinct for language" in preschool children. Finally, the logic of the "glass theory," according to which the child of preschool age does not perceive the sound form of a word beyond its lexical meaning, was clarified.

It was discovered that the development of forms and functions of speech is determined by those new tasks that the child encounters during the process of social interaction with adults and in the course of the development of his own activities. The differentiation of diverse speech forms and functions during preschool age is accomplished on the basis of a new content of social interaction of the child with adults, as well as intensive development during this period of varied types of activities demanding different kinds of participation from adults and presenting the child with new demands.

The so-called egocentric speech does not represent any exception in this regard. Being social in its origin and orientation, it emerges at a given level of the child's development, namely when on the one hand the child is confronted with the demands for independent activity, but on the other still has strong tendencies toward mutual interaction with adults. The significance of egocentric speech decreases to the extent of an increase in the child's independence and conversely, increases in situations in which collaboration with adults still remains a necessity, but for which there are no internal psychological conditions. In addition, one may assume that internal speech is also born out of the impossibility of realizing mutual activity with adults, and at the very beginning of its development appears to be transferred "inside" and formalized "within the brain" by the child's mutual activity with an adult.

Thus, by presenting the child with new tasks that demand new forms of interaction, by regulating the nature of his mutual interaction with adults, and by complicating his independent activity, we are able to direct considerably the development and differentiation of forms and functions of speech during the preschool age.

The development of speech forms and functions during this age is, however, directly associated with the mastering of the grammatical structure and the phonological composition of the native language. Pedagogues and psychologists currently have at their disposal well-substantiated materials delineating the general approach for the child's mastery of the grammatical structure. However, these facts collected by linguists, pedagogues, and psychologists depict only a general sequence, the logic in mastering individual forms, and tell us very little about the process of mastering each one of these forms. It is possible to say that we have access to a program that is adhered to by a child in the process of mastering the native language.

Whereas the general logic of the process of language mastery is reasonably developed, the psychology of the mastery process is still insufficiently developed. We still know very little concerning how the mastering of each separate form attains such a level that the child employs it without errors in his speech. It is quite apparent that this is not a mechanical process in which the child learns each separate linguistic form by the means of sheer repetition. Observations show that the mere mechanical repetition and accumulation of separate linguistic forms is far from being sufficient for their mastery. One cannot, however, undervalue the child's practice of social interaction with adults as the main source from which the child is able to derive new linguistic forms. It is well known that with insufficient interaction, i.e., when children are rarely spoken to and when they do not show the need for linguistic interaction, speech development becomes slowed down in its tempo. The practice of interaction must henceforth remain the basic source of speech development in all preschool children. The children must be presented with more and more complex tasks and should simultaneously receive a sufficient quantity of examples of high quality language. However, this in itself is not sufficient. In the interaction with adults involving objects and phenomena of the surrounding reality, the word emerges before the child first of all in terms of its lexical meaning. In this regard, the adherents of the "glass theory" were right. However, they were incorrect in that they viewed the child as completely incapable of orienting himself towards the sound form of the language. If the child generally were unable to orient himself toward the sound form of the language, then the development of speech would indeed be a miracle, as it appears to be in the theory of "intuitive discoveries" performed by the child in very early childhood. Investigations show that the child's orientation toward sound forms of the language emerges very early. But, spontaneous emergence of orientation is connected with great difficulties that are overcome by the child at the expense of long periods of time and effort. The question concerning the conditions favoring easy occurrence and intensive development of orientation toward sound forms remains unsolved. In this regard, there have been only initial experimental attempts.

Regretfully, one has to generalize that the current practice of speech development in the preschool institutions has paid very little attention to the child's orientation to the sound form of language. The development of speech acquires a somewhat one-sided character, whereby upbringing moves mainly in the direction of developing new forms and functions of connected speech.

The child's recognition of linguistic reality until this time remains unorganized, and the capacities of preschool-age children in this regard are far from being totally exploited. The upbringing does not intervene at all into the organizing of orientation toward the language's sound form, and language learning continues to remain spontaneous. Just as in the process of upbringing, the spontaneously occurring orientation is not supported; the labor related to its development is not organized and having fulfilled its function at a minimal level that is required for the mastery of grammatical structure, it is curtailed and ceases to develop. As a result, we find this state of affairs: having mastered the known "sensitivity" of the language at the very beginning of the preschool age, the child loses his special linguistic "giftedness," and enters school training unable to orient himself to the sound structure of the language. Thus, it becomes necessary to teach him such orientation all over again.

The problem of the psychology of the child's mastery of gram-

matical structure and sound composition of the native language is
one of the most important ones from the theoretical, and to a
large extent, practical points of view. Soviet psychologists have
made only the first steps in this direction. However, even the few
investigations that have been carried out indicate that there exists
a very tight connection between mastery of the grammatical
structure and the orientation to phonological aspects of the
language. The obtained data allow us to assume that formation
of orientation in the phonological system of the language
must represent, in itself, a base for mastering the grammatical
structure.

In this connection it seems apparent that is is necessary to reex-
amine the negative attitude observed in practice toward various
exercises that take place sometime in the child's developmental
period within the family in the form of playful manipulation of
words, which is supported by the orienting-exploratory reflex,
and which, at the same time, serves to increase a child's orientation to the sound form of words. Such exercises are treated by
some pedagogues as nonsensical because lexical meanings of
words are either delegated to a secondary position or are absent
altogether. However, such exercises have a great deal of meaning
for the child. In them, first of all, are imitated changes in the
sound form per se and the child, having had the opportunity to
observe them, has an opportunity for developing his perception
of linguistic reality.

Most distinctly these questions are being raised at the present
time in connection with the evaluation of grammar teaching in
preschool institutions. The possibility of teaching literacy to
preschool children with the aid of correct methodology is unquestionable. It is possible to expect that, with the correct utilization of different aspects of speech development during this
period, the mastery of literacy can progress more easily than
during the school period.

There is no doubt, however, that teaching literacy cannot be
simply attached in a mechanical fashion to the existing system of

speech development in preschool institutions. It requires real changes, first of all, in the program and organization of work related to the mastery of the grammatical structure and the sound composition of the language. Designation of the correct content and organization of this kind of work in preschool institutions requires intensive research of the issues concerning psychology of language mastery by preschool-age children.

References

1. Aleksandrovskaya, M. A. Nedostatki proiznosheniya u detey starshego doshkolnogo vozrasta. (Inadequacies in pronunciation among older preschool children.) Kand. diss. Moscow, 1955.

2. Arkin, Ye. A. Doshkolny vozrast. (Preschool age.) Moscow. Uchpedgiz, 1948.

3. Bernshtein, S. N. Voprosy obucheniya proiznosheniyu. (Questions of training in pronunciation.) Leningrad, 1937.

4. Bogoyavlensky, D. N. Psikhologiya usvoyeniya orfografii. (Psychology of mastering spelling.) Moscow. Izd-vo APN RSFSR, 1957.

5. Chukovsky, K. I. Ot dvukh do pyati. (From two to five). Izd. 11. Moscow, 1956.

6. Dettsova, A. V. Razvitiye osoznaniya zvukovoy storony rechi u detey doshkolnogo vozrasta. (Development of awareness of the aural aspect of speech in preschool children.) Rukopis. (Manuscript.) Moscow, 1953.

7. Elkonin, D. B. Osobennosti vzaimodeystviya pervoy i vtoroy signalnykh sistem u detey doshkolnogo vozrasta. (Aspects of interaction between the first and second signaling systems in preschool children.) Izvestia APN RSFSR. Vyp. 64, 1954.

8. Fausek, Yu. N. Obucheniye gramote i razvitiye rechi po sisteme Montessori. (Training in literacy and the development of speech according to the Montessori method.) 1922.

9. Fradkina, F. I. Vozniknoveniye rechi u rebyonka. (Emergence of speech in the child.) Uchyonyye Zapiski LGPI. (Scientific notes of LGPI.) Vol. XII, 1955.

10. Galperin, P. Ya. Opyt izucheniya formirovaniya umstvennykh deystvy. (A study of the formation of mental activity.) Doklady na soveshchanii po voprosam psikhologii (3-8 Iyulya, 1953g). (Presentations at the psychological conference, 3-8 July, 1953.) Moscow. Izd-vo APN RSFSR, 1954.

11. Gvozdev, A. N. Usvoyeniye rebyonkom zvukovoy storony russkogo yazyka. (Child's mastering of the aural aspect of the Russian language.) Moscow. Izd-vo APN RSFSR, 1948.

12. Gvozdev, A. N. Formirovaniye u rebyonka grammaticheskogo stroya russkogo yazyka. (Child's formation of the grammatical structure of the Russian language.) Ch. I & II. Moscow. Izd-vo APN RSFSR, 1949.

13. Istomina, Z. M. Vliyaniye slovesnogo obraztsa i naglyadnogo materiala na razvitiye rechi rebyonka-doshkolnika. (The influence of verbal image and visual material on the development of speech of the preschool child.) Rukopis. (Manuscript.) Moscow, 1950.

14. Karpova, S. N. Osoznaniye slovesnogo sostava rechi rebyonkom doshkolnogo vozrasta. (Realization of the verbal composition of speech by a preschool child.) Voprosy psikhologii. (Questions of Psychology.) 1955, No. 4.

15. Katz, D. and R. Gespräche mit Kindern; in Untersuchungen zur Sozialpsychologie und Pädagogik. Berlin, J. Springer, 1928.

16. Khokhlova, N. A. Sravnitelnoye psikhologicheskoye izucheniye zvukovogo analiza slov detmi-doshkolnikami. (Comparative psychological study of preschoolers' sound-analysis of words.) Rukopis. (Manuscript.) Moscow, 1955.

17. Kislyuk, G. A. Obrazovaniye dvigatelnykh navykov u detey doshkolnogo vozrasta pri naglyadnom pokaze i pri slovesnoy instruktsii. (Formation of motor habits in preschool children under conditions of visual presentation and verbal instructions.) Kand. diss. Moscow, 1953.

18. Krasnogorsky, N. I. K fiziologii stanovleniya detskoy rechi. (Physiological bases of children's speech.) Zhurnal vysshey nervnoy deyatelnostsi im. I. P. Pavlova. (I. P. Pavlov Journal of higher mental activity.) Vol. II, Vyp. 4, 1952.

19. Leushina, A. M. Razvitiye svyaznoy rechi u doshkolnika. (Development of connected speech in the preschooler.) Uchyonyye zapiski LGPI. (Scientific notes of LGPI.) Vol. XXXV, 1946.

20. Levina, R. Ye. Nedostatki chteniya i pisma u detey. (Children's deficiencies in reading and writing.) Moscow. Uchpedgiz, 1940.

21. Luria, A. R. O pathologii grammaticheskikh operatsy. (Concerning pathology of grammatical operations.) Izvestia APN RSFSR. Vyp. 3, 1946.

22. Lyublinskaya, A. A. Prichinnoye myshleniye u rebyonka y deystvii. (Causal thinking of the child in action.) Izvestia APN RSFSR. Vyp. 17, 1948.

23. Marx, K., and Engels, F. N. Nemetskaya ideologiya. (German ideology.) Sochineniya. Vol. III, 1955.

24. McCarthy, D. Language development in children. In "Manual of Child Psychology," ed. L. Carmichael. New York: Wiley, 2nd. ed. 1954, 492-630.

25. Morozova, N. G. Razvitiye otnosheniya detey doshkolnogo vozrasta k slovesnomu zadaniyu. (Development of attitude of preschool children to a verbal task.) Izvestia APN RSFSR. Vyp. 14, 1948.

26. Piaget, J. Language and Thought of the Child. (Translated from French.) New York, 1959.

27. Popova, M. I. K voprosu ob ovladenii grammaticheskimi elementami yazyka detmi preddoshkolnogo vozrasta (ovladeniye soglasovaniyem v rode). (Concerning the question of mastery of the grammatical elements of the language in preschool children, mastery of correspondence in gender.) Kand. diss. Moscow, 1956.

28. Rubinshtein, S. L. K psikhologii rechi. (Toward a psychology of speech.) Uchenyye zapiski LGPI im. Gertsena. (Scientific notes of Hertzen LGPI.) Vol. XXXV. Leningrad, 1941.

29. Rubinshtein, S. L. Osnovy Obshchey psikhologii. (Basis of general psychology.) Moscow. Uchpedgiz, 1946.

30. Rzhevkin, S. N. Slukh i rech v svete sovremennykh fizicheskikh issledovany. (Hearing and speech in terms of current physical investigations.) Moscow, 1951.

31. Shvachkin, N. Kh. Razvitiye fonematicheskogo vospriyatiya rechi v rannem detstve. (Development of phonemic perception of speech in early childhood.) Izvestia APN RSFSR. Vyp. 13, 1948.

32. Sokhin, F. A. Nekotoryye voprosy ovladeniya grammaticheskim stroyem yazyka v svete fiziologicheskogo ucheniya I. P. Pavlova. (Certain questions concerning the mastery of grammatical structure of the language in terms of the physiological teachings of I. P. Pavlov.) Sovietskaya pedagogika. (Soviet pedagogy.) 1951, No. 7.

33. Sokhin, F. A. Nachalnyye etapy ovladeniya rebyonkom grammaticheskim stroyem yazyka. (The initial stages of the child's mastery of the grammatical structure of the language.) Kand. diss. Moscow, 1955.

34. Stern, C., and W. Die Kindersprache. Eine psychologische und sprachtheoretische Untersuchung. (Speech of children.) Leipzig. Barth, 1907.

35. Syrkina, V. Ye. Problema egotsentricheskoy rechi v issledovaniakh Piaget. (Problem of egocentric speech in the investigations of Piaget.) Rukopis. (Manuscript). LGPI, 1934.

36. Ushinsky, K. D. Sobraniye Sochineny. (Collected works.) Moscow. Lzd-vo APN RSFSR, 1950.

37. Vygotsky, L. S. Izbrannyye psikhologicheskiye issledovaniya. (Selected psychological investigations.) Moscow. Izd-vo APN RSFSR, 1956.

38. Yegorov, T. G. Psikhologiya ovladeniya navykom chteniya. (Psychology of mastering the reading habit.) Moscow. Uchpedgiz, 1953.

39. Yendovitskaya, T. V. Rol slova v vypolnenii prostykh deystvy detmi doshkolnogo vozrasta. (The role of words in the execution of simple actions by preschool children.) Izvestia APN RSFSR. Vyp. 64, 1954.

40. Zakharova, A. V. K voprosu o razvitii grammaticheskogo stroya rechi u detey doshkolnogo vozrasta. (Concerning the development of the grammatical structure of speech in preschool children.) Kand. diss. Moscow, 1955.

41. Zaporozhets, A. V. Izmeneniye vzaimootnosheniya dvukh signalnykh sistem v protsesse razvitiya rebyonka-doshkolnika. (Change in the interac-

tion of two signaling systems in the process of development of the pre-schooler.) Doklady na soveshchanii po voprosam psikhologii (3-8 Iyulya 1953g). (Presentations at the psychological conference, 3-8 July, 1953.) Moscow. Izd-vo APN RSFSR, 1954.

5. Development of Thinking

During the preschool years great changes occur in the thinking of a child. By observing simpler phenomena of nature and social life understandable to him, by participating in given patterns of family and kindergarten interactions, and by playing and getting used to organized activity in a preschool institution, the child expands his mental outlook and acquires new knowledge from which the basis for his consequent mental development and learning in a school setting is formed. This process, however, is not limited to a simple expansion in the scope of ideas or to a simple increase in the quantity of knowledge. Along with the change in content, restructuring of the character of the mental activity occurs and new forms of thinking emerge. The preschool child uses different approaches to an intellectual problem, utilizes other methods for its solution, and makes different generalizations from the observed phenomena than, for example, does a pre-preschool child.

Thus, in investigating the development of a preschool child's thinking it is necessary to take two mutually interrelated aspects of this process into account: the change of its content and the emergence of new forms in the child's intellectual activity.

In studying these aspects, it is necessary to establish more precisely what is meant by the term "development of thinking." Occasionally this term is used in a very broad sense, implying the development of any cognitive activity of the child, and even the development of any form of behavior, since it implies an adaptation to new surroundings. Such an unlawful extension of the term is quite frequently observed among American authors who treat the development of thinking as a "formation of new connections" (Thorndike) or an "acquisition of new types of behavior" (Harriman), etc.

Even though the development of thinking is directly connected with the development of other cognitive processes and also with general changes in the child's activity, it does not mean that one can ignore the specific character of the child's intellectual development and refuse to subject it to special investigation. Therefore, the attempts of certain authors to relate questions about the genesis of children's perception, cognition, and memory to the problem of the development of thinking are unsound. For example, Rubinshtein wrote, "The child thinks whenever he turns away from 'a strange woman' and happily extends his hands toward his mother—he perceives intelligently, distinguishes, recognizes, determines certain connections, actively selects" (42). However, in this instance no specifically mental acts are noted for solving the given problems, as they require only the processes of perception and memory.

Russell (1956) also expands the area of children's thinking, including in it: 1) "material of thinking"—sensation, perception, images of memory, cognitions, etc.; 2) "motives of thinking"—sensitivity, needs, relationships, etc.; 3) "processes of thinking"—selection, exploration, manipulation, solution of problems, creativity, discovery, etc.; 4) "capabilities of thinking"—habits, techniques, etc. (43). The above-mentioned author assumes that there are no rigid boundaries among the enumerated component parts of thinking. The total act of thinking is characterized by the organization and integration of these elements. Consequently, even at the beginning of his book Russell refuses to accept a unified terminology for the analysis of thinking and for the isolation of specific intellectual processes.

Along with such an unlawful expansion of the term "thinking," some authors restrict it severely in an attempt to examine the development of thinking only as the development of ability, "conceiving through considering and reasoning" (Bühler, 7). Limiting the area of intellectual processes by the higher forms of logically successive deductions prevents psychology from genetically exploring the problem, and it leads essentially to rejecting the presence of thinking in younger children. Sometimes such conceptions are implicitly expressed. For example, Piaget points out that even though there is thinking in a child, it is alogical (37).

(The question to what extent a preschool child is logical in his reasoning will be an object of our evaluation later on.) However, the thesis of existence of alogical thinking contains a well-known error. It is almost the same as asserting that even though the child possesses meaningful mental activity, it is void of any kind of meaning.

Lower forms of thinking that are detected in the youngster qualitatively differ from those complex forms of reasoning formed in the fully developed adult. However, this does not mean that they are discretely separated and do not have anything in common. Genetic investigation of thinking should encompass all these stages of development and should show how more complex, more perfected forms emerge out of more elementary ones.

In determining the distinctiveness of thinking activity and the process of its development, one primarily has to rely on its content. For, as classic writers of Marxism-Leninism indicate, thinking is a mediated and generalized reflection in the subject's head on things and events of objective reality, encompassing their connections and interrelationships. The development of thinking may be defined as the development of this type of reflection.

This kind of definition allows one to exclude from the series of issues associated with thinking a number of questions not having any direct relationship to it and to partially exclude the question concerning adaptive changes in behavior occurring automatically, without awareness. One can also exclude issues related to developing the elementary forms of a child's cognitive activity, which pertain to direct perception of the surrounding reality and reproduction of this sensory experience in simpler forms of memory.

Furthermore, it would be inappropriate to examine the child's intellectual development by limiting oneself only to the analysis of its higher forms, such as acts of thinking occurring in a discursive form. In many instances of solving some kind of a practical problem, the preschool child does not arrive at highly developed deductions. However, his activity is of an intellectual nature as much as he through a mediational path establishes certain relationships among objects, relying on generalizations from his previous experience.

General Questions Concerning the Development of Thinking of a Preschool Child

The problem of development of the child's thinking long ago attracted the attention of philosophers and pedagogues. However, for a long time attempts at its solution were based primarily on naturalistic observations or on theoretical conceptions. A significant step in clarifying the problem was taken when the materialists of the seventeenth century began to examine human thinking as a product of development, the sources of which are localized in sensations experienced by the child as a result of the influence of external objects on his sensory organs. This empirical theory of the development of thinking was in contradiction on the one hand to the Cartesian theory of "innate ideas," and on the other to the theory of spiritual abilities that had been retained from medieval metaphysical psychology. The sensory ideas of Locke as applied to the development of thinking were liberated from idealistic aspects and were developed in their materialistic orientation by the founders of association psychology, Hartley and Priestley. The empirical theory of thinking development lacked factual material concerning systematic observations related to the psychic evolution of the child, as well as understanding the actual reasons for such a development. Representatives of this orientation did not venture beyond the structure of available mechanical schemes of the development of thinking, according to which common ideas and also their unification are established through reasoning by way of associative connections.

A considerable influence on the formation of scientific propositions about the child's intellectual development was exerted by experimental investigations in the area of the physiology of sensory organs undertaken during the middle of the last century. Sechenov took the leading role in clarifying issues concerning the development of thinking based on these new psycho-physiological data. He primarily emphasized genetic investigations in the analysis of basic problems related to the physiology of nervous activity and to psychology. "In the mental life of a man," wrote Sechenov, "only early childhood presents instances of actual emergence of thoughts or ideational constructions out of psychological products of lower form, not having the character of thought. Only here does observation uncover actual periods when man does not think and thereafter, little by little, he begins to show this ability" (44).

In characterizing the usual path of the child's intellectual development, Sechenov argues that its sources lie in the perception of the external world: "Most simple observations further indicate that the roots of thought in the child lie in one area of sensation. This is apparent from the fact that all the mental interests of early childhood are focused primarily on objects of the external world, and that these objects are apparently recognized initially only through sensation (mainly through the organs of vision, touch, and hearing)" (44).

Sechenov rejected the idealistic concept of thinking, which considers the reasoning aspects of thinking as "inherited forms or the laws of the perceiving and knowing brain" on the grounds that it is unrealistic. Furthermore, he emphasized the weakness of naive sensationism, which was attempting to explain the entire process of intellectual development only by the nature of external influences, totally leaving out characteristics of the subject and his neuro-physiological organization.

The progress in evolutionary teaching and physiology of the sensory organs permits one, according to Sechenov, to overcome this limitation of the classical sensationism and to approach the problem of the child's intellectual development in a new manner. In examining the origin of different intellectual constructions in ontogeny, Sechenov points out how complex spatial conceptions, understanding of causal relationship, and abstract conceptions of numbers, etc., emerge out of elementary sensory processes. In contrast to the associationists, who viewed the child's mental development as a result of passive contemplation of reality, Sechenov attributed decisive meaning to the child's practical experience, i.e., to the process of activity in relation to the perceived objects serving as the means for forming adequate understanding of the external world. He considered logical forms appearing at a certain level of the child's development the quintessence of the child's experience of activity with objects, a result of the reflection of his awareness of multiple perceived relationships among objects. In pursuing the child's development of understanding causal relationships, Sechenov states:

After the child has learned how to walk, speak, and use his hands, his entire life is absorbed in so-called tasks and games. Here, every moment he is an active agent who, according to his own will, changes objects of the external world and obviously cannot fail to notice himself as such. In other words, in every moment through his awareness pass such sensory series (more appropriately 'series of personal action'), which in comparison with one another differ in general terms (in terms of the law of similarities), and which ultimately break up into elements, the corresponding counterparts of which in the abstract form of conception are: an animated subject with willingness and ability for action, actions themselves, and effect. All this is repeated hundreds or even thousands of times and the type of an active man, effecting events or changes in the external world, being most habitual becomes for the child a model for explaining such changes and events (44).

In clarifying the meaning of objective activity in the process of concept formation, Sechenov was far ahead of prevailing notions in international psychology concerning ontological development of thinking. He demonstrated new productive ways for a really scientific, materialistic resolution of the problem. However, because the investigation of children's activity at different ages lacked sufficient systematic observational and experimental data, Sechenov was able to designate only general tendencies in the development of the child's psyche.

A shift in psychology to systematic observations and experiments in the study of child psychology created new opportunities for the investigation of thinking. Thus, Darwin's publication of "A Biographical Sketch of an Infant" (8) set the stage for a series of works based on careful recording of long, planned observations related to the child's psychological development. At the end of the last century, the experimental approach was applied to the study of the child's thinking. One of the pioneers in this area was the Russian investigator, Sikorsky, who undertook the study of the child's capacity for mental activity (45).

In a short time child psychology, having armed itself with new methods of investigation, accumulated a great deal of material concerning the nature of the child's thinking activity. These materials provided for the first time a possibility for differentiating the characteristics of thinking processes at various stages of ontological development and, in part, an explanation of specific aspects of thinking in the preschool child. However, the massive accumulation of factual material concerning the intellectual activity of children in various countries of Western Europe and the United States did not lead, contrary to expectations, to the formation of a streamlined scientific conception of children's thinking.

The reason for this shortcoming may lie in the observation indicating that the period of extensive application of experimentation and observation in the area of the child's psychological development coincided with a deep methodological crisis encompassing bourgeois psychology. In connection with this, various idealistic and mechanistic theories appeared in America and Western Europe. These theories interfered with the correct understanding of facts already established within child psychology, as well as with the correct orientation for further investigations of the child's thinking.

In addition, one must take into account that almost to the beginning of the twentieth century, the study of thinking was based on formal, logical analysis of intellectual processes and on the explanation of associations that lie at their base. The place and role of associations in thinking are still being debated, and a number of authors have reversed the attempts of associationists to reduce the processes of mental development to the formation of associations. Thus, Pratt (1928), having examined forty-six investigations concerning the thinking and reasoning processes, concluded that such identifiable factors of thinking as selectivity and directionality serve as the base for the rejection of associationism (41). Associationism was criticized in foreign psychology for its atomism and mechanism, for ignoring the specificity of intellectual processes and motivation, and for ignoring the wide context of mental activity. Humphrey (1951) summarized all these criticisms as follows: "The classical theory was criticized on the basis that experience is not reproduced through the same path, that thinking is directional, that mental elements undergo changes whenever they enter into a new combination, that we are aware of connections—all this would have been impossible if there were only isolated ideas—that, in view of this, images and sensations are partial and thoughts general" 15; p. 28).

In criticizing associationism, Lashley relied on generalization as one of the basic functions of the organized nervous tissue. This fact, according to Lashley, negates the simplicity of a connection between stimulus and response. Associationistic understanding of thinking was subjected to a critique by the representatives of the Würzburg School. Bühler correctly asserted that the process of abstraction from the associationistic series cannot be viewed as the conclusive act of causal thinking. However, while Bühler recognized that semantic dependencies of goal-oriented action are the first dependencies comprehended by children, he treated these cognitive processes in terms of an idealistic point of view, one in line with his general concept of development governed by bio-social principles. According to his views, the child comprehends dependencies of goal-oriented action through instinctual, psychic interaction—"intuitiveness"—and thereafter employs them in his understanding of natural events.

Russell in a special monograph writes that contemporary knowledge indicates that the hypotheses about the role of associations in thinking are undoubtedly divergent from the nature of thinking (43). Nonetheless, he includes in his book a chapter on associationistic thinking.

Associationism is an antigenetic conception that does not concern itself with problems of internal motivational forces in the individual's development, which does not recognize any qualitative changes in its course, and for which the problems of training and development also do not exist. The driving force in one's development according to orthodox associationism is training, i.e., actions and influence of the trainer, the teacher, and not the child's activity such as playing, learning, working, etc. The focus of attention is on quantitative changes—accumulation of associations. Thus, Ling (1941) assumes that the perception of form merges with or is directly translated into the understanding of form; the perception of small groups—into the understanding of small numbers, etc. (22). Training and development in essence are identical for associationists.

Representatives of Gestalt psychology (Wertheimer, Köhler, Koffka, Duncker, and others) emphasized productivity in contrast to the reproductiveness of thinking in various problem-solving situations (51, 18, 17, 11). Even though to a large extent their cricicism of associationistic and behavioristic understanding of the development of thinking is valid, they nevertheless did not present any more satisfactory solution to the problem. In reality, furthermore, they displaced the main problem of development by substituting for it the establishment of the principles of transformation of form or structures, which are given a priori. Thus Köhler, relying on the theory of "gestalt," excluded from thinking the presence of groping and exploring that precede a solution, as well as the corrections and controlled actions that follow it. Rejecting the importance of external activity in the representation and solution of problems, Köhler, Koffka, and others have introduced the concept of insight—sudden understanding of the relationship based on the emergence of new phenomenological structure.

Piaget, in analyzing the principles of Gestalt psychology, indicates that the laws of structural organization and their transformations are accepted by the Gestaltists irrespective of their development and appear to be the same in all spheres of the exploratory process. As a result, one obtains something similar to an analogy of water in a canal, subdivided by the locks into separate segments. Even though the water in various segments is maintained at a different level, it acquires one and the same horizontal position in all segments.

Among the theories of the child's thinking attracting much attention in Western European and, in part, American psychology is the theory formulated by Piaget.

In contrast to other investigators who noted the separate distinctive features of child psyche, Piaget made an attempt to explain the entire variety of expressions in the child's thinking by one principle; to present a general conception of the thinking of a preschool child. In the psychology of the nineteenth century, one's development was best understood in terms of a mechanistic orientation, with the difference between the thinking of a child and an adult postulated as mainly a quantitative distinction; by contrast, Piaget distinctively separates the thinking of the child from that of an adult.

In their own time, such authors as Baldwin and Stern stressed the separate distinctive features of the child's logic (3; p. 38). Piaget made an attempt to ascribe a universal meaning to these facts. According to his point of view, the logic of an adult and the logic of a preschool child are absolutely different. The thinking of the latter is syncretic; the preschooler thinks in terms of global schemes, analyzing and contrasting instead of synthesizing. His judgments are based on the subjective connections acquired through direct impression and not on objectively established relationships between things. Syncretism of the child's thinking is connected organically with the transductory nature of his reasoning. The latter means that the preschool child acts as if he does not utilize either deduction or induction, but moves in his reasoning from particular to particular missing the general. The main reason for this special aspect of the child's thinking is, according to Piaget, the weakness of the child's introspection, the unawareness of his intellectual operations. This circumstance makes the child insensitive to contradictions, evokes a noncritical orientation toward his own judgments, and excludes the opportunity for giving it a logical base.

The source of the child's introspective weakness, i.e., the absence of critical orientation toward his own thought processes, lies in the peculiarity of the child's approach to the surrounding phenomena, in his seemingly antisocial, egocentric orientation. The preschool child, according to Piaget, reasons about everything from his own subjective point of view, not taking into account objective conditions, and is not able to assume another human being's point of view. Thus, the syncretic structure of the child's thinking is explained by Piaget through the child's egocentric orientation. "The child thinks for himself, not being disturbed either by the concern to be understood by those surrounding him or by the concern to take the point of view of another" (37; p. 231).

From this viewpoint, the egocentric thinking of the preschool child appears to be an intermediary stage of intellectual development between the autistic thinking of a youngster and the logical, socialized thinking of an adult. As outlined by Piaget, the youngster's autistic thinking is in complete agreement with the psychoanalytic constructs of Freud. Characteristically, the child during this stage of development behaves as if he does not conform at all to reality but, living in a world of his own subjective experiences, makes an attempt in his thoughts to satisfy his wants through illusionary methods. Subsequently, having become a preschooler, the child begins to direct his mental sight toward objective reality; however, he evaluates it from his own subjective, egocentric point of view. And only subsequently does the child learn to take the point of view of another person and to conform his thinking to generally established logical norms.

What is the cause then for the intellectual development of a child? What makes him change from one type of thinking to another? Answering this question, Piaget in his previous works has rejected the significance of experience. Knowledge about objective reality has almost no meaning for the developmental process of the child's thinking. From his point of view, "it is not the things that influence the mind, but the things themselves are influenced by the mind." The reason for the development of the child's thinking, according to Piaget, lies in the psychic interaction of a child with other people, in the submission of his thinking to the commonly accepted forms of reasoning in the mutual interaction of the thoughts of a child and an adult.

Thus, Piaget contrasted the biological and the sociological. The biological is the emergent beginning that brings about the psychological substance. The sociological is something outside of the child that appears as a confronting force exerting pressure on the child and producing forms of thinking familiar to him. Piaget did not take into account the fact the the child from the very beginning of his life is plunged into interaction with the surrounding people, i.e., he is a member of the human collective. On the other hand, the socialization process itself was presented by Piaget as the interaction of the child's consciousness with the consciousness of others, which is in the tradition of the French sociological school (Durkheim and others).

A series of propositions in Piaget's theory are so contrary to facts that even some bourgeois investigators, themselves far removed from a systematic materialistic understanding of the child's psychology, have referred to them in a critical manner. In this connection, it is interesting to note the remark by Stern that the principles founded by Piaget are not intransitive laws of nature, but a product of a particular system of upbringing adopted in the kindergartens where Piaget conducted his investigations (37).

In Switzerland the upbringing of preschoolers is conducted according to a system closely resembling that of Montessori, and the absence of collective games and exercises brings about the familiar egocentrism of the child and evokes verbal expressions with an increased number of monologic forms of speech, conversations with themselves, reasoning out loud, etc. With a different system of upbringing in the preschool institution and usually in the family, egocentric orientations are found significantly more rarely, and the dialogic form of expression clearly predominates in children.

While Stern was criticizing the concept of egocentrism and the proposition about the dominant role of egocentric expressions in the preschooler's speech, other authors have raised their views against the theory of the child's syncretic thinking.

It is necessary to note that the term "autistic thinking" is used differently by different authors and appeared long before the work of Piaget. It was introduced by the American psychologist, Moore (1910). Moore defined autistic thinking as a tendency to make conclusions based on false premises rather than on the basis of logical common sense. On the basis of his experimental investigation, Moore concluded that autistic thinking is a well-defined, very transitory phenomenon of childhood. This term was then used by Bleuler (1924), who used it to define thinking directed toward the realization of wishes and goals, as in poetry, fantasy, sleep, etc. Murphy emphasized the role of need gratification as a more specific emotional factor of such thinking. He was doubtful that thinking in general encompasses autistic factors (34). Piaget's formulation did not make a significant impression on many American authors and by utilizing the term, "autistic thinking," they are emphasizing the role of needs and emotions in the child's thinking, and by the way, not only in the child's thinking.

However, a number of authors—McHugh (31), Russell (43), Dennis (9)—who have investigated the child's conceptions support Piaget's point of view and do not agree that autistic thinking is a very transitory phenomenon of childhood. It is interesting to note that some authors, for instance, Abel (1), distinctively refute

Piaget, showing the presence of illogical factors in the thinking of adults.

Still earlier, Kin and Deutsche (10) ran into difficulties trying to classify the child's explanations of various kinds of events according to Piaget's categories. While working with the preschoolers, both authors found that many explanations offered by the children were naturalistic and phenomenological. Kin failed to substantiate the existence of differences in methods used by different age groups in forming an explanation of natural events.

The work of Isaacs, which encompasses a great deal of factual material concerning the thinking of three—eight-year-old children, supports a discrepancy in Piaget's theory with regard to the realistic path of the child's intellectual development. Excerpts of the children's reasoning based on the observed facts show that in simpler instances even the youngest children (three-four years) catch the objective connections between events, and one does not find any egocentric premises or tendencies toward a syncretic approach in their reasoning. Isaacs rejects the thesis of the existence in the child of a separate logic, distinctly different from the logic of an adult, and points to the dependence of the child's thinking on concrete situations and on the demands of practical activity.

Isaacs's investigation also discloses that children strive to give a physical interpretation of the facts and that they are able to master the correct explanation of many events.

On the other hand, some authors (Isaacs and others), while disputing the presence of the separate syncretic logic of a child, at the same time ignore the specificity of form in the child's thinking and lean toward a mechanistic interpretation of the child's intellectual development as a process of purely quantitative changes.

In subsequent works, Piaget's proposition concerning the path of the child's mental development was substantially changed. He acknowledged an obvious shortcoming of his term "egocentrism" in characterizing aspects of the child's thinking. In his reply to criticism by Vygotsky Piaget explained the meaning of this term, which he utilized at a given stage of investigation. This meaning, writes Piaget, distinctively differs from the generally accepted understanding of egocentrism as a hypertrophic individual awareness and does not have anything in common with the individualistic theory of J. J. Rousseau. According to Piaget, the process of an organism's adaptation to the environment is not always successful and adequate to the conditions. For example, the child might still be lacking means or organs for the adaptation necessary for the solution of given problems. As a consequence, attempts in adaptation lead to systematic errors. Errors of this type are found not only in the sphere of man's mental activity, but also in other areas of psychological life.

I have introduced the phrase 'egocentrism of cognition', in order to express the thought that the progress of knowing is never accomplished by means of the simple addition of parts or new levels, as if a more complete knowledge would be a simple complement of a less formalized, previously acquired knowledge; this progress requires a constant reformulation of former points of view via a process that moves forward as well as backward, continuously correcting not only the initial systematic mistakes, but also those that arise within the process of cognition itself (40; p. 3).

Thus, the factually specific term "egocentrism" is used by Piaget to denote restrictiveness, one-sidedness of the cognition process in the historical as well as the developmental sphere, dependence of awareness on the subject, or relativity of his knowledge, i.e., such aspects which indeed are present in cognition. Piaget has also agreed with Vygotsky's interpretation of the phenomenon of egocentric speech—the beginning form in the development of internal speech.

After his initial studies, Piaget departs from attempts to deduce the child's mental development from the relationship of thinking with language. He writes:

I knew quite well that thinking processes spring from activity; however, I believe that the language directly reflects the activity and that the understanding of the child's logic is only possible in the area of reasoning and verbal interaction. Only later, while studying the forms of the intellectual conduct of one- and two-year-old children, did I understand that for the full comprehension of the genesis of intellectual operations, first of all one has to explore the child's activities with objects and his attempts at such activities.*

Subsequently, Piaget also arrived at an idea that was being explored in the 1930s among a series of Soviet investigations (Bozhovich, Zaporozhets, and others), that as a prerequisite to the learning of verbal interaction, it is necessary to have learning of the forms of objective activity.

From these new premises, Piaget together with his co-workers conducted a large number of concrete experiments. In the 1940s as a result of these studies, Piaget formulated a proposition regarding the structure of the intellect and the general directionality of its development. Thinking, according to Piaget, represents a system of operations. The operation is defined as internal activity. Originally activity has an external objective character that, having been carried out with objects, shifts into an internal plan; it is executed mentally but does not lose its original character of activity. Thus, in reality, operations and objective activities are only different categories of activity. Operation differs from an objective activity not only by its form of internal action, but also by having a series of other characteristics. One of these is condensation. In comparison with realistic activity, operation is condensed activity. The internal activity is performed not with the realistic object, but with the images, symbols, and signs. However, not every mental activity is an operation. An internal activity becomes an operation, then, when it is in interaction and interconnection with other activities, organized into a definite system. Such a system of operations represents a totality in which some operations are balanced by others, due to such characteristics as reversibility. Only reversible action is an operation. Reversibility

*Piaget, J. Autobiography. In E. G. Boring et al., *History of Psychology in Autobiography*, Vol. 4, Worcester, Mass., Clark University Press (1952), p. 247.

means that for each operation there is a symmetrical and opposite operation that springs from the results of the first, reconstructing the initial situation or the point of departure.

According to Piaget, there are four basic stages in the development of thinking from birth to maturity. The first stage corresponds to the period of development in the child from birth to two years of age. This is the stage of sensory-motor thinking; at this period there are no operations. However, based on external behavior, one can isolate the beginnings of reversibility (for example, crawling across the room, the child is able to return to the point from which he began his movement). The child becomes aware of the course of objective actions through relatively stable, constant signs. The objects become for him *invariants.* Invariance, the constancy of an object, is the result of definite organization of the child's movements, coordinated for the purpose of attaining some goal. The second stage encompasses the period of development from two to seven years of age. This is the stage of preoperational thinking. Speech development, concept formation, and internalization of activity into thought occur during this period. This is the time in which the child exhibits the formation of the concrete thinking that Piaget calls intuitive. The third stage includes the ages from seven-eight to eleven-twelve years; this is a period of concrete operations. Mental actions acquire the characteristics of reversibility and are formed into a definite structure. These operations are logical according to their structure. However, they are performed on objects and not in relation to verbal expression. Although they can correctly solve a problem involving concrete objects, the children have difficulty in solving the same problem whenever it is given to them only in verbal form. Finally, the fourth stage in the development of thinking—from eleven-twelve to fourteen-fifteen years of age—is the stage of formal operations with sentences or expressions. This period is characterized by an organization of operations into a structural whole. An ability to reason according to a hypothesis appears: that is, possible hypotheses for carrying out an activity are formed and then the activity is structured in relation to these hypotheses. There emerges, as Piaget puts it, a synthesis of the possible and the necessary.

Thus, during preschool childhood Piaget refers only to the first two stages. Let's focus a little more in detail on their characteristics. The sensory-motor stage is characterized by the absence of specifically intellectual operations. During this period one notices the development of movements, in part coordination, which provides for the possibility of transferring activity into an internal plan. Toward the end of this stage one observes the beginnings of representations. However, for the appearance of thinking the child must free himself from the egocentrism that is characteristic of his perception and motor activity.

The second stage—the appearance of speech, the inception of symbolic function, and the progressive internalization of concrete actions—is subdivided by Piaget into two periods: the period of symbolic and precognitive thinking and the period of intuitive thinking. The first period represents the precognitive thinking connected with the transduction of precognitive reasoning. Piaget thinks that symbolic play or imaginative play in the child's process of reality assimilation is the base that is used for the acquisition of collective signs, i.e., speech. The symbols themselves are individual determinants and represent the most pure form of a child's egocentrism. Intuitive thinking—in distinction from the symbolic—is accomplished through a form of images. However, it retains in general the characteristics of symbolic thinking. Egocentrism is also its basic feature. Intuitive thought remains phenomenological, as it imitates the contours of reality, but does not reflect it.

In the past years, Piaget and his co-workers published a series of experiments pertaining to perception of space, speed, and time, in which they present a concrete characterization of the preoperational thinking stage. During this stage intuition is a necessary condition for the perception of speed, space, and time (36). These investigations by Piaget were subjected to experimental verification and critique by Fraisse and Vautrey (12), who showed that Piaget overvalues the significance of intellectual factors in the nature of the child's perception.

Wallon, in a book "From Action to Thought" (50), characterizes Piaget's conception in the following manner: 1) Piaget regards not sensations but movements as primary elements of psychological life; 2) the development of awareness emerges out of the development of motor schemes; how does one show in these transitions from one scheme to another, a moment during which movement becomes cognition?; 3) taking this premise, awareness in fact is not the final point but the initial one—it emerges because it was assumed to exist from the beginning, even though this in itself is not mentioned.

Furthermore, it is necessary to add that the introduction by Piaget of the new line, "action—thinking" does not remove but inversely assumes preservation of his former line, "from egocentrism to socialized thinking." The thinking of a child up to seven-eight years of age continues to remain egocentric, syncretic, and turns into logical thinking only as a result of socialization (full presentation of this second line of thought is given in the work of Piaget's pupil and follower, Joanno, 16).

In an article, "Logic and Balance in the Behavior of a Subject," Piaget examines a question concerning equilibrium-type systems in this application to the analysis of the structure of logical operations and their development. The structures of logical operations may be conceptualized as a system balancing itself in response to the impact of external influence—information. Their development may be conceptualized as an objective distinction in the formation of structures that emerged as a result of transition from one level to another. In this case, the appearance of logical structures, as such, cannot be understood as the consequence of some kind of inborn structures or qualities, uncovered through experimentation with objects, or some type of social and linguistic structures (even though all these circumstances play a definite role in intellectual development). The appearance of logical structures is the result of the activity of an objective factor—equilibration of a system. Thus, the external aspect—equilibrium—Piaget accepts as the driving force in the development of logical operations, logical structures. Under such conditions, as correctly pointed out by Wallon (50), changes from one stage, or one structure to another structure, disappear. The development does not unfold as a realistic process as solving and resolving of contradictions.

In spite of the fact that the basic thesis of Piaget's entire conception is the study of the genesis of logical structures, thinking, perception, etc., it cannot be recognized as really genetic. The matter is this, that his main method is the description of sections of maturational development. The real driving forces of development are not explored. The influence of the French sociological school was marked and Piaget could not overcome its impact, even to the end. Piaget defers the impact of a child's social surroundings only to later stages of ontogenetic development and only to higher processes. As Leontiev and Tikhomirov point out in the epilogue to the Russian translation of the book by Inellder and Piaget, "Genesis of Elementary Logical Structures" (1963), Piaget, having introduced a thesis concerning objective activity, did not fully overcome abstract sociologism, which reduces social interaction to mental interaction. He bypassed the main fact that the child's first objective activities are accomplished by himself under conditions of interaction with adults, who organize his activity in correspondence with the generally established function of the object. Inconsistency in the construction of genetic principles also exists in Piaget's practical refusal of an active formation of psychological functions as a method for their investigation. His contrast of training with the independent mental development of the child is indeed excessive. Finally, while speaking about the emergence of mental operations from concrete actions, Piaget does not analyze the process of internalization, the transition from practical to intellectual activity.

The task of constructing a scientific theory of the child's intellectual development has been given special consideration in Soviet psychology.

During the first stages of the development of domestic psychology in the post-October period, some Soviet psychologists viewed noncritically different Western European and American theories and, in part, Piaget's theory. Prominent Soviet psychologists, Blonsky and Vygotsky, while making significant contributions to the study of the child's thinking and critically evaluating bourgeois theories of the child's intellectual development, nevertheless during certain stages of their work committed serious errors and were not critical enough in their approach to false assumptions by Piaget, Stern, Bühler, and others. However, in the course of reworking basic problems in child psychology in terms of Marxist-Leninist philosophy, in the process of generalizing on the basis of data obtained from Soviet preschool institutions, and in view of the accumulated experimental material, Soviet psychologists subjected a series of bourgeois theories on the child's thinking to a thorough critique. They outlined a positive approach to the solution of the main problems concerning intellectual development during childhood.

Of great value are Blonsky's studies, who, having shown an error in Piaget's methodology used in the investigation of thinking processes, has developed original ways of investigating the child's intellect (4). Vygotsky also critically analyzed certain theories of the child's thinking that have received wide coverage in bourgeois psychology. He examined the structural theory of the development of the child's thinking, Stern's intellectual conception, Bühler's biological theory of the maturation of the intellectual mechanism, and Piaget's theory of egocentric thinking, etc. An extensive critical analysis of various mechanistic and idealistic teachings pertaining to the child's thinking was also conducted by Rubinshtein (42).

A series of investigations were instrumental in charting a new course based on experimental data for studying psychological problems involved in intellectual development during childhood and in providing a new approach to experimental investigation of the process of mental development in ontogeny. Of particular importance are: Blonsky's experimental investigations on concept formation and forms of reasoning in a child (4); Vygotsky's investigations on concept formation and the development of thinking and speech in children (49); and the studies of Basova, Natadze (35), Leontiev (20,21), Rubinshtein (42), Luria (25), and other Soviet psychologists, pertaining to various issues in the formation of the preschool child's thinking.

Many Western European and American authors examine the development of the child's thinking separately from the common content of his activity, apart from the conditions of his life and from the character of ongoing training activity. Thinking is treated as some type of mental ability, found in the child either since birth (Freud and others) or appearing at the later stages of ontogeny as a result of maturation of some kind of intellectual mechanism (Bühler and others).

In reality, numerous observations and experiments indicate that the child is born without any signs of intellect and that the first thinking processes become available to him only during the end of the first year, as a result of experimentation with his own activities and acquaintance with a series of phenomena in the surrounding environment. These first sparks of the child's thinking are neither characteristics of "dreams of fantasy" (Freud and Piaget) nor "discovery of common principles" (Stern and others), but they represent the purely practical nature of the child's thinking directly related to his objective activity.

In his time Marx, ridiculing Stern's idealistic constructs, pointed out that it is absurd to imagine the child as a metaphysicist to whom "the nature of things" is closer than his toy and concrete events that occur in his immediate surroundings. A child's life does not begin with the solution of theoretical problems. He satisfies his present needs, manipulates and plays with various objects, and in the process of these simple activities gets to know the surrounding reality. Based on this are the initial generalizations that allow the child to employ mediational, intellectual approaches to solving certain elementary practical problems. Thus, the simpler forms of the visual-motor type of thinking are observed even in a preschool child. However, this thinking is still directly connected with his objective activity. Within this activity, however, no special intellectual problems have as yet been identified, and the child has not yet formed special methods for their solution.

In the course of the child's development as a result of his accumulation of knowledge and abilities, new modes of activity and new, more complex forms of interaction with the people around him become available. The place that the child occupies in the system of human relationships also changes.

Preschool childhood is a time of life when the surrounding world of human reality becomes increasingly open to the child. Through his own activity and, first of all, through his games, which have now gone beyond the narrow limits of manipulation of surrounding objects and interaction with people around him, the child enters into a wider world, mastering it in its realistic form. He masters the objective world just like the world of human objects, conducting human activities with them (21).

The expansion of his sphere of activity and an increased complexity of its form exert new demands on the child's thinking and mediate the transition to qualitatively new, distinctive stages of intellectual development.

The Development of Visual-Motor Thinking During the Preschool Age

Genetically, visual-motor thinking is the earliest form of thinking. Already, at the end of the first year and at the beginning of the second, it is possible to observe intellectual solutions of the simpler types of practical problems in the child.

As Menchinskaya indicates, the child's initial intellectual solutions consist of the application of earlier formed habits to new surroundings. Somewhat later, more complex actions involving the construction of a solution method corresponding with the new problem is observed. She cites a series of examples of this type of solution taken out of diaries by Russian authors:

Barbara (one year ten months, who was raised by Boldyreva) was not able to reach a lamp with her hand; taking a cover from a box into her hand, she was then able to reach it. Walter Bransburg-Chaykovsky (one year eight months) was making an attempt to reach something in the cupboard; at the beginning he stretched his hand upward, however, seeing that nothing would become of it, he pulled the chair over and got up on top of it. Helen (one year one month, who was raised by Boldyreva) utilized a step stool to obtain peanuts lying on the table; she was unsuccessful; then, she pulled over a chair and reached the desired goal (32).

An investigation by Köhler on the behavior of anthropoid apes, which in part contributed to the understanding of the psychological structure of an animal's primary intellectual operations, showed the independence of primitive visual-motor forms of thinking from speech. This led Köhler, as well as a number of other investigators, to assume that there exists a special type of "practical" thinking that, contrasted with the more developed logical thinking, is not directly connected with speech.

Experimental investigations of visual-motor thinking in the small child, by K. Bühler, Sh. Bühler, Reem, and other Western European psychologists, were conducted mainly by transferring Köhler's methods of investigation of the anthropoidal intellect into the area of child study. The data obtained in these studies were utilized to defend the biogenic conception of the genesis of children's practical intellect, which received wide coverage in Western European and American psychology. Bühler simply stated that "there exists in the life of the child a phase which may be quite appropriately called a chimpanzeelike age" (7). Ray, in developing this conception, wrote that the behavior of a child from four to five years of age closely resembles the behavior of the lower monkeys, and the behavior of anthropoids approximates the behavior of children from five to six years of age.

Bühler, Lippman, Bogen, and others ignored the significance of speech in the formation of the child's practical thinking. While analyzing the intellectual behavior of a child who was solving "monkeylike" problems, they were making an attempt to find in it the same psychological principles that are characteristic of an animal's intellectual behavior. They were attempting to find in the child's intellect, to use Köhler's expression, only a different range of possibilities and not a principally different structure of psychological activity. In order to be able to explain the appearance in a human being of new—in comparison with animals— forms of practical thinking, while maintaining their own positions, these investigators had to accept the appearance of certain new abilities in the human being. For example, Bühler admits "an ability to comprehend mechanical connections and attachments of things, an ability to think up the mechanical means for the attainment of mechanical goals" (7). Lippman and Bogen introduce an ability for the operation "of physical structures" (23). Contrasting visual-motor thinking with the discursive, reasoning type, the above-mentioned authors assume that visual-motor thinking is stripped of cognitive meaning and serves only for the solution of everyday, constricted practical problems. On the other hand, it appears that discursive thinking does not have anything to do with concrete things but consists of constructions of formal relationships between ideas and is directed to the solution of purely theoretical problems.

Studies by Russian psychologists have demonstrated the lack of a basis in the biogenic conception of the development of a child's thinking. Such a concept is contrary to facts.

An experimental investigation by Shapiro and Gerke (coworkers of Bosov) showed that the nature of the solution for the child's practical problem is basically determined by the generalized schemes in his experience, which have been acquired under the specific conditions of general interaction with other people and under the influence of nurturing activity on the part of the adults. In connection with this, certain individual tasks that are attempted by a child (for example, when a child hesitates in deciding whether to climb on top of the table in order to reach an object suspended high above) are explained not by slow wits, but by the assertion that such an activity is contrary to the acquired norms of social behavior. Here the social experience of the child hinders the solution of the problem; in other circumstances it suggests to him multiple ways for the attainment of a goal that are entirely unavailable for animals.

The originality of the ways in forming the psychological mechanism of children's thinking was investigated in a series of experimental studies directed by Vygotsky. In contrast to a series of bourgeois investigators, who conceive the young child as an autistic, antisocial being, Vygotsky emphasized situational conditions, stating that beginning with the first days of the child's life the social situation exerts a pronounced influence on the character of his behavior. In his initial intellectual solutions, the child constantly orients himself toward an adult, turns to him with requests, demands and quite often attains the necessary results only directly through another human being. A more complex structure of activity where aspects of intention and its execution acquire relative independence is formed very early in the child's life as a result of the influence of social conditions on his development.

For a pre-preschooler, verbal expressions are realized in the course of executing action; their place and function in the structure of the intellectual act have not yet been determined. However, for a preschooler the processes for considering the conditions of a problem and the formation of intention already begin to precede its practical solution. These processes serve the function of planning subsequent actions. The specific human forms of intellectual activity, formed on the basis of the social conditions in a child's development, unfold before him entirely new possibilities for solving problems that in principle are not possible for an animal. The experimental studies by Vygotsky indicate that a child, in contrast to a monkey, is considerably less attached to the directly perceived situation, "the visual field" (49).

Bozhovich, in a study directed by Vygotsky, defines the prac-

tical intellectual activity of a child as one directed to the solution
of new problems, which are solved or basically broken down
within the visual-motor plan (6). Thus, practical intellect is not
contrary to the gnostic intellect but is only a separate form of
man's cognitive function. Therefore, the main issue emerging
from Bozhovich's study and other studies directed by Vygotsky
consisted of exploring basic changes that the primary forms of
intellectual activity undergo under the influence of speech.

An experimental study by Levina explored this issue further.
She employed the following methodology: the child, having been
given a practical task (a situation with a detour), in one case acted
freely, i.e., without the interference of the experimenter, in a
second was actively encouraged to speak, and finally, in the third
case was not permitted to speak. Thus, in these investigations
intellectual activity was studied under the conditions of inclusion
and exclusion of speech.

Whenever the child encounters difficulty with the task the percentage of egocentric speech increases almost twofold. This observation by Vygotsky led him to assume that egocentric speech,
conceived by Piaget as only a product of the child's specific
emotionality, an epiphenomenon of his activity and experience,
in fact fulfills a certain objective function in his intellectual behavior. This assumption by Vygotsky served as a departure point
for the analysis of experimental data obtained by Levina. She
came to the conclusion that is is not possible to refer to egocentric speech as something entirely permanent. Conversely, its
place in the child's behavior constantly changes and with it
change its character and its content.

The egocentric expressions of three—four-year-old children make
up a definite stage in developing a relationship between speech
and thinking. The analysis of transcripts of studies with children
of this age shows what appears to be a lack of connection
between the child's speech and the process of solving a given
problem. During this stage, speech represents what appears to be
an independent and self-sustaining process, and in the child's

behavior one discovers what seem to be two independently on-going types of activity: speech activity and intellectual activity, directed to the solution of practical problems. Expressions of emotional nature, echolalia, accidental and purely verbal associations, recollections, and appeals to others are the basic content of speech activity in this period. This is most likely speech apropos of the problem rather than about it. Such speech frequently distracts the child and leads him away from the presented goal.

Among older children a different relationship exists between speech and intellectual activity. Expressions are more directly related to the child's activity in a given situation. During this stage, speech becomes the means for reflecting the situation. The experimenting child while executing a movement (for example, reaching out for candy suspended on the wall) immediately states it in his speech, thus describing what appears to be a verbal form of the activity, a copy of his behavior and the situation. As it appears at first glance, this is the same accompanying speech, i.e., it seems that the child speaks and acts simultaneously; however, if one were to subdivide his entire behavior into a series of internal segments, one can observe that the verbal expression is found always at the end of the activity and contains some of the verbal totality.

In examining this form of speech, Levina indicates that reflected in it most frequently are not the details of the situation and activity but their common scheme. This observation clarifies the psychological meaning of this form of speech. Speech, having been connected to the intellectual activity and having reflected it, separates it from the situation in exactly the same fashion as it isolates and abstracts the individual elements of the situation. By these means the child translates the essence of the task into a verbal plan and envisions new conditions for the flow of the entire intellectual process. These conditions permit him to abstract from the actual situation, the visual field, and to act in terms of the new verbal plan.

Analysis of experimental data concerning the third stage of the development relating speech and thinking indicates a movement of this development along the direction of greater and greater verbalization of intellect and intellectualization of speech. Speech, which earlier concluded activity, now begins to anticipate it. The child begins to think out loud. Thus, at this stage of development the child's egocentric speech may be characterized, as was done by Piaget, in the form of the child's monologue. It may be defined by his formula, "The child talks with himself as if he were thinking out loud." Speech here no longer follows the child's activity, copying it as was the case during the initial stages of development, but now dictates and determines the child's activity. Whenever the child at this stage of development participated in a game called "silence," in which he was not permitted to talk, all his attempts at play were paralyzed; his behavior became disorganized and he experienced complete failure in the solution of given problems (studies by Levina). Conversely, whenever the child, while making attempts to act directly, was given an instruction, e.g., "Tell me how are you going to reach that," a positive effect on the problem's solution was observed. The insertion of verbal expression into the process of solving practical problems permits the child to grasp mental connections that go far beyond the limits of the visual field, creating opportunities for solving problems that present unsurmountable difficulties for anthropoids.

Lyublinskaya, having analyzed a preschool child's expressions in the process of solving a problem, also isolates two forms of speech that seem to fulfill distinct functions in the child's activity. On the one hand is the "speech of play," expressing a child's emotional relationship to a situation, and on the other is the "speech—question" form of speech, directed toward the establishment of new connections and relationships that have not yet been obtained by the child. The planning function belongs primarily to the second form of the child's expressions, which directs his activity (28). Lyublinskaya's investigation indicates that in the process of solving practical problems and overcoming difficulties associated with the fulfillment of practical activity the child, for the first time, begins to form questions pertaining to the reasons for such difficulties. The appearance of such questions is extremely important, for it demonstrates the emergence of the child's initial ideas concerning causative connections. Furthermore, the questions exert an essential influence on the process of solving a practical problem, adding to the activity an aspiration for the search for correct solution and to the processes of thinking a definite directionality.

The greatest ability for inquiry at this age is formed in connection with the nurturing influences of the adult. Whenever in a practical problem-solving situation a preschooler encounters difficulties in discovering causes, for example, for the breakdown of his toy, and his attempts at fixing the mechanism are of chaotic nature, a question from an adult makes his search for the causes and the activity related to removing the impairments in the mechanism more goal-oriented and organized. As a result of such mutual activity with an adult, where the adult only guides the child in the search for causes and the child independently discovers them and executes the necessary practical actions to remove them, he forms an ability for inquiry prior to the commencement of practical activity. Such a preliminary inquiry even in its general form—"What interferes? What is broken?"— contributes to a more organized and directional nature of the activity. Granted that in the process of solving practical problems the preschool child can fairly easily raise a question and his actions due to this impact will begin to show a directional character, in the sphere of mental activity his logical reasonings emerge appreciably later and are connected with the demarcation of cognitive problems, with the appearance of cognitive relationships to reality.

Vygotsky's studies have raised several questions for future investigators: by what means do verbal expressions lead to basic changes in the child's intellectual functioning, and how do verbal expressions in the process of solving practical problems acquire planning functions essentially influencing the course of such a solution? Vygotsky has expressed a general conception pertaining to the direction in which one should move in order to search for the answer to these questions. He wrote: "Speech enters as a necessary integral aspect into the judicious activity of the child, is intellectualized, engaging the mind in these initial goal-oriented actions, and begins to serve as a means for the formation of intention and of a plan in the more complex activity of the child" (49). However, he did not investigate the basic mechanisms of the intellectualization of speech in the course of practical activity, focusing his attention on the study of the influence of aspects of speech on the course of the child's thinking processes. This brought about in due time the appropriate reproach concerning his overevaluating the role of speech in the course of the child's intellectual development.

Investigations by Luria in the area of semantic analysis of the child's speech have shown convincingly that, during the early stages of development (younger preschool age), the child understands the expression or verbal instruction directed to him only to the extent to which it is directly related to a given concrete situation and does not contradict the elementary logic of practical activity mastered by children (24, 27). The experiments by Zinchenko and Kontseva (19) indicate that children three-four years of age understand quite well, for example, the relation "over" and "under," and carry out the corresponding instructions if the demands embodied in them correspond to the customary relationships of things and to the accustomed activity with them. So, the children unmistakably carry out such instruction as: "Put the cover on the ink bottle" or "Put a checker-piece under the table." However, they show a lack of ability and begin to make mistakes whenever they are told: "Put the ink bottle under the cover" or "Do things in such a way that the table would be under the ink bottle." If one takes such instructions literally, then they contradict the accepted logic of action—and this disorients the child.

Thus, during the early stages of development, speech moves along as if immediately following the actions and only subsequently, after the child has had experience with practical actions, may it exert an influence on their later course. The words of the child's speech may fulfill a planning function only to the extent to which they have acquired a specified meaning and have become the carriers of well-known generalizations. Initially, the child forms these generalizations in the process of his objective activity, during practical acquaintance with the surrounding environment.

In a series of investigations directed by Leontiev (Bozhovich, 6; Zaporozhets, 52, 54, 55; Asnin, 2, and others), the process studied was that of the formation and the utilization of generalizations by preschool children and those of younger school age during the solution of a series of similar practical problems. In contrast to the intuitive type theories linking the intellectual solution with a "direct observation of relationships" to "the closure of integral structures," etc., these studies showed that the intellectual process becomes available only on the basis of transferring the method of action, which was formed in the course of solving one problem, to a second problem—similar but not identical with the first. Initially, the child accomplishes transfer only on the basis of the external similarity between situations; however, later—in the preschool age—he begins to catch the internal mechanical connections in relation to objects and, while solving a series of similar simpler types of mechanical tasks, grasps the principle that unites them and forms the corresponding generalization.

This process was thoroughly studied by Bozhovich (6). In one series of experiments, the child sat at a table that had a lever on a metallic axis attached to its top. The lever in the form of a wooden ruler was positioned frontally in relation to the child at a distance longer than the length of his arm. A picture that the child was required to reach was fastened to one of the ends of the lever. To the other end, attached by a movable connection, was a stick, the end of which was in the sphere of his arm's reach. A preschooler three-five years of age attempting the solution of this problem usually tries at the beginning to reach the picture directly with his hand. Then, whenever this fails he pays attention to the lever and the attached stick, grabs it, and pulls it toward him. As a result of this action, the lever turns on its axis and the picture moves further away from the subject. Direct perception of the situation leads the child to believe that one should pull the obtained object toward himself, but under the conditions of the task this leads to the negative result—the logic of the instrument requires that one should perform an opposite action. The child makes an attempt first to get out of the predicament utilizing, as one may say, reserve capacities of old methods of action. Only subsequently—as a result of the experience with application of several similar instruments—does he catch the common principle of their use.

A new aspect of the problem of interrelationship between thinking and speech, as contrasted with the one observed by Levina in her work, was discovered in the next series of experiments.

An investigation by Bozhovich introduced corrections into the existing notion concerning the interrelationship of thinking and speech. According to Levina's study these relationships came about in the following sequence. Initially, a solution is obtained within the realm of direct action. The subject makes a series of movements, which lead to a result through one way or another. This stage only anticipates intellectual activity. Thereafter, a higher level of solution is noted, consisting of the inhibition of impulsive actions and the appearance of dynamic displacements in the perceptual field, as a result of which there emerges, enclosed and seemingly preplanned, the motor solution as a whole. Further development consists in this, that the movement of visual images in the subject's perceptual field is replaced by a "movement" of words, i.e., movement of signs representing objects. Now it is not the combinations of things (first stage) nor the visual representations of these things (second stage) that is formed, but words as realistic substitutes for both. This, then, is the stage for inclusion of speech as an indispensable link in planning the intellectual process.

Bozhovich made an attempt to shift children to the stage of solving problems intellectually independent of the direct influence of the actual situation. This he did by employing inclusion of speech for the purpose of guiding the planning of actions, by relying on the instruction of the experimenter: "You first tell me how are you going to go about getting it and then you will do it." The investigation showed that such an inclusion of speech does not in principle change the course of the process. Some of the children simply refused to fulfill the instructions, i.e., not paying attention to it; they again renewed direct and impulsive attempts and only as a result of these attempts came upon a solution to the problem. Another group of children, though planning their actions, made the same kinds of mistakes in their verbal plan that occurred in their movements. Finally many children were expressing only verbally the already-obtained solution. Here speech did not direct the intellectual process but was itself determined by it. Bozhovich writes:

Thus, the results of this investigation from the point of view of our proposition concerning the function of speech in the solution of problems, involving mechanical connections and relationships, appear negative. If the child did not catch the actual relationships in a given situation, then in his speech he only reinforced his own initial incorrect understanding; however, if he immediately understood the principle of the activity correctly, then in his speech he also gave adequate answers. Thus, in the process of our investigation it became clear that the child does not simply 'think via speech', but that there are more complex relationships in which quite frequently we have what appears to be a reverse process of the translation of a child's thoughts into speech. The pure mechanical inclusion of speech, i.e., substitution of a movement by a word, was found to be ineffective in changing anything in the nature of the intellectual operations, and conversely the speech itself, taken from its external side, was found to be subservient to the activity and seemingly dragged behind the intellectual act (6; pp. 52-53).

Further investigations were needed to resolve the question concerning the internal mechanisms of man's intellectual behavior, relatively independent of the influence of the immediate situation. The solution of this problem called for new methodological applications.

The preliminary observations by Bozhovich showed that not every kind of speech that externally appears to be homogeneous is such in reality. This raised the issue of analyzing the meaning of the word, i.e., that generalization conveyed by the word. On the basis of her own experimental data and the results of investigations on the formation of understanding directed by Vygotsky, Bozhovich formed the following connection between speech and thinking:

A word is indeed a necessary intermediary link in thinking. Its inclusion in the intellectual operations is of principal significance to the development of human forms of thinking. However, the word enters not as a replacement of a thing, not in the quality of an element composing only 'the verbal field', but as a pivot in the development of generalization and a material carrier of generalization, i.e., as an internal aspect, and not only as an element in the material composition of thinking (6; p. 63).

Using these assumptions as a point of departure, Bozhovich further studied the dynamic relationships between the level of development of the child's verbal generalizations and the extent of transfer, i.e., the level of development of his intellectual operations.

The investigations by Leontiev and Asnin indicate that the child's intellectual solution of a problem concerning mechanical connections and relationships emerges as a result of the child's generalization of his experience in utilizing a series of analogous implements by transferring the principle related to the solution of one problem to another, similar to the first one.

An investigation by Zaporozhets showed that older preschoolers (five-seven years), having acquired a corresponding practical experience, are able to solve complex tasks pertaining to mechanical connections and relationships. The child during this age not only succeeds with a problem requiring the use of ready-made mechanical systems, representing a combination of levers, blocks, etc., but he can also introduce an essential change into the mechanical system for the problem's successful solution (52, 55). For example, whenever it is necessary, he changes a lever of the first kind into a lever of the second kind. In another case, he places a ruler with an opening on the nail that is driven into the table, thus constructing the lever that is necessary for the goal's attainment.

The utilization of mechanical connections and relationships becomes so common for some older preschoolers that even in those circumstances where a straightforward method of activity would be more appropriate, the child consistently makes an attempt to apply a complex principle. Thus, one child was constantly trying to use a pivot as a lever instead of simply taking it off the nail and using it as a long stick.

The formation and application of generalizations during various stages in the development of thinking are directly connected with the solution of practical problems. In their content, structure, and method of functioning these generalizations are determined by the nature of practical activity and depend directly on those changes which the activity undergoes.

The thinking of the preschool child undergoes restructuring along with expansion of the sphere of his objective activity and the formation of new systems of operations, associated with a common purpose of objects within the household and with simpler types of instruments used in everyday life.

Already by his second year, the child begins to utilize primitive means in reaching for a distant object, e.g., a rope, a stick, a pencil, etc., thus widening the sphere of his hands' movements. Thereafter, under the influence of adults he gradually learns to use simpler instruments in the household—cup, bowl, spoon, fork. By the end of the pre-preschool age, some children begin to use a hammer, scissors, etc. The simpler forms of manual labor thus become accessible to the preschooler. These facts are commonly known, but their psychological significance has not been fully uncovered. In part, the question is raised whether the application of various means is only a common accumulation of new motor abilities, or whether it evokes the qualitative reconstruction of the child's activity. The results of investigations that have been conducted recently favor the second alternative.

In order to understand the significance of instrument utilization in the child's psychological development, it is necessary to distinguish the internal and the external aspect of the matter. To make judgments concerning the emergence of instrumental operations in a child, it is not sufficient merely to point out the external fact—the child's utilization of instruments. It is necessary to determine to what extent his actions have been restructured in correspondence with the new methods of solving a problem, since not every kind of operation with an instrument is a proper instrumental operation.

A failure to recognize this has led some authors (Köhler, Bühler, and others) to a false resolution of the question. Having determined that in the second year of life the child already guesses how to utilize a stick for the attainment of a given goal, they assumed that the child had mastered the principle of instrumental operation and that it only remained for him to expand this principle further to a more encompassing range of human instruments.

In reality, the development follows another path. An instrument in the initial stages actually enters into the composition of the child's manual movements without changing their structure. In actions with instruments, the child initially utilizes the reservoir of manual operations that he has already formed during the period of his development involving grasping movements and direct manipulation of objects. And only later, under the influence of his experience in the utilization of instruments, does there appear a restructuring of his activity; instrumental operations are formed in the literal sense of the word.

Until such a time as children begin to utilize implements like a stick, they have no special needs for restructuring their manual movements. The stick normally serves only as the extension of an arm, and its movements in the process of solving a problem only reproduce the typical manual movements of reaching, etc. The use of differentiated human instruments is quite another matter. Even some of the most elementary ones are constructed according to principles of the simpler types of physical machines, and the hand that uses them must quite often execute movements contradictory to those it would be executing under analogous conditions if it were to operate independently. It is necessary to press downward in order to raise something upward and push something away from oneself in order to bring something else toward oneself. Here the hand movements must submit themselves to the logic of the instrument's movements, which makes up the nucleus of instrumental operations. A shift to a new type of constructing operations creates great difficulties for the child. Initially the child, even during utilization of differentiated human instruments, makes an attempt to use the old reservoir of manual operations; however, this leads him to a series of situations with negative results.

A shift to instrumental operations is quite clearly evident in the child's use of a spoon—one of the first instruments of the culture that he learns to utilize. In the beginning the little one acts as if he were raising to his mouth not a spoon but his fist. From a functional point of view, at this stage the spoon is nothing more than an extension of his hand. He carries it to his mouth not worrying about the position in which the spoon is found, and most of the stuff contained in the spoon is spilled. The logic of this elementary instrument, which the child masters only as a result of relatively prolonged training, is that through any movements of the hand it is possible to accomplish lifting a full spoon in a horizontal postion to his mouth's level and only thereafter putting it into his mouth.

An experimental investigation of different manual and instrumental operations was conducted by Galperin (13). In special trials children of different ages were required to retract from the bottom of a wooden box ("a well") different kinds of objects with the help of a special little shovel, the blade of which was at right angles to the handle, just as in a hoe. In order to get the object, it was necessary to put the blade of the shovel under it, to secure it on the blade, and then to lift the shovel so as not to drop the object. As indicated by the results, this complex co-ordination of movement created considerable difficulties for the child. For the two-year-old children pure manual operations were quite frequent during the solution of this problem. While lifting an object with the shovel, the child bends his arm at the elbow as if the shovel were actually an extension of his arm, and the blade—his hand, holding the toys lying on it. However, since the attributes of a shovel are different from those of a hand, the shift to the conditions of manual operation leads to failure, and the object falls off the blade as soon as it departs from the horizontal position.

In contrast, the four—five-year-old children in this situation en-tirely master the necessary instrumental operation. Their hands' movement rigidly adheres to the logic of the instrument's move-ment. Extremely varied movements of hands and of the entire body are called upon here only to secure the vertical raising of the shovel through a lift. In difficult situations the child leans forward and to the side, twisting his chest to the right and twist-ing his right hand by the movement of the elbow upward. He moves around the instrument; this line of movement becomes the axis for the child's entire system of movement.

Of special interest is the shift between these two extreme points in the formation of instrumental operations. It was found that the two-year-old child somehow finally succeeds with the task presented to him. However, at the beginning he approaches it by applying the old system of manual operations to the new condi-tions. The reserve possibilities of the old system are utilized, which are mobilized in the sphere of the arm's direct movement only under conditions of special difficulties (for example, when-ever it becomes necessary to support the object with the elbow because the hand is occupied, or whenever it becomes necessary to support the object on the back surface of the hand). In a simpler case the little one, while lifting the object, stops thoughtlessly tilting the shovel into different directions and acts with greater carefulness, making an effort not to change the position of his hand, similar to what he does whenever he retracts an object from somewhere directly with his hand, having grasped the object not quite adequately and being afraid that with a different position of the hand he will drop it. Applying the old system of manual operations to the new conditions provides a realistic motor background for the formation of a new system of instrumental operations and mobilizes certain motor components that will enter into the composition of the newly formed entity. However, as the investigation shows, this shift, even though prepared by the antecedent development of the child's activity, does not occur spontaneously and includes in an overt or a covert form the training of the child by an adult who demonstrates certain commonly formed methods of utilizing the instrument.

An investigation of the development of instrumental movement in pre-preschool and preschool age conducted by Neverovich demonstrates that at a given level of development, having mastered the system of movement connected with the use of an object (spoon, comb, scissors, hammer, etc.), the child discovers a means of transferring the acquired method of activity to a series of similar things and is even capable of executing it, simulating it, in the absence of the object.

A practical familiarization with the commonly formed methods of utilizing objects of the domestic environment during the preschool years undergoes a special process of "crystallization," which imparts a specific human character to the child's initial ideas that reflect relatively simple connections and relations between objects. These originally practical, objective, or, as some authors call them, functional concepts compose the semantic aspect of the child's speech, permitting him to fulfill that planning function in relation to activity that was discussed above. The verbal expressions of a preschooler during the solution of practical problems may fulfill a planning function only when the meanings of the words reflect a known general experience in activities with definite objects. If such a type of generalization is absent, then verbal expressions do not help in solving the problem facing the child.

This proposition has to be especially emphasized since some psychologists tend to ascribe to speech the function of primary reason in the intellectual development of the child. In discussing this, they cite the evidence available in the psychology of the deaf and dumb, which apparently shows that with a retardation in the development of speech the thinking of a child remains at a very primitive level, corresponding to the intellectual level of some higher animals.

Zaporozhets (54, 56) studied the visual-motor thinking of deaf and dumb preschool children who were quite untrained in speech or were at a very early level of such development. The intellect of these children was investigated by the method of transfer. The child was required to solve a series of elementary mechanical problems similar in principle but not identical in their external form. This method permitted one to observe the formation of generalizations and the nature of their utilization in a situation involving the solution of new problems.

The investigation showed that the content and the structure of actions of a deaf and dumb child, one who has not yet been taught speech, differ essentially from the most complex actions of higher animals that always retain a direct instinctual character. Relying on his experience in acquiring the use of objects that have a definite, commonly fixed purpose, the child learns to depart from the external similarity between objects and to generalize according to their functional cues. The generalizations obtained in this fashion have a specifically human character (functional ideas) and present the child with possibilities for solving mechanical problems involving connections and relationships that remain inaccessible to higher animal anthropoids. Furthermore, generalizations of the new type serve the deaf and dumb child as a prerequisite for the cognitive mastering of acoustic and mimical speech and for a transfer to higher forms of interaction with other people. The investigation results point to the inappropriateness of examing the role of speech in the child's intellectual development apart from the general character of his activity, apart from his experience of practical familiarization with the objects and events of the surrounding environment.

The data indicate extensive changes in content as well as in forms of visual-motor thinking during the preschool age. The structuring of relationships with people and the objective world and the appearance of new types of activity expand the child's mental horizon and thereby make available to him, as well as permit him to comprehend, more penetrating existing connections between phenomena. In his own actions the child begins to orient himself not only toward the external, directly perceived relationships of objects, which is commonplace in the pre-preschool age, but also toward more penetrating, often not directly observable, simpler mechanical connections. A more important role in this transfer is attributable to the generalization of the child's experience in the area of practical familiarization with the methods of utilizing objects, simpler types of domestic instruments, and their publicly formulated purposes. A change in the content of the child's visual-motor thinking leads to a change in its structure. In using his general experience, the child, while reasoning in terms of a verbal plan, is capable of mentally preparing and stipulating the nature of his subsequent actions.

Thus, the preliminary consideration and subsequent execution—aspects of intellectual activity—still undifferentiated from one another during the pre-preschool age, acquire for the preschool child relative independence and enter into complex relationships with one another.

In contrast with the notion of many bourgeois psychologists who treat practical intellect as a lower, primitive form of mentality, as if it developed in isolation from the general formation of the child's thinking, it is necessary to emphasize that between the visual-motor and so-called discursive thinking there exists a deep and two-sided connection. On the one hand, the child's experience of direct actions with objects during the solution of simple practical problems prepares the necessary foundation for the emergence of discursive thinking. On the other hand, the development of discursive thinking changes the nature of objective actions and creates the possibility for a change from the elementary form of visual-motor thinking to the more complex form of an adult's intellectual activity, which is observed during the solution of practical problems.

The conditions for and the mechanisms of a change from a visual-motor to a discursive type of thinking were studied by Minskaya under the direction of Zaporozhets (33). The methodology of the investigation was constructed according to the principle of transfer developed by Leontiev and Zaporozhets. The materials consisted of problems in establishing simpler mechanical connections and relationships under different sets of conditions.

In the first series of experiments, the children solved problems in a practical fashion, operating real levers which were attached to the experimental table; in the second series, they narrated, by relying on their imagination, how it was possible to solve the problem; in the third series, the children narrated the possibilities of solving similar problems whose conditions were presented to them or were described to them verbally. Table 24 presents the data pertaining to the problem solutions by the preschoolers in the three series of experiments (percentage of solved problems is indicated).

The highest percentage of solved problems is found when the problems were presented in terms of a visual-motor plan. Even the youngest preschoolers under these conditions attain 55 percent correct solutions; among the older ones these problems are solved almost totally (96.3 percent). In presenting the children with analogous problems via a visual-figurative plan, the number of correct solutions throughout the entire preschool period is

Table 24.
Change from Visual-Motor to Discursive Thinking in Problem Solving

Age (years)	Problems		
	Visual-Motor Plan	Visual-Figurative Plan	Verbal Plan
3-4	55	17.5	0
4-5	85	53.8	0
5-6	87	56.4	15.0
6-7	96	72.0	22.0

smaller than in the experiments of the first series. The number of problems solved under the conditions of a verbal plan is even smaller than the number of the second series. The children three-four and four-five years of age who gave a relatively high percentage of correct solutions within the visual-motor plan were not able to solve the problems under the verbal plan conditions. The data obtained indicate the presence of a definite sequence in the development of specific forms of thinking during preschool age. Initially, visual-motor thinking is formed; right after it visual-figurative thinking; and finally, verbal thinking.

According to this investigation, the effectiveness in solving the problems presented in terms of the visual-motor plan depends essentially on the nature of the orienting-exploratory activity performed by the children in relation to the objective conditions of the problem. Four types of orienting-exploratory activity were identified. In the first type (primitive-chaotic), orienting reactions toward conditions of the problem are absent; the children explore the furnishings of the room and look at the experimenter. However, they do not pay any attention either to the goal or to the lever with the help of which the goal may be reached. In the second type, the child focuses completely on the goal which has to be reached; however, the lever still remains unexplored. The third type of orienting activity (visual-motor) is associated with the exploration of not only the goal, but also the lever connected with it. The fourth type has a purely visual character; the child observes the relationships of the lever's individual components and then, on the basis of this preliminary investigation of the problem's conditions, immediately performs the correct practical solution.

It was observed that the orienting-exploratory type of activity exerts the decisive influence on the solution's effectiveness. Among all age groups, the number of correctly solved problems increased according to the degree of change from the chaotic orientation (the first type) to the visual (the fourth type). The greatest number of problems solved by the children of all age groups were under the conditions of visual orientation (the fourth type). Further, correct solution of certain problems is even possible under conditions of the lower types of orientation if they are presented in terms of the visual-motor plan.

Thus, the study demonstrates that there is a history to the solution of problems in terms of a visual-motor plan. Under the conditions of the higher, fourth type of orientation (visual orientation), it approaches in its nature the solution of problems given under conditions of a visual-figurative plan.

It is possible to assume that the experience accumulated by the child during the solution of problems presented to him under the conditions of a visual-motor plan may, under certain conditions, exert a decisive influence on the shift to visual-figurative and verbal thinking. The shift from visual-motor thinking to visual-figurative and verbal thinking depends on the degree of forming higher types of orienting-exploratory activity. Consequently, problems presented in terms of a visual-motor plan may be solved by the child on the basis of different forms of orienting activity—from simpler to most complex. But the problem presented in terms of a verbal plan cannot be solved under the conditions of an orienting activity of a lower type.

Minskaya's investigations also indicate that the experience obtained by the child in the process of the visual-motor solution of the problem is necessary for his shift to visual-figurative and verbal thinking; however, not just any kind of such experience facilitates transfer. The visual-motor experience of solving the problems per se is not of main significance, but what form and content of orienting-exploratory activity the child has formed as a result of such an experience is important.

It is obvious that solving problems according to the verbal plan demands orientation not only toward immediate conditions, but also toward a plan involving representations connected with speech. Minskaya, in another series of experiments, trained children to solve problems according to the visual-motor plan in such a way that first there emerged an orienting-exploratory activity related to the essential components of the lever, and secondly, there was verbal interaction among the children. Such training showed a great influence in the shift to solving problems presented in terms of visual-figurative and verbal plans. The number of younger children who were able to solve the problems within these plans increased considerably; the number of older children solving these problems reached 100 percent. The data of these series of experiments indicate that the shift from visual-motor thinking to visual-figurative and verbal thinking is performed on the basis of a change in the nature of the orienting-exploratory activity, first as a result of the replacement of chaotic and motor orientation by visual, and thereafter, by mental thinking.

Thus, during the preschool age there is a shift from visual-motor thinking to visual-figurative, and thereafter, to verbal thinking. The decisive condition for such a shift is the child's acquisition of experience of solving problems in terms of the visual-motor plan. However, such an experience exerts its influence only in the case when in solving problems according to the visual-motor plan higher types of orientation toward the conditions of the problem are formed and the verbal forms of interaction become activated. The latter is especially important for a shift to solving problems in terms of a verbal plan.

The Development of Reasoning in a Preschool Child

Just as the thinking of pre-preschool age children operates exclusively within the visual-motor form and is not separable from his practical and playful activity, the intellectual processes of a preschooler acquire a relative independence and appear in the form of special theoretical action-reasonings.

Near the end of the pre-preschool age, the child expresses judgments while observing one or another set of phenomena or while acting with objects. These judgments are best characterized as isolated instances in the general flow of practical and playful activity and are not yet united into one whole, i.e., they do not form any particular plan of thinking. The unification and agreement of separate judgments among themselves that lead to the formation of simpler deductions, i.e., the emergence of thoughts relatively independent of the direct perception and manipulation of objects, occurs during the preschool age.

The pre-preschool age child, in forming generalizations regarding the observed phenomena, does not present himself with any kind of specific cognitive tasks. His generalizations appear, one may say, as a by-product of practical and playful actions. A special cognitive task only begins to be isolated during the preschool age. A characteristic expression of the emergence of such a task are the endless questions of "why," which the preschooler raises with the adult and which touch upon all kinds of different aspects of reality. "Why is the rain falling? Why do we have to water the plants? Why is the doctor examing the patient? Where do the stars come from? Can a tractor carry a little house if one were to put the house on a set of wheels? If all the water from the river goes into the sea, then where does it go from there?" Such are some of the questions of a six-year-old child.

One can't assume, as Piaget suggested, that the preschooler raising such questions is not concerned with the trustworthiness of responses and is ready to be satisfied by any kind of fabrication. Obviously, in such cases, whenever the adult refuses to help him and the area of the facts in which he is interested is totally unknown to him, the child is forced sometimes to resort to accidental analogies and constructions of fantasy. For example, a girl of five, sitting under the window in the evening when her mother was busy baking a shortcake, asked: "Where do the stars come from?" Mother, being occupied by her own task, did not find an answer to this difficult question immediately. Then the child said: "I know how it is done. They make them out of the leftovers of the moon." Apparently, the girl saw how her mother was cutting a large circle out of the dough and from the leftovers was making little ones. This then served as a basis for her theory of the origin of the stars.

However, in a case where the child is able to rely on already-known facts, he is stricter in his judgments and demands more from the adult's explanation. For example, a five- and one-half-year-old boy who lives in a mountainous region asked: "Where did the rain come from?" The adult responded that the wind brought the rain. The child remained unsatisfied with the answer and said: "If the wind has brought it, then it means that it was there earlier, when the wind was still not there. The rain is made in the mountains [apparently he had in mind the clouds that were covering the tops of the mountains], and later the wind brings it here." Following the question "why?" the child is confronted with a definite congitive task, and he makes an attempt to solve it by any kind of means at his disposal.

The cognitive problems of a preschooler acquire a distinctive character. As a matter of fact, the solution of intellectual problems is carried out by him not in a context of cognitive activity or learning activity, as it is by a schoolchild, but in connection with practical and playful motives. In the younger preschoolers, there is a general tendency to convert an intellectual problem into a playful one. In Boguslavskaya's experiments (5), the little ones, rather than classifying the objects in terms of specific signs, began instead to spread them out on the table in a certain order and played with them, i.e., performed actions quite different from the ones involved in solving an intellectual problem. But even when the child takes on a cognitive task and attempts to solve it, the practical or playful motives that arouse him to a particular type of activity transform the problem and provide a distinctive characteristic to the directionality of the child's thinking. It is very necessary to take into account this particular aspect of the child's thinking in order to be able to evaluate correctly the potentialities of his intellect.

Frequently it appears to an adult that the reasons for the child's inability to solve problems presented to him is his insufficient mastery of corresponding intellectual operations or his inability to attain the necessary level of thinking. In reality, a distinctive solution is given because the child has changed the perception of the problem to correspond with the motivation stimulating him. In experiments by Kontseva directed by Zaporozhets (19), the child was required to select from stories one whose content resembled the plot of a fable by Krylov, "A Swan, a Crab, and a Pike." Among the stories there was one that resembled the fable in its internal content: this story told how the children were quarreling with one another and were not able to agree on some type of mutual play, and to what unpleasant results the whole thing led the children. Another story resembled the fable only externally: it included detailed descriptions of a crab's life in a river and of its relationships with the pike. It was found that for the majority of small children, the content of the second story most closely resembled the content of the fable. Why did the children come to this conclusion? Initially, it may appear that the cause lies in the relatively low level of generalization ability in a child. The children equated events on the basis of external similarity and did not understand the deeper essential connections and relationships between them. Because of it, the allegorical meaning of the fable remained inaccessible to them.

However, subsequent conversations with the children showed that such a proposition is meaningless. The whole matter is not that the child was unable to observe the internal similarity between the stories; he did not do that because from the point of view of the problem confronting him these relationships are non-existent. When the child was further questioned whether or not there is a similarity between the story and the fable, then without hesitating too much he responded that there is: "In both they were all not cooperating with one another and not accomplishing anything." However, in spite of this the story about the crab and the pike is more similar to the fable since "in it, there is a further description about how they lived in the river and what they were doing there." It appears that the children under a certain set of conditions are capable of performing a juxtaposition of things in relation to the external as well as internal connections. But at times they prefer external connections as corresponding more to the problem confronting them. Consequently, they responded to the fable as a fairy tale in which the story is being told about the adventures of a swan, a crab, and a pike, and being taken in by their fate, they attached a special significance to the story of the animals' subsequent life. The content of this story, in reality, appeared to them closer to the content of the fable than the story of quarreling children.

The original relationship of a child to the intellectual task also emerges during the necessity for object classification. Vygotsky cites as an illustration the following case of grouping objects. Before the six-year-old child playing the game, "fourth is an odd one," were four pictures with images of a cup, a glass, a saucer, and a piece of bread. Whereas the school-age children under such a set of conditions separate the image of the bread and say that the remaining pictures may remain because they represent dishes the little one approaches the whole thing quite differently. He relates to the problem not as a pure problem in generalization, but is guided by the motives of experiential, practical expediency. He rejects the picture of the glass, arguing his actions in the following manner: "If I were to have breakfast, I would pour the milk into the cup and would eat the bread. Therefore, the glass is not necessary here. It's extra." It is necessary to point out that from the point of view of logical operations, the above-stated reasoning is irreproachable. Only the child's relationship to the problem, which leads him to substitute a mental solution of a lifelike problem for classification, is original.

Experiments by Kontseva (19) indicate a distinctive treatment of an arithmetic problem by preschoolers. Thus, they first are taken in by the experiential content of the problem, while deferring purely mathematical aspects for a later part of the plan. For example, a child was asked to finish a problem that had the following question: "Six tanks were rolling along, two of them got broken . . ."—and the child continued: "They were fixed and they continued on their way." New problem: "Mother ate four candies and gave two to her son. How many candies did they eat together?" The little one does not solve this problem, since he is disturbed by the description of the inequality depicted in it. He says: "And why did she give Michael so little? It should have been equally divided." While perceiving the content of the problem, the child first of all sees in it a description of certain realistic events in which specific numerical facts have only a secondary, auxiliary meaning.

The progress in the development of the preschooler's thinking presupposes extensive changes in the character of his activity, which is associated with the appearance of new cognitive motives different from the motives of play and practical activity. As experience from our institutions for children indicates, such changes indeed occur by the end of the preschool period with the corresponding organization of the developmental work. On the one hand, along with play activity there begin to form new types of learning activity; on the other hand, in the play itself there appear such newly formed activities as intellectual play, puzzles, etc.

Observations by Kistyakovskaya on puzzle-solving by preschoolers in the context of a playful situation indicate the following: whereas among the younger children playful elements predominate under these conditions, among the older children a goal to understand the principle of the puzzle's solution is observed. Other aspects, for example, the interest toward the process of the game itself or toward winning, which may appear as a consequence of a successful solution, clearly are placed as the last of priorities. Thus, for the older preschoolers new forms of intellectual activity are shaped, which are aroused by the motive of learning to solve difficult problems. Without this process of motive changes in a preschooler, it is impossible to understand the formation of the intellectual operations. The emergence of a cognitive problem brings to life a special internal intellectual activity that is directed toward solving a problem, namely, the process of reasoning.

In the little ones, these internal processes are not yet formed. For them, to solve a problem means first of all to act. So, in one of the experiments a three-year-old child was not able to figure out how to use a ruler in order to obtain an object that was placed very high. Then the experimenter told him, "Why are you always jumping, it is better that you stop and think how you can reach that!" The child answered to this quite assertively, "No need to think, one ought to reach." The problem presented itself to him from a purely practical, active aspect, and thinking about it appeared out of place for him.

However, gradually the child begins to encounter relatively complex, practical problems that require not only physical activity, but also preliminary thinking and analysis of the situation.

Some foreign psychologists have asserted that the preschooler is not capable of logical thinking, that he cannot reason sequentially, and consequently gets into contradictions with himself and reality without being aware of it. Thus, Stern thinks that the reasoning of the preschooler is transitional, i.e., that he moves from particular to particular bypassing generalization (46). Piaget assumes that the preschooler is alogical in his reasoning, that he does not even attempt to match his own judgments with one another (39). In discussing this, they usually refer to the accidental expressions of a child or else compel one to judge him on the basis of phenomena that are not known to the child, as was done by Piaget in his clinical conversations. For example, the child is asked: "Why does the sun hold itself up in the sky and not fall down to the earth?" He replies: "It is because it must shine." To the question; "Why doesn't a ship sink," the child replies, "Because the ship constantly spins its wheels and throws the water from underneath itself."

Material of this type does not permit one to formulate a correct proposition concerning the thinking of a preschool child. Our observations show that even the younger preschoolers under a specified set of conditions exhibit simple forms of reasoning, containing a movement of thought from partial to general as well as elements of deduction. However, these intellectual processes emerge only under specified conditions. A special organization of activity is necessary, providing the child with a realistic acquaintance with those connections and relationships between phenomena that must become the object of his reasoning. In this regard, the child's accidental expressions about the causality of a certain type of event or his answers to an adult's questions related to facts very little known to him cannot give a basis for characterizing the child's thinking. An investigation of the child's thinking has to be conducted under conditions such that one can be quite sure that the child is solving an intellectual problem presented to him, and that he is provided with concrete facts for corresponding generalizations.

In an experiment conducted by Zaporozhets and Lukov (56), the child was presented with a pan of water placed in front of him on a table along with a variety of different objects made out of metal, cellulose, wood, etc. The experiment was conducted in the form of a game that involved guessing. The experimenter showed an object and asked the child whether this object would swim or sink if it were placed in water. After the child had answered the question, he was given the opportunity to throw the object into the water. This served as a clarification as to whether or not the child guessed correctly. The trials continued for approximately half an hour so that the child was able to experience many objects. Among the objects there were many that resembled one another in some dimension (size, form, material); therefore, there was the possibility of forming certain generalizations and being guided by them in subsequent judgments. In order to clarify the extent to which the child was capable of substantiating his judgments, he was given additional questions, such as "Why do you think this will swim?" or "Why will this sink?" during the course of the experiment.

Under these conditions, even the younger children made an attempt to solve the problem, to guess correctly which object would sink and which would swim. However, the nature of their reasoning was very peculiar. Let us give corresponding illustrations from the inquiry with a child of three years three months:

Experimenter: (shows the child a match) "Will it swim?"

Child: "Yes."

Experimenter: "How about this disk?" (showing a brass disk) "Will it swim?"

Child: "No, it will not swim." (He throws it into the water and it sinks.)

Experimenter: "And why doesn't it swim?"

Child: "It doesn't hold itself on water."

The child is subsequently given a demonstration of a metallic needle, a nail, and a safety pin. He throws them into the water and argues that they sink because they are small. Then he is shown a piece of a match and he is asked, "Will this swim?"

Child: "No, it will sink."

Experimenter: "Why?"

Child: "It doesn't know how to swim."

Here a certain connection of judgments was formed that led the child to an unexpected conclusion. After it was observed that the nail and the needle had sunk, the child decided that the match would also sink, basing his thinking on the assumption that all little things sink. In this case, the child made a mistake. However, this mistake indicates that his separate thoughts are not integrated with one another but are connected on the basis of a simpler generalization. It is interesting that initially the child does not recognize the basis for his reasoning. He does not say that the match will sink because it is little. He simply declares that "it cannot swim." But, even here one clearly detects an elementary connection of judgment about a singular phenomenon through a known generalization.

For the four—five-year-old children, the reasoning about the objects that swim or sink acquires a more complex character. Thus, the experimenter in a conversation with a five-year-old girl, especially selected small objects that would swim in order to observe whether or not the child forms a corresponding generalization. He showed the child a pine needle, a piece of papier-mâché, and a little splinter. And the child replied: "It will swim. It is little and it is light." Here, on the basis of specially selected facts, the child not only arrived at a given generalization but consciously utilized it in the solution of the problem: "A splinter swims because it is little and it is light."

Such a generalization begins to exert an influence on the subsequent judgments of the child. However, since it is not quite fully perfected, the child makes certain characteristic mistakes. For example, the experimenter showed the child a small safety pin. In preliminary trials the subject correctly guessed that the pin would not swim. But now having come to the conclusion that small, light objects swim, she asserts that the safety pin will also swim. Having thrown the pin into the water and discovered that what happened did not support her supposition, the girl becomes a bit witty. She says, "The little pin is not so small. It expands in water." And in order to support her assertion she immerses her hand in the water and opens the pin. The child is so convinced of her own judgment that is is difficult for her to refute it even in the light of contradictory facts. However, does it mean then that the child is not aware of the contradictions, that she ignores reality whenever it does not correspond to her understanding? The observations show that this is not so.

The experimenter shows the child a small nail. The child says, "It will not swim even though it is small. You won't fool me anymore." The experiment with the safety pin was not carried out in vain. Under the influence of new facts, she rejected the initial generalization and is searching for a new basis for her reasoning. It is interesting that the child, even though arguing her own thinking and relying on the known generalization, does not make this generalization an object of her analysis. She only utilizes it as a means for guessing in the ongoing game. Whenever a particular means is found to be unacceptable, she rejects it and searches out another one.

Among six—seven-year-old children, the reasoning in a given situation acquires an even more complex and realistic character. The most characteristic aspect of this period consists of the fact that, along with the judgments concerning separate phenomenon, there is an ongoing detailed analysis of the understanding itself. The child not only forms generalizations but also corrects and perfects them. The formation of generalization becomes a special problem. Let us illustrate this with the following example:

The experimenter shows the child a key.

Child: "It will sink. It is heavy and it is made out of iron." (Experimenter shows a chunk of wood.)

Child: "It will swim. It is made out of wood."

Experimenter: "But earlier you said that heavy things sink. This chunk of wood is heavy."

Child: "Yes, I said that. But things made out of wood will swim anyway, even if the whole log is there." (Experimenter shows the child a tin box.)

Child: "It will sink. It is made out of iron."

The experimenter throws the box into water and the box swims. The child is dejected. He takes the box into his hand, looks at it, and says, "Even though it is made out of iron, it is empty inside. That's why it swims. Even an empty bucket swims."

Here, in the process of reasoning the child gradually works out an understanding that was brought into agreement with the observable events. Obviously, the understandings that the child uses to support his judgments are still far from perfect and are distinguished from understandings that he will acquire later in the course of studying physics. In spite of this, they include the generalization that was formed as a result of observing separate facts, which will be utilized in a series of subsequent deductions.

Thus, under appropriately facilitating conditions the preschooler forms relatively complex forms of reasoning. Gradually he learns to think independently, to align his judgments with one another and with reality, and not to fall into contradictions. Whenever the preschooler finds himself confronted with an interesting problem that he comprehends and when he can rely on the observation of facts that he understands, he then forms simpler types of logically correct reasoning.

Ulyenkova investigated the extent to which preschool children are capable of solving certain syllogisms (47). It was discovered that a correct independent deduction is available to only a few children at the third year. Noticeable gains are observed among children four years of age. Among the five—six-year-old children, more than half are capable of solving similar problems. However, the success of solving individual syllogisms varies even among the same children. This depends on the affinity of the problem to the child's experience, on the presence of the necessary general judgments in children, and on the degree of their exposure to concrete experience. For example, a general judgment such as "Wood burns" was present in all four-year-old children, whereas at the same time such an analogous general judgment as "Wood swims" was found only among a few (only among 4 percent of children of the same age).

The children with the smallest number of correct solutions were given additional training experience. Essentially, on the basis of direct actions with the objects or with the help of the experimenter's leading questions that actualized the child's previous experience, the training consisted of guiding the child in the formation of the necessary general supposition. After this, the children were again given the corresponding syllogisms. The results of training exerted a noticeable influence on the effectiveness of solution (Table 25: Roman numerals show the type of syllogisms-I or II; Arabic—percentage of solved problems).

After the training, only the youngest group of children (three-

Table 25.
Effect of Training on Solving Syllogisms in Preschool Children

Solution of Problem	Age (years)							
	3-4		4-5		5-6		6-7	
	I	II	I	II	I	II	I	II
Pretraining	0	0	4	4	20	20	38	38
Posttraining	0	0	52	40	96	88	100	98

four years old) showed no improvement; among the four—five-year-old children, the effectiveness of solution increased to 40-52 percent; and among the older children, to 88-100 percent. The results of training indicate that the formation of deductive conclusions in preschool children is directly related to the accessibility of the generalizations that serve as a basis for common judgments, and it is dependent on the child's ability to reflect various aspects of reality.

An analysis of the deductive judgments and of the errors encountered in the process resulted in the discovery of basic stages in the formation of deductive thinking in preschool-age children. At the first stage the child does not employ general propositions, and his assertions are either not supported at all or are augmented by the most casual substantiation. In the second stage the child already employs a general proposition; however, it still reflects reality inadequately. He makes an attempt to base his solutions on a given kind of generalization formed on the basis of accidental external cues. At the third stage the child employs a general proposition that to some extent approximates the existing aspects of reality and is not far from encompassing all possible cases. Finally, during the fourth stage the child employs a general proposition that correctly reflects reality; thus, correct deductions are made.

So, in solving the syllogisms associated with the general proposition that "all wooden objects swim," the children at the first stage do not utilize the generalization and, as a substantiation for the swimming ability of wooden objects, they assert that such objects will swim "because they want to wade," etc.; the children in the second stage rely on such generalizations as "Big ones swim and little ones don't" "Long ones swim, and round ones don't," etc. Children at the third stage use a general proposition of the following type: "The heavy ones sink and the light ones swim"; and finally, during the fourth stage the child operates on the basis of a general point of view that "all wooden objects swim."

These stages in forming deductive reasoning include many mutual transitions and may coexist in the child's mind, depending on the depth of his knowledge of the objects that he employs in his reasoning. It is necessary to point out that the shift from the first stage to the second is in principle different from the shifts to subsequent stages, for it is here that a new form of reasoning emerges, that is, general judgments and a shift from them to concrete cases.

The change from the second stage to the third stage and then to the fourth is defined by the child's deeper and deeper curiosity about reality and by the changes in bases that are used in forming common judgments. In making a generalization concerning the properties of objects, such as the ability of certain bodies to float, the children move from the form and size of objects to their weight and thereafter to their material. It is apparent that the developments from stage to stage are not directly determined by the child's age, but by the extent of his experience and by the perfection of his knowledge of objects and phenomena in the environment.

In examining various aspects of the child's reasoning ability, a related issue is his understanding of causal relationships. Piaget (39), on the basis of a special investigation designed to study the child's understanding of physical causality, concludes that the preschool age is governed by "precausality," i.e., there is an absence of real interest in the causes of physical phenomena as well as in causal explanations of such phenomena. According to Piaget, the first forms of the physical explanation of causality and the first questions about it are concerned with why a particular phenomenon takes place, and they appear around the age of seven. The preschool age is noted for the variety of distinctive forms of explaining causality: 1) psychological in conjunction with finalistic; 2) finalistic; 3) phenomenological; 4) participating; 5) magical; 6) moral; 7) artificial; 8) animistic. In this early investigation, Piaget connected the precausality that governs a child's explanation of physical events with egocentrism, the inseparability of "I" of the child from the surroundings, and as a result of this, with the absence of the occurrence of concrete cause-effect connections.

According to Piaget, only by the seventh-eighth year is a decline in precausality observed. The child then begins to distinguish physical causality, motives, and moral causes. He manifests interest in actual causality and exhibits the first forms of explaining physical causality. Piaget ties in the decline of precausality with the decline in egocentrism. Here, one observes the emergence of a clear understanding of "I" and, as a result, an understanding of the relationship of one's own point of view to those of other people: a possibility of coordinating one's own viewpoint with others. First of all, it becomes possible to exchange one's own individual point of view for a social one that imposes its own norms and patterns of logical thinking on the child. Essentially, one first encounters an opportunity for mastering human experience and subsequently for mastering causal explanations of physical phenomena. Basically, Piaget assumes that the training, the influence of adults, may indeed exert an important effect on the child's further development beginning with the seventh-eighth year of life.

Piaget's views pertaining to the general development of the child's thinking, as well as to the preschooler's understanding of physical causality, have been critically examined by both foreign and Russian psychologists.

An experimental study by Venger (48) investigated the understanding of causality by preschoolers. The first part of the investigation concerned itself with estimating the child's existing level of understanding. In the second part of the investigation, an attempt was made to produce changes in the understanding of causality by training. In order to clarify the existing level of comprehension, children were given a series of problems in which they were required to explain the cause of some physical phenomena. In the first series of experiments, the child was required to explain the reason for the sphere's falling when the cube was tilted (Series I-A) and why it did not fall when the sphere was attached to the cube by a nail (Series I-B); the fourth series required the child to explain the reason for the fall of a rectangular table that had only one leg; in the seventh series, it was necessary to show the cause for the fall of a ball on an inclined plane; during the tenth series, the child had to determine the cause for the flotation or submersion of a series of bodies in water. All of these basic series of experiments were conducted under conditions that provided the child with opportunities for actions with objects and with direct perception of corresponding events. Beside these basic series, I, IV, and VII, two additional experiments were conducted, in one of which the physical event was represented on a picture and in the second one, it was described verbally.

The data obtained in the original, as well as in the additional series, are presented in Table 26 (summary of percentages in all series of experiments). These data show that even children of the youngest age (three-four years) show understanding of causality to some extent. This understanding steadily grows during the preschool years. An obvious change in the understanding of causality comes about approximately at the age of five (the absence of

Table 26.
Understanding of Causality in Preschool Children

Age (years)	Absence of Explanation	Inadequate Explanation	Satisfactory Explanation
3-4	48.7	14.6	37.6
4-5	22.0	16.4	60.7
5-6	4.6	11.8	83.6
6-7	2.7	0.9	96.4

explanations drops to 4.6 percent and inadequate explanations to 11.8 percent).

From the cumulative data, it is difficult to distinguish the events that are more accessible to explanation from those that are less accessible to explanation. A separate analysis of the above data, where the children had the opportunity to act with the objects and to observe these phenomena directly, showed that understanding depends to a certain extent on the characteristics of such phenomena and upon the causal relationships lying at the foundation of these phenomena. Thus, the poorest results are observed in experiments involving the flotation of objects (25 percent of the cases lacked explanations and 47 percent gave inadequate explanations). Under these circumstances, the properties of objects that are necessary for flotation or submersion do not appear on the surface, but they have to be isolated by abstraction from other immaterial properties. This then is the essence of the difficulty confronting children in their explanation of causes for the flotation of objects.

Of some significance in the explanation of causality is the method of familiarization with the phenomenon. Whenever direct observation and action are the means of familiarization with the phenomenon, correct explanations are usually more frequent than when the familiarization is based on imagination or verbal description. Only during the older preschool age does one observe a decrease in this difference, this being connected with the appearance of new forms of orienting activity that permit problems to be solved by mental representation.

Depending on the age of the children, their experience, and the nature of the phenomena, there are different levels of understanding causality. First of all, the children isolate the external signs of the objects that can be easily identified by directly observing the influence of one object on another. Initially, the understanding of external causes is diffuse in nature. The children point to the cause of the entire situation in general without conducting any detailed analysis. Only later do there begin to be isolated elements of the situation that have a more direct relationship to the causes of the observed facts. Gradually, the children begin to understand that the causes of the phenomena may not necessarily be only in the external actions exerted on the objects, but also in properties of the objects themselves. Consequently, the directly perceived and frequently unessential properties of objects are initially identified and isolated. Thereafter, the more essential properties of objects become identified.

An important aspect in the development of understanding causality is the formation of generalizations. During the early stages of development, the children in their explanations refer to a singular analogous case; at a subsequent stage, their explanations acquire a more general character and they no longer rely on a single case, but on a known general proposition; the highest level of understanding observed among preschoolers is best described by the fact that the children begin to isolate and generalize connections and relationships, which exist between the objects or their properties, as causes of the phenomena. Thus, for example, Charles (five years of age), while explaining the fall of a table with broken legs, explained it as follows: "Because it was standing on one leg, it has many edges, it is heavy, and it is not supported."

Even though the levels of understanding the causes of phenomena cannot be closely tied in with age, i.e., among children of the same age one can observe different levels depending on the complexity of the phenomena and their affinity to the child's experience, there is still a clearly expressed general tendency. The development of the preschooler's understanding of causality according to data obtained in investigations by Venger, moves in the direction: 1) from the recognition of the external to the isolation of internal causes of a phenomenon; 2) from the undifferentiated, global understanding of causes to a more differentiated and precise explanation of them; 3) from the reflection of a singular cause of a given phenomenon to the reflection of a generalized principle.

The more inaccessible the phenomenon is to the experience of the child, the lower is the level of explaining its causes. Basically, this accounts for the fact that Piaget, when presenting the children with quite difficult problems whose solutions could not be based on the children's direct experience, obtained an unusually low level of understanding causal relationships in preschool children.

In order to clarify the dependence of the level of comprehension on the child's experience and the influence of adults from its dependence on training, Venger undertook a special experimental investigation in which she studied the influence of training on children's understanding the causes of the flotation of bodies (explaining the causes of this phenomenon seems to be the most difficult one for children). The training was conducted in several ways. In one method, on the basis of specially selected facts, a direct organization of the children's experience was obtained. The children were given pairs of floating or sinking objects selected on the basis of material (wooden and metallic), and they, having acquainted themselves practically with the facts about the floating or sinking of these objects in water, were required to form a generalization independently and to transfer it to other new objects. The experiment showed that under those conditions only half of the children satisfactorily explained the cause for floating.

Under another method of training, the children not only observed different objects floating or sinking in the water but were required also to separate the floating bodies from nonfloating ones on the basis of their experience and to characterize each group. The experimenter strived to make sure that each child would isolate the material from which the object was made and would point to it as the cause for floating. With this set of training conditions, directed toward the formation of adequate generalizations, it was possible to obtain a marked improvement in understanding the causes for the flotation of bodies with children of all ages. After such training even the youngest ones gave 40 percent correct explanations. The comprehension obtained under these conditions was general in nature and was easily utilized by the children in relation to new, formerly unfamiliar objects.

Thus, direct experience in and by itself is still insufficient for forming generalizations necessary for explaining the causes of physical phenomena. The child must be presented with not only a specially isolated problem of generalization, but also an organization for its formation. Only then does the generalization become the base for explanation. This demonstrates that the child is not a little Archimedes; that whereas Archimedes formulated principles independently, the child masters them under the guidance of adults and cannot independently and spontaneously form any kind of generalizations that adequately reflect reality. Furthermore, with an appropriate organization of the child's direct experience and with generalization in the preschool age, the child may reach an understanding of the real causes of certain physical phenomena.

The formation of causal thinking during the preschool age moves along the same path as the formation of thinking in general, as has been shown in a formerly presented investigation by Minskaya (33). The first cognitive problems are isolated in the process of playful activity, and the processes of thinking are entirely subjugated to playful or practical motivation. However, in the older preschooler the cognitive problem may subsequently emerge in its own context as a problem requiring the mastery of new knowledge.

The influence of activity motives on the course of operation of the thinking processes has been investigated in a number of experiments directed by Leontiev. For example, Asnin showed that the differences in the solution of similar intellectual problems among younger and older preschoolers are determined not only by the level of the development of their intellectual operations, but also by their distinctiveness of motivation. Whereas younger children are aroused to the solution of practical problems by a direct desire to reach a picture, a toy, etc., for the older children the decisive meaning acquires motives of competition, a desire to show one's own imagination to the experimenter, etc. (2).

The investigations by Boguslavskaya found that optimal conditions for the formation of understanding among younger preschoolers emerge in situations of play, for example, when the grouping of objects according to given signs is a necessary prerequisite for winning. For the older preschooler, better progress is noted not in play situations, but in exercises where the child begins to be guided by striving for the acquisition of new knowledge about the object. The psychological preparation of the child for school develops following this path. On the one hand, during preschool childhood the sphere of ideas is expanded and the intellectual operations necessary for the subsequent mastery of school subjects are formed. On the other, new motives of cognitive activity develop that make possible a systematic and conscious mastery of new knowledge.

References

1. Abel, T. M. Unsynthetic modes of thinking among adults: A discussion of Piaget's concepts. Amer. J. of Psychol., 1932. 44, p. 123-132.

2. Asnin, V. I. Pro rozvitok naochnodiyovogo misleniya u ditini. (Concerning development of the child's visual-motor thinking.) Pratsi respubl. nauk. konf. z pedagogiki i psikhologii. (Works of republic's scientific conference on pedagogy and psychology.) Vol. II. Kiev, 1941.

3. Baldwin, J. M. Dukhovnoye razvitiye detskogo individa i chelovecheskogo roda. (Mental development in a child and the race.) Moscow, 1912.

4. Blonsky, P. P. Pamyat i myshleniye. (Memory and thinking.) Moscow-Leningrad, 1935.

5. Boguslavskaya, Z. M. Razvitiye poznavatelnoy deyatelnosti detey doshkolnogo vozrasta v usloviyakh syuzhetnoy igry. (Development of cognitive activity in preschool children under conditions of games with a plot.) Izvestia APN RSFSR. Vyp. 64, 1955.

6. Bozhovich, L. I. Rech i prakticheskaya intellektualnaya deyatelnost. (Speech and practical intellectual activity.) Rukopis. (manuscript.) 1935.

7. Bühler, K. Die geistige Entwicklung des Kindes. (Mental development of a child.) Jena, Fischer, 1918.

8. Darwin, C. A biographical sketch of an infant. Mind, 2, 1877. 285-294.

9. Dennis, W. Historical beginnings of child psychology. Psychol. Bull., 1949, 46, 224-235.

10. Deutsche, J. M. The development of children's concepts of causal relations. Univ. Minn. Inst. Child Welfare Monographs, 1937, No. 13, 104.

11. Duncker, K. On Problem-Solving. (Trans. by L. S. Lees.) Psych. Monogr., 1945. V. 58, No. 5, IX-113.

12. Fraisse, P., Vautrey. La perception de l'espace, de la vitesse et du temps chez l'enfant de cinq ans (étude critique des travaux de J. Piaget). Enfance, 1952, 5, 1-20.

13. Galperin, P. Ya. Do pitaniya pro rol nastanovi v mislenii. (Concerning the role of a set in thinking.) Pratsi respubl. nauk. konf. z pedagogikii psikhologii. (Works of the republic's scientific conference on pedagogy and psychology.) Vol. II. Kiev, 1941.

14. Huang, J. Children's conception of physical causality: A critical summary. J. genet. psychol., 1943, 63, 71-121.

15. Humphrey, G. Thinking: An introduction to its experimental psychology. New York, Wiley, 1951.

16. Joanno. Le raisonnement mathématique de l'adolescent (entre 13 et 18 ans).

17. Koffka, K. Die Grundlagen der psychischen Entwicklung; eine einführung in die Kinderpsychologie. Osterwieckam Harz, A. W. Zickfeldt, 1921.

18. Köhler, W. The mentality of apes, New York, Harcourt, 2nd ed., 1927.

19. Kontseva, O. M. Umovi formovannya pochatkiv logichnogo mislennya u doshkilnikiv. (Conditions for the formation of the beginning of logical thinking in preschoolers.) Nauk. zap. in-tu psikhologii URSR. (Scientific notes of the URSR institute of psychology.) Vol. VI. Kiev, 1956.

20. Leontiev, A. N. K Teorii razvitiya psikhiki rebyonka. (Toward a theory of development of the child's psyche.) Sovetskaya pedagogika. (Soviet pedagogy.) 1945, No. 4.

21. Leontiev, A. N. Teoristicheskiye problemy psikhicheskogo razvitiya rebyonka. (Theoretical problems in the psychic development of the child.) Sovetskaya pedagogika. (Soviet pedagogy.) 1957, No. 6.

22. Ling, B. C. The solving of problem situations by the preschool child. J. genet. psych. 1946, 68, 3-28.

23. Lippman, W. Public opinion. New York, Harcourt Brace and Co., 1922.

24. Luria, A. R. (ed.) Rech i intellekt v razvitii rebyonka. (Speech and intellect in the development of the child.) Trudy psikhol. lab. AKV im. Krupskoy. (Works of the Krupskaya Psychological Laboratory of AKV.) Vol. 1. Moscow, 1928.

25. Luria, A. R. Puti razvitiya detskogo myshleniya. (Paths of development of child's thinking.) Yestestvoznaniye i marksism. (Natural science and marxism.) 1929, No. 2.

26. Luria, A. R. Razvitiye konstructivnoy deyatelnosti doshkolnika. (Development of constructive activity in the preschooler.) Sb. Voprosy psikhologii rebyonka—doshkolnika. (Questions of psychology of the preschooler.) Moscow-Leningrad, 1948.

27. Luria, A. R. and Yudovich, F. Ya. Rech i razvitiye psikhicheskikh protsessov u rebyonka. (Speech and development of psychic processes in a child.) Moscow. Izd-vo APN RSFSR, 1956.

28. Lyublinskaya, A. A. Prichinnoye myshleniye rebyonka v deystvii. (Causal thinking of a child in action.) Izvestia APN RSFSR. Vyp. 17, 1948.

29. Lyublinskaya, A. A. Vospitaniye myshleniya u detey. (Cultivation of thinking in children.) Doshkolnoye vospitaniye. (Preschool upbringing.) No. 12, 1951.

30. Lyublinskaya, A. A. Rol yazyka v umstvennom razvitii rebyonka. (The role of language in mental development of the child.) Uchyonyye zapiski LGPI im. Gertsena. (Scientific notes of Hertzen LGPI.) Vol. 112, 1955.

31. McHugh, G. Autistic thinking as a transitory phenomenon of childhood. Child devel., 1944, 15, 89-98.

32. Menchinskaya, N. A. Voprosy razvitiya myshleniya rebyonka v dnevnikakh russkikh avtorov. (Questions of development of the child's thinking as reported in diaries of Russian authors.) Uchyonyye zapiski in-ta psikhologii. (Scientific notes of the institute of psychology.) Vol. II. Moscow, 1941.

33. Minskaya, G. I. Perekhod ot naglyadno-deystvennogo k rassuzh dayushchemu myshleniyu. (A shift from visual-motor to discursive thinking.) Kand. diss. Moscow, 1954.

34. Murphy, G. Personality: A biosocial approach to origins and structure. New York; Harper, 1947.

35. Natadze, P. G. Genezis obrazovaniya ponyatiya. (Genesis of the formation of understanding.) Trudy Tbilisskogo gos. in-ta. (Works of Tbilisi State Institute.) Vol. XII, 1940.

36. Piaget, J. Child's Conception of Physical Causality. (Translated from the French.) New York, 1930.

37. Piaget, J. Problemy geneticheskoy psikhologii. (Problems of genetic psychology.) Voprosy psikhologii. (Questions of psychology.) 1956, No. 3.

38. Piaget, J. Origins of Intelligence in Children. (Translated from the French by Margaret Cook.) New York, 1956.

39. Piaget, J. Language and Thought of the Child. (Translated from the French.) New York, 1959.

40. Piaget, J. Comments on Vygotsky's critical remarks. Cambridge. MIT Press, 1962.

41. Pratt, K. C. Experimental studies of thought and reasoning. Psychol. Bull. 1928, 25, 550-561.

42. Rubinshtein, S. L. Osnovy obshchey psikhologii. (Basis of general psychology.) Moscow. Uchpedgiz., 1946.

43. Russell, D. H. Children's thinking. Boston. Ginn, 1956.

44. Sechenov, I. M. Izbrannyye filosofskiye i psikhologicheskiye proizvedeniya. (Selected philosophical and psychological studies.) Moscow, 1947.

45. Sikorsky, I. A. Psikhologicheskiye osnovy vospitaniya i obucheniya. (Psychological basis of upbringing and training.) Kiev, 1909.

46. Stern, W. Psikhologia rannego detsva. (Psychology of early childhood.) Izd. 2, 1922.

47. Ulyenkova, U. V. Psikhologia deduktivnykh umozaklyucheny u detey doshkolnogo vozrasta. (Psychology of deductive conclusions in preschool children.) Kand. diss. Moscow, 1954.

48. Venger, A. A. Razvitiye ponimaniya prichinnosti u detey doshkolnogo vozrasta. (Development of understanding of causality in preschool children.) Kand. diss. Moscow, 1958.

49. Vygotsky, L. S. Izbrannyye psikhologicheskiye issledovaniya. (Selected psychological investigations.) Moscow. Izd-vo APN RSFSR, 1956.

50. Wallon, H. De l'acte à la pensée; essai de psychologie comparée, Paris. Flammarion, 1942.

51. Wertheimer, M. Productive thinking. New York. Harper, 1945.

52. Zaporozhets, A. V. Rol elementoy praktiki imovi v rozvitku mislennya u ditini. (Role of elements of practice and speech in the child's thought development.) Nauk. zap. Khark. derzh. ped. in-tu. (Scientific notes of Kharkov's state pedagogical institute.) Vol. I, 1939.

53. Zaporozhets, A. V. Mislennya i diyalnist ditini. (Thinking and activity of a child.) Pratsi respubl. nauk. konf. z pedagogiki i psikhologii. (Works of the Republic's scientific conference on pedagogy and psychology.) Vol. II Kiev, 1941.

54. Zaporozhets, A. V. Razvitiye rassuzhdeny v doshkolnom vozraste. (Development of judgment in preschool age.) Doshkolnoye vospitaniya (Preschool upbringing.) 1942, No. 5-6.

55. Zaporozhets, A. V. Razvitiye logicheskogo myshleniya u detey v doshkolmom vozraste. (Development of logical thinking in preschool children.) Sb. Voprosy psikhologii rebyonka doshkolnika.(Questions of the psychology of a preschooler.) Moscow, 1948.

56. Zaporozhets, A. V. and Lukov, G. D. Pro rozvitok mirkuvannya u ditini molodshogo viku. (Concerning development of thinking in a young child.) Nauk. zap. Khark. ped. in-tu. (Scientific notes of Kharkov's pedagogical institute.) Vol. VI, 1941.

6. Development of Imagination

The emergence and the formation of one of the most basic psychological processes can be observed in the preschool child, namely, imagination, or the ability to form new representations on the basis of previous experience, which allows for the planning of future actions.

The questions associated with the development of a child's imagination are being investigated by many psychologists in our country as well as abroad.

Various types of idealistic conceptions exist in Western European and American child psychology, according to which imagination seems to be some kind of innate ability that develops gradually and is independent of life's conditions and upbringing (Karl and Charlotte Bühler, 3, 4). Presumably, imagination is not a reflection of reality but only an expression of the child's internal subjective states, affect, worries, and wants (psychoanalytical directions in psychology). Such an understanding of the nature of imagination leads some bourgeois psychologists to appreciably overvalue the role of imagination in the preschooler's life, assuming that at different stages of ontogeny the innate ability to fantasize manifests itself most clearly and thereafter is suppressed by the conscious intellect.

Soviet psychologists examine imagination not as an innate ability, but as a complex psychological activity that is formed as part of the child's overall development within the context of his environment. Imagination is a distinctively creative reflection of reality. Its growth requires accumulation of corresponding experience and the development of the ability to unify mentally different images into new contexts and combinations and to conceive possible changes in reality. These abilities are constructed gradually and undergo a series of stages in their formation.

Experimental investigations indicate that the observed richness of the child's fantasy is an expression of the weakness of his critical thinking, an inability to differentiate the possible from the impossible. Disregarding its apparent strength, the child's imagination is poorer, more monotonous, more unstable, and consists of fewer constructive elements than an adult's.

The rudiments of imagination appear during the preschool years. Its development at this age is connected with the increasing complexity in the kinds of interactions the child has with adults and with the shift of the preschooler from the elementary forms of activity to more complicated ones. As a result of verbal interaction with an adult, the child develops a need for conceiving what extends beyond his immediate perception, for example, that which is conveyed by fairy tales, stories, etc. Furthermore, the shift of the preschooler to certain types of productive activity, for example, drawing, construction, and also role-playing, requires planning of the forthcoming activity and the development of preliminary intention.

In the process of drawing and construction the child must be able to conceive the ultimate result of his activity—an image of an object appearing on a drawing or of a planned structure—and to preserve that imaginary picture until the end of the activity. In a play it is necessary to think up a plot and its development, to be able to put one's self into an assumed role, and to act in terms of an imaginary situation. While listening to fairy tales or stories, looking at pictures, or listening to songs, the child has to imagine objects that he has never previously perceived, although their representations do not exist in his previous experience. The above-stated problems confronting the child in all of these kinds of activity cannot be solved without imagination.

Features of Imagination in Children of Pre-Preschool Age

The child already displays imitative games by the middle of his second year of life. It would be possible to assume that this particular instance is the beginning of imagination. However, special investigations indicate that the initial games of pre-preschoolers still do not include elements of fantasy. Thus, Fradkina, having analyzed play activity of children this age (7), concludes that whenever the child "drinks" out of an empty glass, "eats" out of an empty plate, or "waters" out of an empty watering can, the objective activity performed by the child is in its entirety determined by the existing conditions. The child carries out one and the same action irrespective of whether a spoon is empty or full, for example, merely because it is a spoon and is to be lifted to the mouth—here the child masters the objective activity as such.

Sometimes one object outwardly appears as a substitute for another to the pre-preschooler. However, as observations show, in such a substitution the object retains its usual (for the child) name and no renaming occurs. Fradkina describes the case of a year and a half old girl who, while playing, picks up a pillow and sings "ah, ah, ah" (just like a lullaby), and sequentially puts a spool, a ring, a toy cat, or a toy dog "to sleep" on it. The child acts as if she replaces one object with another, much in the same manner as does the preschooler. This is, however, only an external impression, and the nature of the child's activity here is different. The action here is determined by the pillow, which is associated with putting something to bed, and not by the toy objects which are being put to bed on the pillow.

The appearance of the rudiments of an imaginary situation in the child's activity is relegated by Fradkina to the third year of life, when the content of a child's realistic actions is supplemented by *naming* actions of imaginary objects. At this age the child not only plays with concrete objects and toys but also supplies them with his own fist or the doll's hand as substitutes for an imaginary candy or an apple.

It is significant that the children in such instances *name* these imaginary objects. For example, they name the imaginary food as if it were present in the toy dishes with which they are playing.

An investigation by Slavina (20) indicates that the imagination in pre-preschoolers is poorly developed, passive, and reconstructive. In this connection their games are imitative in character and basically involve the manipulation of objects. At this stage, unfolding a plot and execution of a role are only contemplated.

Furthermore, the observations show that toward the end of the pre-preschool age, the child is capable of comprehending a short story or a fairy tale, especially when they are accompanied by illustrations, and when the description of the heroes' activity is of an unfolding nature. Slavina, while studying perception by pre-preschoolers of a literary text under different conditions (19), has discovered that with an unfolding, dramatic description of events the understanding of the text sharply increased and the children were able to conceive of the events about which they were told.

Features of the Imagination of Preschool Age Children

Characteristics of a Preschool Child's Imaginative Images

During preschool childhood basic changes in imaginative images occur. In contrast to the pre-preschooler, whose fantasying is limited to supplementing an existing situation by previously perceived images, a preschooler exhibits gradual development of an ability to create entirely new images of objects through a complex restructuring of previous experience. These images acquire a generalized character. The preschooler learns to isolate that which is characteristic in objects, in connection with which the images of fantasy, while remaining concrete and observable, begin to reflect whole groups of similar objects and phenomena.

Some foreign psychologists view the world of a child's imagination as a special world emancipated from reality, a miragelike construction in the area of unreality to which the child turns as if escaping from reality (Piaget and others). They assume that the images of a child's imagination are not a reflection of the objective world but only a representation of its symbolic designation (Stern and others) or in general have no relationship to reality, only expressing a child's subjective state (Volkelt and others).

An investigation by Soviet psychologists of a child's imagination has indicated that during playful activity, in the perception of fairy tales as well as in figurative activity, one can clearly detect the child's peculiar realism. Zaporozhets, in criticizing the theory of symbolism, asserts that the child prefers an umbrella for a ready-made toy horse not because it is a symbol, but because one can "ride" on an umbrella whereas one cannot on a toy horse, and that in this the actual realism of a preschooler is expressed.

Elkonin (6) has specifically clarified the extent to which preschoolers in play follow the logic of real life and to what extent they are steadfast in implementing this realistic tendency. Thus, the preschoolers while playing the game "lunch" were asked to eat the second or the third dish first, and then the first dish. For the middle and older preschool age children, this invitation evoked a violent protest on the basis that "it is not so" in everyday life. Elkonin proposes that the appearance of the images of fantasy is brought about by the confrontation of a realistic idea with the limited means for its realization, which then creates a necessity for supplementing the missing elements in the situation by the imaginative images.

Studies of preschool children's perception of fairy tales reveal numerous examples of a realistic approach to their content. Zaporozhets (26) discovered that the preschool child while listening to a fairy tale approaches its evaluation from his own particular realistic position; that from the child's point of view in the fairy tale not everything is possible. Thus, whenever certain realistic elements of the fairy tale are distorted, for example, typical properties of objects and the nature of activity performed with them, this tends to evoke a negative attitude in a child. A child, having been raised with popular tales, senses a certain limit that should not be surpassed by creative imagination. Whenever certain objects are assigned functions that are not characteristic of them, for example, when in a fairy tale cereal is cooked in a pant leg or an ink bottle that is guarding a house barks, concern is evoked in a child, and he remarks that one cannot cook cereal in a pant leg and that an ink bottle cannot bark. "It would have been better having it spit ink," he suggests to the storyteller.

Realism of imaginative images is distinctively observed at the older preschool age. The younger preschool-age children cannot always separate the possible from the impossible; therefore, one sometimes gets the impression that their fantasy is of a carefree nature. This carefree nature, an uncritical relation to images of imagination, is explained by the lack of previous experience and by not knowing what and how things exist in reality. Younger preschool-age children frequently do not distinguish images of fantasy from the realistic ones and are sometimes ready to agree with any kind of imaginary production. However, the older the preschooler, the greater is his previous experience, the more fully reality is reflected in his games and in his conceptual activity, and the more critical is his approach to the images of his fantasy.

Experiments by Repina (14), who studied the features of a child's imagination within the context of a play corresponding to the fairy tale, "The rooster with a golden comb and a magic mill," demonstrated that the younger preschoolers show a lack of critical analysis in their selection of playful material. Their selection follows the principle "Everything might be something else." For example, a large pine cone might be "a pea plant," a little rock—"a cake," a long wooden stick—"a boy," a large toy bear—"a rooster," etc. However, at the older preschool-age the selection of material was in line with the special requirements.

The first requirement stipulated that the selected object must be able to replace the imaginary object or a character in function. Thus, the main function of a rooster according to the children is pecking; therefore, for its representation the children chose an acute-angled cube, the edge of which was the rooster's beak. For a windmill, whose importance is that it must turn, they used, for example, a toy cat that could be rotated by its tail as if by a handle. The second requirement entailed that the selected item would have at least some kind of external resemblance to the imaginary object. Thus, a toy elephant with a golden cloth and a yellow paper hat were utilized by the children as a mill since they were similar in color to the golden mill. The third requirement specified that correspondence in dimensions between play objects be reflected to some extent in the dimensions of the imaginary object.

A realistic approach to the fairy-tale type of fantasy is developed only at a definite stage of a child's development (Zaporozhets relates it to the middle preschool age). The realism of a child's imagination requires an active upbringing. It is imperative that the child's imagination be developed in connection with enriching his experience by knowledge of reality, and that it not turn into a unfruitful fantasy that serves as an escape from reality.

Repina (15) studied children's understanding of certain fairy-tale images in the preschool age (a child's retelling the fairy tale, "The rooster with a golden comb and a magic mill," drawings, and games related to this fairy tale were analyzed). The younger preschool children imagine the magic mill most frequently in the form of a simple vertical stick or in the form of the same kind of stick with a little cross at the top, and the miraculous pea as a vertical stick with small rings adhering to it or placed on it. The rooster is also imagined very schematically, most frequently being a head with a beak and feet which come out directly from the head. Among the middle age preschoolers, the content of the drawings and individual representations becomes somewhat richer; the miraculous pea is not simply sticks with circles—its stalk contains branches on which leaves and pods are symmetrically distributed. The representation of the rooster also becomes more complete (in some cases, the children depict the comb and the chin sack). There are also changes in children's images of the magic mill. The middle preschoolers most likely imagine it as a circle with a handle that can be used to spin it. In the older preschool children, portrayal of fantastic images becomes even more complete. Thus, the pea is most frequently imagined in the form of a large, fully developed tree from which pea pods are hanging; the content of drawings depicting the mill also becomes more complex and enriched.

Developmental work dealing with enrichment of the preschoolers' representations, through familiarization with different aspects of reality, shows that widening the scope of representations exerts an influence on the content and number of imaginative images. Rybakova (17), while studying the imagination of preschoolers, worked extensively with the children on enriching the sphere of representations, and thereafter he compared the way the stories were originally told by the children with the way they were retold. It was shown that the narrations composed by the children after the enrichment were distinguished by a more complex content and plot.

A distinctive feature of a preschool child's imaginative images is their concreteness, clearness, and insufficiently generalized nature. The study of this feature is connected with the problem of the interrelationship between an image and a word.

Leushina (8) asserts that in the process of perceiving a fairy tale or a story the children construct visual images on the basis of a verbal description. Given a task to tell about something or to retell what the child has already heard from adults, "a picture" appears in his consciousness, and only under these conditions is he in a position to tell a story.

Vygotsky (25) appropriately points out that the development of a child's imagination is directly associated with the acquisition of speech, which facilitates the formation of representations about objects and permits the child to imagine an object that he has never seen before. Vygotsky indicates that the children who are retarded in speech development also exhibit a retardation in the development of imagination.

A characteristic feature of a child's imagination is its vividness, its intense emotionality. Numerous observations show that in his playful, as well as conceptual, activity and in his verbal creativity the preschooler reproduces the objects and events that arouse his imagination or emotionally involve him. An interesting story, a play, or events that have agitated the child are reflected immediately in his drawings and play.

As a rule, the plots of the preschoolers' creative games are determined by the scope of events that are emotionally meaningful for them. In a game it is very important to the child that the role he assumes be emotionally attractive to him. Quite frequently preschool children refuse to assume the role of some kind of negative personality or play it out with a great deal of unwillingness.

Some foreign investigators assume that the world constructed by the child's imagination competes in its vividness, distinctiveness, and detail with the directly visible world, and that the child confuses the images of his fantasy with reality and lives in a world of illusions. Investigations of Soviet, as well as a series of foreign, authors indicate that no matter how clear or emotional the child's imaginative images, he nevertheless distinguishes quite clearly the imaginary from the realistically perceived. No matter how involved the preschooler might be in playing with a doll daughter for example, an illusion that it is not a doll but a living child is certainly not present. And if the doll were to suddenly bite off a piece of a presented cake or were to talk or walk, the child would become extremely frightened.

In studying the play of pre-preschoolers, Fradkina correctly notices that the absence of illusions does not interfere with the child's ability to be engrossed in his own fastasy and to vigorously protest against various attempts by adults to disturb the imaginary play (7). The children strongly react to their partners in play who for one reason or another refuse to play and depart from the play situation.

In the process of a child's imagination the previously seen presentations are combined and reformulated; this being accomplished through the analysis and synthesis of the available images. In their imagination a separation of individual characteristics of images that emerged in the process of perception takes place, which leads to construction of new images.

Of special interest is the child's image construction during the perception of fairy-tale material. Urusova (21) studied how in their drawings preschoolers reflect such fairy tale characters as

Koshchei the Deathless or Baba Yaga, a witch; how they imagine the magical transformation of Ivan into a goat; Vasilisa the Beautiful into a cuckoo bird, etc. The investigation showed that conceiving the fairy-tale characters—Koshchei, the witch—is a simpler task for children than conceiving magical transformations. The aspect of transformation as such is imagined by only a few children, and even at that they imagine it realistically, emphasizing the gradualness of transformation from one state into another.

Combinational methods are not the main ones used by preschoolers in reformulating fairy-tale images. Repina's observations indicate that conceiving a combinational image on the basis of a description is a very difficult task for a preschooler. Almost none of the preschool children was able to construct such an image from a description and to isolate it from the integral parts of the segmented game. In order to find a way out of the predicament, some children attempted to characterize an image according to some aspect of its integral part. Thus, when they were given a description of two images at the same time, each one of which consisted of three parts, some children picked up these parts correctly but were not able to combine these parts accurately into a correspondingly described image.

The Development of Voluntary, Creative Imagination in Preschool Age

In discussing the beginnings of the preschoolers' imagination, we noted that it is expressed through an involuntary transformation of images that is independent of any cognitive goal. It is only during the preschool years that along with involuntary imagination the children begin to form a voluntary, active imagination.

Operations with images that are subordinated to a cognitive goal initially (especially among the younger preschool children) are very unstable and of short duration. The child is unable to hold the goal and the intention of imagination for a long period of time.

However, the goal orientation of a child's imagination and the stability of his intentions gradually increase from the younger to the older preschool age. This has been reported by numerous investigators of play and conceptual activity in preschool-age children.

Repina (13), in one of her investigations, has demonstrated that the younger preschool-age children, while beginning to draw according to a prescribed theme, do not fulfill the task (the children were required to illustrate the fairy tale, "The rooster with a golden comb and a magic mill"), due to the instability of intention. For example, Mike (three years of age), while working on a task set up by the experimenter to depict the magical mill, draws a vertical stick and thereafter draws additional sticks attached to the first one—"mills." After that, he connects a few horizontal ones to all the vertical sticks. Thus, one gets "pine trees" out of "mills." A subject of the same age, Natalie, in response to instructions to draw a picture of how the rooster was thrown into a well, initially draws a circle ("a well") and thereafter turns it into a "pea plant." Subsequently, the girl attaches a stalk and a few additional pods to the circle. However, older preschool-age children exhibit relatively stable intentions in their imaginary activity. They are capable of conveying the themes assigned to them or reflecting the content of a narrated story or fairy tale in their pictures and cut-outs.

Growth of an imaginative goal orientation during the preschool years is evidenced by an extension in the ability to continue a game having one theme and by a greater stability of roles. Usova (22) has shown that for three—four-year-old children the typical length of a game is from ten to fifteen minutes. For the middle preschool age children continuation of a game reaches forty to fifty minutes; for the older preschoolers it extends to several hours, and even up to several days.

A study by Repina (14) demonstrated that in contrast to older preschool children, who exhibit relatively stable playful intentions that are frequently completed, younger preschool children under the influence of external distraction frequently depart from the main intention and divert their attention to some kind of tangential activity. In such situations, the initial playful redesignation of objects is forgotten and the child begins to act with objects in accordance with their realistic designation.

At first, the images of voluntary imagination in preschool children emerge from the verbal influence of adults. Thereafter, the elements of voluntary imagination begin to emerge in collective games with an intention and in drawings about particular themes, i.e., where there is the necessity for a preliminary plan. An investigation by Repina has shown that in play based on the theme of a recently heard fairy tale the younger preschool-age children exhibit only elements of planning—each one of the children takes on the role he likes most. Furthermore, the child selects from the play materials two or three items to represent objects that are necessary for the beginning of the game. At the older preschool age, the stage of preliminary planning is of a more developed nature. Before beginning the game the children assign roles, clarify for what kind of roles there are insufficient people, and agree how they will perform each individual role. For example, they decide whether one of the children should perform it pluralistically, transforming himself from one role into another, or whether the unavailable actor should be replaced by a toy. At the beginning of the game all the objects necessary for its full unfolding are selected from the available materials.

In the middle and older preschool child, the elements of planning are observed in drawing and, in part, in decorative drawing (Sakulina, 18).

The creative imagination of a preschooler is tightly associated with the development of voluntary imagination. The initial elements of creative imagination are encountered in the child's reproduction of something previously heard. For example, he supplements the image of the hero of a fairy tale by thinking up new characteristics and events. In drawing, the elements of creative imagination are apparent in the composition of the drawing and in the utilization of color. Additional creative aspects of imagination are found in the role playing of preschoolers.

Some authors overemphasize the creative abilities of a child. On the other hand, some psychologists (Montessori, Gaupp, Ribo, Wundt, and others) generally deny any creativity to the child. Thus, Gaupp assumes that for the most part the child possesses a passive and visual fantasy. Montessori points out that in play the child only copies adults, changing the images of reality in terms of his own ignorance. On the other hand, Mendzheritskaya (11) holds that the preschooler's play is not just a simple stimulation but an expression of creative imagination that manifests itself in the selection of a plot for the game, in how the plot is developed, and in the method the child utilizes in constructing various images.

The elements of creative imagination and inventiveness are also observed in the constructive building games of preschoolers, such as construction of toys out of paper, cardboard, pine cones, or other materials.

Mirenova and Kolbanovsky (12) have investigated the effectiveness of different methods in the development of combinatory functions in the preschooler's constructive building activity. The first method based on imitation did not stimulate the child's activity: he was required to produce a structure according to a given model consisting of cubes of a definite form. The second method, which stimulated the child's activity, consisted of giving the children only the general contour of the structure in place of a model. In this case, the children were required to select their own building materials in order to produce the structure of a given form. It became apparent that under these conditions the preschoolers were required to perform a series of detailed constructive steps, exchanging one set of cubes with another in the process of construction. The controlled experiment demonstrated a greater effectiveness of the second method in development of the combinatory ability because the many and varied manipulations by the children with the cubes were much more conducive to the development of creative imagination.

The initial forms of creative imagination in children were studied by Rybakova (17) under conditions of verbally restating the content of pictures. The younger preschool-age children, while telling a story based on the content of a picture, made it quite apparent that their narration depended totally on the external content of the plot. Preschoolers in the fourth and fifth year, while restructuring the content of the picture, were able to compose a simple plot to the story. However, they were not able to go beyond the limits of the directly perceived. The older preschool-age children attempted not only to recreate the perceived, but also to supplement their stories by aspects that were not directly perceived but were subsumed in the created plot, as for instance, thinking up a beginning and an end to the story.

Dependence of the Formation of a Preschool Child's Imagination Upon His Activity

Some foreign psychologists assume that the formation of a child's creative activity, as well as partially his playful activity, is dependent upon development of his fantasy (Stern, Bühler, and Piaget). Herein imagination enters as the explanatory principle of play.

In contrast to this, Soviet psychologists propose that imagination is formed and developed within the context of the various kinds of a child's activity, largely determined by his environmental conditions. The formation of imagination in the process of play, construction, and other forms of children's activity has been studied by many Soviet scientists (Elkonin, 6; Luria, 10; Lukov, 9; Zaporozhets, 26, and others). Their investigations revealed that the child's imagination functions and develops quickly whenever he is playing, cutting things out of paper, drawing, and constructing, and that it extinguishes as soon as the child stops acting. The child's imagination finds external support, for example, in playful but realistic actions with play material in an imaginative situation. The process of a child's imagination in role playing depends on the nature of the toys and on the presence of role attributes.

Of special importance is the nature of toys for younger preschoolers. Fully developed play is only possible for them when the necessary toys for the plot are present. In older preschool-age children, this connection between play and material for the plot does not exist. Conversely, Repina (14) has shown that the most creative play is developed with natural material. In these experiments, the children's play followed the plot of the fairy tale presented to them. In one situation, they were given natural material (cones, leaves, sticks, and rocks) as a material for play. In the second—building materials of different forms and sizes were presented; and in the third situation, toys for a plot, not corresponding in their content to the represented objects, were made available.

It was demonstrated that for all of the preschoolers play developed most easily in the presence of natural material. Under these conditions, an especially clear indication of the development of creative imagination was obtained with the older preschoolers. In the situation where the construction material was used, the latter aroused children into independent constructive activity. For the older preschoolers, this activity followed the content of the fairy tale. Utilizing the cubes, the children constructed a well, a stove, etc. However, the imagination of the younger children was diverted away from the developing plot by the features of the play materials. Children began to select the cubes according to color or form, and were making stairs, trains, accordions, and pianos out of them. As a result, their play obtained an independent content.

In the third situation contradictory data were obtained. On the one hand, the younger preschool children did not exhibit any difficulty in renaming the available toys into play objects. They were acting according to the principle "Everything can be something else," substituting for the necessary play object the first toy that met their eyes, not paying any attention to its characteristics.

Older preschoolers, while changing the names of the toys presented to them, conducted a careful selection, substituting for the play objects a toy that had at least some similar characteristics—external or functional in nature—with the substituted play object. On the other hand, renaming by the younger preschoolers did not lead to the development of play. Because, due to the influence of the object's external cues, the new name was forgotten and the children resorted to playing with the toys according to their realistic designation.

The above-mentioned investigation has also shown that if one gradually deprives the child of external supports for his imagination, such as toys, by removing them a point is reached when the play becomes impossible. For the younger preschoolers, this moment arises much earlier than for the older ones.

If for the younger preschoolers the external support in play is primarily found in toys, then for the middle and older preschoolers such support lies in the fulfillment of the assumed role. A child's reliance on the attributes of a role as supports for his imagination is of great significance in his assuming a given playful personality and in sustaining such a role (Vityaz, 23).

The imaginary activity of the preschooler is quite distinct, containing various playful aspects. In his drawings and cut-outs the preschooler frequently attempts to convey the imaginary character's chain of actions. If, however, he fails to resolve this task through representational means, then he turns for assistance to words, gestures, or play, such as conversing with the imaginary characters and evaluating their behavior. For example, in investigations by Repina a four-year-old, Valerie K., while illustrating a fairy tale, attempts to reproduce the entire chain of actions and the dynamics of their transformations in one of the drawings. Initially, she imagined how the slave is carrying the rooster in order to throw it into the well; at the same time, how the rooster is drinking water out of the well. Then she crosses out the figure of the slave, explaining that the slave has already gone. Thereafter, she crosses out the representation of the rooster; this means

that "the rooster has drunk all the water and has flown away."
The same girl, while drawing an old lady with the magical mill
that has now been brought by the rooster, vigorously talks with
the imaginary characters and gives them advice: "Now see how
nice the rooster is" she tells the old lady, "he brought you the
mill and you were crying."

Volkova (24), in studying younger kindergarten children's activities with modeling clay, indicates that for this age group such
activity is based on play. In exercises with modeling clay, the
child's activity frequently consists of pinching off separate pieces
of clay, and if these pieces even remotely remind him of some
kinds of objects he then begins to play with them, move them, or
imitate the sounds of these objects. In such cases, the play substitutes for the child's imagination of an object.

In the case of listening to fairy tales or stories, the child's imagination is not reinforced in realistic action. Here, the child must
experience the described events mentally; he has to act in his
mind. This is a complicated problem for his imagination. In forming the ability to empathize with imaginary characters, the structure and nature of the artistic text plays a major role. Investigations by Slavina (19), Zaporozhets (26), Aronovskaya (1), and
Boguslavskaya (2) indicate that for an adequate perception of the
fairy tale's images, it is necessary that the plot be exposed in an
extensive and a dramatical form.

In investigations by Repina, the child was required to reproduce
in his imagination a spatial distribution of objects and agglutina-
tive pictures on the basis of description. In one case, the fairy tale
description had an epic character, in the second, dynamic and
emotional. In the latter case, involving a change in the structure
of the fairy tale and an increase in the emotionality of the text,
the children's imaginative images were much more accurate. Thus,
graphic representations and illustrations are of great importance
in the formation of imaginative images.

The work of Repina (16) indicates that, in the younger preschool age, a drawing does not merely fulfill a supportive and

narrow illustrative function but assumes the role of the basic material, in the absence of which the little child cannot imagine the events described in the fairy tale. The words of the text serve merely as indicators of actions and circumstances, which the child has to follow visually step-by-step while examining the corresponding pictures. Here the drawing represents reality, which for the child cannot be replaced by verbal description. Subsequently, the words of the text without the pictures begin to evoke images. Thus, older preschoolers understand the plot of a fairy tale or a relatively simple story without the illustrations. However, understanding the inherent meaning of the story is difficult for him, and in overcoming this, illustrations again begin to play an important role by visually representing those actions and interrelationships of characters by which one most clearly discovers their inherent features.

The transition of the child's imagination activity in need of external supports to independent internal activity is basically accomplished in the older preschool age. Characteristic of older preschoolers is the appearance of intellectual or verbal games, i.e., the development of independent verbal creativity. A typical example of play requiring a high level of imaginative development is the game of travel. In essence, the child is required to compose a story about his travels in compliance with the given rules of the game (that the story be composed in terms of a given theme with the utilization of previously given words, etc.).

The verbal creativity of children is extensively observed in the middle and older preschool age. Elements of verbal creativity are also noted at a much younger age. However, as a rule they are connected with some kind of external activity, like a game or a dance. Chukovsky (5), studying younger preschooler's poems, which he calls "ekikiki," views such poems as a characteristic aspect of connections with movement. In some cases, three—four-year-old children are able to compose a short, two-line verse without movement. However, this is usually accomplished in the context of emotional arousal, such as the great joy associated with an accomplished or forthcoming pleasure, like a New Year's party, an interesting excursion, etc. For example, a three-year-old child when given a beautiful paper-made boat places a little cube into it and while dragging the boat over the table, sings: "Lodochka plyvet kubika vezet." (The little boat swims carrying the cube.)

Toward the fifth and sixth year of life, as indicated by Chukovsky, the children switch to real poems that are especially composed and invented. Compared with the poems of the younger children, these poems are much more intellectual, their connection with external activity not being necessary.

Among the most widely known types of preschoolers' poetry are the child's teasing limericks and counting limericks. The teasing limericks comprise original childish forms of satirical lyric. Each of the limericks contains some boasting, which reflects the child's striving to assure himself while underscoring the inadequacies of someone else.

Counting and witty elements are the characteristic features of childish limericks. Many of the well-known limericks begin by counting: "raz, dva, tri, chetyre, pyat—vyshel zaychik poguluat" (one, two, three, four, five—the rabbit came out to play) and "raz, dva, tri, chetyre—menya gramote uchili" (one, two, three, four—I was taught literacy"). Limericks in a dialogic form are very popular with children:

"Zayats bely, kuda begal?
V les dubovy!
Chto tam delal?
Lyki dral!"

("White rabbit, where did you go?
Into the oak forest!
What were you doing there?
I was barking the trees!")

In another type of limerick there is no singular content, but there are separate forms, poorly connected with one another.

For example:

"Ana-duna-zhest,
Kandi-rimdi-rez,
Ana-duna-raba,
Kandi-rindi-zhaba."

The children like fairy tales and happy poems, which deliberately contain different kinds of contradictions. The presence of elements of unreality and transformations is also characteristic of a child's verbal creativity.

Chukovsky is quite correct in pointing out that unreality is necessary for the child only when he is quite sure of reality, and that in transformations the child manifests his initial humor.

Fairy tales and continuous stories are another type of a child's verbal creativity. Under the influence of books read to preschoolers by adults, the children begin to compose their own fairy tales and stories, even though these are very naive and imitative.

The fairy tales the children tell are similar to those which they have heard, and therefore quite frequently they preface their fairy tale with a warning: "I will tell you about a little boy, but this is not about a little boy made out of a toy." The children like to think up stories about the past that never really happened, in which they themselves are active characters. Thus, a four-year-old boy, having been affected by the fairy tale, "The Wolf and the Seven Little Goats," begins to compose: "Well, one time I was a blacksmith. The wolf came to me, but I refused to make his voice soft. I knocked out all of his wolfian teeth."

Among the stories composed by children the continuous ones are especially noteworthy. These stories are characterized by great dynamics and dramatization.

Toward the end of the preschool age, the imagination of the child becomes relatively independent of external activity, the basis from which it was formed. At about this time, creative elements appear in imagination. These imaginative features of older preschoolers are of great significance in preparing the child for school training, when it becomes necessary for him to form images of objects that he has not previously perceived on the basis of accumulated concepts.

The imagination of the preschooler does not develop by itself. It is composed and developed on the basis of play and imaginary activity, in the course of perceiving artistic productions. Therefore, it is necessary that adults, relying on an appropriate approach, organize and guide this activity.

References

1. Aronovskaya, D. M. Zavisimost ponimaniya rebyonkom skazki oyyeyo kompozitsii. (Dependence of the child's understanding of a fairy tale on its composition.) Kand. diss. Kharkov, 1945.

2. Boguslavskaya, Z. M. Psikhologicheskiye osobennosti usvoyeniya znany v usloviyakh doshkolnykh zanyaty. (Psychological attributes of mastering knowledge under conditions of preschool training.) Rukopis. (Manuscript.) Moscow, 1956.

3. Bühler, Charlotte. From birth to maturity: An outline of the psychological development of the child. London. Kegan Paul, 1935.

4. Bühler, K. Die geistige Entwicklung des Kindes. Jena. Fischer, 1921.

5. Chukovsky, K. I. Ot dvukh do pyati. (From two to five.) Moscow, 1956.

6. Elkonin, D. B. Psikhologicheskiye voprosy doshkolnoy igry. (Psychological questions of preschool play.) Sb. Voprosy psikhologii rebyonka doshkolnogo vozrasta. (Questions of the psychology of the preschool child.) Moscow. Izd-vo APN RSFSR, 1948.

7. Fradkina, F. I. Psikhologiya igry v rannem detsve. Geneticheskiye korni doshkolnoy igry. (Psychology of play in early childhood. Genetic roots of preschool play.) Kand. diss. Leningrad, 1945.

8. Leushina, A. M. Razvitiye soyuznoy rechi u doshkolnika. (Development of connected speech in a preschooler.) Uchyonyye zapiski LGPI. (Scientific notes of LGPI.) Vol. XXXV, 1941.

9. Lukov, G. D. Ob osoznanii rebyonkom rechi v protsesse igry. (Concerning realization of speech by the child in the process of play.) Kand. diss. Kharkov, 1937.

10. Luria, A. R. Razvitiye konstruktivnoy deyatelnosti doshkolnika. (Development of constructive activity in the preschooler.) Sb. Voprosy psikhologii rebyonka doshkolnogo vozrasta. (Questions of the psychology of a preschool child.) Moscow. Izd-vo APN RSFSR, 1948.

11. Mendzheritskaya, D. V. Razvitiye tvorcheskoy igry rebyonka. (Development of a child's creative play.) Doshkolnoye vospitaniye. (Preschool upbringing.) 1942, No. 9.

12. Mirenova, A. N., and Kolbanovsky, V. N. Sravnitelnaya otsenka metodov razvitiya kombinatornykh funktsy u doshkolnika. Eksperimenty na odnoyaytsovykh bliznetsakh. (Comparative evaluation of the methods of development of the preschooler's combinatory functions. Experiments with monozygotic twins.) Trudy mediko-biologicheskogo institute. (Works of the medical-biological institute.) Vol. III, 1934.

13. Repina, T. A. Osobennosti voobrazheniya doshkolnika pri vosproizvedenii v risunkakh obrazov skazki. (Aspects of the preschooler's imagination in reproducing images of a fairy tale.) Rukopis. (Manuscript). Moscow, 1956.

14. Repina, T. A. Osobennosti voobrazheniya doshkolnika v igre po syuzhetu skazki. (Aspects of the preschooler's imagination in a game according to the plot of a fairy tale.) Rukopis. (Manuscript.) Moscow, 1956.

15. Repina, T. A. Osobennosti voobrazheniya doshkolnika pri slovesnom vosproizvedenii im skazki. (Aspects of the preschooler's imagination under conditions of verbal reproduction of a fairy tale.) Rukopis. (Manuscript.) Moscow, 1956.

16. Repina, T. A. Rol illustratsii v ponimanii khudozhestvennogo teksta detmi doshkolnogo vozrasta. (The role of illustration in the preschool child's understanding of an artistic text.) Voprosy psikhologii. (Questions of psychology.) 1959, No. 1.

17. Rybakova, M. M. Nachalnyye formy tvorcheskogo voobrazheniya detey doshkolnogo vozrasta na osnove izucheniya detskogo slovesnogo tvorchestva. (Initial forms of preschool children's creative imagination based on a study of children's verbal creativity.) Kand. diss. Moscow, 1952.

18. Sakulina, N. P. Metodika obucheniya risovaniyu i lepke v detskom sadu. (Methodology of teaching drawing and modeling in kindergarten.) Moscow. Uchpedgiz, 1953.

19. Slavina, L. S. Nekotoryye voprosy vospriyatiya rechi malenkimi detmi. (Certain questions pertaining to perception of speech by small children.) Doshkolnoye vospitaniye. (Preschool upbringing.) 1943, No. 12.

20. Slavina, L. S. Razvitiye syuzhetnoy igry v doshkolnom vozraste. (Development of a play with a plot in preschool age.) Doshkolnoye vospitaniye. (Preschool upbringing.) 1949, No. 5.

21. Urusova, E. K. Razvitiye voobrazheniya doshkolnikov v protsesse slushaniya skazki. (Development of preschoolers' imagination in the process of listening to a fairy tale.) Rukopis. (Manuscript.) Moscow, 1954.

22. Usova, A. P. K voprosu o kharaktere tvorcheskikh igr detey v doshkolnom vozraste i pravilakh rukovodstva imi. (Concerning the nature of preschool children's creative games and rules for their implementation.) Uchenyye zapiski LGPI. (Scientific notes of LGPI.) Vol. 56, 1947.

23. Vityaz, M. G. Razvitiye tvorcheskoy igry v mladshey gruppe detskogo sada. (Development of creative play in the younger kindergarten groups.) Sb., Psikhologicheskiye voprosy igry i obucheniya v doshkolnom vozraste. Pod. red. D. B. Elkonina. (Psychological questions of play and training in preschool age. Ed. D. B. Elkonin.) Moscow. Izd-vo APN RSFSR, 1957.

24. Volkova, A. A. Lepka v mladshey gruppe. (Modeling activities of the younger group.) Doshkolnoye vospitaniye. (Preschool upbringing.) 1952, No. 8.

25. Vygotsky, L. S. Razvitiye vysshikh psikhicheskikh funktsy. (Development of higher psychological functions.) Moscow. Izd-vo APN RSFSR, 1960.

26. Zaporozhets, A. V. Psikhologiya vospriyatiya skazki rebyonkom-doshkolnikom. (Psychology of perception of a fairy tale by a preschooler.) Doshkolnoye vospitaniye. (Preschool upbringing.) 1948, No. 9.

7. Development of Movements and Formation of Motor Habits

Development of Movements of the Preschooler
The development of movements in the course of preschool childhood is one of those phenomena in ontogeny which first attracts the attention of the observer. In reality, the newborn is a completely helpless being, not having at his disposal even the simplest voluntary movements. Without continuous attention and constant care from the adult he cannot even last a day. An older preschooler, on the other hand, is an independent human being. He walks, runs, jumps, accurately throws a ball, executes simple gymnastic exercises, and carries out with the help of a spoon and a fork such refined coordinating movements as eating. And the child has accomplished all this in only six-seven years! It is not surprising that some authors assume that the development of movements exerts a leading influence on the development of all other functions during the first year of life and is the dominant one during the first three years of life (Bergeron, 2).

Mastery of movements provides the child with independence, i.e., relative lack of dependence, permitting him to satisfy some of the simpler needs on his own. However, simultaneously, the development of the motor sphere exerts a strong influence on the general development of the psyche in ontogeny. Thus, the motor functions are necessary for organization of different types of perception (for example, movement of the eyes is necessary for the perception of form) and comprise the basis for the development of many representations about time and space (for example, the understanding of order and sequence may occur only on the basis of a succession and ordering of actions executed by the child—Sechenov, 60, already alluded to this). Interesting material regarding this question may also be found in Piaget's writings. Even the simple ability to sit, to stand, and to walk is extremely important, for it leads to an immeasurable expansion of the sphere of reality accessible for the child's comprehension (Wallon,

74). Of special significance in the psyche's development is the mastery of hand movements from the simplest to the most refined, for the hands embody into actions a man's intentions. In performing or simply manipulating, the child acquires, verifies, and refines his knowledge about the world.

Apparently the movements and resulting tactual sensations are of great value to the child in themselves and according to many specialists become a continued source of satisfaction for him, especially during the early stages of ontogeny. Observations of a series of authors (for example, Solomon, 67) indicate that breast-fed children show a real need for kinesthetic sensation and, especially when adult interactions are lacking, they begin to execute a series of stereotypic movements (rolling the head across the pillow, banging the head on the wall of the bed, or rolling back and forth.

The development level of the child's movements and their nature leave a definite impression on the personalities of children, for they are an important, integral part of their temperament (Wallon, 74).

Therefore, one can understand the interest which has been expressed, and continues to be expressed, by many investigators of different specialties (pedagogues, physiologists, hygienists, physicians, and psychologists) about the questions pertaining to the child's motor development. The literature about this topic is quite extensive. For the most part, it consists of studies that employ the method of observation basically represented by recording the sequence of occurrence, execution, and identification of separate movements in the process of ontogeny. On the other hand, the number of studies pertaining to the investigation of principles in the development of the motor sphere—especially studies supported by experimental data—is relatively small. This one-sidedness of material pertaining to the ontogeny of motor behavior creates difficulties in formulating the principal question concerning conditions and motivational causes in the development of movements.

Conditions and Causes of the Development of Movements in the Process of Ontogeny

How and why does the development of movement occur in the process of ontogeny? What kinds of conditions support it? Numerous investigators have made an attempt to provide answers to these questions.

No one doubts that in order to be able to master human movements one must be born a man with the characteristic, specific, neurophysiological features of the neuromuscular apparatus. Beside articulated movements and speech, even the upright mobility, diapason, preciseness, and the nature of a human being's hand movements are unavailable to even the closest of his relations—monkeys—under conditions of even the most prolonged and ingenious training.

Investigations of histologists, anatomists, and physiologists indicate that at birth the human being's apparatus for movements is still not completely formed. According to certain data, (Bernshtein, 3), this apparatus finalizes its development not earlier than around two—two and one-half years of age. A question arises: Is not the process of a human being's motor development determined by the maturation of the neuromuscular substrata? Such a point of view is shared by a number of investigators. In short, it may be formulated as follows: The specifically human aspects of a human being's movements are biologically inherited from his ancestors, and they gradually enter into his activity and are manifested outwardly to the extent to which the neuromuscular substrata of the motor sphere have progressed to a necessary level of maturation.

What is understood here by the term maturation? This, for example, is how McGraw defines it: "Maturation is a change in behavior occurring as a consequence of anatomical or physiological development of the nervous system, the appearance of which is not associated with any kind of known external stimuli" (46; p. 120). This definition is quite characteristic. Probably the most definitive expression of the theory that stipulates that maturation has the leading role in the child's psychological development was presented in the studies of the American investigator Gesell. It is quite obvious, according to him, that from the very moment of inception the internal and external factors interact with one another, but the initial impetus and the base for development are provided by the internal factor. "The so-called medium—be it internal or external—does not account for progressive development. The factors of the media sustain, reject, and specialize but do not bring about either the basic forms or the sequential steps of the ontogeny" (17; p. 354). The directionality and the force of growth are already embedded in the zygote. The process of maturation determines the basic connections, sequence, and formation of behavior structures. Gesell supports his deductions by data obtained from observing the ontogenetic development process of the behavior of many children. The most convincing, according to him, are the data pertaining to the development of monozygotic twins.

First of all, these data attest to the striking similarity of movement and behavior of the twins at different stages of childhood. In comparing 612 acts of behavior of the twins, S. and T., negligible differences were observed in 99 instances and fully, or almost fully, identical behavior was observed in 513 of the remaining instances (19, 20). Thus, after 28 weeks both twins reached for a cube and did not pay any attention to a small tablet, 8 mm in diameter. When it was presented to them at the age of 38 weeks, both of them took it. In this situation, the position of arms, hands, separation of the thumb, and the nature of grabbing movement in both children coincided to the finest detail.

All changes in the reactions of grabbing occurred in the twins simultaneously and in the same direction. This was shown by an experiment conducted with the same pair of twins at another time. The children were seated back to back and two experimenters simultaneously threw a tablet into a glass bottle (separate for each twin) right in front of their eyes. During the first two trials, the twins did not react to the tablet. On the third trial, they made an attempt to reach it with a finger through the glass, and finally, in the last trial, they stuck a finger into the neck of the bottle. All changes made by both children ran extremely parallel (21, 22). The similarity of the twins' behavior was preserved even at school age, manifesting itself not only in the character of penmanship, but also in such aspects as mistakes made while writing simple monosyllabic words to dictation (18).

It is necessary, however, to emphasize that in all of the above-described situations the twins lived under the same set of conditions and obtained essentially the same experiences. In cases when the upbringing of monozygotic twins was accomplished under a different set of conditions, one could observe fairly early the divergence in the nature of their behavior, especially in instances pertaining to habits and abilities. Thus, studies by Mirenova and Luria (42, 43) showed that training the twins in constructive activity via the method of passive copying of prepared models or by active reproduction of these models (in this case, the model was enclosed by paper that prevented one from seeing its structure) led to a difference in the development not only of constructive ability, but also of speech, perception, relationship to the surrounding environment, etc. Different conditions of life exerting an influence on the children in the course of many years lead to big differences in the motor-psychological development of monozygotic twins (Gesell, 16).

In support of the dominant role that he attributes to the factor of maturation, Gesell presents additional evidence—stability of individual attributes occurring at a very early age—that he ascribes to the continuous action of some type of constant factor. Thus, a multifaceted investigation of four children in the course of their first years of life showed stability in the indicators of psychomotor abilities expressed by children at an early age (18). Especially emphasized is the influence of maturation on the development of the motor sphere during the first stages of childhood. Thus, Gesell states that the role of maturation, even though preserved for the full utilization of potential in the development of human being, is most evident in the fetus and the child (17). This line of thinking is supported by Carmichael (5), Stone (68), and others.

One cannot disagree with facts and evidence concerning the importance of maturation of the neuromuscular apparatus and the changes in body proportion in the development of a human being's locomotion. However, even though being a necessary and inseparable condition in the development of motor activity, maturation is not its motivating cause. Most of all this is supported by facts. Thus, it is known that when left alone, i.e., being excluded from socialization with adults, children do not master the more important features of human movements—upright movement, typical human postures, etc. This, in part, is supported by data on the training of Indian girls who were raised among wolves (for example, Gesell, 16). This is also corroborated by Dennis's experiment, even though its length was limited to fourteen lunar months (7, 8). While raising a pair of female twins under conditions of social isolation and without special training, the author registered sponteneous emergence of 154 reactions. However, under this condition neither one of the girls exhibited any one of the following three reactions: grabbing a suspended circle, independent sitting, and assured vertical standing. It appears that for the emergence of even these quite elementary motor reactions maturation of the neuromuscular structures in itself is insufficient. Furthermore, study of the higher nervous activity of premature children (for example, Kasatkin, 30) indicates that their brain begins to function prior to the time of the normal arrival of children into the world, and that the early functioning accelerates the maturation of the neural structures.

Consequently, keeping in mind the importance of the maturation factor, it cannot be recognized as the motivating cause of development. It constitutes only one of the very important conditions of the ontogeny of motor movements. The course of the latter is determined by something else.

A long time ago, many investigators pointed to learning as a motivational cause for the development of motor activity, as well as the psychological functions of a human being in general. Here, first of all, we have to remember the supporters of the behavioristic orientation in psychology. The authors who adhered to the doctrine of orthodox behaviorism of the Watsonian type assumed that there is a very limited number of inherited components of behavior. Out of these through the path of multiple conditioning grow all the complex acts of behavior, which are subsequently chains of simple reflexes. According to this point of view, the child can be taught anything that one desires. One must only show adequate patience and ingenuity for this. On this basic assumption, behaviorists almost went to the extreme in generally rejecting the role of maturation. In other words, theories that attribute the primary role to maturation appear to a large extent to be reactions to the behaviorists' position.

What is understood here by learning? As a characteristic of this phenomenon, behaviorists limit themselves to the description of its external aspect. Learning is the appearance of a reaction to a stimulus, which prior to the beginning of exercises did not evoke this reaction (Carmichael, 5). The specific content of the activity of a human being's learning thus disappears; its essential nature remains undiscovered. The process of learning in a human being, in principle, is identified with the process of the acquisition of experience in animals and is transformed into the means of the organism's simple adaptation to the surrounding environment.

In reality, many facts confirm that the norms and limits defined by adherence to the maturation theory based on anatomical-physiological indices are not rigid, and that under certain sets of conditions in experiments with children they can be greatly surpassed. Thus, for example, Dusenberry (10) showed that when training children to throw a ball, it is possible in children three-seven years of age to reach much higher indices than could be expected on the basis of maturation and usual practice. In an interesting work, Williams and Scott (75) have shown that the assumed racial difference between Negro and white children, consisting apparently in the acceleration of motor development, in reality is determined by the conditions of social order. A careful observation of 104 Negro boys, ages four to eighteen months, resulted in the determination that in the families that belonged to a lower social strata the children had greater freedom, their life was much less regimented, and their contacts with adults and surrounding children were much tighter and much more frequent than among children of the higher social level. Not racial features, but namely these social determining conditions of life and, subsequently, experiences acquired by the child during the first few months of life, exerted influence on the motor development of children—it's speed, directionality, and level. Consequently, out of this work one can deduce that learning, to a large extent, exerts an influence on the ontogenetic development of a child's motor sphere.

However, a complete rejection of the influence of maturation, treating the facet of learning as absolute and most important in its behavioristic treatment as a one-to-one process between man and his surrounding media, is just as incorrect as the theories of maturation. It is necessary to note that the majority of authors recognize the importance of learning as well as maturation in the development of the child's behavior, even though many of them place a special emphasis on one of the many factors. Thus, Dennis (7, 8) emphasizes that all the reactions of children during the first year of life are acquired or else contain elements of learning. The role of maturation consists in its making learning possible. Maturation in itself, according to the thoughts of the authors, seldom leads to the appearance of new reactions. This point of view is supported by McGraw, who declares that "maturation and learning are not different processes, but simply different facets of the same process of growth" (46; p. 131). In exploring the mutual relationship of learning and maturation, the author conducted an experiment (45) in which he made an attempt to determine how early training influences the mastery of voluntary urination. Two groups of monozygotic twin boys were used as subjects. The study encompassed a period from the 23rd day to the 470th day of life. One of the twins was put on a pot every hour, the other was not put on it until a specified time. The exercises with the second twin were begun at 430 days and older. It was found that the children who did not receive any training caught up with their brothers very rapidly if not almost immediately. On the basis of these data, the author makes the following deduction: In order to be able to change a function with the help of special influences, it is necessary that the nervous mechanism has attained a certain level of maturity. Perfection of a function in the process of practice or exercise apparently coincides in time with inclusion of the cerebral cortex into the work. Initiation of exercises prior to the attainment of minimal maturation of corresponding structures to some extent is a waste of effort, and sometimes it may even be detrimental. Thus, daily exercise of a year-old child in riding a tricycle up to the 19th month only interferes with his attaining this habit, since the interest that undoubtedly would have arisen at a given age disappeared as a result of the previous, difficult exercises (Neverovich, 49).

There is no doubt that maturation and learning, or mastering, are factors that are found in continuous interaction with one another. An especially significant influence on learning is the maturation of the cortex since it is the material substrata in the mastery of individual experience. McGraw (46) points out the fact that changes of external behavior depend on maturation of the cortex. She has described in detail the gradual suppression or disappearance of innate unconditioned reflexes of the newborn with the subsequent development of motor functions that are under the control of the cortex. According to her data, each function acquires features of learning simultaneously with the inclusion of the operations of the cortex into its practice. Thus, the newborn already has reflex movements of the feet if he is placed on a solid surface while being supported under his arms. Exercises during the period of the presence of this reflex obviously do not speed up mastery of walking. However, one does not doubt that the vertical movement becomes effective only gradually and is acquired as a result of prolonged training.

The importance of the cortex as it related to the activity of acquisition of individual experience is especially emphasized by Shchelovanov (61, 62). Experiments by Kasatkin (30) showed that toward the end of the first months of life it is possible to form initial conditioned-reflexive connections. This is explained by the prime importance of the conditions of life in forming of even the most elementary and initial qualities of behavior. Shchelovanov writes:

It is impossible to reject that for the development of these or other movements of a child, having a corresponding level of maturation of his nervous system is necessary. However, this is not a singular condition. Complex nervous processes lying at the base of emerging movements are organized with a direct and marked participation of the cerebral cortex. And the functional structure of the cortex of the main brain, as it is known, is not defined from birth by its anatomical structure but develops as a result of functioning (63; p. 25).

Shchelovanov emphasizes principal differences between the development of children and the offspring of animals. The first and the basic difference consists in this, that the correct development of the child from the moment of birth is not possible without special nurturing actions on the part of adults. Even when speaking about a child two-three months of age, one cannot assume that correct feeding and hygienic care insure his motor development. Also necessary is a planned system of nurturing measures directed toward the development of the child's movements through construction of favorable conditions for his displacement, e.g., placement of attractive objects into his visual field within the limits of his reach. The adults must create and sustain for children a satisfactory emotional condition without which, as observations show, general psychological development of children is greatly hindered. Emotionally dull children, as a rule, move around very little and inactivity leads to the weakening of the muscular system. The absence of positive emotions serves to reduce the intensity of the work of the heart and circulatory system and the respiratory and endocrine systems.

In a special investigation directed by Shchelovanov, Kistyakovskaya (33) produced data indicating a dependence of the development of movement in children in their first year on their kind of upbringing, along the four following qualities: 1) tempo of the development of movements; 2) order of their occurrence; 3) presence or absence of these or other movements; and 4) variability of the content of different categories of movements. With regard to the tempo of movement development, the author observed that with a fairly weak nurturant approach the children, toward the end of the first and the beginning of the second year of life, had a very weak footing or were not able to discover it at all, were unable to raise and hold up their heads while lying on their stomach, were not able to grasp and hold a toy in their hands, etc. Kistyakovskaya observed cases of frequent changes in the occurrence of movements in relation to upbringing conditions. Thus, under certain conditions, at the end of the first year the children are able to stand on their feet quite steadily while hanging onto a barrier. However, they still do not sit independently. The presence or absence of these or other movements in a child is also determined by the actions of upbringing. In nurseries, the children in a majority of cases crawl prior to walking. This behavior is determined by several factors, such as, the clothing not constricting the child's movement; furthermore, in the play area with plenty of toys and sufficient space, there naturally arises an impulse to crawl, which is also facilitated by the encouragement of attempts to crawl by the attending adults and by special exercises conducted with the youngsters. Under the condition of home upbringing, the parents quite frequently do not provide conditions for their children that would favor the development of crawling but instead begin to teach them how to walk early. Therefore, the children raised in a family frequently bypass the crawling stage. Variability of the content of different categories of movements (for instance, forms of crawling) also depend to a large extent on the conditions of upbringing.

Thus, the first difference in the child's development in comparison with the development of animal offspring consists of the fact that development is accomplished under the influence of upbringing in the form of acquisition of adults' experience and not as a simple accumulation of one's own individual experience.

Furthermore, the development of movements in a child occurs under the control of distal receptors—vision and hearing—at the time when among animals the vestibular, proprioceptive, and, in part, skin apparati exert the dominant role for a long time. Due to the sequence in which various receptors enter into activity, the child early attains the ability for focusing, which is necessary for the establishment of contact with surrounding people, and the development of movement is accomplished as the formation of objective actions directed toward grasping and exploring different objects. "Thus," writes Shchelovanov, "in the young one distance receptors are first formed (visual and auditory) up to their cortical divisions, and only thereafter do movements begin to develop; in the majority of animals the order is reversed" (64). In another instance he states: "There exists a gross difference in the functional interaction between the motor and analyzing centers in children and in animals, especially in ones that are born blind. At the time when the child's analyzing centers become functionally operational or dominant and the motor centers are not functionally constructed, the majority of animals exhibit the opposite relationship. In their development motor centers are formed earlier than analyzing centers, even when the analyzing centers do not receive an inflow of stimulation from the periphery because of lack of eye and ear formation. Therefore, the child readily develops attendant inhibition from the analyzers innervating the musculature (fixation); whereas in the majority of animals the action upon analyzers (eye and ear) after the established functional connections with movements easily transmits impulses of motor reactions" (63).

Finally, the third feature of the child's development in comparison with an animal comprises a very important role that is acquired by the functioning of the cortex of both hemispheres. "In comparing the factors that characterize the development of movements in animals and in men, there emerges the following rule: the greater the role of the cortex of the brain's hemisphere in the development of movements, the less organized are the movements of the newborn, the longer is the period of their development, and the more final is the result. This is the complexity and diversity of movement of adult individuals" (Figurin and Denisova, 13).

On the basis of the above-stated brief theoretical views of Shchelovanov and the data of his collaborators, a new system of educational work has been developed and introduced into institutions housing children from birth to three years of age. Its practical application led to a complete eradication of the so-called hospitalism in homes for children and in nurseries and to the full-fledged physical and psychological development of children in these institutions.

The views of psychologists concerning the explanation of motivational causes of children's development is close to Shchelovanov's position. In Soviet psychology, a proposition has been affirmed concerning the formation of all human, specific, psychological characteristics and abilities in one's lifetime. "Everything specifically human in the psyche," emphasizes Leontiev, "is formed in the child in his lifetime" (38; p. 25). According to Leontiev's hypothesis, the development of the psychological functions of mankind as a result of the accumulation of sociohistorical experience is crystallized in the form of objects manufactured by people. In part, the development of the hand's motor function finds its expression in the process of the historical development of hand tools and instruments. The child is able to master human movements only by achieving an adequate form of active interaction with these tools and instruments. Consequently, the process of the development of the child's motor sphere is essentially a process of mastering the sociohistorical experience of preceding generations operationalized by objects, tools, and instruments. This is why the mastering process is characterized by Leontiev as the process of humanization of the psyche.

On his own the child cannot comprehend the purpose of objects and cannot master an appropriate form of activity with these objects, for these qualities of objects are not directly perceivable. Only with the help of an adult can the child master the sociohistorical experience of a given object. However, he does not find himself one-to-one with the world of objects. His relationships with the world of objects are conditioned by his relationships to other people and are included in the process of socialization. Consequently, socialization—in its initial form of mutual activity or in a form of verbal interaction—comprises a necessary condition in the process of the individual's mastery of the attainments of mankind.

According to data of Shchelovanov and Aksarina (65), observations by Figurin and Denisova (13), and others, the child enters into interaction with adults very early—in just a few weeks after birth. Under normal conditions at the age of two months the child exhibits a definite complex of arousal at the sight of an adult or the sound of his voice. This arousal complex is the first evidence of contact between the child and surrounding people.

In the course of childhood the form and content of the child's interaction with adults and other children change, but the process of mastery appears to be always included in the context of interaction.

Thus, the development of the child's motor sphere is realized through learning and through mastery of static and dynamic structures of behavior produced by mankind in the course of its sociohistorical development. However, mastery is only possible in the context of the child's interaction with surrounding adults.

Ontogenetic Development of the Motor Sphere and its Content

What is the course of the development of movements in the process of ontogeny? Is it a continuous process of quantitative expansion, an accumulation of motor reactions that are under a child's voluntary control, or are there in the course of development certain qualitative changes in behavior?

In this respect there are divergent points of view. They were clearly expressed, in part, in a colloquium on the work of Wallon concerning the significance of movements in the child's psychological development (6) and in the presentations by participants in the Geneva conference of the Association of Educational Psychology of French-speaking countries (Zazzo, 79). Tanner asserted that in the process of the child's growth, it is not possible to isolate separate stages. The development is realized in a continuous manner following a regular curve without radical accelerations with the exception of the adolescent age. According to Osterrit, in support of the absence of clearly defined qualitatively different stages is the fact that when an attempt was made to construct a composite diagram of stages described by eighteen prominent psychologists, a total overlap of one stage by another occurred, and as a result an absence of correspondence in even some of the basic points was found to exist. Essentially, the same point of view is shared by Gesell. The process of development, according to his views, is continuous. Separate stages can be isolated only conditionally. Therefore, any investigator may subdivide a period that he is studying into as many segments of such duration as is convenient for him.

However, numerous authors acknowledge the presence of qualitatively different stages in the process of development—differences that cannot be accounted for only by the quantity of motor reactions that are at the disposal of the child of a given age. Wallon (6, 72, 73, 74), for example, adheres to such a point of view. Obviously, he asserts that in the course of the entire development the unity of personality is preserved entirely. However, qualitative characteristics of behavior change at different stages of childhood. The separate stages are not rigidly fixed. Each one of them has a series of alternative phases, but there is some kind of a sequence typical of the overwhelming majority of children. Each stage is characterized by the prevalence of movements of a given type, by the meaningful content and context in which they occur, and by its own characteristic construction of movements, their structure, and means of regulation. At each developmental stage, one of the forms of activity takes on a dominant role; namely, it defines the qualitative peculiarity of a given stage. Qualitatively distinctive stages are not only characteristic of behavior in general, but also of each function, such as grabbing and locomotion.

The stagelike nature of development is acknowledged by McGraw (46). She emphasizes that in the development of each function there are critical periods. These periods are characterized by the emergence of readiness for the execution of some function. Interestingly, McGraw mentions that with the emergence of such a readiness the child experiences an insatiable desire to exercise for the purpose of realizing a specific function. Numerous repetitions of a given reaction—exercise in its realization—are apparently an essential part of the development of the function that has just attained a threshold sufficient for its external appearance. Consequently, the initial readiness of structure leads to the appearance of function, and the execution of the latter exerts a reverse positive influence on the final formation of structure. Whenever a pedagogue or an educator is able to detect the appearance of readiness, he is in a position to attain unusual success in forming the child's corresponding reactions. Thus, McGraw was able to attain much success in training the twins, Johnny and Jimmy, to roller skate, jump, climb a ladder, and turn the pedals of a bicycle at an age of less than two years (44). After the child has mastered the functions, the need for its realization diminishes and gradually becomes nil. Usually this moment corresponds to the occurrence of the readiness for some other function. Even though the basic functions occur in all normal children at comparable times, the periods of readiness for each reaction may be considerably different for individual children depending on a series of circumstances.

In Soviet psychology, on the basis of extensive factual data and theoretical investigations, a proposition has been put forth concerning qualitative changes of behavior in the process of its ontogenetic development with identification of certain basic stages. These stages are not totally separate from one another but frequently overlap and coexist over an extended period of time, even though one of them maintains a predominant role during this time.

Each stage is characterized first of all by a definite type of interaction with the surrounding people: for it is in the nature of interaction that the specifically human aspects of the child's motor activity are actualized. The nature and content of the interaction changes significantly in the course of childhood, beginning with a passive acceptance of the adults' actions associated with the sophistication of the child's needs, and ending with a fully developed educational activity and the beginnings of cooperative, productive labor at the end of the school age.

The type of interaction is determined by the context of activity that relates to the main problem confronting the subject. Thus, the problem of behavior confronting a youngster is the expression of his needs so that an adult may satisfy them, as well as accomplishing simpler adaptational goals. However, the problem of a schoolchild's activity lies in the conscious mastery of knowledge and the experience of mankind through socially useful labor.

In correspondence with the basic task of behavior, an activity is formed that is the predominant activity for a given period of development, this activity being the most adequate for attaining the goals confronting a child of this age. The construction of movements at each level takes place depending on the goals and tasks set for the child's activity (Bernshtein, 3). Here, Bernshtein's notion concerning the association between the level of movement construction and the task of the predominant activity is extremely relevant and fruitful, for it permits one to uncover the pithy, psychological process of changes of biomechanics, the internal construction of movement in the process of ontogenetic

development. According to Bernshtein's theory the level of movement construction is characterized first of all by the composition
of the predominating afferentiation. The latter subsumes, according to the author, not just isolated sensations that serve as the
basis for regulating movement, but also their fusion—merging—
into one inseparable sensory synthesis that contains imprints of
the immediate experience of various modalities, as well as traces
of former impressions interwoven into a unified whole. Furthermore, sensations, as well as the resulting elements of synthesis,
are not represented in their raw form but are preliminarily recon-
structed in the central apparati of the nervous system of some
level (depending on the construction level of the motor activity).

On the basis of the predominating afferentiation, an adequate
construction of movement is realized; movement that provides
for internal coordination and continuous sensory correction of
motor elements, as well as alignment of movements in correspondence to the external conditions of the activity. Finally, each
stage of the development of movements is characterized by a
typical form of mastering movements that is basically determined
by the nature of the predominating activity. Thus, at the preschool stage when play is the child's predominating activity, mastery of movements is primarily realized through the imitation of
adults' actions, the functions of which have been accepted by the
child in play. For a child of school age, mastery is primarily accomplished in the course of goal-oriented educational activity.

Thus, the external image of the ontogeny of motor activity
represents a sequence of qualitatively distinctive phases or stages,
conditioned by the type of social interaction and the tasks of
activity emerging from it. The internal content of the ontogeny
of motor activity is the development of afferentiation and, determined by it, a change of levels in the construction of movement
with a gradual shift from lower to higher levels.

Development of the Motor Sphere of Preschool Children
Let us shift to the factual description of how motor activity is
realized from birth to seven years. The quantity of the corre-

sponding data is here inversely proportional to age. Therefore, we are able to characterize the development of infant movements in great detail; but for the children of preschool age (three-seven) only scanty data are available. Such a state of affairs apparently is not accidental. The fact is that the infant attracts attention by his individual motor reactions, which are initially altogether absent from the repertoire of his behavior; they then emerge and are modified, gradually perfected, and finally relatively stabilized. At this stage, the semantic content of these reactions is relatively elementary. At the same time, transformation of the structure of these movements unfolds almost directly in the observer's view. Therefore, experimenters have a tendency to describe and analyze not the motor acts, actions, and deeds, but motor activity in the actual sense of the word. The matter is intensified by the unquestionable role that is assumed by the maturation of the neuromuscular and anatomical apparatus of movements in the development of motor activity during the first year. In the forefront at the preschool age is the mastery of different kinds of habits, including motor habits (correct posture, etc.), via imitation and planned teaching of the child by adults. The complicated behavior resulting from the child's immersion into a more complex system of interaction with the surrounding people attracts attention mainly to the psychological content of the motor acts, and it delegates to a secondary position the biomechanic aspects of movement. This is why, in the formation of the question concerning the movements of preschool children, the central position is allocated to data concerning the formation of motor habits.

Development of Movements of an Infant (Birth to One Year)
A newborn arrives in the world as a helpless being. Any kinds of movements designed for assuming and maintaining a given posture are absent, particularly the ones responsible for displacement in space. The dominant tonus of the newborn is that of the contractive muscles. Consequently, at quiescence the fingers of the infant are usually pressed up toward the stomach. Individual movements of the extremities are abrupt and sharp. During the

short periods of a wakeful state, the newborn apparently finds himself in a negative emotional state manifested by restless movements and crying (Elkonin, 11).

Among the movements of the newborn, two types are dominant: First, according to Bernshtein, there are disorganized chaotic movements of the synkenetic type, i.e., movements representing combinations of various uncoordinated, frequently antagonistic motor acts. Secondly, there are unconditioned reflexes of a different nature—distinguishable by a sequence and strict coordination of the elements that compose them. Among these, it is necessary to point out the sucking reflex. Other unconditioned reflexes do not have any adaptive characteristic and represent atavistic reactions. Such, for example, are the grabbing or palmer reflex, swimming movements, shuffle reflex, etc.. Apparently, subcortical formations are primarily involved in the implementation of the initial motor acts. Because of this, some authors refer to the newborn as a thalamopallidal being (Bernshtein, 3; Irwin and Weiss, 28). Indeed, the cortex of the main brain at the time of birth is still morphologically not completely formed.

However, according to Krasnogorsky (36), Kasatkin (30), Shchelovanov (65), and others, this is not an obstacle for cortical functioning shortly after birth. Consequently, the formation of the child's movements from the very beginning is carried out under the control and participation of the cortex of the hemispheres.

The First Half-Year. How does the development of a child's movements proceed during the first six months of life? First of all, it is essential to emphasize that from the very beginning, this development is realized within the context of the child's interaction with the surrounding people. Wallon is especially emphatic about this. "The life of a human being," he writes, "begins with an affective or emotional stage that fits well with the general and prolonged helplessness of childhood; it orients his initial intuitive movements toward others and puts interaction in the primary scheme" (72; p. 131). In another instance, Wallon notes that the initial

movements of a child are essentially expressive gestures, with
which he is successful in his attempts to attract the attention of
those around him toward recognizing his needs (72).

During the first months of life, the child's interaction with
adults in the context of which his behavior is developed is very
primitive; the child expresses his needs to an adult and signals
whenever these are satisfied. But even this primitive interaction is
important in the lifelong development of a child. This is supported by data indicating that "with insufficient or inadequate
nurturing influences, as early as second-third months of age, one
would observe retardation in the child's development" (Elkonin,
11; p. 61).

What kinds of means does the child employ in attaining the
solution to his basic problem; how does he fulfill his role in the
interaction with an adult? During the initial months he develops
all the basic forms of fixation—auditory and visual—aside from
nutritive and labyrinthian, which were already present at birth.
Dominant states of an extensive irradiation of arousal now occupy the central position. Due to this, the perception of stimuli—
auditory and visual—presented by adults becomes effective. Data
of Figurin and Denisova indicate that initially the reaction of
fixation and later the arousal reaction are evoked by the sight and
voice of a human being and not by other types of stimuli within
the same modalities. This once more underscores the association
of the emergence of these reactions with the problems of interaction.

Based on the visual and auditory fixation, toward the second-
third month one observes the appearance of a characteristic reaction of a complex nature that was identified as an arousal complex by Figurin and Denisova. This reaction occurs only with the
sight of an adult or with the sound of his voice and includes smiling, movement of extremities (raising of arms, quick shuffling of
the legs, and bending of the legs at knee and hip joints), and hum-
ming (utterance of low, quiet sounds). The appearance of the
arousal complex is the first clear-cut evidence of the child's inter-

action with an adult. Its essence is the basis upon which grabbing movements of the hand, speech, and emotional reactions are formed in the future. Soon after the final formulation of the arousal complex it begins to fall apart, to be differentiated into separate inherent components. In part, the movement of grabbing becomes differentiated out of its context.

It is well established that one can easily evoke a reaction of hand flexing in a newborn by simply touching the palm of his hand (snapping movement, or the palmer reflex). The evoked grabbing or clenching of the object touching his palm is so intense that it allows the child to suspend his body in the air for some time. During the first month this reflex gradually intensifies, apparently due to the maturation of the subcortical centers that bring it about. However, thereafter its strength begins to diminish each day, and subsequently, it becomes totally suppressed.

The grabbing reaction as such is of a complex conditioned-reflexive nature and is formed gradually. During the arousal reaction, the child executes numerous disorganized hand movements. During this time he occasionally and accidentally makes contact with nearby objects and grabs them. This is the beginning of the grabbing reaction. However, before this reaction is finalized it undergoes a lengthy developmental sequence. At two and one-half—three and one-half months, the child for the first time exhibits reactions that are preparatory for grabbing. They consist of groping movements. It is interesting that the first objects to be explored by groping are the infant's own hands. Subsequently, he shifts his groping movements to other objects (diaper, blanket, etc.). The groping is conducted without looking.

Two to three weeks later, the child exhibits a visual exploratory reaction to hands that happened to fall into his field of vision. At this time, the hands are maintained for a rather long period in a position conducive to their exploration. Subsequently, the child begins to stretch himself toward the surrounding objects and, having reached them, examines them by feel under the control of vision, alternating his fixation between the object and his hand.

This preparatory period is ended by the appearance of the reaction of grabbing an object right after the visual and groping exploration. It is a bit premature to talk about an actual grabbing reaction, for while extending his hands toward objects, the child does not yet arrange them into a position specifically for the purpose of grabbing. Only at four-five months does the actual grabbing reaction appear for the first time, which is characterized by a preparatory arrangement of the hand and fingers in a semi-bent position necessary for quick and accurate implementation of the reaction.

This type of grabbing is characterized by numerous authors as sensory-motor and not an objective reaction (Bernshtein, 3; Wallon, 74); the most typical aspect of it is the establishing of coordination between the visual stimulation, still rather inaccurate and diffuse, and the movement of the hand. Up to the first year of life, grabbing basically remains at this initial stage of development. Only considerably later does grabbing become an objective reaction manifested by a refined and unusually extensive differentiation of hand positions, which is being readied for taking an object of a given size, form, and designation. (See an interesting study on this topic with adult subjects by Kotlyarova, 35).

Development of hand movements is extremely important for the general psychological development of the child, for it permits him to shift from a purely contemplative, visual perception of the world to an active, effective, and therefore much more total and accurate knowledge of it.

Furthermore, in this period one observes a rapid formation of imitative movements—smiling, which occurs during the second month and sometimes even at the end of the first, crying with tears, and laughing. Simultaneously, there is a gradual suppression of all innate behavioral reflexes. Having attained a maximum toward the thirtieth-fortieth day after birth such reflexes as Moro's, Robinson's, swimming, shuffle, etc., begin to be rapidly extinguished. All of these changes in the child's motor sphere basically serve the goals of interaction with adults. However, even in the initial stage of his existence the child may be confronted with an independent although secondary, task of mastering his own body. According to an assumption made by Pavlov, there is apparently an absence of a connection between kinesthetic and motor cells of the cortex at birth. "It is realistic to assume," he writes, "that the initial stage of individual existence of higher animals and especially man, when the latter spends months in learning how to operate his own beginning movements, is consumed in the formation of this connection" (53; p. 317). It is possible that in the course of the disorganized, widely spread movements that are observed right after birth, there is an accumulation of experience necessary for the establishment of these connections. Aside from this, while discussing the infant's spontaneous movements, would it be accurate to reject totally their adaptational significance, for they, even though not intentionally, are able to satisfy the child's needs in that they provide for a change in a position, allow him to adopt a more comfortable posture, increase circulation, improve digestion, etc. It is possible that gradually as a result of these exercises there is a change in the general nature of the movements—they become more flexible and there is a more appropriate distribution of tonus among the muscles—flexors and extensors.

Very early during the first month the distal receptors, the eye and the ear, assume a great and ever-increasing role in regulating behavior. This phenomenon is cited by Shchelovanov (63) as one of the essential differences of the ontogeny of man from that of other higher animal species. However, the dominant afferentiation during this stage is of another type. According to Bernshtein, it may be identified as proprioception in a broad sense of the word, i.e., synthesis of sensations of various modalities arising in one's own body and almost entirely unrelated to the external space. Due to the afferentiation of this level, the child is successful in gradually abandoning synkenesis and shifting to movements of the synergetic type, i.e., complex motor acts, the individual elements of which are strictly and correctly coordinated with one another.

The Second Half-Year. During the second half of the first year, there is a drastic change in the child's development, which initially is manifested by a change in the form of interaction with adults. Instead of one-sided contact where the adult took on an active role and the child to a large extent a passive role, participation by the child in mutual activity with the adult now emerges. This activity unfolds primarily in connection with objects—toys and simpler types of everyday things. Usually, the adult shows the toy to the child, names it, hides it or extends it to the child, manipulates it, and encourages the child to manipulate it. This type of interaction demands the child's perception of himself and of objects in relation to one another and the ability to bring his movements into correspondence with the objective conditions of the activity. Furthermore, the change of the nature of the child's interaction with an adult is also manifested by the fact that the child no longer just becomes aroused by the sight of an adult and delighted by him whenever the adult turns to him on his own initiative, but he now arouses an adult to contact, extends his arms to him, and pulls him toward himself, therefore attracting the adult's attention by a persistent, summoning shouting.

Bernshtein characterized this stage of motor development as a stage of spatial field. The leading afferentiation at this level is an orderly perception of the surrounding media, i.e., perception of oneself and objects within accurate coordinates of time and space and their mutual relationship. The pithy characteristic of objects, the sociohistorical experience crystallized in them at this stage, does not occupy a prime position of importance. The child derives satisfaction from being able to reach the object, examine it visually, manually, taste it, listen to it, and perform some of the simpler manipulations with it. Actions with objects at this level are very primitive in their content and can be reduced basically to displacements of objects. According to observations by Kistya-kovskaya (33), a child of this age acts about the same with all objects and toys. In spite of this primitive level of manipulation, it permits the child to obtain some initial information concerning the attributes of the objects and thereby prepares the child for a shift to essentially specific actions with the objects.

The development of the child's hand movements during the first year of life would be impossible without simultaneous formation of typically human postures—sitting and vertical standing. Children begin sitting with assistance at approximately six months of age. In the majority of children, sitting independently is observed not earlier than seven or eight months of age. An interesting aspect of the genesis of this reaction is its entirely experiential formulation. While the newborn exhibits an innate shuffle reflex, observed whenever the child is supported under his arms and is placed with his feet down on some solid surface, no such unconditioned reflexive elements of sitting are noticed in a newborn. Apparently, this indicates that in phylogeny, sitting reflexes are the last ones to appear.

Until quite recently, it has been assumed that children learn initially to sit and subsequently to crawl. Such is the case under appropriate conditions of upbringing. However, it is much more convenient for the child to learn to crawl initially, for it makes him more active and more independent and it expands the world available for his exploration quite extensively. This is especially emphasized by Shchelovanov (for example, Vygotskaya, 71). The works of Ryss (58, 59) indicate that under conditions favoring the development of active movements (sufficient area for unrestricted displacement; clothing free enough to prevent restriction of movement; supplies and toys; attention of adults to the motor activity of the child; and daily massage and gymnastics) children begin crawling significantly earlier than sitting, and this is positively reflected in their general physical and psychological development. Crawling is the child's first locomotor reaction. However, it has only a temporary significance. Toward the end of the first year of life, children begin to walk. Walking has two aspects: maintenance of the body in a balanced and vertical position and displacement forward. Subcortical reactions of overstepping and the supportive reaction (pushing off from the base), which are already present during the initial months of life, are not the initial stages of erect movement and gradually become extinguished. A precondition for the formation of walking is the mastery of the posture of standing.

According to Figurin and Denisova, the act of standing undergoes the following stages in its formation:

1. While supported under his arms, the child does not bend his legs but bends himself at the hip joints.
2. Whenever pulled, the child is lifted by his hands.
3. Whenever held by the hands, he stands for a short time.
4. Does not bend his legs and stands upright.
5. Stands for a long time whenever he is held by the hands.
6. Picks himself up whenever taken by the hand.
7. Stands, while holding on to a railing.
8. Kneels, while hanging on to something.
9. Lifts himself, while hanging on to something.
10. Sits down from a vertical position.
11. Makes an attempt to stand without support of his hands.
12. Stands without support of his hands.
13. Lifts himself without hanging on to something.
14. Squats, while standing without support.

The final formulation of the sitting posture and the dynamic reactions connected with it are accomplished in ten-eleven months. With the development of raising and standing is associated the development of walking. The formation of walking begins with attempts at overstepping (at approximately five months). Toward eight months the child is proficient at overstepping, taking a large number of steps whenever held under his arms. Thereafter, children begin to walk while hanging on to a railing or a moving chair with both hands or while supported by adults. From nine to eleven months, walking is possible while holding the child by only one hand. Only by the age of one year or sometimes later do children learn to walk quite independently, taking only a few steps at first and subsequently conquering large distances.

Sitting, standing, getting up, and walking represent complex motor acts constructed out of a chain of reflexes. Their mastery and voluntary execution on the child's initiative attest to considerable success in the development of his motor activity.

A summary of the child's motor development during the first year of life may be expressed by the words of Sechenov: "Being armed with an ability to see, hear, grab, walk, and command the movement of his hands, the child ceases to be, one might say, nailed to one spot and enters into an era of a more free and independent interaction with the external world" (60; p. 265). During the first year, the number of movements performed by the child sharply increases and the individual aspects of his motor activity change drastically; movements become more coordinated, more precise, more adapted to external circumstances, and as a result of this, more arbitrary.

By what means, then, are the new movements mastered and their new qualitative aspects acquired during the first year of life? According to all the authors studying the development of movements in the first year, goal oriented training of a child by an adult in any form does not have any significance for the child's acquisition of new actions (for example, Bergeron, 2). New actions are basically a by-product of the child's practical activity in the course of which useful movements, successful from the point of view of confronting the child's problems, become reinforced and fixed, while adverse movements—or the unnecessary ones— become inhibited without receiving positive reinforcement. Reinforcement of movements during the first year of life may be of two basic types.

The satisfaction of basic organic needs may be viewed as reinforcement. We have already mentioned that even the uncoordinated, spontaneous movements of the infant facilitate the well-being of the organism, influencing its breathing, circulation, and digestion. Furthermore, they might occasionally fulfill a direct adaptational role by producing a change in an uncomfortable position of the body. This type of reinforcement occurs in connection with the secondary task of mastering one's own body that we alluded to previously. Included in this task, apparently, is the selection of the most effective biomechanical movements, since they reduce unproductive energetic expenditures of the child's organism. However, "satisfaction of organic need in and by itself," as emphasized by Elkonin, "does not lead to either new actions, understanding of speech, or walking. All those acquisitions come about in connection with the need for interaction and on the basis of forms of cognition and actions with objects associated with it" (11; p. 92). Thus, a more important type of reinforcement of movements during the first year of life is the satisfaction of the child's needs in the course of interaction. In contrast with the first direct reinforcement, the second type of reinforcement might be conditionally called social. Consequently, the basic formative role in the development of motor activity is attributed to reinforcement emerging in association with interaction.

Development of Movements in a Pre-preschooler (One-Three Years)

Toward the end of the first year of life, the child's interaction with the surrounding adults becomes complicated. As before, the child cannot get along without the help of an adult, for he is just beginning to learn how to walk, cannot yet dress himself, eat unassisted, etc. However, in comparison with an infant he is more independent. He exhibits certain needs and wants. He directs some of them to an adult because he is still not able to satisfy them himself (to obtain a toy or a different object; to go out for a walk; to be fed his favorite dish, etc.). Therefore, the child is confronted with the necessity for expressing his wants—making them known to an adult. The complexity of a pre-preschooler's needs in comparison with the needs of an infant, demands that he master more effective means for the outward expression of his needs—to refine his gestures, to diversify them, to enrich his

mimicry. However, soon even this is insufficient: A need arises
for verbal interaction. This is the base for the formation of
speech. Simultaneously, there is a change in the adult's approach
to the child; the adult for the first time begins to confront the
child systematically with certain demands and shows him how
these demands can be fulfilled. He teaches the child or helps him
with his independent attempts. Basically, the demands of an adult
toward the child consist of expecting the child to master specifically human and historically conditioned forms of behavior (eating out of dishes, observance of neatness, simpler rules of cohabi-
tation, etc.). Of prime significance becomes mastering the correct,
i.e., adequate, methods of handling different objects (for example, utilization of a spoon, a cup, etc.). The predominating activities of the child at this stage are objective actions and games
based on them—manipulation of objects in which the child
attempts to reproduce methods of using different objects observed by him—rolling a buggy, feeding a doll, etc.

In correspondence with the new forms of interaction and associated with their problems of activity is a change in afferentiation
of movements. Now it is impossible for the child to be limited to
proprioception or even to simpler extraceptive afferentiations of
the spatial field variety. The primary position is now taken up by
an object not only as a physical body, but as a specified thing
with its own designation. There is a formation of objective actions directed and regulated by a precise, intelligent perception of
the objects of action. Naturally, the task of mastering one's own
movements from the point of view of the internal "economy" of
the organism and with respect to the relationship to external
space retains its significance. However, instead of having the primary role, it becomes subservient—secondary.

The beginnings of objective actions are observed initially at the
age of ten-eleven months in the form of specific activity with
various types of objects. Thus, Vygotskaya (71) was able to observe how, toward the end of the first year, the child begins to
manipulate various objects in different ways—for example, swing-

ing a rattle, throwing a ball, squeezing or squeaking a rubber toy, etc. Certainly, these manipulations are still very simple and few in number. However, they are of great significance in the child's development. In the process of these initial objective actions, there is an increasingly deeper analysis of objects and identification of their different attributes. The child's knowledge of the qualities of objects becomes increasingly enriched. On the basis of specific actions with objects there arises isolation of their permanent features and a formulation of initial generalizations. Of great importance in this process are words, which reinforce the obtained generalization.

The formation of objective action is characteristic of the pre-preschool age. During this stage, not only is the formation of hand movements accomplished, but also general motor activity of the body.

Actual bipedal locomotion (Bernshtein, 3) develops at the beginning of the second year of life. Initially, the movements of walking are awkward and unstable, a condition that is aggravated by purely anthropological difficulties (weakness of the lower extremities, weakness of their musculature, high position of the body's center of gravity with respect to the hip axis). Walking and running are still not differentiated. The child appears awkward and clumsy. During the second year, walking becomes an insatiable need, which is only diminished toward the third year after automatization of the act of walking. Along with the ability to walk on the floor the ability gradually develops for overcoming such obstacles as hills, ladders, slopes, narrow passages, small planks, and vacillating surfaces. Walking does not entirely absorb the child's attention—children enjoy transporting objects and in the course of such activity perform all kinds of simple actions. At twenty months the child generally masters all types of locomotion with the exception of running, the formation of which is not finalized until school age.

Thus, in the course of pre-preschool childhood objective acts

appear and develop and all basic locomotor movements are formulated.

What are the methods for the mastery of these motor acts by
the pre-preschooler? Meaningful studies are absent in this area. A
characteristic form of mastering new movements by a pre-preschooler is determined by the nature of his predominating activity—objective play in the context of which one basically accomplishes mastery of motor habits and abilities at this age. The child
acquires knowledge, abilities, and habits in an offhand manner as
a result of some kind of goal-oriented play activity. A decisive
role in this is attributed to imitation of adults' actions, which the
child frequently observes and attempts to reproduce.

Ability to imitate is not present at birth. It first appears during
infancy and undergoes a series of qualitatively diverse steps during
the course of its development. Evident at the beginning of the
second half of the first year is a frequent repetition of reactions
that Figurin and Denisova (13) identify as the differentiating sign
of the last, fourth period of infancy. These reactions usually
consist of petting an object with a hand or tapping it and of repetitive pronounciation of sounds and syllables. These reactions
attest to the fact that, due to a presence of connections between
kinesthetic and motor cells of the cortex, the child is able to
reproduce movements that he just executed a short time ago. This
seems to be imitation of oneself, or that which Wallon calls
echolalia and echopraxia. Practice in repetitive reactions is very
important, since it permits the child to clarify or to establish
connection between a given movement and its sensory (most
often) or objective result. Reinforcement of some of these movements by encouragement on the part of adults, by a smile or just
simply by attention to the child's activity, may lead to selectivity
and to a subsequent reinforcement of some of these acts. However, to speak of imitation at this age is still not possible, for as a
matter of fact, imitation is a process directed at the reproduction
of action observed as it is being performed by someone else and

copying the observed movement, not a simple exercise in the execution of one and the same action. The role of the repetitive reactions consists possibly in the fact that they prepare certain copying mechanisms, aligning one's own movements with a model, the function of which is assumed here by traces of kinesthetic stimulations of just-executed acts.

Shortly after the appearance of echolalia and echopraxia, there begins to develop an initial, most primitive form of actual imitation, which consists of reproduction of a well-mastered act executed before the child by an adult. This form of imitation is especially evident in prespeech vocalization by the child: Children of nine-ten months listen attentively to adults, pronouncing syllables that the child has already learned to speak and with readiness now repeats. At the same time, pronunciation of new syllables by adults does not evoke attempts at imitation.

However, by the end of the first year of life, the child attempts to repeat movements of an adult that are new for him, but this occurs only under two sets of conditions: 1) whenever the model is presented directly, i.e., whenever the adult performs the necessary movement right in front of the child, and 2) whenever movement is quite simple in its composition and the child is able to execute its individual elements. Through this type of imitation the child learns, for example, how to do patty-cake, usually in combination with a method of passive movements. Slow progress in imitation at this stage may be explained by the weakness of the visual-motor coordination mechanism, without which it is impossible to coordinate the observed movement with the one being performed.

Only at the next stage does there emerge imitation having a formative function. At this time, while observing people's movements around him, the child masters movements that are new to him. Transformation of imitation into a means for mastering entirely new, socially constructed forms of behavior and its acquisition of the decisive role in the development of motor behavior, emphasizes Zaporozhets, occur initially in phylogeny at the human level. At this stage of development, for the first time one observes a complex structure in the imitation process. It begins with observation of the object for imitation and a formation, on these bases, of a model of the necessary action. Thereafter follow attempts at reproduction of the model that at first are not very successful. A coincidence of the actions occurring during practice with the model serves as a distinctive reinforcement. As a result of a series of repetitive attempts, the child attains more or less accurate reproduction of the action model. The entire process of imitation is built on the basis of the combined reflexive mechanisms under a great influence of the orienting exploratory activity. With the latter, imitation has much in common (78).

Further development of imitation occurs in the preschool age and follows two paths: The first is along the line of complicating the models available for reproduction. This advancement becomes possible subsequent to improving activity related to exploration of the model and to its reproduction with the assistance of sensory corrections. Secondly, imitation becomes possible in the absence of a direct model on the basis of an idea, and finally, on the basis of only the verbal description of the required action.

Imitation is one of the simplest forms of learning. With the help of this process, a planned mastery of socially derived forms of movements becomes possible. In part, the actual mechanism of imitation is the basis of the child's mastery of his initial objective reactions.

Another simpler way of learning is the method of passive movements. Certain data (for example, Vygotskaya, 71) permit one to assume that the method of passive movements may already play a definite role in the infantile period, for example, when the child is learning grabbing. However, gains attributable to this method of learning are rather limited and are smaller the younger the child. Toward the end of the first year it is possible by employing the method of passive movements to teach the child to wave his hand for departure, to do patty-cake, etc. In pre-preschool childhood it becomes possible by relying on this procedure to master more complex movements, for example, the ones of everyday experience (drinking out of a cup, eating with a spoon, etc.). However, this method of passive movement does not acquire especially independent significance and basically occurs as a facilitating one in the mastery of new, difficult, imitative movements.

Development of Movements in Preschool Age (Three-Seven Years)

By three years of age the child's motor activity has developed considerably. Children of this age are lively, agile, and graceful. However, the general level of body and manual dexterity is still quite low. This was the basis upon which Bernshtein (3) characterized the motor activity of the preschooler as "graceful awkwardness."

The type of interaction of children this age with adults differs considerably from the one observed at earlier stages of development. The earlier forms of mutual activity between the child and the adult are torn down. The degree of independence in the preschooler reaches a high level. In his striving for independence, the child frequently opposes the dictates and requirements of adults, while assertively expressing his own wants and interests. Furthermore, children want to participate in the life of the adults—to be their equal—even though their resources, knowledge, and abilities are obviously insufficient for this. The child satisfies his striving for independence and for participation in the adults' activity through role playing, which becomes the primary activity in the preschool age.

On the other hand, there is a change in the relationship of the adults to the child—they increase their demands of the child and at the same time their trust in him. Therefore, they invite children to perform individual tasks, to increase their participation in a task, and occasionally present them with simple, permanent instructions related to everyday life. Thus, the child acquires serious responsibilities. Finally, at the preschool age, for the first time the child is being taught, even though his learning activity is only beginning to emerge.

New problems require mastery of new movements by the preschooler. Along with the movements of the types mentioned above, the preschooler for the first time begins to master a new type of movement—instrumental. In contrast with the former levels, i.e., the objective movements where there was nothing separating the child and the object of his activity, the characteristic aspect of the instrumental movement is that the influence exerted on an object is carried out or mediated by a tool or an instrument. Depending on the structure and attributes of the tool, the hand must function in a new manner—in line with the logic of the instrument. A complete mastery of instrumental movements is accomplished in the course of learning and professional working activities. However, the beginnings of this important and specifically human type of movement begin to be formed considerably earlier, at the time when children begin to utilize a spoon, a fork, scissors, and other relatively simple instruments.

Each tool's socially constructed means of utilization and man-made origin are the main differences between man's tools and other facilitating means used by other animals. Therefore, mastery of instrumental movements signifies acquisition of a sociohistorical method of work. In school as well as at work, this mastery is obtained on the basis of systematic training. In preschool age and earlier, mastery of instrumental movements is accomplished basically through imitation and in practical activity through self-help.

Simple household tools are available even to the pre-preschooler. Initially, however, in his actions with them the child constructs his own movements of the manual type and will therefore, for example, turn the spoon over on its way to his mouth, spilling its contents. Only gradually does he master the logic of a tool's application and begin to act accordingly.

What is the afferentiation at the base of instrumental movements? There is a gradual isolation of afferent impulses informing
the subject of the most essential conditions of the problem and
which orientation may best secure the attainment of the desired
result. Such are the impulses evoked by movements of the operating tool, which primarily represent the kinesthetic signals. However, these signals now begin to inform one not only about the
positions of his own body, but also about the displacement of the
tool. There seems to a "displacement" of the hand's sensitivity to
the tool being guided by it. Consequently, there emerges afferentiation specific in content designated by that which is being sig-
naled.

In an investigation by Ginevskaya (24) it was possible to distinguish quite clearly the presence of a series of stages in the
mastery of instrumental movements at the preschool age. Children were asked to drive a nail into a board. Initially, they exhibited nonspecific reactions with the hammer as if just acting
with a heavy object. At the second stage, children were already
reproducing an external picture of the activity with the hammer.
However, at this point the trajectory of the hammer's movements
exactly reproduces the trajectory of the hand. Only at the third
stage does the child utilize the attributes of the tool (in part, its
weight and the momentum of the swinging hammer), so that the
hand begins now not only to move the tool but also to regulate
reactive forces occurring in the process of its displacement.

Galperin (14) demonstrated the attributes of instrumental movements in an example of the formation of artificial instrumental
action with two—seven-year-old children, involving retrieving toys
out of a box with the help of a special little shovel without any
directions from an adult. Initially, the child made attempts at
succeeding in his goal—obtaining the toy—without special consideration for the attributes of the tool. He performed various
probing movements without observing them, isolating them, or
reinforcing them. Successful applications occurred without intent
on his part. Consequently, the child began to identify acciden-

tally occurring, favorable positions of the shovel and to preserve them, but he was still not able to produce them himself. At the third stage, the child was already isolating successful applications and frequently, even importunately, was making attempts to employ them. But, only at the fourth stage was the child beginning to take into extensive account objective properties and associations of objects. At this stage, the development of instrumental movements in the preschool age comes to an end.

During the preschool age the development of locomotor movements continues. According to the data of Levi-Gorinevskaya (39), walking and running of the younger preschooler (three-four years) is quite imperfect; the length of steps is not constant, development of the concordant movements of the arms is just beginning, and the straightforwardness of the movements is inadequate. In running there is an absence of "flight." Toward the end of the preschool age, all qualitative and quantitative indices of locomotor movements are increased. In 93-94 percent of children six-seven years of age, one observes consonant arm movements in the course of walking or running, running becomes straightforward and rhythmic, flight is expressed in 84 percent of the children, speed of running is increased, and the length of a step also increases.

In the preschool age, children for the first time master jumping; initially just jumping up and down in one place, subsequently jumping from a slight elevation, and finally, jumping straight up from one spot. The length of a jump and its height increases (97 cm and 52 cm, respectively). Children master throwing, and with systematic practice in this type of movement they attain considerable success. However, accuracy of a throw still remains poor. In general, movements of a preschooler suffer from a lack of precision and ability to overcome resistance, since types of activities accessible to preschoolers do not demand these qualities. Only with the shift to learning and especially work do children master strength and accuracy.

In conclusion, let us characterize the methods of mastering new movements that are characteristic of the preschool age.

According to Elkonin, "At preschool age, the reconstruction of movements and actions of a child consists in that they begin to be practically executed, controlled, and regulated independently by the child on the basis of an image of the anticipated activity and the means for its realization" (12; p. 226). At the preceding stages of development, the function of controlling the child's movements was basically fulfilled by an adult. Such a change became possible only with the accumulation of experience and with the development of the child's orienting-exploratory activity necessary for the analysis of a model in relation to the actually performed actions. In correspondence with this change in the nature of regulating movements, the method of passive movements is displaced to a secondary position. Data of Kirillova (31) indicated that after five-six years the effectiveness of the method of passive movements decreased considerably in comparison with the effectiveness of imitation. Data obtained by Ginevskaya (24), Kozlovsky (34), and Poddyakov (54, 55) support this deduction. Apparently, the crux of the matter is that with the method of passive movements the tonus of the nervous system is lowered and there is a weakening of the orienting-exploratory activity. At the same time, that method produces satisfactory results in cases when insufficiency of visual-kinesthetic connections hinders the mastery of new movement through imitation.

Imitation during the preschool age remains one of the basic methods in the mastery of movements. An expanded imitation activity at the preschool age is attained in the course of role playing. In the course of the game, the child identifies himself with a given personality or a person of some profession and strives to reproduce their characteristic actions and sometimes their gait, posture, etc. Furthermore, the success of imitation gradually increases as a result of the development of observation, which enriches and refines the image of the action being copied; and, as a result of greater precision of the visual-motor coordination, the child is permitted to attain a more accurate reproduction of the desired model.

In addition, the preschool-age child experiences for the first time the possibility of goal-oriented mastery of movements and methods of action through systematic training by adults. Up to this stage, mastery of new movements in all instances was a by-product of some kind of practical activity, and the process of mastery was directly connected with the execution of the goal-oriented operation. In correspondence with the general attributes of the afferentiation of movements at this age, one of the first and most effective forms of teaching the child movements is demonstration, for it presents the child with an opportunity to employ a method of imitation familiar to him. Teaching children by demonstration has been investigated by numerous authors. Thus, experiments by Dimanshtein (9) and Grebenshchikova (26) indicate that even the younger preschoolers are able to reproduce a demonstrated, simple type of gymnastic movement even though they encounter certain difficulties in such a task. Polyakova (56) taught children to move through a table maze. In some series of the experiments she silently indicated the correct path before-hand. Inclusion of demonstration—permitting the child to rely on imitation—accelerated the process of mastering the general con-figuration of movement, especially for the younger preschoolers. For six—seven-year-old children the influence of imitation was considerably decreased and to the forefront came the child's independent orientation to the situation, which allowed him to bring his movements more quickly and with greater accuracy in correspondence with the objective conditions of activity. Thus, visual demonstration gradually abandons its leading role, giving place to verbal instructions. Polyakova's experiments indicated in part that introduction of verbal explanations—designation of the orientators of the path—considerably accelerates the mastery of motor habits through imitation.

In the preschool age, formation of the ability for conscious, goal-oriented training and, in part, for teaching movements through gymnastic exercises brings to the forefront the problem of habits, the investigation of which will not be reviewed.

Formation of Motor Habits in Children of Preschool Age

The mastery of motor habits has great significance in the child's development. It is possible in forming the qualities required of a future builder of life to teach him to act in a given manner and to obtain in his action a certain result through the most economical method.

Active motor activity characterizes the child's behavior in early childhood. During this period there is an intense development of the neuromuscular apparatus; also, the basic manual and loco-motor functions are formed—sitting, standing, walking, running, jumping, grabbing, throwing, etc. On the basis of these movements the child subsequently masters complex and diversified movements of the hands, requiring great proportionality and strict coordination, which is acquired through systematic training and constant exercises.

Habits are formed in childhood and have significance not only for the future but simultaneously are antecedents for the development of independence, which provides for the practical realization of various types of activities characteristic of preschool childhood. The presence of habits makes possible realization of intention, that is, the planned attainment of a given outcome in activity.

During preschool childhood, both the attributes of the process of motor training and the nature of the formulated habits undergo distinctive changes. Not only an increase in quantitative indices of learning is apparent, but also the appearance of new methods of mastering habits and a change in their internal structure.

In spite of the great number of studies pertaining to habits, the question of their genetic attributes still remains relatively unexplored. For the most part, the problem of habits has been studied within the scheme of the psychology of learning and very little within the framework of developmental psychology.

The majority of American authors investigating this problem emphasize a general increase in the effectiveness of motor learning with age, explaining this phenomenon in terms of maturation of the corresponding neurological mechanisms (Skinner, 66). A series of experimental facts indicate, however, that the quantitative indices of motor learning alone cannot characterize the process of development. Thus, for example, according to the data of Ivanov-Smolensky, the speed of the formation of elementary conditioned associations during the shift from preschool to school age decreases at the same time that the effectiveness of the formation of more complex systems increases during the same period.

Similar data have been cited by some of the foreign authors as a reason for establishing various pluralistic theories of developmental changes in the processes of motor learning. Thus, Hilgard (27) assumes that there are different forms of learning, which apparently are of a different nature and may be explained from the point of view of different psychological and neurological theories. Among the most elementary forms of learning Hilgard includes the process of forming the conditioned reflex, which he treats in terms of the behavioristic theory of conditioning. A higher form of learning from his viewpoint is the process of the formation of habits by trial and error, which he treats in terms of the well-known concept of Thorndike. Finally, the highest form of learning according to Hilgard is "cognitive learning," which is explained in terms of Gestalt psychology and the neobehaviorism of Tolman. According to Hilgard, there is a replacement of one form of learning by others in the process of development. With age, the relative weight of the lower forms of learning (conditioning and mastery through trial and error) decreases, and the significance of the higher forms, cognitive learning, increases.

This is an eclectic conception of ontogenetic changes of motor learning, arising from the treatment of its stages in terms of different and, in essence, mutually exclusive theories. It does not provide an adequate explanation of the problems being examined.

In assuming the psychological characteristics of the formation of motor habits at preschool age, it is first of all necessary to mention the following: A change in the nature of habits depends decisively on a more general change in the content and structure of the child's activity at a given developmental stage.

A shift from elementary objective actions of the manipulative processing game to a more complex game with a plot, constructions, and elements of educational and working activities creates new demands on the child's motor activity and compels him to master new motor habits and abilities. Thus, the preschooler masters the utilization of certain tools and instruments (pencil, brush, scissors, hammer, etc.), which demand precise coordination. Simultaneously, there is an increased demand for locomotor movements (jumping, running with obstacles, etc.) and for free gymnastic movements executed without any objective supports. The child cannot master these complex habits simply in the course of his practical play activity, so typical in the pre-preschool age. For their successful mastery, it is necessary that the motor learning as such be separated into a problem of its own.

To the extent that the main path of development of the child's motor activity consists of mastering socially constructed forms of behavior, the latter soon have to appear as models to which he conforms in his motor behavior. Isolation of this specific problem takes place in the preschool age, which in turn adds new qualitative attributes to the process of habit formation at a given genetic level. During this period, the orienting-exploratory activity of the child increases in complexity. From the orientation of a pre-preschooler, which was realized in the course of action and served to clarify the immediate conditions of this action, it is transformed into a preliminary detailed inspection of the situation and leads up to the emergence of the entire picture of that which now has to be performed. Regulation of the subsequent motor behavior on the basis of these images increases its effectiveness and facilitates the process of forming new motor habits.

Furthermore, as investigations of Luria (40, 41), Zaporozhets (78), and others indicate, during preschool childhood the role of words in the formation and realization of motor habits gains in importance. In connection with this, the effectiveness of motor learning increases, and the formed habits acquire a more concrete and generalized nature; they are easier to transfer to new, constantly changing situations than the habits that are formed in pre-preschool childhood.

In order for the child to master a habit, a single action is usually not enough; a frequent exercise of the same action is necessary. As a result of exercise, individual movements are unified into a system of coordinated motor acts, leading to a solution of a given problem. Repeated exercises directed at realizing the methods of the action's execution lead to the making and automatization of the most perfected systems. Thus, exercise is the basic condition that provides for the formation of a habit.

The course of exercises, their number, the time involved, and the mistakes allowed characterize the success of the process of forming a habit, which may be expressed quantitatively and subjected to objective analysis.

The essential changes in the process of habit formation during preschool age occur along with the course of exercises. There is a decrease in the number of exercises, quantity of error, and time required for the mastery of a new system of movements. At the same time, the process of motor learning acquires new qualitative attributes. As we have already mentioned, the increased participation of words and a change in the nature of the orienting activity add a goal-oriented, planning characteristic to the process of habit formation.

All these attributes of motor learning depend on the methods of formation, the nature and the structure of the habit being formed, and on the problems and motives of activity within which the given habit is formed.

Aspects of Habit Formation by a Preschooler under
Different Conditions of Training

At all levels of his development the child learns habits; he masters socially formulated methods of motor behavior under the guidance of an adult. However, the method of mastery differs at various stages.

Experimental data and systematic observations indicate that in early ontogeny (infancy and pre-preschool age) visual demonstration and verbal instruction even more so are only slightly effective methods of training. In connection with this, simple methods of guiding the child's actions are of importance, which are referred to by American authors as mechanical guidance. As the experiments of Vygotskaya (71) indicate, the application of this method produces positive results in the teaching of elementary motor habits at an infantile age.

Mechanical guidance is widely applied in pre-preschool childhood when other methods of training do not bring about the necessary results. It also plays a role in the formation of more complex motor habits at a younger preschool age. However, in general the methods of mechanical guidance are relatively ineffective. Whenever an adult executes some kind of action by movement of the child's hands, the child remains in a passive state. The lowering of the activity level under passive instructions is mainly manifested by the extinction of the orienting reaction and by an insufficiently intensive exploration of the conditions of the problem. Training by the method of passive movements results in a decreased level of orienting activity, which constitutes the main reason for its limited effectiveness.

During infancy and in part at the pre-preschool age, when the experience of the child is limited and the orienting activity is still of an elementary nature, passive training plays an important role since more accomplished methods of habit formation are still inaccessible to the child. However, by preschool age it becomes possible to employ other, more effective methods of training, which are no longer characterized by a mechanical guidance of the child's movements, but consist of directing and organizing his orienting activity so that the child will construct an accurate conception of the actions that he is required to perform. Here is the beginning of mastering habits through imitation.

Formation of Habits in the Process of Imitation. An investigation by Kirillova (31) demonstrated the drop in the effectiveness of the passive method in forming motor habits during the preschool age and, at the same time, relative increases in the success of imitation. Children of different preschool ages were given an opportunity for perfecting a system utilizing four motor reactions (depressing reaction keys) in response to a system of multicolored light signals. In one series of experiments, the habit was formed by the method of passive movements and in the other by imitation (Table 27).

The data presented in Table 27 indicate that in the case of younger preschoolers training in habit formation is more successful when the means are passive movements rather than imitation. In spite of the fact that three—four-year-old children are constantly and carefully observed, the actions of those whom they are trying to imitate, the limitation of their motor experience, and the absence of the necessary visual-motor connections result in a situation in which their visual impressions do not evoke the corresponding movements. Thus, imitation is a less effective method of training than are passive movements. In contrast, older preschoolers manifest visual impressions based on demonstrated movements that immediately evoke motor representations, and

Table 27.
Comparison of Methods of Passive Movements and Imitation in Forming Motor Habits

| Age (years) | Number of Trials in Training | |
	Passive Movements	Imitation
3-4	8	12
4-5	8	8
5-6	5	3
6-7	3	1

the indicators of mastery of a habit via imitation in this case are significantly higher than in the case of training by passive movements.

At preschool age, the child masters numerous elementary habits related to self-help and the utilization of simple household objects by directly imitating the actions of those around him. While observing the movements and actions of adults, the child repeats them in practical and playful activity and by doing so masters them to some degree.

While investigating the aspects of imitation in preschool age, Gorbatenko (25) has demonstrated that it occupies an essential place in the general development of children. Children, while imitating a teacher or one another in practical activity and especially in creative games, follow the examples of those around them in their relations, in actions, and in content and form of verbal interaction. On occasion, as an object of imitation, they were given movements. In a game entitled "mirror," the leader performed movements and the children standing around in a circle (mirrors) repeated these movements. The first leader was the teacher, and his movements could have served as an example for the subsequent leaders—children. Thus, the task for the child consisted of showing movements to the surrounding mirrors, and in doing so, he could rely on reproduction of the teacher's movements or show a bit of independence and come up with his pattern of movement.

The experiment revealed that imitation of the movements demonstrated by an adult is characteristic of all preschool children. At the same time, it was observed that during this period of childhood there is an essential change in the content of imitation. Thus, the majority of children in the younger preschool age—87 percent of the children taking part in the experiment—mechanically copy the teacher's movements. Among the older children, direct reproduction of the model is appreciably reduced (only 26 percent in the middle age and 10 percent in the older age). These children replace literal imitation by general imitation, i.e., adopting in their image a general picture (for example, that the movements are performed by hands), and they thus demonstrate a certain independence.

Some authors, Porembskaya (57) for example, note that even the simple acts, which the child frequently sees being performed by adults, cannot be reproduced correctly without special training. For example, in setting a table, children imitate the actions of adults but are not able to establish an internal connection between individual operations—they generally know what to do but not how to do it.

A study of the development of object movements performed by Neverovich (32) indicated that, while observing everyday actions of adults in real life, the child pays attention first of all to the result of the action—directs his attention to the goal reached by such actions and does not isolate the methods of action and the movements realized in such actions. In his own activity (for example in self-help), while imitating the observed activity, the child also strives to obtain a given result—to wash, to dress, etc.—and he performs this by various primitive methods including many additional, non-goal-oriented movements. According to the data of this investigation, changes in children's actions in the planning of isolation and comprehension methods of action and the mastery of precise, correct movements are connected with the expansion of children's practical experience, the increase in demands for proper utilization of various objects, and the training of children in the methods of fulfilling action.

Consequently, in order that the child be able to master the method of action and the habit, it is not sufficient for him just to see the actions of another person and to repeat them on his own. A special organization of the child's activity is needed with the guidance of an adult.

Investigations pertaining to the development of voluntary movements at preschool age, conducted under the guidance of Zaporozhets (78), indicated that the development of the child's movements depends on that concrete process in which they are included and the nature of the problem confronting the child.

New, more complex forms of motor reactions, according to Zaporozhets, which are to be mastered by a preschooler, cannot be formed now by the method of simple adaptation to the conditions of the problem as observed at the lower levels of development. It is necessary first of all to master the movement consciously, to learn to execute it, and only thereafter to utilize it for practical needs. The elementary forms of direct learning accessible to the preschooler, realized via the method of direct demonstration of a new movement or by the demands for the fulfillment of a given task under well-structured conditions, are the basic sources of new motor formations at the preschool age (78).

Thus, complex motor habits are mastered by the method of direct training under conditions of specially organized exercises. Imitation plays an essential role in this process. However, imitation acquires new qualitative attributes under conditions of goal-oriented training. From an impulsive, elemental copying of the individual aspects of activity surrounding the children, it is gradually transformed into a method of conscious mastery of the assigned motor pattern. At the same time, there is a shift from reproductive imitation, involving duplication of already-known actions, to a productive imitation through which new habits are mastered.

The influence of imitation on the process of habit formation was the object of inquiry in a study by Polyakova (56). In this study a comparison was made of the effectiveness of forming the habit of traversing a maze by hand either by following the movements of an adult or by the child's independent attempts. Prior to the experiment, the children were given an explanation as to the goal and conditions of movement—that it is necessary to move from one point to another, that one cannot cross the wall, that one must follow the outlined path, etc. The methods for executing these movements were not specified. Some children were developing the habit on their own through independent trials; others prior to independent actions were given the opportunity to observe how the maze was run by the experimenter and, imitating his movements, could have mastered the habit. The results of these experiments are presented in Table 28.

The data indicate that throughout the entire period of preschool childhood a motor habit is formed more quickly and effectively through imitation than through independent attempts. The number of exercises necessary for habit formation, as well as the number of mistakes made, is smaller in the first case than it is in the second. The children's movements based on independent attempts are of a more chaotic and less confident nature than the ones in the context of imitation. Polyakova explains this difference in the success of habit formation on the basis that the experimenter's demonstration presents the child with an opportunity to visually observe the correct path and to compare a visual image of the demonstrated movement, prior to his independent attempt to traverse the maze. With the shift to a practical activity this image serves as a measure of the correctness or incorrectness of his movements, as a result of which the incorrect movements become inhibited prior to their execution. This is the rationale used to explain the special effectiveness of habit formation via imitation.

The results obtained by Polyakova indicate that imitation in the form of special training by example is one of the methods of forming motor habits at the preschool age.

In comparing results obtained by Gorbatenko and Polyakova we detect seemingly contradictory facts. Thus, according to Gor-

Table 28.
The Influence of Imitation on the Process of Habit Formation

Age (years)	Independent Attempts		Imitation	
	Trials	Errors	Trials	Errors
3-4	21	56	14	24
4-5	17	43	11	20
5-6	10	23	8	12
6-7	7	12	7	7

batenko, a majority of the younger preschool children, in contrast
to older ones, easily and directly imitate adults' actions. In line
with this it could be expected that in a training situation where
imitation is employed, the formation of motor habits in younger
preschool children should be faster than in the older ones. Results
of Polyakova's experiments, on the other hand, indicate that in a
habit formation using imitation younger preschool children required twice as many exercises as 6-7 year olds.

However, this contradiction is only an apparent one. The little
children, while getting acquainted with the surrounding objects
and mastering their designation and utilization by imitating
adults, carry out manipulations reflecting adults' actions. However, these actions are not confronted with demands for certain
precision and coordination. As soon as another problem confronts the child—the necessity to execute exact, coordinated
movements, as was the case in Polyakova's experiments—one
encounters significant difficulties, and the child requires a greater
number of repetitions of the exercise than do the older ones in
order to master the given system of movements.

Learning via the method of imitation is, in essence, learning by
visual demonstration, whenever the child observes directly what is
done by someone else, and thereafter, reproduces what has been
observed. More complex forms of habit mastery are directly
associated with the development of the child's speech and its
increased role in regulating the child's behavior. To the extent
that the child masters the language and utilizes it for interaction,
verbal instructions of those surrounding him begin to play an
ever-increasing role in his general development and, in part, in the
development of his motor sphere. With the assistance of language,
the shift from direct actions to actions mediated by the child's
experience and the experience of humanity is realized: The latter
is generalized and is passed on to the child through speech.

**The Role of Visual Demonstration and Verbal Instruction in the
Formation of Habits.** First of all, let us examine the data characterizing the influence of a word on the speed of habit forma-

tion. In order to do this, we will compare the effectiveness of learning under conditions of verbal instructions with that of visual demonstration. In studies by Kislyuk (32) and Neverovich (48), the child was taught a motor habit under laboratory conditions. In one instance, the child's practical activity was preceded by a demonstration of what he was required to perform; in a second case, the experimenter informed the subject about the signals that would appear and how the subject was expected to react to them, and only after this was the child given the opportunity to perform the exercise. Neverovich's experiments investigated the more elementary motor habits, consisting of a system of uniform depression of keys in response to light signals occurring in a predetermined order. In Kislyuk's experiments, more complex habits were studied, consisting of a system of various types of motor reactions (turning one key forward and backward and a second key clockwise and counterclockwise), which were performed in response to a system of various light and sound signals.

The comparison of the data obtained in the formation of the two various habits indicated that the speed of forming a new habit is not of constant magnitude: It changes not only with respect to the methods of training but also is determined by the structure of the habit—by the system of stimuli at hand and the corresponding reactions. In the experiments by Neverovich, the movements per se (depressing a key with a finger in order to extinguish a light) did not create difficulties for the child. The basic difficulty was found to be in the ability to relate spatially the order of the presented stimuli with the corresponding sequence of keys. Such a connection is established better and quicker with a verbal plan, and the child then quickly realizes it in practical activity. Therefore, in this experiment, learning through preceding verbal explanation is significantly more effective than visual demonstration. Analogous data were obtained in studies by Strazhnikova (69) and Barkhatova (1) in which spatial motor habits were formed.

Contradictory results were obtained in Kislyuk's experiments. In these trials, the child was required to form a connection between signals, qualitatively different from one another (an electric bell and a buzzer, a red and a green light), and the corresponding movements, opposite in directionality. As the experiment indicated, establishing such different types of connections within the framework of only verbal designations, without visual support, is quite difficult for the preschooler; therefore, for their formation a greater number of exercises is required than in the case of visual demonstration. Similar conclusions are obtained by Dimanshtein (9) and Grebenshchikova (26), who studied the execution of gymnastic exercises according to verbal instruction with a visual demonstration. They report that in the formation of gymnastic habits the direct signals are of essential significance.

As further investigations have shown, verbal instructions and direct perception of the situation for action are, in the case of habit formation, a more complex relationship than it may initially appear. For example, it was observed that the child does not remain indifferent to the verbal explanation, even in the case where the visual method of learning the habit is identified as the preferred one. Furthermore, learning through verbal instruction does not exclude visual support, and conversely, visual observation makes it easier for the child to establish the connection between the stimuli and the corresponding movement.

The studies of Polyakova, Strazhnikova, and Grebenshchikova include an additional series of experiments in which verbal instruction was linked with visual demonstration. The child simultaneously watched the actions of the experimenter and listened to his explanation. In such a case in the experiments of Strazhnikova, a comparison of verbal and visual methods of training has demonstrated the great effectiveness of preliminary verbal instruction, whereas in the experiments of Grebenshchikova, teaching the children gymnastic exercises, the advantage of visual training was noted.

A comparison of the results obtained from the series linking verbal instructions with visual demonstration indicates that at the preschool age the best conditions for habit formation are obtained by combining verbal instructions with visual perception of the conditions of action and the nature of the movements. Table 29 presents Strazhnikova's data and Table 30 the data of Grebenshchikova.

A comparison of the experimental data characterizing the speed of forming motor habits under various conditions of learning indicates that, during the preschool period, the effectiveness of habit formation under any method of learning increases with age—the older the child, the fewer the number of exercises necessary. However, the method of learning is of no little significance in the success of habit formation. The effectiveness of the method is determined first of all by the nature of the habit. Some habits are perfected quicker under conditions of visual demonstration (Kislyuk, Grebenshchikova), others under verbal instructions (Neverovich, Strazhnikova).

We are not concerned here with the material characterizing the biomechanical structure of these habits and their components, which are already found in the previous experience of the child and which would allow one to relate the effectiveness of one or another method of training with the nature of the habit. Only certain data may be used as grounds for asserting that habit formation on the basis of verbal influence is successful only when a similar type of connection between signals and movements has occurred in the preschooler's experience, and that therefore

Table 29.
Number of Trials (mean) Necessary for Habit Formation through Visual Display and Verbal Instructions

Age (years)	Visual Display	Verbal Instruction	Verbal-Visual Instruction
3-4	19	14.5*	12.5
4-5	10	7.5	6.0
5-6	5	5	3.5
6-7	3	3	3

*Out of 10 children, 6 mastered the habit.

Table 30.
Number of Children Correctly Performing Exercises Under Various Conditions

Age (years)	Visual Display	Verbal Instruction	Verbal-Visual Instruction
3.5-4.5	40%	0%	50%
4.5-5.5	60	40	70
5.5-7.0	70	60	100

words, arousing already-consolidated connections, facilitate their detection under new sets of activity conditions. Thus, three and one-half—four and one-half-year-old children in Grebenshchikova's experiments were not able to fulfill a new exercise on the basis of verbal instruction, consisting of several elements (to stretch out both arms forward, then to lift one upward and to move the other one to the side), but whenever they were given a simple task (to raise both arms upward), all children executed it correctly right after the first presentation of instruction. Addition of a new element—to raise both arms upward and then to move one leg backward—created difficulties for the children, and this exercise was completed by only four out of ten children. It became apparent that combining the verbal with the visual demonstration of the action considerably increases prospects for fulfilling the task, and even the most difficult task, which was impossible for children to achieve on the basis of verbal instructions, was fulfilled at once by half of the younger children under these conditions.

Thus, the mastery of an unknown, formerly unrealized system of movements, corresponding to a complex verbal instruction, is accomplished with difficulty by a child. Under these conditions, visual perception of the action serves as support for the formation of a new system of connections.

The effectiveness of the training method depends not only on the attributes of the habit that is being trained, but it is also determined by a mutual relationship of verbal and visual influences at each developmental level of preschool childhood. During the period from three to seven years, their role in the process of habit formation gradually changes, and even greater significance is placed on the verbal signals. Whereas children of the younger age (three-four years) encounter great difficulties in fulfilling an action on the basis of preliminary instructions, such a problem creates relatively little difficulty for older children (five-seven years). Furthermore, the older the child, the less the difference in the effectiveness of mastering a habit by various methods of training. The latter, as may be interpreted on the basis of data of Neverovich, Strazhnikova, and others, is explained on the grounds that the older children employ words while visually perceiving experimenter's actions; they independently name the stimuli, mark the sequence of signals and the responding movements, and simultaneously reflect the direct influences in their verbal scheme. All this facilitates habit formation.

One does not observe such a sequence of events at a younger age. Under conditions of visual demonstration, younger children do not utilize verbal designation of the perceived action, but attempt to execute the movements right there in the course of the experimenter's demonstration. One gets the impression that the child, being afraid of forgetting what he directly perceives, mirrors the experimenter's actions. However, since the child is asked to observe first and then act, he executes only parts of the exercise correctly in his independent attempts, not being able to remember everything under such conditions. Usually, this is the beginning or the end of the demonstrated action, i.e., that part whose visual image has been preserved. Therefore, in order to master the entire system of movements, the younger preschoolers require considerably more repetitions of visual instructions than do the older children. According to Strazhnikova's data, under the visual method of training, three—four-year-old children require ten repetitions of the demonstration of action and nineteen independent trials, whereas older children (six-seven years) require only one demonstration and three trials for mastering a habit.

The limited possibilities of the younger preschooler for regulat-

ing his actions by words and the primary effect of the direct
influences are observed not only under conditions of visual training. These facts are also applicable to the verbal-visual method of
habit formation. Thus, studies of Polyakova and Grebenshchikova
present instances when the younger preschoolers only with difficulty unite the two components of the instruction (explanation
and demonstration) and initially prefer to react to the visual
demonstration. Only in the course of exercises is there the beginning of correlation and unification of these two components.

Yendovitskaya (76) studied in detail aspects of the execution of
action based on preliminary verbal instruction. After playing with
a table set of construction materials, the children, being guided
by the form and size of the figures, were asked to put it away in a
given sequence into three boxes. In this experiment, Yendovitskaya determined that it is possible to delineate the essential
differences among preschoolers in their ability to execute actions
based on preliminary verbal instructions, and in this regard the
children may be subdivided into four groups. The first group of
children, consisting of three–four-year-olds, can neither independently organize its activity on the basis of preliminary verbal
instructions, nor attain the result indicated in the instruction. In
performing the task, these children follow only directions related
to the general goal of the action, and the entire order of action is
distorted. The figures that happen to be at hand are taken and are
placed without order or consideration of form or size. However,
if these children are presented with instructions in the form of
elemental dictation—"Put the pyramids into this box. First of all
put the large ones in"—the child's actions follow the adult's
words, and then such partitioned instructions evoke and organize
separate motor acts of the child.

The second group of children is just beginning to be guided by
the verbal instructions given prior to action. In the process of its
execution they temporarily become influenced by the direct
stimuli (take the figure that is directly in the line of vision) and
therefore cannot yet perform the task totally. The third group

includes children for whom preliminary verbal instruction serves as a base for realization of the goal-oriented actions. However, in performing the action, they follow instructions pertaining only to the goal of action, ignoring the instructions pertaining to the organization of activity, i.e., pertaining to the method of action. For example, knowing that initially it is necessary to reassemble and sort out the figures on the table and only thereafter place them in a box, these children pick out of the mass of the figures one that is needed, in spite of the experimenter's reminders.

Finally, the fourth group consists of children who in their actions follow the preliminary instructions (goal as well as method) completely. The children's activity in this instance moves along as a whole (in a temporal sense) process, as if executed in terms of a singular plan, emerging prior to actions on the grounds of the verbal instruction.

Table 31 presents the data (in percent) pertaining to the distribution of children of various ages into different groups in correspondence with their ability to execute action on the basis of verbal instruction.

The materials reviewed indicate that in some cases verbal instruction serves as a base for the fulfillment of action, planning it, and regulating it, whereas in others, it does not exert the necessary influence. The latter is very characteristic of the youngest preschooler. But even these children are capable of fulfilling actions according to verbal instruction whenever such instruction is not given all at once, but in sequential parts, after which the child

Table 31.
Distribution of Preschoolers According to Their Ability to Follow
Verbal Instructions (in percent)

Age (years)	Groups			
	1st	2nd	3rd	4th
3-4	43	43	14	--
4-5	--	57	21.5	21.5
5-6	--	35	15	50
6-7	--	--	14	86

immediately executes the elements of the complex action. Instruction in this case seems to be an order for a particular action and yet cannot regulate the entire course of realizing the task. Only at a somewhat older age is it possible to direct and regulate the preschooler's actions by verbal instruction.

Having analyzed experimental investigations pertaining to the formation of habits, Zaporozhets makes the following deduction: As long as the child is not able to respond correctly to a singular verbal instruction, words play an essential but limited role in his activity. At this level, verbal actions actualize old connections but cannot as yet by themselves bring about new ones. At later stages of the child's development a system of verbal actions produces arousal of traces of previous impressions in new combinations, and for essentially the first time there is an opportunity for the formation of new temporal connections, for the formation of new knowledge and ability on the basis of purely verbal instructions and explanations (78; p. 277).

The possibility for forming habits on the basis of verbal influences not only increases the speed of their mastery, but the words also exert a penetrating influence on the quality of the mastered habit. This is manifested by the extent of the child's awareness of the performed actions, committed errors, and by how he utilizes the acquired method of action in new, changed conditions of activity.

In this connection, of special interest are the results characterizing the level of awareness of the perfected habits.

In a study of Neverovich (50), after the child's having perfected a habit, a verbal inquiry was used to determine the child's degree of awareness of the system of stimuli and the reciprocal movements. It was revealed that the youngster's awareness falls behind the process of habit-formation development. The observed divergence, however, is minimized with age. It is of smaller degree in the case of training by verbal instructions than by visual demonstration. Thus, 60 percent of the younger children who have reached a criterion of errorless performance of the instructions after ten trials following visual demonstration are not aware of either the order of presentation of the stimuli or the order of their corresponding practical movements. Only after fifteen additional trials do they begin to become aware of what they are actually performing. Under conditions of verbal instructions, awareness is obtained much quicker. Even the youngest children begin to reflect awareness of the system of stimuli and movements in their verbal reports after only six additional trials, and older children come to this realization three times faster.

Thus, a complete and adequate account of movements comprising the habit is not immediately obtainable. Errorless awareness of the connection between stimuli and the corresponding motor responses is formed in children slowly and gradually. According to Kislyuk's data (32), the correct actions are the first ones to be included in the verbal framework, whereas the incorrect reactions, intermixed with the correct ones in the process of habit formation, are reflected only to a minimal degree. Table 32 presents data concerning the number of cases of an adequate verbal account of correct and incorrect actions (percent in terms of the total number of reactions). These data indicate that the verbal instruction has a much more facilitating effect than the visual in developing awareness of the executed actions. It is interesting that this is applicable even in cases in which the habit is formed more rapidly on the basis of the visual demonstration as reported in the previously mentioned studies.

As noted by Kislyuk, an adequate verbal account of correctly executed actions may be a result of a sample reproduction of the

Table 32.
Number of Cases of Adequate Verbal Accounts of Correct and Incorrect Actions Following Visual or Verbal Instructions

Age (years)	Visual Display		Verbal Instructions	
	Correct Reactions	Incorrect Reactions	Correct Reactions	Incorrect Reactions
3-4	18	8	30	9
4-5	40	13	50	16
5-6	44	17	60	20
6-7	60	50	76	52

mastered material (verbal instruction or visual demonstration) and still does not indicate that the child's behavior as such has been reflected in verbal activity. As far as the adequate account of the incorrect actions is concerned, it may only appear as a result of a reflection of the performed actions in terms of a verbal framework, and therefore, the intensive growth of the corresponding indicators is quite essential.

An analysis of the awareness of the incorrect instances of one's actions, across children of all age groups, indicates that the nature of the inadequate verbal accounts depends to a certain degree on the method of training. If at the early stages of learning, the child, while incorrectly reacting to a stimulus, inaccurately but differently accounts for this reaction (which occurs under both conditions of learning), then in the process of perfecting a system of reactions the content of the inadequate accounts begins to change and is determined by the method of learning. Thus, in experiments involving visual demonstration, in which awareness of actions falls considerably behind the process of habit formation, the child qualifies his correct responses as incorrect. The opposite cases, when the child while reacting incorrectly reports his inaccurate reactions as correct (executed in line with the instruction), are basically encountered in experiments with verbal instruction. However, while relying on the verbal instructions, the children are quicker in noting their mistakes and in correcting them in the subsequent trials. Analogous facts are cited in the experiments by Barkhatova, Strazhnikova, and others.

A realistic indicator characterizing the qualitative aspect of the mastered habit is the ability to use the developed system of action in new, modified conditions. In the corresponding experiments, modification in the conditions consisted of rearranging the order of previous stimuli, which in turn led to a restructuring of the system of actions. Table 33 presents data from the experiments of Kislyuk, I, (32) and Barkhatova, II, (1), concerning the number of trials (arithmetical mean) necessary for the reconstruction of the formed system of reactions under various conditions of learning.

The data presented in Table 33 indicates that the older the child the more successful is the restructuring of the formed system of reaction under both conditions. Furthermore, a habit developed from verbal instruction is more flexible than one formed on the basis of visual demonstration. The observed difference in the number of trials required for restructuring a habit in the Kislyuk experiment as compared with the Barkhatova experiment may apparently be explained by the difference in the structure of the habits being formed, which would then require a different number of trials for their formation as well as their restructuring (a detailed treatment of the structure of a habit will be presented shortly). In this particular case, as far as the possibilities of restructuring a given system are concerned, the relative and not the absolute indicators are of interest.

In this connection, it is necessary to examine another aspect of the reported data characterizing the process of restructuring. On the basis of the studies of Pavlov's students, it is known that restructuring a dynamic stereotype is an exceedingly difficult task for the nervous system, frequently beyond its strength and requiring divergence from its normal work. Even just a change in the order of formerly presented stimuli creates a difficult problem for an animal. Other data obtained in the experiments, studying habit

Table 33.
Number of Trials (mean) Necessary for Restructuring Reactions under Various Learning Conditions

| Age (years) | I | | II | |
	Visual Display	Verbal Instruction	Visual Display	Verbal Instruction
3-4	1.7	1.5	--	--
4-5	1.4	0.4	27.0	13.5
5-6	0.9	0.4	12.5	11.8
6-7	0.3	0.2	9.0	7.7

restructuring in preschool children, indicate the relative ease with which a new system of movements is formed on the basis of previous connections. Furthermore, the positive impact of the old system on the formation of the new one is noted. It is manifested in the reduction of trials necessary for the development of the new habit. Thus, at a younger age, 11 trials are needed for the development of a habit according to verbal instruction, but for its restructuring in line with a new order of stimulus presentation only 1.5 trials are necessary (Kislyuk). In the case of restructuring, one also observes a reduction in the number of errors and a qualitative change in their nature. There is a total absence of chaotic movements and gross incorrect reactions, but one observes new errors representing movements that were previously utilized in the realization of old connections of the previously formulated system, but even these are corrected rapidly. The positive influence of experience, acquired in the development of one motor system, on the formation of another new system apparently may be explained on the basis of the dynamic reflection of direct influences within the verbal scheme.

The above-cited data pertaining to the child's awareness in the course of his executing correct and incorrect movements indicate that, in one form or another, verbal mediation took place under various conditions of learning. This in turn resulted in awareness of the formed habit and its generalized nature and led to an understanding of a general principle of work under a given set of conditions. The latter facilitated the subsequent restructuring of the formed system of actions. Consequently, participation of speech in developing a preschooler's habit facilitates its transfer to other conditions, reduces difficulty in restructuring it in line with new conditions of activity, and removes those specific difficulties in restructuring a dynamic stereotype in animals, which were indicated by Pavlov.

Experimental data concerning aspects of the process of habit formation under verbal and visual methods of learning indicate an increased influence of words with age on the success of habit formation, as well as on its generalization and flexibility. However, these developmental attributes in the formation of habits, obtained by comparing the arithmetical means, characterize only a general tendency in the development of the regulatory role of words. An analysis of individual cases indicates considerable individual departures from the mean with respect to the process of habit formation, as well as its effectiveness under various conditions of learning. All age groups included children who were able to form a habit very quickly, as well as children who were relatively very slow in forming a habit compared to other children of the same age group. These data are presented by Kislyuk, Neverovich, Barkhatova, and others. For example, among the children of younger ages there were cases where, under a given set of conditions, the children were not able to form a habit at all. Furthermore, some younger children were able to perfect a habit quicker than some of the older ones. The latter was observed among the children who showed a well-developed facility for speech and those who, at the time of the experiment, were able to rely on the active orienting-exploratory activity.

Thus, the effectiveness of the habit formation, process of awareness, and generalization of actions cannot be specifically anchored to any particular age and seems to be dependent on the complexity of the problem at hand and the conditions of the environmental experience of the child.

The Role of Orienting-Exploratory Activity in the Formation of Habits

A series of investigations, directed by Zaporozhets, reveal the dependence of habit formation upon the nature of the child's behavior during experimentation, that is, the extent of intensity and organization of orienting-exploratory activity. If, for example, the child attentively listens to the experimenter's explanations, looks at objects named by him, and follows movements performed by the experimenter, which the child subsequently has to execute himself, then the habit formation moves along more successfully than when the child does not perform such a preliminary exploration of the surroundings but instead immediately attempts to act.

Experiments by Tsvetkova revealed that under conditions of intensive orienting-exploratory activity children's motor reactions in the initial stages of habit formation are slowed down. In the first trials the appearance of the signal does not evoke immediate pressing of the key. Instead, the children examine the signal and the key, choose which one to depress, and only after this execute the movements. They permit only a small number of errors, which exclude reactions that would be totally unrelated to the conditions of the problem. In the course of exercise, the presentation of the signal results in quicker and more assured pressing of the key, and the habit is formed with a relatively small number of trials.

In an opposite situation, when the child inattentively listens to the instructions, does not follow the experimenter's demonstration, and does not conduct a preliminary exploration of the surrounding conditions, but immediately after the first demonstration begins to act (depresses keys out of order, frequently two at a time), he makes a large number of errors and the habit is formed very slowly. Sometimes these children are just not able to master the required system of movements.

A detailed exploration of conditions that precede practical activity and permit the child to orient himself to the way the initial motor reactions will be executed under experimental conditions has an essential influence on the process and the effectiveness of habit formation. In the behavior of a child who is attempting to master a given motor habit, according to Zaporozhets, one observes two types of components. First of all, the child performs a series of manual, executive movements, which simply serve the attainment of the required external result as defined by the experimental conditions. Secondly, he performs a series of actions that in their nature and role in behavior essentially differ from the manual, executive movements. Following Pavlov, who introduced the concept of orienting reflexes, we call this type of activity orienting-exploratory. Not leading directly to the external results required of the subjects, this reaction permits one to become more precisely oriented in the situation and facilitates the execution of manual movements corresponding to the conditions of the problem (78).

A further investigation of the role of orienting-exploratory activity in the child's behavior indicated that as a result of the preliminary orientation, he constructs an image of the task—an image of the conditions of the action and of what he will be required to do under those conditions. With the formation of such an image, incorrect movements begin to be inhibited at the very beginning of their appearance as not being in correspondence with the formulated notion as to what and how things must be done, and the correct movements are reinforced as being in correspondence with such a notion. Thus, an image formulated in the process of orientation directs and organizes the child's activity, and habit formation proceeds more rapidly acquiring a more goal-directed nature. Let us examine the results of some of the investigations that explore the role of orienting-exploratory activity in habit formation.

Ovchinnikova (51) studied the process of habit formation in three- to seven-year-old children in connection with movement through a maze. The child was given a problem, to transport a cart from "the store" to "kindergarten." This was to be done through a maze that included bushes, fences, and roads in three dimensions, thus easily detectable by touch. The transporting had to be done "at night," i.e., with the eyes closed, and in such a way as not to run into dead ends. One blindfolded group of children was allowed to examine the maze beforehand and to identify by touch the path to be used in transporting the cart. Another group was given an opportunity to explore the maze visually and thereafter to transport the cart while blindfolded. The third group was required to transport the cart through the maze while blindfolded without any kind of preliminary training.

These experiments showed that the formation of motor habits is accomplished much quicker with an orientation than without it. If one were to combine all the exploratory tactual movements (first series) or the quantity of the visual familiarization (second series) with the number of performance movements necessary for the habit formation, then one would get a smaller average number than the number of movements executed without the preliminary orientation. For example, five-year-old children required thirty-one trials for the formation of a habit without preliminary orientation; in the case of motor-tactual orientation—thirteen trials (ten orienting and three performance); and in the case of the visual familiarization—eleven trials (five orienting and six performance).

The positive influence of the preliminary familiarization had an impact not only on the effectiveness of habit formation, but also on the nature of the children's motor behavior in the very process of habit forming. Performance trials of children exposed to preceding orientation acquired special characteristics; they were executed on the basis of the preliminary account of the conditions of action. Children quite assuredly, without any gross errors even at the beginning of trials, pushed the cart in the required direction, announcing beforehand the points in which direction they would be moving shortly. Consequently, they showed a better conception of the maze as a whole, as well as of the directionality of their movements. In contrast to this, the motor behavior of children without preliminary orientation was chaotic in nature. Performance trials only slightly corresponded with the conditions of the task; they were performed with a large number of errors, which were slowly overcome. Even after twenty-thirty trials, the children failed to form a distinct conception of the maze as a whole or its details, and of the directionality of their movements. The habit was formed in only half of the four- to six-year-old children. It is interesting that in this series of trials children constantly made attempts to disrupt the instructions; leaving the cart alone, they began to feel the walls of the maze. It seems that they had a need for preliminary exploration of the maze.

The results of Ovchinnikova's experiments also indicate that at the younger preschool age of primary significance is the motor-tactual orientation (manual examination of the conditions of the problem), and only subsequently on its basis is the visual orientation formed, which becomes sufficient for familiarization with the surroundings.

Boguslavskaya (4) specifically investigated the changes occurring in orienting activity in the course of the child's development. It was determined that only a detailed examination of the object by hand may provide the child with the necessary knowledge that subsequently directs the execution of actions. For example, in order to construct a distinct conception of an object, to compare and differentiate its individual characteristics and qualities younger children require taking the object into their hands, feeling it, testing it in action, etc.

Subsequently, the eye, which previously pursued the movements of the hand, begins to overtake the hand movements and to fulfill orienting activity independently. During the shift at the middle preschool age from motor-tactual orientation to visual, it is sufficient for a child under usual conditions to view the object and to examine its contours visually in order to carry out a subsequent independent action. During the shift to the older preschool age, that which is perceived by the eye finds its expression through words. At this level of the orienting-exploratory activity, one can evoke by a word an orientation in connection with the directly perceivable circumstances and, thereafter, even in their absence. The possibility of mental orientation in a situation is a precondition for the fulfillment of action corresponding to verbal instruction, presented without visual demonstration of the conditions of action. Verbal directions isolate the most essential aspects of action for children, which may be difficult for the child to isolate out of the totality of circumstances from visual observation.

Data obtained in a study by Kislyuk, Polyakova, Pantina, and others indicate that verbal instructions may change the content of the orienting-exploratory activity; they may direct it to cues, which under different sets of conditions would be unnoticeable, and thus lead to a higher organization of the motor habit.

Since, in the course of the investigations it was determined that the formation of the motor habit depends largely on the nature of the orienting-exploratory activity, experimenters specifically organized the orienting-exploratory activity of children in some studies. Thus, a study by Kislyuk (32) included experiments in which the orientation of children was activated. The child, while being given instructions, was invited to look in the direction of the signals and keys named. These were pointed out to him; he was required to point to them with his finger and to indicate the movement that would be necesssary to perform, etc. Executional movements were absent during that period. Table 34 presents data from these trials.

These data indicate that under conditions of special organization of orienting activity it is possible to increase considerably the effectiveness of training in children of all ages. Furthermore, under such conditions mastery of the system of movements is much more goal-oriented, without accidental chaotic movements. An error committed is noticed immediately by a child, and he reports where the error occurred and what should have been done instead. As a result, incorrect movements not in correspondence

Table 34.
Number of Trials (mean) Necessary to Form a Habit from Verbal Instructions under Various Conditions

Age (years)	Visual Conditions	Special Organization of Orienting Activity
3	11.0	4.7
4	6.4	1.8
5	4.9	1.5
6	3.5	0.4

with the existing image become separated and inhibited at the very beginning.

Habits formed on the basis of detailed visual and tactual examination of the experimental surroundings and on the basis of perceiving the essential signs through instruction, which one has to orient oneself to, are easier to realize, more flexible, and can be more rapidly restructured by changing the order of stimuli than those that were formed without preliminary familiarization with the conditions of the problem.

The process of habit formation and the quality of the constructed activity are essentially changeable, depending on what extent and at what level the orienting-exploratory activity unfolds. In analyzing the content of the orienting activity in the process of action regulation, Galperin concludes that "the first condition in the success of forming this action is the presence of a conception concerning what this action consists of and what the product represents, which must come about as a result of the action . . . Of great significance is the notion concerning the system of directions, as to what it is that one should orient oneself to in order to execute the action correctly and to arrive at the anticipated result" (15; p. 43).

Orienting activity represents in itself a complex formation. It occurs beforehand, prior to the beginning of habit formation (during perception of instructions) as well as in the course of habit formation, and includes a series of processes: constructing the preliminary notion about the process of the action and its result (not only about the final one, but also about a series of the intermediate ones); registering the present conditions of action and its factual flow; and identifying and eliminating the constantly impinging departures from the model. Preliminary notions concerning the forthcoming actions, which facilitate the executional movements, may reflect various aspects of the task as well as the process of action itself and may be complete or incomplete, correct or incorrect. Galperin points out that the success of the formation, as well as the quality, of the formed habit depends to a large extent on this.

In learning a simple motor system, orienting activity is apparently not as complex, for it is sufficient just to activate the child's attention to perception of the instruction in order to obtain the necessary result. However, in the formation of a complex motor habit, especially that which assumes the use of tools (for example, scissors, pencil, hammer, etc.), when the quantity of cues in the surroundings, the material, the tool, and the process of action itself increases considerably, the registration of their interrelationships in attempts to fulfill the task correctly becomes considerably more difficult. In such a case, as indicated by the studies of Neverovich and Pantina, habit may be formed either as a more primitive one or a more accomplished one, depending on the organization of the orienting activity; that is, depending on how clearly and distinctly the main cues necessary for orientation and formation of the correct image concerning the action process are isolated.

As an example of a complex motor habit, one may use writing letters of the alphabet. A study of the nature of the orienting activity and its influence on the quality of correct writing of the letters by six—seven-year-old children was conducted by Pantina (52), under the direction of Galperin.

In the presence of a correct visual image of the letters' configuration (i.e., a notion about the product to be obtained as a result of writing), the child encounters great difficulties in his attempts to reproduce manually a given form in a three-line booklet with slanting guidelines. Under these conditions, the child is required to plan correctly each segment of a letter in the corresponding part of the coordinates in a booklet. The latter is possible through a detailed visual orientation, by comparing visually the separate segments of the letter being written with the segment of the letter represented in the model. In learning how to write, children under usual sets of conditions orient themselves to the general form of the letter and reproduce it with wide departures from the model.

In a study by Pantina, it was established that the quality of writing letters depends to a large extent on how the child is oriented toward the task whether he is able to analyze the picture of the letter in a model and, in reproducing it, can find those places on the coordinates of the booklet where the line of the letter sharply changes its direction. Experimental training in writing was conducted under three different types of orientation to the task.

The first type presents only a model, which is reproduced by the experimenter in front of the child with only the most general directions on how to write. The second type includes, in addition to the above-stated, an indication of all the basic points of the contour, the beginning and the end of each line in the process of writing it, and an explanation of a shift from point to point. The third type entailed training the child to independently identify the supportive points by analyzing the presented model and thereafter to fulfill the action on the basis of the model.

The data obtained indicate the essential advantages of the third type of training. Whereas training according to the first type required, on the average, 1,238 presentations for the mastery of 22 letters, 265 were needed for training by the second type, and only 48 were required for mastery of 13 letters, when the training was of the third type. Thus, the superiority of the third type is quite apparent.

The differences became especially apparent in a shift to writing the letters of an entirely unknown alphabet (Georgian or Latin). The group of children trained by the first type was not able to write correctly a single letter of the unfamiliar alphabet, and they also grossly distorted the configuration of the already-learned Russian letters when writing in different coordinates (one, two, or three lines). Consequently, even after a prolonged training with the first type, only partial ability was attained—ability to write correctly only each given letter. Children trained by the second type were able to correctly write the unfamiliar letters; however, the percentage of correct writing was very small. The constructed habit was unstable and sensitive to the changes of surroundings: a shift to different coordinates evoked significant variations in the results of separate actions. Those trained by the third type shifted to writing the unfamiliar letters within various coordinates without much difficulty and with insignificant variations.

Thus, just a general arousal of orienting activity cannot provide for the success of training in the formation of a complex habit. What is needed in addition is the isolation of the basic cues to which the child must be oriented and, which by so doing, specifically direct the child's orienting-exploratory activity. In the experiments of Pantina, just such an isolation of the basic cues (partitioning of the model, identification of locations where the lines change their directions, marking these locations by periods and their transfer to the neighboring square) facilitated broad generalization of action and the most successful habit formation.

However, in the formation of complex habits there may not be enough indications as to what one should orient himself. In a complex combination of various stimuli the child finds it difficult in the course of his action to orient to the stimuli that are indicated in the instructions. Thus, in Neverovich's experiment (50) in which the child was trained to drive a nail into a board with a hammer, it was found that the child cannot fulfill instructions pertaining to handling the hammer and the hand movements. Over successive trials, the child strived for a goal of quickly driving the nail into the board, and his orienting activity was directed at the result of this action, namely, how the nail goes into the board, why it bends, etc. The nature of the hand movements and the ways of handling the hammer, despite the experimenter's directions, commanded no attention from the child, even though only the correct utilization of the instrument could have led to successfully driving the nail.

It is clear that the child had difficulty attaining the necessary result of action and thus simultaneously learned to use the hammer, utilizing it in the actual sense as a work tool. The construction of special conditions, which aroused the child's attention to the movement of the hand holding the hammer, essentially changed the process and the result of training. To accomplish this, the child was trained to strike the board with the hammer—"a blank trial." Under these conditions, the necessity for arriving at an objective result of an action was not present, and the child began to orient himself to the movements of the hand holding the hammer and to follow the experimenter's directions pertaining to the nature of movement. As a result of special motor exercises, the effectiveness of forming a given habit increases sharply. Table 35 presents data pertaining to the number of strokes necessary for driving one nail into a board under various conditions of training (percent in relation to the number of strokes necessary for training).

Thus, special organization of the orienting-exploratory activity in situations of activity is an important condition in forming motor habits in preschool age.

Dependence of the Formation of a Habit on Its Structure
The dependence of a habit's formation on its nature and structure has not been investigated in child psychology. However, as preschool pedagogical experience indicates, the nature of the habit and its structure play an essential role in teaching children habits. We have available only certain tangential material obtained in studies investigating other issues, which indicates the dependence of a habit's formation on its structure.

Poddyakov (55), while studying the process of automation in preschool children's actions, trained them by the method of verbal-visual instruction to execute one system of movements

Table 35.
Number of Strokes Necessary for Driving a Nail under Various Training Conditions

Age (years)	Training with the Result of Action	Training of Movements (simulated)
3-4	40	7
6-7	28	7

under different conditions of presenting stimuli and reinforcement. In the first series of experiments, a system of motor reactions was developed in response to light signals, appearing in the same order in various points of space. In response to each one of these signals, the child was required to depress a disc of the corresponding color and, by so doing, extinguish the light, which in turn served as reinforcement for the right action. In the second series, everything remained the same as in the first with the exception of supplementary reinforcement; with the correct extinction of the light, a miniature automobile appeared accompanied by noise. Consequently, the last link of the developing system was simplified—the child did not have to check the bulbs to see whether the light extinguished: it was sufficient to listen to the noise of the automobile. In the third series the conditions of presenting the light signals were simplified. All four signals were presented in the same order as in the first two series, not however from different places but from a single window situated directly in front of the child. The correct reaction was also reinforced by the extinction of the light and the automobile's noise (Table 36).

The results indicate that the most favorable conditions for the formation of a habit were present in the third series of experiments, in which it was not necessary for the child to search on the screen for a window in which the light would go on—it went on in the same place all the time, and it was not necessary to see whether the light extinguished. Thus, if the work to be performed by the child is distributed among analyzers (for example, the signals for action are perceived visually and the result of action is

Table 36.
Number of Trials Necessary for Correct Reproduction of the Order of Depressing Discs

Age (years)	Series		
	I	II	III
3.5-4	40	20	10
5	14	10	5
6-6.5	10	10	5

evaluated aurally, simplifying the perception of the system of
signals), then the success in forming habits increases appreciably—
and the older the child, the greater the success. The results obtained by Poddyakov indicate that the structural components of
the habit and their organization exert an influence on the process
of its formation. The same conclusions are obtained from results
of the comparative data of Neverovich and Barkhatova.

An investigation by Barkhatova studied the formation and restructuring of motor habits in preschool children. Experiments
were conducted in analogous conditions and with the same methodology as the above-mentioned experiments of Neverovich (48),
in which the child was required to depress four keys on a control
panel in the following order: 2-3-1-4 in response to four sequential light signals, appearing in different places on the screen. However, in Barkhatova's study, instead of four light stimuli there
were five, and correspondingly it was necessary to execute five
motor responses in the following order: 3-2-4-1-4. Thus, the
fourth signal and the corresponding reaction were repeated twice,
and the action itself consisted of five elements. In essence, this
was the difference in the two habits that were formed. A comparison of the results indicates that the introduction of the fifth,
in this case repeated, element considerably complicates the task
and that the child requires more trials in order to master the
habit. Table 37 presents the number of trials (mean) necessary for
the formation of a habit, consisting of four elements (Nevero-

Table 37.
Number of Trials (mean) Necessary for Formation of a Habit

| | Series | | | |
| | I Neverovich | | II Barkhatova | |
Age (years)	Visual Instruction	Verbal Instruction	Visual Instruction	Verbal Instruction
4-5	10	5	58	35.4
5-6	11	2	46.5	19.7
6-7	11	1	14	11.3

vich-I) and of five elements (Barkhatova-II) under various conditions of training.

The quantitative data indicate only the fact that mastery of the habit consisting of five elements proceeds slower and consequently is more difficult. A more essential characteristic of labor encountered by a child in such a case is uncovered through the analysis of attributes of a given habit's formation process and the mistakes committed by a child. Indeed, such an analysis indicates that with the introduction of the fifth repeatable element the structure of the habit is changed, and for its mastery a more refined differentiation of the spatial sequence of movements is needed than was present in the experiments by Neverovich.

The analysis of errors, according to Barkhatova, indicated that the children correctly reproduce the first two elements of action from the initial trials, but beginning with the third—repeatable element—they make mistakes: 3-2-*1-4*, 3-2-*4-1*, 3-2-*1-4*-4, 3-2-*1-4*-1-4 (needed 3-2-4-1-4), i.e., the children have difficulties in identifying the sequence of the repeatable element. Removal of this stable error requires a large number of trials. For some children four-five years old, the number of trials under visual methods of training approached eighty. What the essence of the difficulty is in forming the habit—the repetition of an element or simply an increase of elements—at the present time is difficult to determine, for we still do not have the necessary data at our disposal.

Sparse empirical data pertaining to the structure of habits permits us to make only a general conclusion: that the nature of movements composing the habit (either objective or gymnastic), their number, the combination of the sequence of directions, and other attributes are determined to a great extent by the process of habit formation, its success, and the methods of training that are the most effective in each concrete situation.

Dependence of the Formation and Realization of Motor Habits on the Aims and Motives of Activity

The mastery of motor habits, as well as the implementation of already-learned habitual movements, is a part of the general context of the child's activity and depends on its aims and motives. So far as the activity of the preschooler is distinctive with respect to its aims and its content, it imparts specific attributes to the formation and functioning of motor habits at a given level of development.

We shall begin the examination of the above-indicated dependence by analyzing experimental data, obtained in a study investigating the influence of the nature of a task on the process of fulfilling already-mastered movements. In the experiments of Ginevskaya, children of different preschool ages were asked to jump from a spot under a variety of conditions (24). In one series, the child was merely asked to jump as far as he could. In another series, he was asked to jump up to a line drawn with chalk on the floor. The effectiveness of performance was higher in the second series than in the first. An increase in the extent of movement during a shift from a free jump to a jump of determined distance is especially evident among younger children. These differences become equalized with age, even though throughout all stages of preschool childhood, a directly perceived goal and the conditions for its attainment can mobilize much greater locomotor possibilities in a child than a goal stated in a generalized verbal form (e.g., to jump as far as you can).

In contrast to Ginevskaya, who studied the dependence of the effectiveness of executing already-mastered movements on the form of the task's presentation, Elkonin (11) investigated the influence of the content of a given task on the realization of movements. In his experiments children of different preschool ages were required to perform the same movements in the solution of various problems. In one series of trials, they were simply required to strike a board with a hammer; in a second—to drive a nail into the board; in a third—to nail two boards together; in a fourth—to make some kind of meaningful thing (a playhouse, a wagon, etc.). It was found that the nature and productivity of the executed movements depend on the meaningful content of activity, with an increase in such indicators corresponding to the increase in the everyday meaning of the tasks being performed.

Attributes of the problem confronting the child exert an influence not only on the fulfillment of already-mastered motor systems, but also on the mastery of new motor habits. In Neverovich's (50) formerly presented experiments in which children were taught to drive nails into a board, the following was found. Whenever in the process of forming a complex habit the child is confronted with several tasks (e.g., to drive a nail into a board quickly and well, and in the process to learn how to use the hammer correctly), then such a combination of tasks is insurmountable for the preschooler. It appears that a more realistic task for him is the productive task—to drive the nail in—rather than the motor problem—to hold the hammer correctly and to execute specific hand movements. Under these conditions the training was only slightly effective, and the habit formed was of a primitive nature.

Only in another series of experiments, in which an attempt was made to present the child with a special task of mastering the means for attaining a prescribed result and to master the necessary system of movements, was the child confronted with a motor task—to learn how to use a hammer in the way it was used by the experimenter. Under these conditions training proceeded much quicker, and the habit being formed was much more complete than the one developed in the first series (see Table 35).

In speaking about the influence of the task on the formation and realization of children's motor habits, it is necessary to take into account the fact that the task assigned by the surrounding adults may be accepted by the child or not, depending on the nature of the motives that arouse him to activity. The same task may be either totally unfulfilled by children or may be fulfilled with differential activity, corresponding to different motivations for action.

In the course of development, the child's motivational sphere undergoes changes. Whereas in the beginning of the preschool age playful motives are of primary significance, motives of an educational nature become of greater importance toward the end of this period of childhood. In line with this, at different stages of preschool age the most favorable conditions for the formation and realization of motor habits are constructed under different motivations for activity.

In a study by Ginevskaya, it was shown that the same previously mastered movements associated with the striking operations are realized more successfully through motives of play than through educational motives. Table 38 presents the mean indicators of the effectiveness of the preschooler's striking movements under conditions of play and under conditions of learning exercises (in centimeters of the driven nail).

As the data indicate, the differences between the indicators are reduced with age, which attests to the increasing influence of learning motives in the realization of motor habits toward the end of preschool childhood.

In foreign psychology there is a widely spread false point of view, according to which the prevailing role in the behavior of a small child is assumed by various types of social biological inclinations. Contrary to this, a series of Soviet investigations showed that at the very early stages of development of great significance are social motives of activity, which in part also exert an influence on the children's motor behavior. Experiments by Neverovich (49) indicate that the manual movements performed by preschool children in the course of simple labor operations (making a napkin or a small flag attached to a pole) are executed with various degrees of effectiveness under different motivational conditions.

Table 38.
Effectiveness of Striking Movements under Conditions of Play and of Learning Exercises

Age (years)	Learning Task	Play
3-5	0.08	1.12
5-7	1.05	2.03

In one series of trials, the children were required to perform a system of movements associated with executing a prescribed elementary task for the sake of direct interest in the activity. The second series had as a goal the personal utilization of the product of such an activity; and finally, the third series included a goal of helping others (to prepare a gift for youngsters). It was found that the children in the third series showed higher indicators of work than those in the first two series.

Thus, already in the preschool age social motives in their simpler forms—as doing something useful for others—exert a genuine influence on the activity and, in part, on the motor behavior of children.

It is interesting to note that the nature of motivation exerts an influence not only on the quantitative indicators of the motor habits performed by a child, but also on their qualitative attributes. So, if in the first two series of trials in the study conducted by Neverovich, children did not strive for a high quality product and therefore performed the required movements carelessly and inaccurately, then in the third series of trials the picture of their motor behavior changed fundamentally. Striving as much as possible in making something for a gift, the preschooler tries very accurately and pedantically to master the necessary movements, which in the final analysis is reflected in the results of his activity.

The motives arousing the child to activity in one way or another are satisfied through it. The process of their gratification serves as a reinforcement for the ongoing motor reactions. In the course of the child's development, along with changes in motivation there is a change in the nature of the reinforcements that may be the best means for acquiring new habits. In the first stages of the ontogenetic development, nutritive reinforcement is of decisive importance in the formation and realization of temporal connections. Shortly thereafter, as indicated by Shchelovanov, it is replaced by orienting reinforcement as well as by the reinforcement of another human being's positive emotional reaction. To the extent to which the child acquires mastery of words verbal reinforcement in the form of verbal demands and evaluations of the child's behavior begins to play an ever-increasing role in the formation and realization of motor habits.

Certain data pertaining to the role of various reinforcers in habit formation of children of different preschool ages are reported in the study by Tsvetkova (70). This study utilized the same reinforcers that are widely used in experiments with children—nutritive reinforcement, orienting, and verbal. A definite system of motor reactions (depressing keys in response to a system of sequentially lighted bulbs) was given a different reinforcement in each series of experiments. In one series of trials, nutritive reinforcement was used (whenever the child correctly executed the required system of movements, he received a piece of candy); an orienting reinforcement was used in a second series (a demonstration of an interesting picture was presented); in the third, verbal reinforcement was used (correct reactions were encouraged by the experimenter's verbal praise). The investigations showed that during the preschool childhood, along with the general increase in the effectiveness of learning, there is a change in reinforcement that plays the leading role in forming motor habits (Table 39).

These data indicate that in the formation of habits during the preschool age there is an increase in the role of the higher, specifically human forms of reinforcement—in the form of gratification of curiosity, as well as in the form of praise or reproach from others. It is necessary to note that the subjective meaning of the

Table 39.
Number of Trials (mean) Necessary for the Formation of a Motor Habit with Different Reinforcers

Age (years)	Reinforcement		
	Nutritive	Orienting	Verbal
3-4.5	6	8	12
4.5-5.5	5	6	3
5.5-6.5	4	3	3

same reinforcements also changes. If a young preschooler is attracted by the candy because of its taste then for an older preschooler it is a reward received from an adult for successfully completing a task.

In examining the dependence of the preschooler's habit formation on the problems and the motives of their activity, it is necessary to underscore the following. In contrast to behaviorists, Soviet investigators (Leontiev, Zaporozhets, Guryanov, and others) showed that habits are not independent units of behavior but represent a result of the automatization of meaningful actions, most of all the method of these actions. In correspondence with this point of view, a genetic investigation must examine habits not in isolation, but in connection with that activity within which they were formed and are functioning. In part, in investigating habits in preschool age, it is necessary to take into account the types of activity that are the dominant ones at a given stage of development and within which the motor training of a child mainly takes place. Such a dominant activity in the preschool age is play. Its attributes, tasks, and motives impart a special character to the motor habits that are formed in the course of this activity.

In the form of play, the child for the first time is confronted with the task of mastering a definite motor model. He is required to master the method of another person's activity and, in connection with this, the effectiveness of motor learning increases considerably in comparison with the formation of habits in the pre-preschool age. However, within the bounds of play, the mastery of a motor image never acquires an independent meaning, as a result of which the precision in the construction of the required movements, as well as the stability of the forming habits, is still relatively low. In order to increase effectiveness in the mastery of habits, new motives have to emerge—educational motives, which begin to be formed toward the end of preschool age and which develop fully during school age.

References

1. Barkhatova, S. G. Vyrabotka i perestroyka dvigatelnykh navykov pri naglyadnoy i slovensnoy instruktsii u detey. (Devélopment and reconstruction of motor habits in children under conditions of visual and verbal instructions.) Rukopis. (Manuscript.) Moscow, 1952.

2. Bergeron, M. Le développement psychomoteur de l'enfant. In Debré R. Course de pédiatrie sociale, 825-842.

3. Bernshtein, N. A. O postroyenii dvizheny. (Concerning the construction of movements.) Moscow. Medgiz, 1947.

4. Boguslavskaya, Z. M. Osobennosti orientirovochno-issledovatelskoy deyatelnosti detey pri oznakomlenii s novymi predmetami. (Attributes of the orienting-exploratory activity of children during familiarization with new objects.) Rukopis. (Manuscript.) Moscow, 1947.

5. Carmichael, L. Ontogenicheskoye razvitiye. V kn. "Eksperimentalnaya psikhologiya." Sost. E. Stevens. (Ontogenetic development. In "Experimental Psychology." Ed. E. Stevens.) Moscow. Izd-vo inostrannoy literatury. (Publishers of foreign literature.) 1960.

6. Colloque sur "L'importance du mouvement dans le développement psychologique de l'enfant." Psychologie française. Vol. 2, No. 1, 1957, 24-30.

7. Dennis, W. Infant development under conditions of restricted practice and of minimum social stimulation: A preliminary report. J. of genet. psychol. 1938, 53, 149-158.

8. Dennis, W. Infant development under conditions of restricted practice and of minimum social stimulation. Genet. psychol. monogr. 1941, 23, 143-189.

9. Dimanshtein, I. G. Vypolneniye gimnasticheskikh dvizheny detmi doshkolnogo vozrasta pri naglyadnoy i slovesnoy instruktsii. (Execution of gymnastic movements by preschool children under conditions of visual and verbal instructions.) Rukopis. (Manuscript.) 1950.

10. Dusenberry, L. A study of the effects of training in ball throwing by children ages three to seven. Res. quart. Amer. Ass. Hlth, 23, 9-14, 1952.

11. Elkonin, D. B. Razvitiye konstruktivnoy deyatelnosti rebyonka v doshkolnom vozraste. (Development of constructive activity in a preschool child.) Rukopis. (Manuscript.) Moscow, 1948.

12. Elkonin, D. B. Detskaya psikhologiya. (Child psychology.) Moscow. Uchpedgiz, 1960.

13. Figurin, N. L., and Denisova, M. P. Etapy razvitiya povedeniya detey v vozraste ot rozhdeniya do odnogo goda. (Stages of the child's behavioral development from birth to one year.) Moscow. Medgiz, 1949.

14. Galperin, P. Ya. Psikhologicheskoye razlichiye orudy cheloveka i vspomogatelnykh sredstv u zhivotnykh i yego znacheniye. (Psychological differentiation of a human being's tools and of the facilitating means of animals and their significance.) Kand. diss. Kharkov, 1937.

15. Galperin, P. Ya., and Pantina, N. S. Zavisimost dvigatelnogo navyka ot tipa orientirovki v zadanii. (Dependence of the motor habit on the type of orientation toward a task.) Doklady APN RSFSR. (Presentations of APN RSFSR.) 1957, No. 2.

16. Gesell, A. Wolf child and human child. New York: Harper, 1941.

17. Gesell, A. The ontogenesis of infant behavior. In "Manual of child psychology." Ed. L. Carmichael. Wiley, New York, 2nd ed., 1954, 332-369.

18. Gesell, A., and Ames, L. B. Early evidence of individuality in the infant. Scientific Monthly. New York, 1937, 45, 217-225.

19. Gesell, A., and Halverson, H. M. The development of thumb opposition in infants. J. genet. psychol. 1936, 48, 339-361.

20. Gesell, A., and Halverson, H. M. The daily maturation of infant behavior. A cinematic study of posture, movement, and laterality. J. genet. psychol. 1942, 61, 3-32.

21. Gesell, A., and Thompson, H. Learning and growth in identical infant twins: An experimental study by the method of co-twin control. Genet. psychol. monogr. 1929, 6, 1-124.

22. Gesell, A., and Thompson, H. Twins T and C from infancy to adolescence: A biogenetic study of individual differences by the method of co-twin control. Genet. psychol. monogr. 1941, 24, 3-121.

23. Ginevskaya, T. O. Izmeneniye dvizheny detey v zavisimosti ot kharaktera stoyashchey pered nimi zadachi. (A change in children's movements depending on the nature of the confronting problem.) Rukopis. (Manuscript.) Moscow, 1948.

24. Ginevskaya, T. O. Osoznaniye rebyonkom svoikh deystvy v protsesse vyrabotki navyka. (A child's realization of his own actions in the process of habit formation.) Rukopis. (Manuscript.) Moscow, 1949.

25. Gorbatenko, G. I. Osobennosti podrazhaniya u detey doshkolnogo vozrasta. (Attributes of imitation in preschool children.) Kand. diss. Moscow, 1955.

26. Grebenshchikova, Ye. D. Rol slovesnoy instruktsii i naglyadnogo pokaza v vypolnenii dvigatelnykh uprazhneny u detey doshkolnogo vozrasta. (The role of verbal instruction and visual demonstration in the execution of motor exercises by preschool children.) Rukopis. (Manuscript.) Moscow, 1952.

27. Hilgard, E. R. Introduction to psychology. New York. Harcourt, 1953.

28. Irwin, H., and Weiss, M. A note on mass activity in newborn infants. J. genet. psychol. 1930, 38, 20-30.

29. Kanayev, I. I. Bliznetsy. Ocherki po voprosam mnogoplodiya. (Twins. Essays concerning multiple births.) Moscow-Leningrad. Izd-vo AN SSSR, 1959.

30. Kasatkin, N. I. Ranniye uslovnyye refleksy v ontogeneze cheloveka. (Early conditioned reflexes in human ontogeny.) Moscow. Medgiz, 1948.

31. Kirillova, S. A. Rol oryientirovochno-issledovatelskoy deyatelnosti pri vyrabotke navyka putyom podrazheniya. (The role of orienting-exploratory activity in habit formation through imitation.) Rukopis. (Manuscript.) Moscow, 1954.

32. Kislyuk, G. A. K voprosu o formirovanii dvigatelnykh navykov u detey doshkolnogo vozrasta. (Concerning motor-habit formation in preschool children.) Voprosy Psikhologii. (Questions of psychology.) 1956, No. 6.

33. Kistyakovskaya, M. Yu. Vospitaniye detey pervogo goda zhizni v yaslyakh i domakh rebyonka. (Raising children in the first year of life in nurseries and homes.) Kand. diss. Moscow, 1946.

34. Kozlovsky, S. M. Rol orientirovochno-issledovatelskoy deyatelnosti v formirovanii dvigatelnykh navykov u mladshikh shkolnikov. (The role of orienting-exploratory activity in the motor-habit formation of younger school children.) Doklady APN RSFSR. (Presentations of APN RSFSR.) 1957, No. 2.

35. Kotlyarova, L. I. Znacheniye dvigatelnogo momenta v protsesse vospriyatiya. (Significance of the motor aspect in the process of perception.) Kand. diss. Lvov, 1946.

36. Krasnogorsky, N. I. O nekotorykh vozrastnykh osobennostyakh fiziologicheskoy deyatelnosti golovnogo mozga u detey. (Concerning certain developmental attributes of the physiological functioning of the cortex in children.) Tezisy dokladov nauchnoy sessii, posveshchanoy 10-letiyu so dnya smerti I. P. Pavlova. (Theses of presentations at the meeting of the 10th anniversary of the death of I. P. Pavlov.) Moscow. Izd-vo AN SSSR, 1946.

37. Krasnogorsky, N. I. Trudy po izucheniyu vysshey nervnoy deyatelnosti cheloveka i zhivotnykh. (Studies pertaining to higher nervous activity of man and animals.) Moscow. Medgiz, 1964.

38. Leontiev, A. N. Biologicheskoye i sotsialnoye v psikhike cheloveka. (The biological and social factors in man's psyche.) Voprosy psikhologii. (Questions of psychology.) 1960, No. 6.

39. Levi-Gorinevskaya, Ye. G. Razvitiye osnovnykh dvizheny u detey doshkolnogo vozrasta. (Development of basic movements in preschool children.) Moscow. Izd-vo APN RSFSR, 1955.

40. Luria, A. R. Osobennosti vzaimodeystviya dvukh signalnykh sistem v obrazovanii dvigatelnykh reaktsii pri normalnom i anomalnom razvitii. (Attributes of two signaling systems in the formation of motor reactions under normal and abnormal development.) Doklady na soveshchanii po voprosam psikhologii. (Presentations at the conference on the questions of psychology.) Moscow. Izd-vo APN RSFSR, 1954.

41. Luria, A. R. (ed.) Problemy vysshey nervnoy deyatelnosti normalnogo i anomalnogo rebyonka. (Problems of higher nervous activity of a normal and an abnormal child.) Moscow. Izd-vo APN RSFSR, 1956.

42. Luria, A. R., and Mirenova, A. Issledovaniye eksperimentalnogo razvitiya vospriyatiya metodom differentialnogo obucheniya odnoyaytsovykh bliznetsov. (Investigation of the experimental development of perception by the method of differential training of identical twins.) Nevrologiya i genetika. (Neurology and genetics.) I, 1936.

43. Luria, A. R., and Mirenova, A. N. Eksperimentalnoye razvitiye konstruktivnoy deyatelnosti. Differentsialnoye obucheniye odnoyaytsovykh bliznetsov. (Experimental development of constructive activity. Differential training of identical twins.) Trudy medico-geneticheskogo instituta. (Works of the medico-genetic institute.) 4, 1936.

44. McGraw, M. B. Growth; a study of Johnny and Jimmy. N.Y. Appleton-Century Co., 1935.

45. McGraw, M. B. Neural maturation as exemplied in achievement of bladder control. J. of pediatrics. 16, 5, 1940, 580-590.

46. McGraw, M. B. The neuromuscular maturation of the infant. New York. Columbia University Press, 1943.

47. Neverovich, Ya. Z. Ovladeniye predmetnymi dvizheniyami v preddoshkolnom i doshkolnom vozraste. (Mastery of objective movements by pre-preschoolers and preschoolers.) Izvestia APN RSFSR. Vyp. 14, 1948.

48. Neverovich, Ya. Z. Obrazovaniye dvigatelnogo navyka na raznykh stupenyakh doshkolnogo detstva. (Formation of motor habits at different levels of preschool childhood.) Rukopis. (Manuscript.) Moscow, 1952.

49. Neverovich, Ya. Z. Motivy trudovoy deyatelnosti rebyonka doshkolnogo vozrasta. (The working activity motives in the preschool child.) Izvestia APN RSFSR. Vyp. 64, 1955.

50. Neverovich, Ya. Z. Rol oriyentirovki v formirovanii slozhnykh dvigatelnykh sistem. (Role of orientation in the formation of complex motor systems.) Rukopis. (Manuscript.) Moscow, 1957.

51. Ovchinnikova, O. V. Rol oriyentirovochnoy deyatelnosti v vyrabotke dvigatelnogo navyka u detey doshkolnogo vozrasta. (Role of orienting activity in the development of motor habits in preschool children.) Rukopis. (Manuscript.) Moscow, 1953.

52. Pantina, N. S. Formirovaniye dvigatelnogo navyka pisma v zavisimosti ot tipa oriyentirovki v zadanii. (Formation of a writing motor habit in relation to the type of orientation to the task.) Voprosy psikhologii. (Questions of psychology.) 1957, No. 4.

53. Pavlov, I. P. Polnoye sobraniye sochineny. (Complete works.) Moscow-Leningrad. Izd-vo AN SSSR, 1951.

54. Poddyakov, N. N. Osobennosti avtomatizatsii deystviy u detey doshkolnogo vozrasta. (Aspects of automatization of actions in preschool children.) Rukopis. (Manuscript.) Moscow, 1957.

55. Poddyakov, N. N. Osobennosti oriyentirovochnoy deyatelnosti u doshkolnikov pri formirovanii i avtomatizatsii prakticheskikh deystvy. (Aspects of the preschooler's orienting activity in the formation and automatization of practical actions.) Kand. diss. Moscow, 1960.

56. Polyakova, A. G. Psikhologichesky analiz protsessa usvoyeniya navykov putyom podrazhaniya u detey. (Psychological analysis of the process of habit mastery in children via imitation.) Kand. diss. Moscow, 1956.

57. Porembskaya, L. A. Bytovoy trud kak sredstvo vospitaniya samostoyatelnosti detey doshkolnogo vozrasta. (Practical activity as a means of cultivating independence in preschool children.) Uchyonyye zapiski ped. in-ta im Gertsena. (Scientific notes of the Herzen Ped. Institute.) Vol. 126, 1956.

58. Ryss, M. G. Osobennosti motornogo razvitiya grudnykh detey pri razlichnykh usloviyakh vospitaniya. (Aspects of motor development of infants under various conditions of upbringing.) Sovetskaya pediatriya. (Soviet pediatrics.) 1940, No. 3.

59. Ryss, M. G. Razvitiye aktivnykh dvizheny i staticheskikh reaktsy u detey grudnogo vozrasta. (Development of active movements and static reactions in infants.) Kand. diss. Moscow, 1945.

60. Sechenov, I. M. Izbrannyye filosofskiye i psikhologicheskiye proizvedeniya. (Selected philosophical and psychological investigations.) Moscow. Gospolitizdat, 1947.

61.Shchelovanov, N. M. Metody geneticheskoy refleksologii. Sb. Novoye v refleksologii i fiziologii nervnoy sistemy. (Methods of genetic reflexology. In: New developments in reflexology and physiology of the nervous system.) Vyp. I. Moscow. Gosizdat, 1925.

62. Shchelovanov, N. M. Nekotoryye oblichitelnyye osobennosti v razvitii nervnoy deyatelnosti cheloveka po dannym sravnitelnogo izucheniya rannikh stady ontogeneza povedeniya cheloveka i zhivotnykh. (Certain individual aspects in the development of man's nervous activity, according to the comparative study of early stages of ontogeny of the behavior of man and animals.) Trudy 2 vsesoyuznogo syezda fiziologov. Tezisy dokladov. (Works of the 2nd Congress of Physiologists. Theses of presentations.) Leningrad, 1926.

63. Shchelovanov, N. M. O vospitanii v domakh mladentsa. (Concerning upbringing in nurseries.) Voprosy materinstva i mladenchestva. (Questions of maternity and youth.) 1938, 3-4.

64. Shchelovanov, N. M., and Aksarina, N. M. (ed.). Vospitaniye detey v yaslyakh. (Children's upbringing in nurseries.) Moscow. Medgiz, 1930.

65. Shchelovanov, N. M., and Aksarina, N. M. (ed.). Vospitaniya detey rannego vozrasta v detskikh uchrezhdeniyakh. (Young children's upbringing in institutions for children.) Moscow. Medgiz, 1955.

66. Skinner, C. E., and Harriman, P. L. Child psychology, child development and modern education. New York. Macmillan, 1941.

67. Solomon, J. S. Brief communication: Passive motion and infancy. Amer. J. orthopsychiatr. 1959, 29, 650-651.

68. Stone, L. J. A critique of studies on infant isolation. Child development. 1954, 25, 9-20.

69. Strazhnikova, A. A. Obrazovaniye dvigatelnogo navyka pri naglyadnoy i slovesnoy instruktsii u detey doshkolnogo vozrasta. (Formation of preschool children's motor habits under visual and verbal instructions.) Rukopis. (Manuscript.) Moscow, 1952.

70. Tsvetkova, L. S. Rol orientirovochno-issledovatelskoy deyatelnosti i razlichnykh podkripleny v obrazovanii dvigatelnykh navykov. (Role of orienting-exploratory activity and various reinforcers in motor-habit formation.) Doklady APN RSFSR. (Presentations of APN RSFSR.) 1958, No. 2.

71. Vygotskaya, G. L. Razvitiye khvatatelnykh dvizheny u rebyonka na pervom godu zhizni. (Development of grasping movement in a child during the first year of life.) Rukopis. (Manuscript.) Moscow, 1951.

72. Wallon, H. L'enfant turbulent (etude sur les retards et les anomalies du développement moteur et mental.) Paris. F. Alcan, 1925.

73. Wallon, H. De l'acte a la pensée; essai de psychologie comparée. Paris. Flammarion, 1942.

74. Wallon, H. Importance du mouvement dans le développement psychologique de l'enfant. "Enfance." 1956, 9(2), 1-4.

75. Williams, J. R., and Scott, R. B. Growth and development of Negro infants: IV. Motor development and its relationship to child-rearing practices in two groups of Negro infants. Child development. 1953, 24, 103-121.

76. Yendovitskaya, T. V. Rol slova v vypolnenii prostykh deystvy detmi doshkolnogo vozrasta. (The role of words in the execution of simple actions by preschool children.) Izvestia APN RSFSR. Vyp. 64, 1955.

77. Zaporozhets, A. V. Izmeneniye motoriki rebenka v zavisimosti ot uslovy i motivov yego deyatelnosti. (Changes in the child's motor activity depending on the conditions and motives of his activity.) Izvestia APN RSFSR. Vyp. 14, 1948.

78. Zaporozhets, A. V. Razvitiye proizvolnykh dvizheny. (Development of voluntary movements.) Moscow. Izd-vo APN RSFSR, 1960.

79. Zazzo, R. Critique de la notion de stade en psychologie. Psychologie française. 1957, 2, 31-32.

Index

Abel, T. M., 198
Abramovich-Lekhtman, 42
Action, formation of, 75-78, 156, 173, 305
Activity, objective,
  definition of, 22
  memory and, 98
  motor learning and, 290-291, 302-303, 307-308
  sensory development and, 22, 24-26, 28, 42-44, 56
  thinking and, 191, 200-202, 205, 207-208, 221, 227
  with toys, 269-270
Adaptation, 2-3, 21, 188, 200
Adults, interaction with. See Interaction with adults
Afferentiation, 75, 295, 301, 302, 307, 314
Agenosova, N. L., 68
Aksarina, N. M., 291
Animals, development of, 67, 284, 287, 289, 290, 301, 313, 339, 340. See also Apes
Anokhin, P. K., 2
Apes, 209, 210, 211, 214, 226, 280
Arkin, Ye. A., 25, 26, 131
Aronovskaya, D. M., 271
Arshavsky, A. I., 1, 2, 3
Asnin, V. I., 217, 220, 250
Association of Educational Psychology of French-speaking countries, 292
Association psychology, 189, 191, 193-194
Attention
  during action formation, 74-78
  definition of, 65
  distributed, 74
  effectiveness of, 74-77
  involuntary, 68
  organization of, 68, 75-86
  as orienting activity, 68, 70
  as sensory reactions, 65-66
  socio-historical forms of, 78
  span of, 67, 69-74, 263, 266

  stability of, 68-69, 70
  to verbal material, 67
  verbal instructions and, 80-84, 86
  verbalization and, 77, 85-86
  voluntary, 69, 72-74, 78
  words to attract, 66
  see also Orienting-exploratory activity

Baldwin, J. M., 195
Barbashova, Z. I., 19
Barcroft, J., 2
Barkhatova, S. G., 329, 338, 339, 341, 353, 354
Basova, 207
Behaviorism, 194, 284, 360. See also Neobehaviorism
Bekhterev, V. M., 10
Belyayeva-Ekzemplyarskaya, S. N., 32
Benua, 3
Bergeron, M., 278, 305
Bernshtein, N. A., 280, 294, 295, 297, 300, 301, 302, 308, 312
Bernshtein, S. N., 165, 166
Beyrl, 68
Bleuler, E., 198
Blonsky, P. P., 206, 207
Bogen, 209, 210
Bogoyavlensky, D. N., 138, 139
Boguslavskaya, Z. M., 42, 53, 233, 251, 271, 345
Bosov, 210
Bozhovich, L. I., 139, 201, 211, 212, 217, 218, 219, 220
Brazhas, V. P., 25
Bronshtein, A. I., 6, 7, 10
Bruskina, 6
Bühler, C., 255
Bühler, K., 131, 135, 187, 193, 206, 207, 209, 210, 222, 255, 268
Bühler, Sh., 209

Calhoun, S. W., 96
Carlson, 170, 171
Carmichael, L., 7, 283, 284